Radicals in Their Own Time

Radicals in Their Own Time explores the lives of five Americans, with lifetimes spanning four hundred years, who agitated for greater freedom in America. Every generation has them: individuals who speak truth to power and crave, like the air they breathe, freedom from arbitrary authority. This book makes two important observations in discussing Roger Williams, Thomas Paine, Elizabeth Cady Stanton, W. E. B. Du Bois, and Vine Deloria Jr. First, each believed that government must broadly tolerate individual autonomy. Second, each argued that organized religion has been a major source of American society's ills – and all endured serious negative repercussions for doing so. The book argues that part of what makes these five figures compelling is their willingness to pay the price for their convictions – much to the lasting benefit of liberty and equal justice in America.

Michael Anthony Lawrence is Professor and Associate Dean of International Programs at Michigan State University, College of Law, where he teaches courses on constitutional law. He lives with his family in East Lansing, Michigan.

Radicals in Their Own Time

Four Hundred Years of Struggle for Liberty and Equal Justice in America

MICHAEL ANTHONY LAWRENCE
Michigan State University, College of Law

Shaftesbury Road, Cambridge CB2 8EA, United Kingdom

One Liberty Plaza, 20th Floor, New York, NY 10006, USA

477 Williamstown Road, Port Melbourne, VIC 3207, Australia

314–321, 3rd Floor, Plot 3, Splendor Forum, Jasola District Centre, New Delhi – 110025, India

103 Penang Road, #05–06/07, Visioncrest Commercial, Singapore 238467

Cambridge University Press is part of Cambridge University Press & Assessment, a department of the University of Cambridge.

We share the University's mission to contribute to society through the pursuit of education, learning and research at the highest international levels of excellence.

www.cambridge.org
Information on this title: www.cambridge.org/9780521187039

First published 2011

A catalogue record for this publication is available from the British Library

Library of Congress Cataloging-in-Publication data
Lawrence, Michael A., 1959–
Radicals in their own time : four hundred years of struggle for liberty and equal justice in America / Michael A. Lawrence.
p. cm.
Includes bibliographical references and index.
ISBN 978-0-521-19366-5 (hardback) – ISBN 978-0-521-18703-9 (pbk.)
1. Civil rights – United States – History. 2. Civil rights workers – United States – Biography. I. Title.
KF4749.L39 2011
973.09′9–dc22 2010024917

ISBN 978-0-521-19366-5 Hardback
ISBN 978-0-521-18703-9 Paperback

For John, David, and William

In teaching history, there should be extensive discussions of personalities who benefited mankind through independence of character and judgment.

– Albert Einstein, 1953

Contents

Illustrations

Cover
(counter-clockwise from bottom right)

1. Roger Williams. Courtesy of Heintzelman Family Art Trust and Roger Williams University Archives.
2. Thomas Paine. Courtesy of Library of Congress.
3. Elizabeth Cady Stanton. Courtesy of Library of Congress.
4. W. E. B. Du Bois. Courtesy of Library of Congress.
5. Vine Deloria Jr. Courtesy of Philip J. Deloria.

Chapter 1

Chapter 2

Chapter 3

Chapter 4

Chapter 5

Acknowledgments

I gratefully acknowledge the contributions of Troy Brown, Philip Deloria, N. Bruce Duthu, Matthew Fletcher, Elizabeth Price Foley, Niok Frankforter, Del Laverdure, Deanne Lawrence, Geoff Lawrence, Stephen Lawrence, William Lawrence, Cal Mackenzie, and David Stowe, all of whom generously read parts of this book in one form or another and offered helpful ideas, comments, suggestions, and encouragement.

I am grateful also to Senior Editor John Berger at Cambridge University Press, a publishing professional's pro who gave a first-time author a shot, and to all of the other fine folks at Cambridge (including Senior Editorial Assistant David Jou for his friendly assistance) and at Aptara Inc. (including Senior Project Manager Shana Meyer and Katherine Faydash for their stellar copyediting work).

Thanks to my faculty colleagues, staff, and students at the Michigan State University, College of Law, which has been a terrific academic home for more than fifteen years. Special thanks to law librarians Barbara Bean, Chuck Ten Brink, Brent Domann (nice images!), Jane Edwards, Hildur Hanna, Janet Hedin, Lynn Heiden, Jim LaMacchia II, Lara Leaf, and Kathy Prince for their peerless faculty research assistance on this and countless other projects; and also to President Clif Haley and Dean Joan Howarth for their loyal institutional support. I am especially indebted to research assistant Alessa Thomas for her fine cite-checking, technical work, and criticism, and to Head of Research Services Jane Edwards for helping shepherd my numerous (often tedious) research requests.

Finally, I would like to thank my family for their love and support: my late parents, Margaret Sperry and Richard Glenn Lawrence (himself a frustrated radical), who shared a deep passion for learning with their children; older siblings Stephen, Geoffrey, and Susan Lawrence, role models during a rich childhood of moving around the country as our parents improved their professional and personal prospects; sons William, David, and John, forever the apples of their father's eye; and, last but not least, my wife and life partner Deanne, for her support, love, and consummate grace.

Introduction

America in the twenty-first century exists in a perpetual Dickensian sort of best-of-times-worst-of-times state when it comes to putting into practice the sacred principles of liberty and equal justice. On the one hand, the once unthinkable occurred in November 2008, when the nation – a land that had permitted and promoted human slavery for more than half of its four-hundred-year history – elected an African American man president. The symbolic importance alone of placing Barack Obama at the pinnacle of power in the United States, given its sordid past practices, cannot be overstated. On the other hand, on the very same day, a majority of voters in the most populous state in the union, California, voted to deny thousands of their fellow citizens, gay Americans, the equal right to marry. The California experience is only one of numerous legislative-judicial struggles beginning to play out on the issue of gay marriage in other states around the nation.[1]

Taking the long view, if history is any guide (and it is), there is little doubt that the discriminatory laws against gay marriage will eventually end up on history's scrap heap. The current battles will soon go the way of those of some fifty years ago involving interracial marriage, during which one Virginia trial court, in upholding the state's antimiscegenation statute, reasoned: "Almighty God created the races white, black, yellow, malay and red, and he placed them on separate continents. And but for the interference with his arrangement there would be no cause for such marriages. The fact that he separated the races shows that he did not intend for the races to mix." Most Americans today would view such language with a mixture of shock and disbelief – but it was not long ago that legislative majorities in sixteen states gave official voice to such ignorant biases.[2]

Fifty years from now, the current arguments against gay marriage will seem similarly archaic. As the Reverend Martin Luther King Jr. limned, "The arc of the moral universe is long; but it bends toward justice." For all its faults, the U.S. Constitution has, over time, provided a one-way ratchet toward greater, not lesser, liberty and equal justice – every constitutional amendment but one (the eighteenth, itself repealed by the twenty-first just fifteen years later), for example, has, if anything, expanded Americans' freedoms.[3]

America's story *is* remarkable: a nation, sprouting from the seeds of Enlightenment principles by which "tolerance was a moral virtue, even a duty; no longer merely the prerogative of calculating monarchs, but a fundamental element of the 'rights of man.'" For the first time in history a people – coming together toward the common goal of liberty and equal justice, and clearly cognizant of human nature's split personality between good (freedom) and evil (tyranny and oppression) – created a government explicitly designed to resolve the tension in favor of freedom.[4]

That is the myth, anyway. But all is not well in the land of milk and honey; for America's constitutional structure has failed to thwart government's moves to the darker side: its shameful history of slavery and apartheid; its past oppression of women; its systematic subjugation of Native Americans in violation of sacred treaty promises; its pervasive discrimination against immigrants and homosexuals; and, among other more recent repressions, its curtailments of civil liberties and inexcusable use of torture in the ill-considered war on terror. Consider also American geopolitics of the past hundred years: World War I censorship (Congress's and President Wilson's 1917–1918 Espionage and Sedition Acts imposing egregious punishments on political speech); World War II nativism (the president's authorizing of the military to force 120,000 people of Japanese ancestry, two-thirds of them American citizens, from their homes and to quarantine them in internment camps for nearly three years); Cold War McCarthyism (powerful committees of both the U.S. Senate and the U.S. House of Representatives conducting modern-day witch-hunts of thousands of American citizens accused of having communist sympathies); and millennial Cheneyism (the executive branch's aggressively exceeding long-accepted constitutional limits on its power – even while operating in a system that separates powers to provide checks and balances on each coequal branch).

In each case, prejudice, greed, and political expediency took hold before being beaten back – for the time being. It is a constant struggle. As much as America has accomplished in advancing humankind's perpetual quest for greater freedom, it has never completely lived up to its own promise, for whatever reason – whether because of bitter class wars (Howard Zinn), its economically motivated Constitution (Charles Beard), or some combination of these or other factors.[5]

Which viewpoint more accurately describes the true America – the mythic common-interest, pursuit-of-equal-liberty view; the grittier class-warfare explanation; the more cynical economic-interest rationale; or something else altogether? The reality is that there are elements of accuracy in each. And it is useful to keep them all in mind: Lest we become swept-up in misty patriotic myth, we should recall America's ignoble history of injustices and intolerance. Conversely, lest we lose hope, we should remember that the myth and partial reality of America as beacon of freedom has for centuries truly inspired millions around the world. In the end, the goals represented in the positive myth are worth fighting for, both idealistically and practically, for they advance our individual and collective humanity – and offer a model of ambition, idealism, and hope for future generations.

In the spirit of Albert Einstein's words in the epigraph to this book, *Radicals in Their Own Time* discusses the personalities of five important Americans who have led the way in bursting some of America's most inglorious chains of injustice and oppression. As noted, progress toward greater freedom in America has never been direct or easy – democracy is messy, and the nation has had its share of despotic leaders and oppressive majorities, but one constant throughout American history has been the recurring theme of individuals of superior character and judgment who have courageously stood up to lead the fights for freedom and justice, despite considerable hardships to themselves. Every generation has them – men and women who speak truth to power in the face of sometimes overwhelming official and unofficial resistance; people who rebel against stifling orthodoxy and demand governmental tolerance and equal treatment even when it seems they alone are waging the fight; individuals who crave freedom from arbitrary authority like the very air they breathe.

This book explores the lives of five such individuals whose lifetimes, laid beginning to end, together form a nearly continuous sweep of four hundred years of American history: Roger Williams (1603–1683), Thomas Paine (1737–1809), Elizabeth Cady Stanton (1815–1902);

W. E. B. Du Bois (1868–1963); and Vine Deloria Jr. (1933–2005). Radicals all, each did more than anyone during his or her respective era to challenge and ultimately force government to honor Americans' natural birthright of individual liberty and equal justice. Each, as we shall see, has had a profound impact on American history.

These five are especially appropriate for our purposes because all are relatively lesser-celebrated figures in the American historical tableau. None are household names in the manner of a Franklin, Washington, Jefferson, Lincoln, or King. None, moreover, were aristocratic legacies to family political dynasties. Rather, they were self-made, in true American fashion, and so represent well the millions of Americans over the past four centuries who have waged, and wage still, their own battles largely in obscurity.[6]

Part of the reason Williams, Paine, Stanton, Du Bois, and Deloria are less-celebrated is that each was, in a sense, too principled for his or her own good. They were controversial and impolitic. They spoke truth to power in ways irritating to authorities, and all were at times harshly critical of America. They were not approval-seeking, conflict-averse people; rather, they were agitators, and they did not shrink from offending others – not only their enemies but also sometimes their own friends – as they resolutely championed the natural rights of liberty and equal justice. There were no sacred cows for these five – including, for all, the particularly combustible topic of Christian orthodoxy.

Roger Williams, who moved from England to the Massachusetts Bay Colony in 1631 at the age of twenty-eight to escape religious persecution, was expelled from the colony in 1635 for his nonconforming views on religious freedom and separation of church and state. Yet with his views favoring unconditional broad tolerance of the views and practices of all (believers and nonbelievers alike) – "I plead for impartiality and equal freedom, peace and safety to other consciences and assemblies, unto which the people may as freely go, and this according to each conscience, whatever conscience this conscience be" – he set the template for governmental tolerance of religion in the New World in his new state of Rhode Island, which made the guarantee of religious liberty a part of its fundamental law.[7]

Thomas Paine, a corset stay maker's son who moved from England to the colonies as a thirty-seven-year-old in 1774, faced withering criticism from his more appeasement-minded colonial colleagues (such as John Adams) and charges of sedition in his home country of England. Yet with his flair for the written word (Ben Franklin once said,

"Others can rule, many can fight, but only Paine can write for us the English tongue"; and Thomas Jefferson, who for many years sent Paine manuscripts for criticism and correction, wrote him, "You must not be too much elated . . . when I tell you my belief that you are the only writer in America who can write better than your obliged and obedient servant – Thomas Jefferson"), Paine was a key intellectual player in not one but two revolutions – penning in *Common Sense* the words that provided "the January heat of 1776 that balanced the July light of Thomas Jefferson's Declaration of Independence" and lending crucial moral support to the revolutionary cause in its darkest hours.[8]

Elizabeth Cady Stanton, groomed in her upbringing as daughter of a prominent judge in upstate New York to a conventional life as mother and homemaker, long endured mocking disdain from countless strangers and even her own father and husband for insisting that women were morally and legally entitled to equal treatment. Yet with her lifetime of unflinching advocacy for women's rights – including her two singular landmark creations, the *Declaration of Rights and Sentiments* for the Seneca Falls Convention of 1848, and the *Woman's Bible* in 1896 – Stanton did more than any single person to establish the framework for eventual gender legal equality in the United States (including the "right" to vote, gained some eighteen years after her death with the Nineteenth Amendment in 1920).

Controversy followed black radical historian, scholar, and agitator-prophet W. E. B. Du Bois during his life and beyond, to the point that the government of his country of birth, America, effectively disowned him during the last year of his life by denying the renewal of his passport while he was abroad in Ghana; and the town of his birth, Great Barrington, Massachusetts, only grudgingly, after a bitter 1969 struggle, established a memorial park at his boyhood home. Yet Du Bois advanced a principled moral approach to race relations and society that predestined the end of Jim Crow and won the hearts and minds of his successors who carried on the civil rights movement. Long committed to core Enlightenment principles, "Du Bois had a towering sense of the Right, of the Just," explains Du Bois's literary executor Herbert Aptheker, "[and] a basic faith in reason and a passionate commitment toward achieving the just through the use of reason."[9]

The Sioux author, scholar, and activist Vine Deloria Jr., whose views on government naturally came through his own tribal traditions, antagonized the establishment while shaking mainstream America out of its complacency with his provocative works exposing the American government's systematic centuries-long oppression of Indian tribes. Beginning with *Custer Died for Your Sins,* his devastating 1969 critique of the U.S. government and passionate call to action to a new generation of Native Americans, Deloria was a central figure in providing a unifying intellectual, political voice to Indians past, present, and future in their battles for self-determination and reclaiming tribal heritage. As the Indian law scholar Charles Wilkinson comments, "If you mark down the great figures of the American West in recent times, [Deloria] belongs there because of his role in reshaping Indian country. . . . I think in the last 100 years, he's been the most important person in Indian affairs, period."[10]

In discussing Williams, Paine, Stanton, Du Bois, and Deloria, this book makes two important observations. First, each argued in essence that governmental tolerance for the autonomy of all citizens is a fundamental, mandatory feature of American democracy. Second, each believed that organized religion was a major source of society's ills (including American government's regular intolerance of citizens' autonomy), and all five endured serious negative repercussions for saying so.

Regarding the first, they believed government must tolerate the personal autonomy of all citizens on the reasoning that matters involving individual choice not affecting the rights of others are natural rights predating government itself. Indeed, in this context, Roger Williams believed the term *tolerance* is itself a misnomer, as it implies that government has the authority in the first place to decide whether or not to recognize the right, whereas the idea of preexisting natural rights forecloses government interference – period.

Thomas Paine explained the concept in the 1792 *Rights of Man:* "Natural rights are those which appertain to man in right of his existence. Of this kind are all the intellectual rights, or rights of the mind, and also all those rights of acting as an individual for his own comfort and happiness, which are not injurious to the natural rights of others." As for the role of society and government vis-à-vis those natural rights, Paine explained in *Common Sense*: "Society in every state is a blessing, but government even in its best state is but a necessary evil; in its worst state an intolerable one." He elaborated in *Rights of Man*: "Man did not enter into society to become *worse* than he was before, nor to have fewer rights than he had before, but to have those rights better secured." In other words, government, which is merely a useful tool devised to protect every person's preexisting natural rights, simply lacks authority to curtail these rights. Government, one might say, is liberty's servant.[11]

It makes perfect sense that tolerance of natural rights would be a critical governmental attribute in a country formally dedicated to "free[ing] the individual from the oppressive misuse of power, [and] from the tyranny of the state," in the words of renowned historian Bernard Bailyn. "No idea is more fundamental," historian Eric Foner adds, "to Americans' sense of themselves as individuals and as a nation than 'freedom' or 'liberty.'"[12]

Conceptually, this is easy – when it comes to matters of individual free will causing no harm to others, government is not required to do anything; rather, it must simply stay out of the way and do nothing at all. The mid-nineteenth-century English philosopher John Stuart Mill aptly articulated the concept with his harm principle: "The only part of the conduct of any one, for which he is amenable to society, is that which concerns others. In the part which merely concerns himself, his independence is, of right, absolute. Over himself, over his own body and mind, the individual is sovereign." A century and a half earlier, John Locke, the great thinker of the European Enlightenment who was probably the most influential source of revolutionary American political thought (Thomas Jefferson, for example, considered Locke "[one of the three] greatest men that have ever lived, without any exception"), wrote: The care... of every man's soul belongs unto himself, and is to be left unto himself." To Locke, government acts properly in protecting individuals from fraudulent or physical harm but acts improperly when it paternalistically regulates private choice. It must, in other words, tolerate individual free will.[13]

The U.S. Supreme Court has also recognized this principle (albeit too infrequently). As Justice Louis Brandeis intoned in acknowledging the concept in a 1928 case: "The makers of our Constitution... conferred, as against the government, the right to be let alone – the most comprehensive of rights and the right most valued by civilized men. To protect that right, every unjustifiable intrusion by the government upon the privacy of the individual, whatever the means employed, must be deemed a violation." Or, as a majority of the Supreme Court commented in 1943 in striking down a West Virginia law requiring schoolchildren to recite the Pledge of Allegiance, "If there is any fixed star in our constitutional constellation, it is that no official, high or petty, can prescribe what is orthodox in politics, nationalism, religion, or other matters of opinion or force citizens to confess by word or act their faith therein." And in one of its finest moments, in a 2003 case striking down a Texas law punishing consenting adults for certain sexual behavior within their own homes, the Supreme Court majority explained: "Freedom extends beyond spatial bounds. Liberty presumes an autonomy of self that includes freedom of thought, belief, expression, and certain intimate conduct."[14]

To Williams, Paine, Stanton, Du Bois, and Deloria, too, a tolerant government does not interfere, thereby allowing diverse viewpoints and practices the necessary breathing space they require in a free pluralistic society. Roger Williams believed government should stay separate from – that it should tolerate – all religious practices. Thomas Paine was committed to the commonsense principle that government must not abridge – that it must tolerate – the individual rights of all people. Elizabeth Cady Stanton demanded that government replace a legal regime imposing separate, inferior status on women with one that recognizes – that tolerates – the equal legal status of women. W. E. B. Du Bois tirelessly challenged government to repudiate laws and practices that institutionalized white supremacist principles and thereby to accept – to tolerate – black people as equals under the law. Vine Deloria Jr. spent his lifetime exposing the practices of a U.S. government that systematically reneged on its solemn promises to leave alone – to tolerate – Indian tribes with their native lands and traditions and pointed the way forward for how that government should make amends for its egregious breaches of faith.

It is worth noting what governmental tolerance is not. It is not a strict libertarian approach in which government would have little or no role in all matters – instead, as Thomas Paine said, "the Public Good is to be [government's] object." Government has vital, important functions. In exercising those functions, however, elective government acts legitimately only insofar as it respects the individual's "right to be let alone." All government activity must be guided by this test – if the elective government's action abridges individual free will on matters of natural private concern, presumptively it is not legitimate and should be struck down by another branch of government – the judiciary. Outside of such freedom-depriving sorts of actions, however, elective government is free to enact policy as it will – whether progressive, conservative, or of any other description. This is where the people and their representatives exercise the will of the majority in a democratic society. In such cases, judicial intervention is inappropriate, and an intervening court would raise legitimate countermajoritarian-difficulty concerns. Finally, at the same time, when judicial opinions fail to respect liberty and/or equal-justice interests, it is elective government's responsibility to enact legislation to (among other things) guide the judiciary.[15]

One last note on tolerance: as much as one may sing its praises, it is important not to view governmental tolerance as a panacea for all of society's ills. As Professor Michael Walzer notes, "Tolerance brings an end to persecution and fearfulness, but it is not a formula for social harmony. Newly tolerated groups [and individuals], insofar as they are really different, will often also be antagonistic, and they will seek political advantage." The point is that in a governmental tolerance regime, the one thing those groups and individuals will not be able to do, even while seeking political advantage, is to enlist government assistance in denying the other groups and individuals from engaging in their preferred activities. Government, with rare exceptions, must tolerate them all.[16]

The second observation, again, is that each of the five profiled radicals argued that organized religion (especially Christian orthodoxy) has been a significant source of intolerance throughout American history – just as it had been for many centuries previously in Europe. Each admired Jesus Christ the man, and the principles of tolerance, equality, humility, and forgiveness he advocated. "[Jesus] was a virtuous and an amiable man," Thomas Paine explained in *The Age of Reason*. "The morality that he preached and practiced was of the most benevolent kind." Indeed, they admired his stubborn commitment to principle (recognizing, no doubt, some of themselves in Christ's own life experiences): "[Christ] preached also against the corruptions and avarice of the Jewish priests; and this brought upon him the hatred and vengeance of the whole order of priesthood," Paine recalled. "The accusation which those priests brought against him was that of sedition and conspiracy against the Roman government, to which the Jews were then subject.... Jesus Christ [likely] had in contemplation the delivery of the Jewish nation from the bondage of the Romans." For that, Paine explained, "this virtuous reformer and revolutionist lost his life." One might accurately say Jesus Christ was himself a radical in *his* own time.[17]

What Paine and the others objected to were the elaborate superstitions and practices that arose around Christ's teachings in the many centuries following his death, which variously punished, stigmatized, marginalized, and victimized certain individuals or groups. And for daring to challenge the church's dogma – which has always been accepted essentially verbatim by the vast majority of Americans, with marginal variations depending on the particular Judeo-Christian flavor – all five, to varying degrees, were vilified.

Williams railed against the hypocrisy of religious wars: "The blood of so many hundred thousand souls of Protestants and Papists, spilt in the Wars of present and former Ages, for their respective Consciences, is not required nor accepted by Jesus Christ the Prince of Peace." In the end, for having "broached and divulged [such] diverse new and dangerous opinions against the authority of magistrates," Williams was banished – literally to the wilderness – from the Massachusetts Bay Colony.[18]

Paine said, "I do not believe in the creed professed by the Jewish church, by the Roman church, by the Greek church, by the Turkish church, by the Protestant church, nor by any church that I know of," explaining instead: "My own mind is my own church." "All national institutions of churches, whether Jewish, Christian, or Turkish," he added, "appear to me no other than human inventions set up to terrify and enslave mankind, and monopolize power and profit." These are fighting words in a Christian country like America; and in 1888, approaching a century after his death, Paine was still being derided as "that dirty little atheist" by the likes of Theodore Roosevelt.[19]

Elizabeth Cady Stanton charged, too, that the clergy were responsible for much of society's ills, especially for women. "I now see more clearly than ever, that the arch enemy to women's freedom skulks behind the altar," she ruminated in 1886. "No class of men have such power to pervert the religious sentiments and oppress mankind with gloomy superstitions through life and an undefined dread of the unknown after death." But Stanton was convinced the clergy did not truly speak for the Almighty, reasoning, "I cannot believe that a God of law and order... could have sanctioned a social principle so calamitous in its consequences as investing in one-half the race the absolute control of all the rights of the other." To so baldly criticize mainstream Christian orthodoxy at the turn of the twentieth century was too radical even for most women's rights activists – who distanced themselves from Stanton by issuing a formal censure at the 1896 National American Woman Suffrage Association convention, and for decades after her death rendering her persona non grata even while canonizing her longtime collaborator Susan B. Anthony.[20]

Although W. E. B. Du Bois believed the true teachings of Jesus were morally uplifting, he had "no particular affection for the Church. I think its record on the Negro problem has been shameful.... [T]he southern branch of the Church is a moral dead weight and the northern branch... never has had the moral courage to stand against it." "The church of John Pierpont Morgan," he stressed, "[is] not the church of Jesus Christ." "Of course, it is the Churches which are the most discriminatory of all institutions!" The U.S. government sued Du Bois on trumped-up charges after his turn to the avowedly atheist communist nations of China and Russia, and then, as noted earlier, effectively disowned him in the final year of his life for his Communist Party membership.[21]

Vine Deloria Jr. was blunt in his assessment of Christian orthodoxy's deleterious effects throughout history: "From pope to pauper, Protestant to Catholic, Constantinople to the United States, the record is filled with atrocities, misunderstandings, persecutions, genocides, and oppressions so numerous as to bring fear into the hearts and minds of non-Christian peoples." Deloria was caustic in his criticism of America and other Western nations' use of Christian orthodoxy to justify its expansionist goals: "At one time or another slavery, poverty, and treachery were all justified by Christianity as politically moral institutions of the state." These harsh assessments antagonized many in a mainstream American establishment thoroughly suffused with Christian dogma.[22]

In short, all five of the profiled radicals lived implicitly by Christ's uncompromising moral values of peace, goodwill, and forgiveness. All spoke their mind about the hypocrisies and abuses perpetuated in Christ's name – and all, like Christ himself, were punished for speaking truth to power. The lesson? Challenge this most sacred of cows, Christian orthodoxy, and be prepared to pay a heavy price.

Part of what makes Williams, Paine, Stanton, Du Bois, and Deloria such compelling figures is that they *were* ready to pay the price – regardless of the consequences. For them, principle prevailed. As Stanton's collaborator Susan B. Anthony mused in 1873, "Cautious, careful people always casting about to preserve their reputation and social standing, never can bring about a reform. Those who are really in earnest must be willing to be anything or nothing in the world's estimation, and publicly and privately, in season and out, avow their sympathy with despised and persecuted ideas and advocates, and bear the consequences." One should never follow the path, Du Bois suggested, of Galileo Galilei, who renounced his life's work seeking scientific truth when threatened by the Catholic Church. "By that lie, civilization was halted, science was checked, and bigotry was more strongly enthroned on its crimson glory."[23]

As oft-criticized, ridiculed, and even shunned by government and society as they were, Stanton, Du Bois, and the others still lobbied, agitated, and generally made nuisances of themselves in their efforts to correct the injustices they encountered. They knew that behind the self-inflating posturing, government is no more than a collection of mere men and women cloaked in special clothing to serve a defined narrow purpose; and they demanded change to the existing order so that they – and we all – might one day see liberty and equal justice served.

It is no stretch to say that without their efforts, we would not enjoy the scope of freedoms we have today. They knew, along with the nation's founders, that the natural tendency of government is "threatening, pushing and grasping; . . . too often in the end . . . destroy[ing] its benign victim." Alexis de Tocqueville presciently recognized this threat in America as early as 1835, commenting: "The [democratic] sovereign . . . spreads a fine mesh of uniform, minute, and complex rules, through which not even the most original minds and most vigorous souls can poke their heads above the crowd. . . . Rather than tyrannize," this subtle government power grab "inhibits, represses, saps, stifles, and stultifies, and in the end reduces each nation to nothing but a flock of timid and industrious animals, with the government as its shepherd." And the fact is, the flock rarely acts against the shepherd's subtle abridgments, as the Declaration of Independence expressly recognizes. "All experience hath shown," the Declaration observes, "that mankind are more disposed to suffer, while evils are sufferable, than to right themselves by abolishing the forms to which they are accustomed."[24]

Even while the masses may be "disposed to suffer" such a death by a thousand cuts, at the same time, they vicariously enjoy the exploits of the few who refuse to be intimidated. So, in any given holiday-movie-going or summer-reading season, it is possible to find fictional radical characters pushing back against overweening or unjust government. "Who are we to just lie there and do nothing?" asks fictionalized radical James Farmer Jr., for example, in the 2007 movie *The Great Debaters*, during a debate about the morality of civil disobedience in response to Southern lynchings in the 1930s. "There is no Rule of Law in the Jim Crow South," Farmer continues, "not when Negroes are denied housing, turned away from schools, and hospitals. And not when we are lynched. St. Augustine said, 'An unjust law in no law at all,' which means I have a right – even a duty – to resist, with violence or civil disobedience. You should pray I choose the latter."[25]

"Pay no attention to the man behind the curtain," the wizard-government of Oz commands as he madly works the levers and wheels trying to maintain his grasp on power in one of the most popular movies of all time, *The Wizard of Oz* – while radical Dorothy scolds him for his hubris and refuses to allow him to usurp her own autonomy or to mistreat her friends. Dorothy implicitly understands that the wizard is human, no better or worse than herself – and she demands the restoration of justice and tolerance to the land of Oz.[26]

Or, on the lighter side, Theodore (Dr. Seuss) Geisel's radical turtle Mack in *Yertle the Turtle* implicitly knows that King Yertle is not so special that he should be able to cruelly command all of the other turtles to stack themselves up merely so Yertle would have a better view from atop the stack – so he does something about it. Mack "did a plain little thing. He burped. And his burp shook the throne of the king!... And Yertle, the King of all Sala-ma-sond, Fell off his high throne and fell Plunk! In the Pond! And today the Great Yertle, that marvelous he, Is King of the Mud." And best of all – "the turtles, of course... all the turtles are free. As turtles and, maybe, all creatures should be."[27]

There is good reason Americans today are so inspired by underdog stories of courageous individuals who take on an unjust establishment and prevail – it is in their blood. It was their ancestors, after all, who against heavy odds declared and won independence from the mighty British Empire on the audacious principles that government exists only as liberty's servant and that the people may abolish any government that fails to do so:

> We hold these Truths to be self-evident, that all Men are created equal, that they are endowed... with certain unalienable Rights, that among these are Life, Liberty, and the Pursuit of Happiness. That to secure these Rights, Governments are instituted among Men, deriving their just Powers from the Consent of the Governed, that whenever any Form of Government becomes destructive of those Ends, it is the Right of the People to alter or to abolish it, and to institute a new Government, laying its Foundation on such Principles.[28]

This was a bold statement to the world. As Thomas Jefferson wrote on the fiftieth anniversary of the signing of the Declaration of Independence just days before his death, "May [the Declaration] be to the world, what I believe it will be (to some parts sooner, to others later, but finally to all), the signal of arousing men to burst the chains, under which monkish ignorance and superstition had persuaded them to bind themselves, and to assume the blessings & security of self-government."[29]

And it was their ancestors who then crafted a Constitution establishing a governmental structure guaranteeing liberty and equal justice, thereby making America the first nation in the history of the world to break the bonds of feudalism. Although the promises of the Declaration and Constitution have fallen far short in the execution, the mandate for a constitutionally limited government dispensing equal justice is every

American's birthright. "It is the protection of the humblest individual against his own government; [his] bulwark against autocratic power, and against the impulses of an irresponsible majority," Gaspar Bacon rhapsodized in 1928.[30]

So, when Americans are presented with anecdotal reminders of liberty, individual autonomy, and equal justice triumphing over a rigid shepherd, it stirs something familiar from deep within themselves: a welling pride, a visceral longing, a sheer hope, that someone – maybe even oneself or loved ones – will have the courage to claim the full promise of freedom bequeathed by their forebears. Americans are hungry to believe liberty and equal justice will ultimately prevail. Dorothy in 1939, the *Great Debaters* in 2007, and even Yertle the Turtle in 1959, speak to this hunger, and stand – as do their real-life counterparts Roger Williams, Thomas Paine, Elizabeth Cady Stanton, W. E. B. Du Bois, and Vine Deloria Jr. – as timeless American heroes for courageously challenging a powerful, often unjust, and intolerant establishment – and winning in the end.

1

Roger Williams (1603–1683)

Freeborn

I plead for impartiality and equal freedom, peace and safety to other consciences and assemblies, unto which the people may as freely go, and this according to each conscience.

– Roger Williams, 1652

I. The Old World

The thirty-two-year-old man, very ill, stood on October 8, 1635, before the General Court of the Massachusetts Bay Colony, considering how to respond to the court's questions about his role in writing two letters bitterly critical of civil authorities for interfering with church matters. The court was prepared to offer one last chance at leniency.[1]

"Do you wish for the court to postpone action for a month for further conference or disputation?" Governor John Haynes asked the man standing, Roger Williams, a minister with the Salem congregation.

Williams, who had cultivated a devoted following during his two years at the Salem church, was a family man, with a two-year-old daughter and a wife expecting their second child within the month, so he had every reason to hope for a light sentence.

"No, I do not," Williams answered.

"Very well, then. Mr. Hooker will debate the issues for the court," Haynes replied with some wonderment.

The Boston minister Thomas Hooker then attempted to "reduce him from his errors," but Williams – who had been called before the Bay

Colony authorities on numerous prior occasions to answer for his troubling views – was unrepentant.

"I can justify both of these letters; moreover, I maintain all of my opinions," he stated stubbornly.

On earlier occasions, Williams had apologized and sought forgiveness for his nonconforming transgressions, but no longer. No human authorities, preaching their false doctrines, would again come between him and his quest for the true church. The Puritan religious orthodoxy, as practiced in the Massachusetts Bay Colony, was in his view little better than the hated Church of England the Puritans had left behind.

Something had changed in him. No longer was it possible to accept anything other than God's true word; it followed that any interference in the spiritual realm by civil authorities was utterly unacceptable. In short, when it came to matters spiritual, in any civil society, there must be liberty of conscience. Williams knew that his savior Christ Jesus had suffered for spreading God's word and that throughout the centuries others, too, had suffered for preaching the gospel. So the authorities could do what they would with him, but he would not yield.

The next morning, Governor Haynes announced the sentence banishing Roger Williams from the Massachusetts Bay Colony:

> Whereas Mr. Roger Williams . . . has broached & divulged diverse new & dangerous opinions, against the authority of magistrates; [and] has also written letters of defamation, both of the magistrates & churches here . . . it is therefore ordered, that the said Mr. Williams shall depart out of this jurisdiction within six weeks . . . not to return any more without license from the court.[2]

So Roger Williams was to be cast out of the Bay with his two-year-old daughter and long-suffering, pregnant wife. Important decisions would need to be quickly made (how and where to go?); but first, within weeks, the young family had important, happier business to attend to in welcoming their newborn daughter into the world and in deciding what to name her.

Given the circumstances, only one name would do: *Freeborn.*

Roger Williams is remembered today primarily as the person who first advanced the idea of separation of church and state in America, or perhaps as the founder of Providence, Rhode Island. Not as well remembered is the connection between these two seemingly disparate efforts: the reason Williams had the "opportunity" to found Providence in the first place was that just four years after arriving from his native England, he was banished by the Puritans from the Massachusetts Bay Colony for his nonconforming religious views – in particular, for refusing to bow to conventional Puritan religious orthodoxy, which favored heavy government involvement in religion. Once banished, he relocated to the territory now encompassed by Rhode Island, befriended the native Wampanoag and Narragansett Indians (Williams was centuries ahead of his time in identifying the abusive practices of the settling Europeans against Native Americans, especially in matters involving real property), founded Providence, and made the colony a beacon of religious tolerance that became the very model for separation of church and state in the founding of the United States some 140 years later.

We may take for granted religious freedom in twenty-first-century America, but in the early colonial America inhabited by Roger Williams, individual free will and self-determination were still vastly circumscribed (for example, no equal suffrage – that is, only propertied men were allowed to vote; absence of free speech; few criminal procedural protections) compared to what exist today. So Williams's insistence on the individual right of liberty of conscience – the right to practice (or not to practice) religion according to one's own desire, free of government interference – was in his own time a revolutionary concept.

Above all, Roger Williams – like the other four radicals profiled in the following chapters – demanded governmental tolerance, which would in turn allow liberty and equal justice to fully flourish. Where he saw official intolerance, he called it out, regardless of the negative repercussions to himself.

Moreover, Williams observed that those negative repercussions frequently originated with the very people he believed should have known better – ministers and other members of the religious establishment who claimed to have God on their side. Williams's understanding on this point was shared by another preacher some three centuries later, Martin Luther King Jr., who recognized the potential for the repressive uses of Christian values by those seeking to protect the power of an entrenched establishment. Writing from the Birmingham jail in April 1963, King addressed his fellow clergymen:

> I came across your recent statement calling my present activities . . . extreme. At first I was rather disappointed that fellow clergymen would see my nonviolent efforts as those of an extremist, . . . [but p]erhaps I have once again been too optimistic. Is organized religion too inextricably bound to

THE ROGER WILLIAMS MONUMENT
Unveiled at Providence, R. I., 1877

PHOTO 1. Roger Williams Monument, Providence. Courtesy of Google Books.

> the status quo to save our nation and the world? Perhaps I must turn my faith to the inner spiritual church, the church within the church, as the true ekklesia and the hope of the world.

King hastened to add that he was not implicating all clergy, explaining, "[S]ome noble souls from the ranks of organized religion have broken loose from the paralyzing chains of conformity and joined us as active partners in the struggle for freedom." "Yes," he acknowledged, "they have gone to jail with us. Some have been dismissed from their churches, have lost the support of their bishops and fellow ministers. But they have acted in the faith that right defeated is stronger than evil triumphant."[3]

Roger Williams – and Thomas Paine, Elizabeth Cady Stanton, W. E. B. Du Bois, and Vine Deloria Jr. – would fully understand Martin Luther King Jr.'s sentiments. Each of these individuals bemoaned the sometimes-regressive tendencies of organized religion in America, and all were punished in some way for challenging the religious orthodoxy. More generally, all five learned it is not easy being a trailblazer. The thicket is rough, with many obstacles along the way – and the person at the head of the line bears the brunt of the hardship.

Little is known of Roger Williams's boyhood. He was born in London, probably in late 1603, to a well-connected lesser-gentry mother and a textile shopkeeper father, as the middle of three brothers and an older sister. The working-class Williams family lived on Cow Lane in the Smithfield section of northwestern London (Smithfield was notorious as the site where hundreds of religious dissenters were burned at the stake starting in 1555, during the reign of Queen "Bloody" Mary). It is unknown when Roger first became serious about religion, although he said many years later that it had been during his childhood that his soul had been touched with a love of the Father of Mercies, the Son, and the holy Scriptures, and it was at the impressionable age of eight that, practically in his own backyard, the Separatist Bartholomew Legate was burned to death for his religious beliefs in March 1611. Williams later espoused some of Legate's heretical Separatist tenets, as well as those of Edward Wightman, who was burned at Lichfield in April 1612. One might surmise that these gruesome executions were themselves burned into Williams's consciousness. What those impressions might have been we cannot know; what we do know is that in a 1632 letter to John Winthrop, Williams commented on how during his boyhood and early adulthood he was "persecuted even in and out of my father's house these 20 years." Might a headstrong, eight-year-old Roger Williams, voicing horror about the sickening events playing out almost literally in his own backyard, have met with parental scorn or disapproval for sympathizing with seditious traitors?[4]

Williams attended a free grammar school in his youth before enrolling shortly after his father's death in 1621 at the Charterhouse School for indigent boys under the sponsorship of the eminent jurist Lord Edward Coke, who was on the school's board of governors. Lord Coke had hired Williams some years earlier to assist him in taking notes of court

PHOTO 2. Lord Edward Coke. Courtesy of the Daniel R. Coquillette Rare Book Room, Boston College Law Library.

proceedings (in an age when official case reporting had not yet taken hold) in the Star Chamber court of equity, as he himself had done since 1572 to pen the case reports and commentary – *Reports and Institutes* – along the way making himself the foremost legal authority of the seventeenth century. Coke saw a special spark in Williams and considered him "so hopeful a youth"; after being presented with his shorthand work, Coke came to regard Williams as a son.[5]

From 1623 to 1627, Williams attended Pembroke College at Cambridge University (sponsored again by Coke, who may have paid some of his fees there after Williams's excellent record at Charterhouse earned him entrance into the prestigious academy at age twenty – six years older than most of his classmates). Pembroke, one of Cambridge's older colleges, had a reputation as "studious, well-learned, and a good setter-forth of Christ's Gospel and of God's true Word," and for being "strongly Anglican, strictly orthodox and anti-Puritan." In all likelihood, the influence of his benefactor Lord Coke, with his avowed Anglicanism (and sometimes irascible, disagreeable manner), played a large role in his choice of college.[6]

All told, Williams was less than satisfied with his Cambridge experience, believing, as his contemporary John Milton put it, that the rote learning of the classics, to the exclusion of the New World discoveries of Columbus, Copernicus, Galileo, and Descartes, was so much "sowthistles and brambles." A university committed to "Protestantism, classical scholarship and a gentleman's education" was inherently limited, and Francis Bacon criticized the "contentious learning" of memorization as failing to exercise human intellect. Williams later wrote of his time at Cambridge as "monkish and idle," and although he "honour[ed] Schooles for Tongues and Arts," he objected to the notion that a university education was required to understand religion.

Cambridge was far from a hotbed of nonconformist thought in the early seventeenth century; together with its older sibling, Oxford University, it largely hewed to the royal party line. Nonetheless, Williams earned his degree from Cambridge in 1627, signing the required oath of sound religious faith required (since 1623) of all graduates, wherein he pledged to subscribe to King James's "three darling articles" – accepting the Church of England's Prayer Book and Thirty-Nine Articles and acknowledging the king's supremacy in spiritual matters. Over the following two years, he then completed all of the requirements to become a member of the official clergy and earn his master's degree, save one: formal application to the episcopacy – a requirement he simply could not stomach (and so never completed) given his hardening opposition to Anglican orthodoxy.[7]

Williams's resolve was likely triggered in part by the escalated efforts during these years of the Church of England's advocates to eradicate dissent through the royal mandate of King Charles I (who had succeeded to the throne on his father James's death in 1625) "that all further curious search [into church doctrine] be laid aside." Charles elevated William

Laud to increasingly powerful positions on the Privy Council, then to postings as archbishop of London in 1628 and archbishop of Canterbury in 1633 – positions from which Laud instituted a program of strict discipline and uniformity of worship on all parishes in England, severely punishing dissenters. At Laud's urging, in 1629, Charles issued a royal decree imposing Arminianism (that is, favoring the reinstatement of church ritual and ceremony that existed prior to the Reformation) as a test of loyalty to church and crown.[8]

This decree was only the latest in a series of outrages in England over the prior century dating from Protestant King Henry VIII's death in 1547 and his daughter Elizabeth's accession (reinstating Protestantism) in 1558 – during which time Henry's son Edward VI ruled until 1553 (strengthening Protestantism), on whose death Henry's daughter Mary ruled until 1558 (reinstating Roman Catholicism). Although some of the ruling monarchs during the sixteenth and seventeenth centuries were more moderate than others, none, regardless of religious proclivities, was charitable toward those not sharing their views, each persecuting the out-group to varying degrees.[9]

When the first in the Stuart dynasty, James I, ascended to the throne at the end of Elizabeth's long reign in 1603, Protestants could be forgiven for thinking that the new monarch, coming as he had from Calvinist Scotland, would be relatively benign. If anything, however, the reign of the Stuarts was even more tumultuous than that of the Tudors before it. James did embrace Protestantism, but of a strictly enforced, rigid Anglican variety, leaving precious little room for variation or discussion.

A certain group of Protestants was at odds with the official theology as practiced both in its relatively more moderate form under Elizabeth and in its more rigid iteration under James. The Puritans believed that the Protestant Church should be cleansed of all traces of Roman Catholicism, whereas the Protestantism of the Church of England maintained too many aspects of popery for the Puritans' taste. As did Catholics, Anglicans still bowed at the mention of Jesus' name, for example, and at baptisms still made the sign of the cross. Moreover, Puritans believed that clergy should be able to marry and that decisions involving excommunication should be made within the church as a spiritual, not a political, matter.[10]

A small sect of extremist Puritans, the Pilgrims, believed that no royal appointee should sit in a position of power over the church and that Puritans should thus completely separate from the Church of England. For them, the persecution became so intolerable that some chose to leave the land of their births for an uncharted North American wilderness to freely practice their religion. The Pilgrims, many of whom had earlier moved to Leyden, Holland, to escape persecution and establish a congregation, sailed in 1620 from Southampton aboard the *Mayflower,* settling in an area just north of present-day Cape Cod that they called Plymouth, after the English town of the same name. Although the Pilgrim leaders had pragmatically "come back half the way" out of Separatism by presenting an unthreatening document to King James to get the royal blessing for emigrating to the New World in 1620, once in New Plymouth, they were able to practice their own brand of Christianity largely outside the reach of royal oversight.[11]

It was during James's reign and the early years of Charles I's reign (beginning in 1625), in the midst of Archbishop Laud's aggressive efforts to stamp out dissent and compel compliance with approved Anglican practice, that Roger Williams came of age. Such restrictions were surely untenable for young Williams, whose character was beginning to coalesce around principles of individual liberty of conscience. Having implicitly renounced the religious orthodoxy through refusing the ordination rite (which would have provided, in addition to his master's degree, ordination, church preferment, and permanent security), Williams began moving actively within a long-established underground Puritan resistance. In early 1629, Sir William Masham (a member of Parliament whom the king had jailed in 1626 for opposing the king's forced-loan tax imposed on every subject to finance an unpopular war with France) hired Williams as household chaplain at his manor in Otes, Essex County.[12]

Williams had to have been aware that in signing up to serve as house minister in Masham's home he would be joining an underground resistance of sorts. It was through such house ministries that the Puritans attempted to circumvent Laud's dragnet. During the time he worked at the Masham manor, Williams attended meetings at Sempringham and elsewhere, where he met a broad group of ministers and others – many of whom were among the first group of Puritans to eventually migrate as the Massachusetts Bay Company to New England in the 1630s. This group included the squire John Winthrop of Groton, Suffolk; Thomas Hooker; and John Cotton (incumbent minister of a church in Boston, Lincolnshire), all of whom were vocal in favoring the establishment of congregationalist churches in every parish under royal patronage and protection. Each local congregation would rule itself, free from the help or interference of bishops and church councils. King Charles, Archbishop Laud, and the rest of the Anglican Church hierarchy had no such plans, however; they were determined instead to root out questioning voices by banning house ministries. On a happy personal note, Williams met his wife, Mary Barnard, a maid-in-waiting, while in the Masham employ. They married in November 1630, and by accounts, their long union of forty-seven years, which produced six children, was a happy one.[13]

With Charles I and Archbishop Laud turning the screws ever tighter on dissident religious practice, another wave of Puritans was prompted to flee the Old Country for the New. In 1630, nearly one thousand men, women, and children, led by John Winthrop on the *Arbella* with royal charter in hand, sailed on eleven ships to establish the Massachusetts Bay Colony. Soon enough, Williams would feel the need to move as well, as "the *only* minister in the Barrington-Masham family circle of clerics not to suffer some form of ecclesiastical suspension, investigation or similar action from Laud's office" – so in December 1630, he, too, sailed with his bride of one month on the *Lyon*. As Raymond Camp reports, "[T]he Archbishop's efficiency [prompted] Williams's motivation for his hasty exit. Beyond a doubt, [Williams's] concern for his 'libertie' was justified."[14]

II. The New World

> *However in Civil things we may be servants unto men, yet in Divine and Spiritual things the poorest peasant must disdain the service of the highest Prince: Be ye not the servants of men.*
>
> – Roger Williams, 1644 (quoting 1 Corinthians 7:23)

The young couple on horseback ambled along the Thames River on a chilly November day in 1630, making their way westward from London toward the port of Bristol and a date with the *Lyon*, bound for Massachusetts. Roger Williams and his wife, Mary, had been married less than a year, and they were now striking out for parts unknown. Likely traveling together with friends and a few other emigrants, they moved along the Thames and Avon rivers and crossed Berkshire and Wiltshire to Bath and the hills of Somerset before arriving some 120 miles away in Bristol.

Passing Windsor early along the way just a few miles south of Sir Edward Coke's thousand-acre forested estate at Stoke Poges, Roger Williams must have ruminated on his relationship with the esteemed justice, then nearly eighty years old. Lord Coke, after all, had been Williams's father figure and benefactor for the previous dozen years, sponsoring him in his preparatory and university education.

Williams adored Lord Coke, saying years later that the justice had instilled in him the qualities of industriousness and patience; Coke, for his part, was pleased to call Williams his son. So, Williams was "bitter as death" not to tell the esteemed justice, a committed Anglican, of his impending journey. But circumstances in England had deteriorated by 1630 to the point that non-Anglicans practiced their preferred religion only at risk of imprisonment at the hands of the prevailing Church of England orthodoxy, thus leading Williams and other Puritans – who advocated the power of individual congregations as opposed to that of the church hierarchy – to cast their lot elsewhere to freely practice their religion.[15]

Williams's arrival in Nantasket just outside Boston in February 1631 after a hard sea journey met with the initial approval of the Massachusetts Bay authorities, who were pleased to welcome "a godly minister" who could presumably replace John Wilson, who was returning to England later in the year to reunite with his wife. They were most surprised, then, when Williams, demonstrating that his principles had solidified considerably in the couple years since leaving Cambridge, declined the Boston church's plum offer to serve as teacher on grounds that he "durst not officiate to an unseparated people." He openly expressed his opinion, moreover, that the Boston civil government was acting outside its authority in punishing violations of the "First Table" (the first four commandments, dealing with the responsibilities and duties to God), and he refused to take communion with the Boston church membership.[16]

To the Boston Puritans, this was odd behavior indeed. Williams's biographer Ola Elizabeth Winslow paints the picture:

> Here he was in a strange land with a wife to support and a home to establish. He had cut all connections with the first twenty-seven years of his life. He had come with no committals, no plans for self-support. Harvest was still many weeks distant. Here was an immediate way of independence, a position which would take care of his physical needs, give him a work to do, an honored place in the community and perhaps a future. It was a position for which he was professionally trained and in which he had already made a successful start. He was equipped for no other. The offer had come without seeking. But no, he "durst not officiate to an unseparated people," and accordingly he shut the door in his own

> face. He did so not only against his own interest, but against all common sense.... It was unthinkable. [The Boston Puritans could be forgiven for wondering,] "Pray, what kind of 'godly minister' is this who has come among us?"[17]

Put in these terms, what could Williams have been thinking, and what must his wife Mary have thought? Winslow answers: "This was Roger Williams to the life and his brusque refusal of this first offer becomes a clue to his whole career, to his successes as well as his losses.... At the very entrance to the new life he was acknowledging conviction to [stand on principle], whatever the odds might be to him personally."[18]

Williams instead chose to accept the offer of John Endecott to be teacher in the Salem church (about fifteen miles north of Boston), replacing John Higginson, who had died the summer before. There he joined the nonconformist Reverend Samuel Skelton, with whose views he felt more closely attuned. Spurned in Boston, Winthrop and the General Court wrote Endecott a letter warning of Williams's "dangerous opinions," "marvel[ing]" that the Salem church "would choose him without advising the Council" (indeed, the fact that independent Salem would not advise the council aptly describes why Williams would choose to serve there). Williams had already been elected, however, so (by some accounts) he took the Freeman's Oath on May 18, 1631, to join the Massachusetts Bay Colony.[19]

After only a few months, Williams left Salem and Massachusetts Bay Colony, even though it appears he made friends there and was popular in the pulpit. Although the records are silent as to why he left, it is fair to surmise that Salem relented to pressure from the Bay authorities – and Williams was essentially sent packing.

In July 1631, Williams and his wife landed in the seaside town of Plymouth, the home of the original Pilgrims in Plymouth Colony, where he lived and worked for about two years as assistant to the pastor Ralph Smith. Governor William Bradford and the Pilgrims, who were more inclined than the Bay Puritans toward separation from the Church of England, warmly welcomed Williams and his wife. Having moved from Europe in 1620 to escape James's persecutions, the Pilgrims – although they had moderated substantially since those early days – were wary of the later-arriving, perhaps overzealous Bay Puritans; so Williams would seem to have been among more sympathetic company in Plymouth than in Salem.[20]

And indeed he was – earning the Pilgrims' tribute as a good and earnest Christian man, of whom Bradford initially wrote:

> Mr. Roger Williams (a man godly & zealous, having many precious parts, but very unsettled in judgment) came over first to the Massachusetts, but up on some discontent left that place, and came here.... And his teaching well approved, for the benefit whereof I still bless god, and am thankful to him, even for his sharpest admonitions & reproofs so far as they agreed with truth.[21]

As suggested by Bradford's comments, not long after arriving in Plymouth, Williams (more fully exhibiting his trademark brutal honesty) managed to alienate Bradford and the rest of the Pilgrim leadership by writing that the king's charters to colonies in North America – including the Plymouth Colony's just recently renewed charter – were invalid. "Kings are not," Williams reasoned in a later piece, "invested with Right by virtue of their Christianity to take and give away the Lands and Countries of other men." Such a position did not square, of course, with the self-justifying rationalizations taken by the colonies that God had destined that the Europeans settle and subjugate the wilderness.[22]

Williams was not impressed with such reasoning; rather, he saw the plain truth for what it was on the ground – that other human beings were already occupying, and had long occupied, the land that late-arriving Europeans were claiming by God-given right. (Vine Deloria Jr. would make these same observations some three centuries later.) It offended his sense of basic fairness that one set of God's creatures, with nary a second thought, would so presumptuously attempt to steal the property of others of his flock.

No matter that Bradford had requested the comments, Williams's honest assessment cut a bit too close for comfort, and from that date forward, his days in Plymouth were probably numbered. Whether Williams was nudged from Plymouth in August 1633 by Bradford is not perfectly clear – but Williams sufficiently annoyed Bradford that he was moved to write that Williams "began to fall into some strange opinions... [that] caused some controversy between the church & him, and in the end some discontent on his part." Bradford concluded, "he is to be pitied, and prayed for, and so I shall leave the matter, and desire the Lord to show him his errors, and reduce him into the way of truth." The church membership, despite the attempts of some of the congregation to retain him, then accepted Williams's formal request for "dismission."[23]

During his two years in Plymouth, Williams refined the habits of hard work that he would carry through to all of his later stops. True to the congregationalist belief that ministers are expected to earn their own keep rather than rely on the handouts of others, Williams farmed his own land – getting his bread, he said, "by as hard *digging* as most *diggers* in Old or New England have been put to." Also, while developing a trading business, he began learning the dialects of the various native Indians of the area. Although he had no way of knowing so at the time, he learned valuable lessons on governance in Plymouth from Governor William Bradford that would come to good use sooner than he ever might have imagined.[24]

In the summer of 1633, Roger and Mary Williams, expecting their first child (daughter Mary would be born in August), moved back to Salem, which was desperate for a minister (thirty-nine-year-old Skelton was terminally ill with tuberculosis and would die in August 1634). Salem exhibited a fair measure of independence from the Bay in inviting and electing as teacher a figure like Williams, who was already under question from the Bay Governor's Council and was fast on his way to assuming pariah status. Williams jumped right in, preaching both the long morning and afternoon service on Sundays and three weekday services in addition to baptisms and funerals. He continued to work as hard as he had in Plymouth both at the hoe (toiling "day and night in my field with my own hands, for the maintenance of my charge") and with his frequent travels related to his trading and missionary work among the Indians – not to mention his multiple summonses to court in Boston or Newtown – all of which brought him "near unto death," under the care of two physicians.[25]

Despite the "excessive" work, as he described it, it must have been a heady, invigorating time for Williams. Though likely nudged out of Plymouth, he was moving, with a small cadre of his more zealous parishioners, to a setting well suited for his passion and energy. Even though it was technically a part of Massachusetts Bay Colony, Salem had more in common with Plymouth Colony's moderately Separatist, independent tendencies. Salem was, indeed, where Roger Williams began to fully spread the wings of his ministry. But soon, like Icarus, he, too, flew too close to the sun and plummeted back to the earth.[26]

Among the issues that bothered both Williams and Skelton were the ministerial association meetings organized among all the Bay clergy to discuss what John Winthrop described as "some question of the moment." Williams and Skelton believed these meetings "might grow in time to a presbytery or superintendency, to the prejudice of the churches' liberties" – in other words, the sort of centralized control that Laud was using to oppressive effect in England. Ever the peacemaker, John Winthrop concluded that the ministers "all clear[ly]" understood that "no church or person can have power over another church; neither did they in their meetings exercise any such jurisdiction," so the objections went nowhere – this, ironically, despite the pressure Boston had put on the Salem church just two years earlier not to hire Roger Williams.[27]

On most matters of theology, Williams was largely in agreement with the Bay Puritans. Where he (and other Separatists) differed with them was in his belief that the true church should separate completely from the irredeemably corrupted Church of England. And where Williams differed even from the Separatists was in his committed belief that Christ's true church could be redeemed only by Christ himself when he returned to the earth. To Williams, it was all so much hypocrisy, then, for any church – be it the Church of England, the Puritan church, or any other – to claim to be the true church, when in fact the only true church was destroyed more than a thousand years earlier, not to be renewed until Christ's return. Williams truly was, one might say, a Puritan's Puritan.[28]

Another area in which Williams differed from Puritan orthodoxy was in his view of God's rewards and punishments. The Puritans adamantly believed that God rewarded those he favored and punished those he disfavored. It made sense, then, that government would be expected to do whatever was necessary to keep the colony in God's good graces. This was a big responsibility. Responding to the violence experienced throughout the English colonies in 1675 by King Philip's War, for example, the Massachusetts General Assembly passed a number of laws against such "provoking evils" as idleness, long hair, drinking, nonconforming apparel, unruly children, and Quakers. The laws' preamble explained that because the Puritans had not been "pure" enough, God had punished them with war. Therefore, to avoid God's wrath, they needed to pass laws to be more pure.[29]

Williams, by contrast, reversed the Puritan assumption, believing that adversity in a person's life was actually a sign of God's favor. "In fact, it was more likely that the godly were ordinary, poor and even persecuted people," historian Edmund Morgan commented. For Williams, then, it followed that "true Christians should prefer adversity with its fellowship of godly men and shun prosperity, which was most often attained by ambitious, covetous, ruthless, and wicked men. Worldly success was most likely to be a sign of iniquity and of a need for serious soul searching."[30]

To the Bay oligarchy, Williams's outspokenness on these theological issues was troubling enough, but his direct and inflammatory criticisms of the king were simply too much to bear. For its own safety, the Bay simply could not be seen as endorsing or even tolerating Williams's radical views of the colonies vis-à-vis the king. Among his troublesome positions was his insistence that the king's grants of land to the colonies were invalid, and that all English people living under those grants lay under the sin of unjust usurpation. The only way kings could have title, Williams suggested, was to negotiate with the natives for it. Williams also exposed the king's "lies" contained in the Massachusetts Bay Company's charter.

These were the arguments he had first made in the treatise written for Bradford in 1632, which came to Winthrop's attention sometime in the summer or fall of 1633. In reading the treatise, Winthrop was not pleased, disapproving of its excessive "figures and flourishes." The Court of Assistants met in Boston on December 27, 1633, to consider what to do about it. There, "[s]ome of the most judicious ministers much condemned Mr. Williams's error and presumption," and the court ordered him to appear for censure at its next session. On this occasion, several came to Williams's defense. Asked by Winthrop for his input, Salem's Governor Endecott returned a "very modest and discreet answer"; and responding to a request from the assistants for their impressions, ministers John Wilson and John Cotton added that the tract's arguments, "being written in very obscure and implicative phrases, might well admit of doubtful interpretation" and thus were not "so evil as at first they seemed."[31]

Williams himself wrote to the governor and assistants "very submissively," according to Winthrop, professing his intent to have been only to have written "for the private satisfaction of the governor etc., of Plymouth, without any purpose to have stirred any further in it, if the governor here had not required a copy of him; withal offering his book, or any part of it, to be burnt." The assistants decided on January 24, 1634, that, so long as Williams retracted or took an oath of allegiance to the king, "it should be passed over." At the next meeting of the court on March 4, 1634, "he appeared penitently, and gave satisfaction of his intention and loyalty"; Winthrop concludes, "So it was left, and nothing done in it." So Williams escaped this time, but very soon he would conclude that he would not again compromise on principle, regardless of the consequences. In any event, his penitence did not signal a long-term muzzling of his outspokenness.[32]

Another incident – one for which Williams was not directly responsible but to whom responsibility was falsely attributed in the early histories – involved the defacing of the English king's flag by members of the Salem community. The king's flag flown in the English colonies in 1630s contained the red cross of St. George the dragon slayer, given as a gift from the pope as a commemoration of victory to the king of England. Governor John Endecott, no doubt stirred up by Williams's impassioned preaching about popish "badges of superstition" and "antichristian superstition," either himself cut or ordered to be cut the cross from the flag of the militia group he commanded.[33]

Why the Salem residents were so passionate about something as seemingly trivial as flag insignia may be explained by remembering that the early colonial Puritan settlers were a principled lot whose values were central enough to justify transplanting themselves from their home country to a remote wilderness; so after the centuries of Protestant persecution at the hands of Catholics, it was like rubbing salt in an open wound to include the pope's cross on their country's flag. For Roger Williams, the most ideological and principled Puritan of the lot, it was nothing short of blasphemous.

The flag cutting was viewed by some as treasonous or, at the very least, as an impolitic stick in the eye of a king on whose good graces the colonies vitally depended. Responding to complaints from a group of loyalist settlers, the court met in November 1634 to address the issue. Here, the Court of Assistants (which could stand on principle at times), led by a majority of the participating ministers, including John Cotton, who recognized the problematic associations of the pope's flag insignia, conditionally supported Endecott and Williams – despite their understanding that the cutting was technically illegal and could create difficulties with the king.[34]

In the course of their investigation of the flag-cutting incident, with Endecott's fate still pending (the court eventually accepted a recommendation that Endecott, on repenting, be barred from holding public office for a year), the authorities became aware that Williams "had broken his promise to us" by speaking out once again in public about the invalidity of the king's patent and, in his continued ardent advocacy for separation, "for terming the churches of England anti-Christian." Ministers from the neighboring churches held the assistants at bay from proceeding against Williams for the time being, until they could discuss the matter further among themselves. In particular, John Cotton, Williams's later nemesis and foil, who had testified on Williams's behalf when he had first come before the court, again convinced the other ministers to request that the magistrates delay their prosecution until they themselves could inquire "in a church-way" whether his behavior resulted from a "misguided conscience" as opposed to "seditious principle." Then-governor Thomas Dudley reluctantly granted the request for delay, though he warned: "You are deceived in the man, if you think he will condescend to learn of any of you."[35]

It was apparently not until April 30, 1635, that the General Court again summoned Williams, this time to explain his actions in opposing the Resident's Oath enacted by the Bay magistrates requiring all resident males sixteen years or older to promise loyalty to the colony against its enemies in England, concluding with the pledge "so help me God." It was not the obvious affront to the crown to which Williams objected; rather, he objected to the direct affront, inherent in any oath, to God. He believed that an oath was a purely spiritual matter, a "part of God's worship, and God's worship was not to be put on carnal persons." "A magistrate ought not to tender an oath to an unregenerate man," Williams argued, because "we thereby have communion with a wicked man in the worship of God, and cause him to take the name of God in vain." John Winthrop reports that this argument (which was representative of Williams's staunch, lifelong opposition to oaths) "was heard before all the ministers, and very clearly confuted [that is, rebutted]," adding that, though John Endecott agreed with Williams, "he gave place to the truth." Endecott, in other words, agreed to drop his opposition to the oath, whereas Williams, not having given "place to the truth" (*truth* as defined, apparently, by the authorities), did not.[36]

With the list of Williams's challenges to Bay authority mounting, the General Court called on Williams to appear once again in early July 1635, for what was likely intended as a public rebuke for four of his previously stated "dangerous opinions": (1) that the magistrate had no authority in punishing breaches of the First Table (again, the first four commandments, dealing with man's duty to God); (2) that the magistrate had no authority to administer oaths to an unregenerate man; (3) that a churchman was prohibited from praying with unregenerate persons, even wives and children; and (4) the prohibition on giving thanks after a meal.

The first charge especially – that the magistrate lacked authority to punish offenses of the First Table – was a serious threat to the Bay magistrates' authority. They had based their authority to regulate the most minute details of the day-to-day life of residents (and punish nonconformists) on the justification that they were God's own deputies charged with enforcing his mandates. "Since the Bay clergy, magistracy, and deputies agreed with

Calvin that the first purpose of government was to buttress the church, that the church should dominate society," Covey explains, "and that this would be impossible without the coercion of the state, Williams in their view was trying to pull the rug out from under the entire order they had risked everything to erect." Ola Winslow adds, "Had Roger Williams's view prevailed, the magisterial figure of colonial times would have lost much of its terror, and the Monday morning victims for the whipping post, the stocks and the cage would have dwindled to a minority." As Sarah Vowell memorably says of the Puritans' propensity for exercising official control over private affairs, "Threatening to take away a Puritan magistrate's right to punish is like yanking the trumpet out of Louis Armstrong's hands. . . . [P]unishment is what the General Court is *for.*" As for the third item, prohibiting praying with unregenerate persons, as Covey observes, "the controversy over this doctrine brought the Bay back to the same place it had left off arguing with Williams in 1631, and must have convinced his old friends that he would have to be written off as incorrigible."[37]

Following "much debate" before the court, Williams's "said opinions were adjudged by all, magistrates and ministers . . . to be erroneous, and very dangerous." The court added, moreover, that Salem's "calling of him to office" as teacher following Skelton's death in August 1634 "was judged a great contempt of authority" and then directed Williams, at the next General Court session eight weeks hence, "either to give satisfaction . . . or else to expect the sentence." In justifying its position, the court explained that the clergy, when asked for their advice, had "expressly declared that he who should obstinately maintain such opinions . . . were to be removed, and that the other churches ought to request the magistrates so to do."[38]

As for Salem and its temerity in hiring Williams, the court punished the town by refusing to act on an earlier petition from the Salem deputies to have land on Marblehead Neck recognized as belonging to the town. In response, the Salem church, joined (or perhaps prompted) by Williams, forwarded a letter to the other churches asking for support in condemning the civil authorities' "heinous sin" of interfering in rightfully separate church matters. The Boston elders withheld the Salem church's letters from the congregations – prompting an angry letter of protest from the Salem congregation (written by Williams and lay elder Samuel Sharp) to the elders at Boston, complaining, "We have not yet apprehended it to be the choice of the officers of a church, when public letters are sent from sister Churches, to deliver or not to deliver the letters unto the body."[39]

Williams, whose judgment was perhaps colored by persistent illness contracted over the summer that brought him "near unto death" (the Boston elders viewed his illness as a sign from God – "It pleased the Lord," said Cotton, "to stop his mouth, by a sodaine disease"), decided he would not yield and wrote a letter to his congregation urging separation from the rest of the Bay churches, which were "full of anti-christian pollution," for not separating from the Church of England. Explaining first that he would no longer "communicate with the churches in the Bay," he then raised the ante considerably by informing his church that "neither would he communicate with them except [if] they would refuse communion with the rest." Increasingly annoyed, the magistrates barred Salem's deputies from sitting in the General Court until they renounced the letters.[40]

Winthrop reports that "the whole [Salem] church was grieved" by the ultimatum, but under pressure, a majority was, in Williams's words, "swayed and bowed (whether for fear of persecution or otherwise) to say and practice what, to my knowledge... many of them mourned under" and chose not to separate. The congregation "wrote an humble submission to the magistrates, acknowledging their fault in joining with Mr. Williams in that letter to the churches against them, etc." – so the Salem deputies were reinstated in the General Court, and the petitioners eventually got their land on Marblehead Neck. For his part, Williams was true to his word, never again appearing in the Salem pulpit.[41]

By now, the Bay authorities were losing patience. When the General Court met on September 2, 1635, in Newtown, it convened Massachusetts' first grand jury to consider Williams's and others' offenses; then it adjourned for a month to consider the evidence, with numerous meetings between individual magistrates and ministers. On reconvening on October 8 – "with all the ministers in the Bay being desired to be present," along with the magistrates and their assistants – the court, with Governor Haynes presiding, started sternly by jailing Endecott (until he retracted the same day) for his part in writing the Salem church letter and banished another resident, miller John Smith, for "diverse dangerous opinions which he holds and has divulged." Taking up the case of Williams's two letters, the court offered him one last opportunity to recant, but as dramatized at the beginning of this chapter, Williams refused.[42]

For its part, the Bay was finished negotiating, so with Governor Haynes reading the banishment sentence the next morning, the Bay rid itself for good of the threatening nuisance Williams had become – in "dar[ing]... to appeal to the people" directly. For good measure, as he read the sentence, Haynes threw in Romans 16:17: "Mark them which cause divisions and offences, contrary to the doctrine which ye have learned, and avoid them." Williams was given six weeks to leave the Bay's jurisdiction for good; but recognizing his illness, the court unofficially gave him until spring to depart, on the condition he did not "go about to draw others to his opinions."[43]

It is perhaps not surprising that Roger Williams, though ill and with a newborn child imminent, did "go about to draw others to his opinions" in private services conducted in his own home. Credible word reached the Bay authorities that a group of about twenty former members of the Salem church, "especially of devout women" who had joined Williams in separating from the Bay churches, "much taken with the apprehension of his godliness," was organizing to form a plantation around Narragansett Bay, "from whence the infection would easily spread into these [Massachusetts Bay] churches," Bay authorities feared.[44]

This sort of dangerous proselytizing the Bay could not abide, so in early January 1636, the court decided to be rid of the wayward Mr. Williams once and for all. Thereafter, legend informs us:

> The Court therefore sent the marshal, James Penn, to fetch him presently, to be shipped to England on a vessel then ready to depart. Several Salem men returned with the answer that Williams could not come, being so ill, without hazard of his life. Whereupon the Court sent Captain Underhill in a pinnace then anchored at Nantaskett to apprehend Williams and carry him aboard the England-bound vessel. When the officers came to the little two-story dwelling near the Salem meetinghouse, they found he had fled three days before; "but whither they could not learn."[45]

Williams, managing to escape in advance of his one-way ticket back to England, was instead on his way to new and entirely unknown challenges – of "man against the wilderness in an almost strictly literal sense," as Ola Winslow describes it. And the odds he overcame in accomplishing what he did in his remaining forty-seven years are nothing short of remarkable, for, "in the beginning Roger Williams fought for bare survival, and against great odds. Yes," Winslow continues, "he made himself a new home, accepted the new pattern of life in untamed places, met the day's urgencies as they came, . . . [but] to the day of his death he did not know the magnitude of what he had done."[46]

Reflecting on the Bay's action in banishing Williams for his nonconforming views, it is most ironic that a group of people who undertook a harrowing journey to a harsh new country to escape religious persecution were themselves as rigid as they were about other people's free exercise of religion. To be fair, one must appreciate the substantial dilemma Williams's arguments presented for Winthrop and the colonies. The Bay faced a number of vexing issues in 1634–5. Indeed, there was a very real (and justified, on the basis of signals from England) fear that the king would revoke the charter and/or impose greater oversight by installing a royal governor. In July 1634, for example, Winthrop received a letter and official order from Matthew Craddock to return the Bay's charter to England. Winthrop, exercising the possession-is-nine-tenths-of-the-law maxim, dissembled and never sent the charter back. The colonies would not take up arms against England for another 140 years, but even at this early date, they were concerned. To maintain their own grasp on freedom, the colonies needed to keep the king at bay, and Williams was not helping matters. As Winthrop lamented in December 1633, if Williams was really concerned for the colonists' well-being, "he would not (for small or no occasion) have provoked our King against us, and put a sword into his hand to destroy us."[47]

Their experience with Williams led the Bay authorities to rethink their strategies for governing and to impose more rigid discipline after his banishment. Meeting on January 18–19, 1636 (probably at John Cotton's home, with Thomas Dudley, John Winthrop, Richard Bellingham, Thomas Hooker, John Wilson, Sir Henry Vane, Hugh Peter, and Governor John Haynes also attending), Winthrop responded to Haynes's criticism that Winthrop had dealt "too remissly in the point of justice" in his treatment of Williams. "[I]t was his judgment," Winthrop explained, "that in the infancy of plantation justice should be administered with more leniency than in a settled state, because people were then more apt to transgress partly of ignorance of new laws and orders, partly through oppression of business and other straights." The rest of the group disagreed, however, and by the next morning the various points of discussion eventually "all sorted to this conclusion: 'that strict Discipline both in criminal offenses and in martial affairs was more needful in plantations than in a settled state as tending to the honor and safety of the gospel,'" Winthrop concluded. "Whereupon there was a renewal of love amongst them, and articles drawn to this effect: 1. That there should be more strictness used in civil government and military discipline."[48]

The Bay authorities had finally succeeded in silencing the troublesome Roger Williams, simultaneously imposing a more authoritarian top-down approach to governing. Yet, in the court of history, it has been Williams's voice, not the Bay's, that has carried the day on matters of church-state separation.

III. Government in the Wilderness

God's children are like stars, *that look most bright*
When foes pursue them through the darkest night;
Like torches *beat, the more resplendent shine;*
Like grapes *when pressed, they yield luxuriant wine;*
Like spices *pounded, are to smell most sweet;*
Like trees *when shook, that wave but not retreat;*
Like vines, *that for the bleeding better grow;*
Like gold, *that burning makes the brighter show.*
– Daniel C. Eddy, 1860[49]

As the men stepped into their gear-laden dugout canoe, the leader paused for a wistful glance back at the planted plots they were leaving behind.

"After all the work, it is a shame we will not be able to reap the harvest," he thought ruefully.

Turning and climbing into the canoe, Roger Williams then led the men out onto the Seekonk River, north of Narragansett Bay. They paddled toward the west bank, bound for territory clearly out of Plymouth Colony, from which they had been gently urged to depart by Governor Edward Winslow. Seeing a convenient landfall on the western shore, they made their way toward the spot.

"What cheer, Netop?" a Narragansett Indian, standing on a large slate rock with a couple other tribesmen, called out in an odd mix of old English and Narragansett as they approached.

"What cheer!" Williams greeted in reply, grounding the canoe and stepping out onto the rock. Williams, a gifted linguist, had learned a good bit of the Narragansett language over the previous several years and was able to communicate with the men.

"I am a friend of your sachem [chief] Ousamequin, and we need a place to settle," he told them. "Can you help us?"

"Yes," they replied, pointing the way a short distance downriver, around a point to the west, and up another small river to a cove into which emptied two small fresh-water rivers. "There you will find a good place to live."

Grateful, Williams and his colleagues climbed back into their canoe and made their way to the appointed spot – and on that mid-April day in 1636, they began settling a town which would, in the fullness of time, become known as *Providence*.

Roger Williams understood perfectly well the implications of Marshal James Penn's January 1636 visit to his home in Salem – if he wished to remain in New England, he would have to flee immediately. Indeed, he must have left the very same afternoon (or possibly the next), probably on January 8 or 9, to have gotten the reported three-day head start.

The route Williams took during the rugged "fourteen weeks (in a bitter Winter Season)" between the time he left Salem and finally settled in the area of what is now Providence on or about April 16, 1636 – a period when he was so "sorely tossed" that he knew neither what "bread or bed did mean" – is uncertain. He may have traveled partway by boat and partway on foot (possibly traveling with Thomas Angell, a domestic servant he had brought with him from England in 1631). He found his way out of Massachusetts into Plymouth territory – experiencing a succession of Indian "filthy smoke holes" along the way – where he seems to have convalesced for a time late in the winter under the care of Indians at Manton's Neck in Seekonk, near the eastern shore of the Seekonk River near modern-day Rehoboth, Massachusetts. According to Baptist elder James Brown (1666–1732), who grew up near Williams's house in Providence, "[Williams] was forced to great hardships, so that if the Indians... had not helped him he might have suffered death, but they [were] very kind to him and helped him along in his journey until he came to a place since called Montons neck, where he had much kindness showed him from the Indians, [and] there he [made his] abode [for] the latter part of that winter."[50]

The Indians who helped him were the Wampanoag (under the leadership of the sachem Ousamequin – earlier known as Massasoit – with whom Williams had established good communications during his years in Plymouth and Salem), along with the Narragansett, led by Ousamequin's rival sachem Conanicus. Writing in 1677, Williams reports of his relationship with Ousamequin and Conanicus: "I spared no cost, to wards them, and in Gifts to Ousamaquin, yea & to all his, and to Conanicus & his, tokens and presents many years before I, came in person to the Nahiganset, & therefore when I came I was Welcome to Ousamaquin & that old prince Conanicus." Further, writing in 1682, Williams speaks of "my great frjendship with [Ousamequin] at Plymouth" as contributing to the sachem's helping him "when the Hearts of my Countrymen & Friends & Brethrens failed me" after his banishment. Indeed, it was with

Conanicus's, Miantonomy's (Conanicus's nephew and coruler), and ultimately Ousamequin's grace that Williams eventually settled peacefully in the Narragansett Bay area.[51]

Around the time he was in Seekonk, even though he had earlier said he "desired not to be troubled with Englishmen," Williams and Angell were joined by several others whom Williams now allowed "out of pity . . . to come along in my company" – including malcontent William Harris, the banished miller John Smith, Smith's companion Francis Wicks, and Angell (if he had not in fact accompanied Williams from Salem). It was in Seekonk, where Williams had previously traveled and purchased a piece of land from Ousamequin, where Williams "first . . . begun to build & plant" when the weather cleared sufficiently, probably in early April.[52]

Very shortly, however, he received a message from Plymouth Governor Edward Winslow, advising him that the Seekonk location he was sowing was technically still within the Plymouth territory. Williams describes the message as stating that because the Pilgrims "were loth to displease the Bay," Williams should "remove but over the river unto this [other] side . . . and then I should be out of their claim, and be as free [as] themselves, and loving neighbors together." Williams, for his part, immediately then "quietly and patiently departed . . . to my Loss of a Harvest that year."[53]

Precise details about what happened next are sketchy (to the point that the official seal of Rhode Island depicting the scene has changed over time the number of men in the canoe from two to five, from six to three), but as dramatized previously, on or around April 16, 1636, Williams and his companions paddled down the Seekonk and around the bend to the site of present-day Providence. According to Williams's deed of December 6, 1661, the arrangement with the Narragansett consisted of the purchase of "the lands and meadows upon the two fresh rivers called Mooshassick and Wanasquatucket," which itself followed from his "several treaties with Conanicusse and Miantonome . . . in the year 1634 and in the year 1635."[54]

On his previous visits to Narragansett Bay, Williams presumably formed impressions of the Indians who were inhabiting the area, and what he would have observed was a relatively densely populated region. The Narragansett, numbering about five thousand (roughly one-fifth of the Indian population of New England at the time), occupied a fairly small area, about twenty miles wide running west from the Bay roughly to the border of present-day Connecticut (inhabited by the Pequot, their traditional enemies; and, farther west, the Mohegan), and fifty miles

PHOTO 3. Roger Williams Landing at Slate Rock (Rhode Island), 1636. Courtesy of U.S. History Images.

north from the Atlantic Ocean. To the east, across the Seekonk River and the Bay in Plymouth colony territory, were the Wampanoag, another traditional enemy, though smaller in number. The Narragansett were a healthy, industrious people who had figured out how to manage their resources and maintain a steady, year-round supply of food.

Given the Narragansett's limited land, why would Conanicus and Miantonomy have agreed to allow the Englishmen to settle in the Bay area? The answer is mainly strategic: it was in the sachems' interest to enable a friendly English presence to neutralize their enemies to the east and as potential allies against their enemies to the west. Roger Williams, in his prior dealings with them, had already proved useful. Aside from his goodwill and generosity as a trader, he had learned their language and was very helpful when it came to communicating with the Massachusetts Bay and Plymouth colonies. (Indeed, their calculations paid off in fairly short order, when the next year the Narragansett briefly allied with the Puritans and Wampanoag against the Pequot in the Pequot War.) So, when Roger Williams came calling at Slate Rock for permission to settle, Conanicus and Miantonomy allowed him a generous tract.[55]

Williams was no dummy; thereafter, he continued to work hard to stay in the sachems' good graces. Given his earlier statements denying the king's right to issue grants of land in New England, it is no surprise that Williams viewed the term *purchase* of the land in Narragansett Bay in terms other Englishmen would view as unconventional. He "understood what was almost incomprehensible to Europeans that, from Conanicus's point of view, the treaty of 'purchase' did not bestow ownership but only the right to settle on the sachem's land as his subjects," Covey explains. "When Conanicus would help himself to any of Williams's trading stock he pleased in later years, Williams patiently endured the situation, knowing that the grand sachem regarded all property in the Narragansett domain as his own."[56]

In short, Williams skillfully and diplomatically managed the touchy task of inserting an English settlement among a society of five thousand Narragansett. As he later recalled, "I having made covenant of peaceable neighborhood with all the Sachems and natives round about us; and having in a sense of God's merciful providence unto me in my distress, called the place, Providence."[57]

Government and Liberty of Conscience

The rest of 1636 and 1637 were largely consumed with the multitude of tasks necessary in carving a living out of the wilderness – planning, staking, clearing, chopping, building, planting, fishing, sowing, harvesting, and the like. Records of the first couple months in Providence are nonexistent (the first entry in the Providence Records is June 16, 1636); Williams's first letter from New Providence was either to Winthrop in June 1636 or to Governor Vane, dated July 26, 1636. Additional settlers arrived during the spring of 1637, including Williams's wife, Mary, and their daughters, Mary and Freeborn, together with other wives and children from Salem. By the time of Providence's formal incorporation as a town on August 20, 1637, about thirty-two settlers (including anywhere from eight to thirteen householders, or "masters of families") called Providence home. Conditions were not easy. When "that great and pious soul" Winslow, as Williams called him, "melted" and visited the Williams family in 1637, he graciously gave Mary Williams a gold piece (and later spoke of the "prophesier" Williams as "a man lovely in his carriage, and whom I trust the Lord will yet recall").[58]

Not least important among the tasks for the band of settlers was to decide how they would govern themselves. Williams, as de facto leader and novice government builder, seems to have settled within several months on a model similar to that adopted years earlier by the Pilgrims in the Mayflower *Compact*, which relied on majority vote of the householders to decide most matters. Williams reported in an undated letter to Winthrop (probably written in summer 1636) the process as it was already playing out: the "[m]asters of families have ordinarily met once a fort night & consulted about our Common peace, watch, and planting; & mutual Consent has finished all matters with speed & peace." Williams added that he intended to memorialize the governing structure by having all family masters subscribe to the following agreement:

> We whose names are here under written, late inhabitants of the Massachusetts (upon occasion of some difference of Conscience)... do with free & joint Consent promise each unto other, that, for our Common peace and welfare (until we hear further of the Kings royal pleasure Concerning ourselves) we will from time to time subject ourselves in Active or passive obedience to such orders & Agreements, as shall be made by the greater number of the present Householders, & such as shall be hereafter admitted by their Consent into the same privilege & Covenant in our ordinary meeting.[59]

Interestingly, as reflected in the last sentence ("such as shall be hereafter admitted by their Consent into the same privilege & Covenant"), at first Williams envisioned that Providence would not be an entirely open democracy – residence would be limited only to persons agreed on by a majority of present voters. "That as I freely subject myself to common consent," he explained to Winthrop, "and shall not bring in any person into the town without their consent; so also that against my consent no person be violently brought in and received." Because he had subjected himself to the will of the majority, he reasoned, others could be made to do so as well to avoid discord. (Williams at the time was seemingly vexed about what to do about some of the troublesome "young men" who were agitating for land.)[60]

Despite the language of the agreement and his comment to Winthrop, Williams never took official action to prevent anyone from settling in Rhode Island – although given the troubles caused by some, he must have been sorely tempted. Williams fathered the first American haven, open to all – to, if you will, "the tired, the poor, the huddled masses yearning to breathe free, the wretched refuse, the homeless and tempest-tost" (as immortalized centuries later on the Statue of Liberty). "No matter how undesirable their reputations announced them to be," Ola Winslow explains, Providence and Rhode Island welcomed all comers:

"The doors were open to troublesome Samuel Gorton whom nobody wanted ... with his riotous company." Moreover, "[t]hey were open to Anne Hutchinson and her following, and to William Coddington, who became a traitor to the colony, to the Quakers, who in Massachusetts thought, were most undesirable of all."[61]

From the beginning, in its earliest recorded covenant, Providence demonstrated that this would be a different kind of government from the sort practiced by the Bay Puritans, for this government would be limited to "civil things" only, not spiritual:

> We whose names are hereunder, desirous to inhabit the town of Providence, do promise to subject ourselves in active or passive obedience to all such orders or agreements as shall be made for the public good of the body in an orderly way, by the major consent of the present inhabitants, masters of families, incorporated together into a Towne fellowship, and others whom they shall admit unto them, *only in civil things*.[62]

Only in civil things: In the colony Roger Williams begat, everyone agreed (despite any other disagreements they may have had, and most assuredly did have) that the very foundation for the society was liberty of conscience – or, more precisely, protecting religious views from government interference. As Williams himself later explained, the early settlers "agreed that [Providence] should be for such as were destitute especially for Conscience sake." In a 1658 letter to the Massachusetts Bay Assembly, for example, the Rhode Island General Assembly averred that liberty of conscience was the "freedom we still prize as the greatest happiness that man can possess in this world." The General Assembly earlier admitted in a 1657 letter to the United Colonies of New England that it valued liberty of conscience even above the survival of government itself (although, it hastened to add, it hoped such would never occur).

The General Assembly conceded that independent-minded persons left free to express themselves would "overturn relations and civil governments among men," but the assembly reasoned nonetheless that "rational discourse and persuasion were the only weapons a government should employ in its own defense and physical suppression could not be countenanced for the sake of preservation of order." Similarly, in 1657, the General Assembly responded to a request from English authorities to stamp out Quakers, who were espousing an especially radical form of Protestantism, by stating: "We have no law among us whereby to punish any for only declaring ... their minds and understanding concerning the things and ways of God, as to salvation and eternal condition." Indeed, so committed to the principle of liberty of conscience were the residents of Rhode Island that in 1638, Providence punished one man for interfering with his wife's attending, together with other devotees, Williams's religious sessions. (This protection of the free exercise of religion, incidentally, goes substantially further than the contemporary First Amendment, which proscribes infringements by government, but not private, actors.[63])

In short, as Bruce Daniels observes, "when the tension between liberty of conscience and good order grew into conflict it was invariably settled on the side of liberty by this first generation" of Rhode Island settlers. In this regard, the contrast with Massachusetts Bay was stark: "The Puritan vision hoped to fashion a civilization uniform in faith that would come as close as possible to approximating the Augustinian city on a hill." By contrast, Daniels suggests, "the dissenting [Rhode Island] vision hoped to fashion a civilization where man would be freed from religious intolerance and could pursue the mysteries of his soul without restraint. The first vision permitted little religious deviation; the second permitted little enforced religious conformity."[64]

Early Rhode Island's commitment to liberty of conscience can be traced directly to Roger Williams's views on the matter, which he stated succinctly in 1652 in *Hireling Ministry None of Christ*: "I plead for impartiality and equal freedom, peace and safety to other consciences and assemblies, unto which the people may as freely go, and this according to each conscience . . . whether of Jews or Gentiles." Quoting Martin Luther, Williams explained: "The Government of the Civil Magistrate extends no further then over the Bodies and Goods of their Subjects, not over their Souls." In Williams's view, because government officials cannot know which religion is "true," the best protection for true religion is to forbid the state from getting involved in spiritual matters. In short, government extends only to the civil realm.[65]

By contrast, for Winthrop and other Puritans, government had dual purposes, both "civil and ecclesiastical." Explaining the marriage of the ecclesiastical and civil government, Winthrop said on the *Arbella*, "The end [of civil government] is to improve our lives to do more service to the Lord." Government's duty, in other words, is to govern in the church's interests. Williams's antagonist John Cotton explains in *The Keyes of the Kingdom* that civil peace, for which civil government is responsible, includes two components: first, the regulation of earthly affairs involving land, goods, grievances, and so on, and second, "the establishment of pure Religion, in doctrine, worship, and government, according to the word of God; as also the reformation of all corruptions in any of these." And Cotton's disciple John Davenport wrote in *A Discourse about Civil Government in a New Plantation Whose Design Is Religion* that the civil and ecclesiastical are "coordinate States . . . reaching forth help mutually each to other, for the welfare of both, according to God."[66]

To Cotton and the Puritans, Williams's suggestion that government should not regulate religious matters was dangerous – to allow this would "then let all Seducers to Apostacy, Idolaters, & Heretics . . . rejoice in an open door of liberty, & safety [that Williams] has set wide open before them." Rather, Scripture suggests that God favors a civil government that deals severely with such persons: "The punishments executed upon false Prophets, and seducing Teachers, do bring down showers of God's blessings upon the civil State, I Kings 18:40, 41." Look also to Luke 19:27, Cotton suggested: "Those of my enemies, that would not that I should reign over them, bring them hither and slay them before my face."

Williams could not have disagreed more. He reminded Cotton that Christ himself had spoken against religious persecution: "[Christ] charges straightly that his Disciples should be so far from persecuting those that would not be of their Religion, that when they were persecuted they should pray, when they were cursed they should blessed." "I observe the unmercifulness of such doctrines and hearts," Williams rued, "as if they had forgotten the Blessedness, Blessed are the merciful, for they shall obtain mercy, Math. 5." Pointing out the hypocrisy of religious wars, he scolded: "The blood of so many hundred thousand souls of Protestants and Papists, spilt in the Wars of present and former Ages, for their respective Consciences, is not required nor accepted by Jesus Christ the Prince of Peace."[67]

Following from Williams's insistence that government should be strictly limited to civil matters, another entirely novel – and radical, for the times – innovation of Rhode Island government was the level of accountability to which it held its elected officials, which largely predated or occurred roughly concurrently with the great writings of the European Enlightenment (Rousseau, Kant, Voltaire, Locke, and the like) on the topic of consent of the governed. These, in turn, formed the intellectual basis for the American Revolution as articulated by such polemicists and politicians as Thomas Paine, Thomas Jefferson, James Madison, and others.

The historical precedents for this approach were the Magna Carta of 1215 and the Petition of Right of 1628, in the sense that these documents were written by the "subjects" (respectively, the barons and the people,

PHOTO 4. John Cotton. Courtesy of Google Books.

through Parliament) to circumscribe the power of the ruler (the king). But the Rhode Island approach stands apart from any other arrangement to date, including those groundbreaking English precedents, in giving the subjects – the governed – vastly more comprehensive power to dictate the terms under which they would be governed and the suitability of those elected to govern. In Rhode Island, to guarantee that government did not operate outside its allotted narrow authority, officials were to be watched closely and removed at the first hint of abuse of office (including if they infringed on liberty of conscience).

According to the 1647 declaration put together by the towns to organize the Providence Plantations, voting was to be by secret ballot, and officials were expressly warned against "going without, besides, or beyond his commission." Moreover, "no officer," the declaration continued, "shall think it strange or hard dealing to be brought to his fair trial, and judgment for what he has done amiss." (Indeed, William Coddington himself was removed from office when he neglected to provide an acceptable answer to constituent complaints.) In addition, the General

Assembly appointed an attorney general in 1650 with special instructions to prosecute officers who abused their power, and it legislated to define as slander, subject to damages, false statements against an individual by a town official. As Daniels notes, "the whole tenor of the organizational legislation in 1647 which in many ways was the first overall constitution for Rhode Island was to spell out the liberties of the inhabitants and limit the power of the governing officers."[68]

Reflecting on these provisions, the novelty of such enforced sentiments against government corruption and abuse of power, especially as compared with any government that had ever before existed in America or anywhere else in the world, is nothing short of breathtaking. It predated by more than 100 years the state constitutions, which themselves informed the federal Constitution – and that even then did not approach the level of accountability required in early Rhode Island. The principles encompass the very core of the principles of freedom elucidated by Thomas Paine in his monumental works *Common Sense* and *Rights of Man* more than 100 years later, and they would, more than 350 years later, still serve as a good model for all-too-often-overbearing government.

Although the essence of Roger Williams's view was to keep government separate from matters involving liberty of conscience, he was not a staunch civil libertarian in the modern sense of the word. "There is not a man in the world, except robbers, pirates, rebels," he wrote just a year before his death in 1682, "but does submit to government." He believed in the role of a strong government in maintaining law and order – commenting in 1655, for example, that the conclusion of some people that his writing "tends to . . . an infinite liberty of conscience, is a mistake, and which I have ever disclaimed and abhorred." He illustrated the point by drawing an analogy of a ship captain and passengers of various faiths who – though not "forced to come to the ships' prayers of worship, nor compelled from their own particular prayers or worship, if they practice any" – were still subject to the captain's orders on certain other matters:

> The commander of this ship ought to command the ship's course. . . . [Should] any seaman refuse to perform their services, or passengers to pay their freight; if any refuse to help, in person or purse, towards the common charges or defense; if any refuse to obey the common laws and orders of the ship, concerning their common peace or preservation, if any shall mutiny and rise up against their commanders and officers . . . the

> commander or commanders may judge, resist, compel and punish such transgressors, according to their deserts and merits.[69]

Edmund Morgan suggests that Williams saw no problem distinguishing between every government's right to "impose a rigorous standard of behavior in matters that affected civility, humanity, morality, or the safety of the state and individuals in it, but [to impose] no standard at all in religion." The state had no business interfering in its subjects' spiritual lives, "[but] when conscience (even religious conscience) led to practices injurious to the 'life, chastity, goods, or good name' of the state's subjects, the state could legitimately interfere to protect them."[70]

As noted, Williams believed that government's job was to protect, along with their bodies and goods, subjects' morality (that is, of the sort specified in the Second Table, the fifth through tenth commandments) – and could regulate to that end. In this sense, he agreed with the Puritans that it was government's job to lead subjects, for their own good, toward right actions. It was by enforcing good morals that government separated man from beast. "Williams too could play the Puritan game of making distinctions," Morgan explains. "Since [Catholics'] allegiance to a foreign potentate might pose a danger to public safety, Williams suggested that they might be disarmed and required to wear distinctive clothing, but he insisted that they ought to be allowed to worship as they pleased." He also thought the Quakers' God-is-within theology promoted anarchy, but he supported sanctions only for their "incivilities," never for their liberty of conscience.[71]

On this view, biographers' occasional characterizations of Williams's decisions as "always [made] with a high regard for individual human rights" are perhaps overstated – at least under modern conceptions of human rights. Asserting, as does Ola Winslow, in the next breath that he governed under "an assumption (often false) of a comradely solicitude for the good of the whole on the part of his companions" is surely accurate, however. Indeed, Williams demonstrated the latter in his deep concern for the welfare of the community. To him, the community welfare depended, on the one hand, on the authorities not intruding at all on residents' spiritual affairs (and in nonspiritual affairs, treating them fairly and respecting their dignity) and, on the other hand, on the residents behaving civilly within the community (and punishing them if they did not). Writing in 1681 to the Providence town clerk just two years before his death, he asserted, "[I]t is the duty of every man to maintain, encourage, and strengthen the hand of authority."[72]

That said, Williams's "hand of authority" was open, softened with a velvet glove. He was aware, and proud, of the unprecedented liberty enjoyed by Rhode Island residents – writing in 1666 to the neighboring town of Warwick: "[N]either Old nor New England knows the like, nor no part of the World a greater [liberty]." Elaborating further on the defining features of Rhode Island's democracy, he enumerated residents' freedoms:

> Liberty of our persons: No Life nor Limb taken from us: No Corporal punishment no Restraint, but by known Laws and Agreements of our own making.
>
> Liberty of our Estates, Houses, Cattle, Lands, Goods, and not a penny to be taken by any rate [tax] from us, without every man's free debate by his Deputies, chosen by himself and sent to the General Assembly.
>
> Liberty of Society or Corporation: of sending or being sent to the General Assembly, of choosing and being chosen to all offices, and of making or repealing all Laws and Constitutions among us.

Roger Williams's views on government may seem routine from the vantage point of twenty-first-century Western civilization, but in the context of the mid-seventeenth century, they were radical. Regarding views of residents' liberty vis-à-vis their responsibility to the community, Williams, a man ahead of his time, would have appreciated the comments of current Supreme Court Justice Anthony Kennedy before the American Bar Association in 1998:

> Freedom may be born in protest, but it survives in civility.... Civility underscores the idea of individual worth and dignity, the idea which is the first premise of democratic theory.... We are civil to each other because we respect one another's aspirations and equal standing in a democratic society.... Law cannot live in the consciousness of a people without an abiding belief in the principles of individual responsibility, rationality, and civility.... [Such principles are] the basis for us to form ... an alliance not of arms but of belief in uplifting standards that secure the law, the rule of law, the law which is the only means to sustain the progress of humankind.[73]

IV. Rhode Island and Providence Plantations; Legacy

[A] People may erect and establish what form of Government seems to them most [appropriate] for their civil condition: It is evident that such Governments... have no more power, nor for no longer time, than the civil power or people consenting and agreeing shall entrust them with. This

> *is clear not only in Reason, but in the experience of all commonwealths, where the people are not deprived of their natural freedom by the power of Tyrants.*
>
> – Roger Williams, 1644

The entourage passing through the New England woods and pastures on this fine autumn day in 1644 was likely in high spirits, both for the homecoming toward which it moved on its several-day journey and for the precious papers it carried. The path on which it traveled, which had been little more than a deer track when the group's leader had used it in duress eight years earlier in search of a new home, had widened considerably with the thousands of settlers who had since made their way the approximately fifty miles south and west from Massachusetts Bay to Narragansett Bay.

As the group neared the Seekonk River just across from Providence, its final destination, Roger Williams was puzzled to make out in the distance what looked to be a small flotilla of fourteen canoes floating on the river.

"What could this be?" he asked himself, and he then queried of his traveling companions, "Do you know why they are here?"

Some of the group, aware of the plan, feigned ignorance. "We know not," they replied, suppressing smiles.

Coming closer, Williams was able to identify many or most of the smiling people sitting in the canoes, and then he realized that the flotilla was a welcoming party for his triumphant return from England after many months away.

"Oh!" he thought as he absorbed the warm greetings of his friends, family, and fellow townspeople ready to escort him home, "how sweet a homecoming!"

Building a Colony

From the beginning, Roger Williams was an accidental leader of a colony. As early as 1632, Williams expressed to John Winthrop that he had no intention of founding a colony but rather intended to operate a private Indian mission. Circumstances, however, led him to Providence – and essentially by default, he was the leader of the nascent colony. It was not an easy task for a person of selfless temperament. As Ola Winslow describes it:

> The beginnings of Providence Plantations were almost fortuitous. One man, deeply harassed, had come to a remote spot for refuge. Others followed him, and a colony resulted.... It was almost as simple as that.... Mistakenly he

> took it for granted that his fellow settlers shared his high motives, as some of them did not. He seemed to have no understanding of the selfishness of men without a country, when they saw fertile lands spread out, as it were, endlessly before them. He also lacked as yet, a political philosophy requisite for the founding of a state. However, not knowing that he lacked either, he assumed charge, and faced the immediate problems of survival and group peace.[74]

The governmental structure that ultimately emerged after 1636–7 out of the settlement's early mutual-consent arrangement (along the Mayflower *Compact* model) was not a well-articulated organism; rather, it was a patchwork quilt stitched together to deal with various exigencies as they happened to arise as time went on. As for Roger Williams's own management style in those early years, Winslow reports that "he met emergencies as they came, and then as later circumstances demanded, modified the earlier arrangements, added to them, feeling his way as he went. It was a piecemeal adventure at first." This early approach created fertile ground for the emergence of a form of nonauthoritarian, local, democratic governance that provided for greater individual freedom than any government in modern history. The defining characteristic, "[s]tronger than any other principle underneath the structure of early Providence government[,] was the hatred of oppression and the militant resentment at meddling with personal freedom in any form." And the most important principle of all, with which all the settlers in the Narragansett Bay area agreed, was religious liberty for all.[75]

Many of the early settlers were, like Williams, refugees who had been banished from Massachusetts Bay for their unorthodox ideas. These were not meek, mild people. The democracy emerging around Narragansett Bay was a contentious, dissent-riven hotbed of local antagonists, seemingly perpetually near revolt. It was messy and difficult. "The first English Rhode Islanders were eccentric or ultraradical Puritans of bewildering diversity," Sydney James comments. "They squabbled heatedly among themselves. Their tiny communities and churches were constantly split over new doctrines. By and large their beliefs were equally horrifying to orthodox Puritans in the nearby colonies, who began foisting a unity on Rhode Island by defining it as a cesspool of heresy and treating it accordingly." "Rogue's Island" became known as "the place where people think otherwise." Bruce Daniels explains, "Neither democracy nor localism necessarily produce disorder, but both create a political structure that is less unified than a centralized oligarchy, and both in the case of Rhode Island created an institutional milieu incapable of checking the tempers and passions of an independent-minded people."[76]

By the early 1640s, Roger Williams and others had come to believe some form of more central structure was needed to help impose a measure of order. In addition to the internal squabbling, the towns were being politically beleaguered both from within and without – from within by William Arnold, one of the early Providence settlers who sought to place Pawtuxet (an offshoot of Providence) under Massachusetts Bay's jurisdiction; from without by the Massachusetts Bay and Connecticut colonies, who were keen on incorporating the Narragansett Bay territories into their own, and the Massachusetts Bay was soliciting English authorities to allow it to do so. Moreover, when it formed in 1643, the New England Confederacy consciously excluded the Narragansett Bay settlements from its membership.[77]

Meanwhile, England was in political turmoil. With King Charles I reconvening the Short, then Long, Parliament in 1640 after eleven years' banishment, members of Parliament – many with radical independent and/or Separatist sympathies – once again had an official forum for their grievances and ideas, which they used to devastating effect (to the king). (Indeed, when the Parliamentarians ["Roundheads"] and Royalists could not resolve their differences, England devolved into a series of three civil wars from 1641 to 1651, which led to the 1649 creation of the Commonwealth after Charles's execution in 1648 [his copersecutor Archbishop Laud was beheaded in 1645 on Tower Hill] and Oliver Cromwell's elevation to lord protector in 1653.) As it happened, the resumption of Parliament was good news for Williams, for he was well acquainted with some of the more influential of the radical Parliamentarians (including Oliver Cromwell and Sir Harry Vane the younger) from his time as chaplain at the Masham estate in 1629. Others in Massachusetts Bay, who harbored dreams of seeing their own brand of church-state politics take hold in the mother country, were following the events in England with great interest as well.[78]

All of this led Williams to conclude that it would be a propitious time to travel to England to seek a charter for the new colony on Narragansett Bay, sentiments shared by the Assembly of Newport and others, as well. As he sailed in March 1643 from New Amsterdam (New York) (as a banished man, he still could not travel through Massachusetts to the more-convenient Boston, for fear of being arrested), he witnessed fires raging through the Dutch settlement from an attack by the Mohawk (despite attempts by Williams, at the Dutch request, to broker a truce). En route at sea and shortly after his arrival, he took the opportunity to write his first book, a translation of the Narragansett Indian language into English titled *A Key into the Language of America*, published in London to an enthusiastic reception in September 1643.[79]

As summer moved into fall and winter, Williams began lobbying his friends in and out of Parliament for a charter – specifically, petitioning a commission (led by the Earl of Warwick) authorized in November 1643 by Parliament to oversee all English plantations. Among others, he spoke with Cromwell (also discussing theological questions such as the end of the world and when Christ might return to the earth), Vane, and the poet John Milton. As it happened, Williams's petition for Rhode Island was playing out at precisely the same time England was engaged in a great contest over the degree of compulsion (as opposed to toleration) in the new national church. Responding to those who would allow less tolerance (including John Cotton), in early 1644, Williams published a couple of pamphlets (*Mr. Cotton's Letter Examined and Answered* and *Queries of the Highest Consideration*), broadly arguing for an absolute right to free private judgment and complete separation of church and state so as to avoid "a world of hypocrites" and the "wracking and tormenting" of souls. How the members of Earl of Warwick's commission viewed this larger question would determine whether it favored Williams's petition or a competing bid for the Narragansett Plantations from the Massachusetts Bay Colony, led by its London agent Thomas Weld.[80]

Williams's efforts finally paid off on March 14, 1644, when he secured the necessary signatures from the commission to favor his proposal and issue a charter to Providence Plantations. Titled "A Free Charter of Civil Incorporation and Government for the Providence Plantations in the Narragansett Bay in New England," the grant read:

> Whereas diverse well-affected and industrious English inhabitants in the towns of Providence, Portsmouth and Newport... have adventured to make a nearer neighborhood... and society to and with the great body of the Narragansetts, which may in time, by the blessing of God upon their endeavors, lay a surer foundation of happiness to all America.[81]

Most important, for Williams's purposes, there was no mention of religion anywhere in the charter, which meant that the colony could choose whatever kind of civil government it wanted and that the government would have no say in church matters.

As noted, the fortuitous timing of Williams's activities and publications advocating religious tolerance contributed to his success in obtaining the charter. With the strength of his writings, Williams confirmed and augmented his stature among the more radical elements in Parliament, who were at the time themselves ascending in prominence and gaining control.

Further help came in somewhat unexpected quarters, in the form of praise from members of Parliament, English Puritans, and others for his translation work in *Key*. To the disapproval of English Puritans, the New England Puritans had made little effort to learn the language of the natives in attempting "to teach, civilize and convert the Indian Nation." As contemporaneous commentator Robert Baillie remarked, "[O]f all [Puritans] that ever crossed the American seas, . . . I have read of none of them that seem to have minded this matter: only Williams in the time of his banishment from among them, did assay what could be done with those desolate souls, and by a little experience quickly did find a wonderful great facility to gain thousands of them."[82]

Before setting sail in August 1644 for his return to America with the precious charter in hand, on July 15, Williams published *The Bloody Tenent of Persecution for Cause of Conscience*, responding again to the steady drumbeat of advocates for intolerance – including John Cotton's *The Keyes of the Kingdom of Heaven* published in June, outlining how England could create a national church modeled upon the New England experience. In *The Bloody Tenent* – which Parliament saw as exceedingly dangerous and ordered burned – Williams quoted Bacon, ridiculing those who would "pressure" others on matters of conscience as "guided therein by some private interests of their own." Why would reasonable men want to throw off intolerance at the hands of one group only to have it replaced by the intolerance of others? he asked, as he railed against the national church and issued a clarion call for religious liberty as a matter of right. To support his case, Williams argued the radical notion that government depends on the consent of the governed for its legitimacy, explaining that "[g]overnments . . . have no more power, nor for no longer time, than the civil power or people consenting and agreeing shall entrust them with" (quoted previously in full).[83]

In September 1644, in what must have been sweet redemption, Williams landed in the heart of his persecutors' Massachusetts Bay, Boston, possessing a document signed by key members of Parliament and the Council of State requesting his safe passage through Massachusetts. The Bay, though still cool to Williams, grudgingly honored the request. As dramatized earlier in this chapter, he made his way down the then-well-worn

PHOTO 5. Canoe Welcoming Flotilla for Roger Williams, 1644. Courtesy of U.S. History Images.

path from Boston to Providence to a welcoming flotilla of canoes waiting to escort him back home to Providence with the precious charter – as close to a hero's welcome as the irascible people of the Narragansett Bay would likely ever provide. On his return, Williams met for the first time his son Joseph, born while he was in England, to join his other two sons and three daughters.[84]

After his return, Williams was elected "chief officer," where a survey of his actions while in that position shows a benevolent leader looking out for the needy and exercising considerable diplomacy with the Indians and townspeople alike. The difficult task remained, though, to convince the four towns of Providence, Warwick, Portsmouth, and Newport to accept the charter. Three years later, after incessant journeying by Williams from town to town, a majority from each of the four towns voted in 1647 to create a central government, with a general assembly, to handle political and legal matters. "The form of government established is democratical," the organizing document declared, "that is to say, a government held by the free and voluntary consent of all, or the greater part of the free inhabitants." At the same time, the declaration acknowledged the argument by some that a society as free as theirs would inevitably lead to anarchy but emphasized that the towns were "unwilling that our popularity should prove (as some conjecture it Will) an anarchic, and so a common tyranny, but [are] willing and extremely anxious to promote every man safe in his person, name, and estate." The colony recognized that it was walking a fine line between freedom and anarchy.[85]

Even though the towns had organized a central authority, they were skeptical of giving it too much power lest it infringe on their liberties. Before and after the 1647 agreement, the towns effectively held the upper hand over the colony government – in practical terms, the towns' agreement on a particular matter was necessary for the colony government to act – even until after the subsequent 1663 charter. Procedurally, the towns would "agitate and fully discuss... matters in their town meetings," and only if all voted favorably would the matter be taken up by the General Assembly (or, alternatively, the General Assembly could propose a matter, which would become law only if all the towns agreed).[86]

The 1647 arrangement was quite soon circumvented, however, by William Coddington's successful scheming in 1651 to obtain from the Council of State in England a separate charter for all of Aquidneck Island (on grounds that he had been the sole discoverer and sole owner by purchase), which made him "governor for life" of the island. Coddington's charter of 1651 thus superseded Williams's charter of 1644. Concerned for the fate of the colony and for their own property and freedoms, residents prevailed on Williams, on behalf of the mainland towns, and John Clarke, on behalf of the island towns' residents loyal to Williams and the one-colony model, to travel to England to try to undo Coddington's work and ratify the 1644 grant. Williams, providing for a large family of three sons and three daughters, was hesitant (indeed, it had taken at least six years to be paid by the towns for his previous visit to England in 1643–4). He would have preferred to stay and tend to his business interests, which now consisted of a trading post, a goat-raising operation on an island in Narragansett Bay, and a speculative ironworks venture in the planning stages. In writing his friend Winthrop Jr. in Connecticut in October 1651 that "my neighbors of Providence and Warwick... have [prevailed on] me to endeavor the renewing of their liberties upon the occasion of Mr. Coddington's late grant," Williams relented and sold his properties in preparation for the journey.[87]

Once again, Williams went hat in hand to the Massachusetts Bay authorities to request safe passage through their territory. This time, the Massachusetts General Court decided that Roger Williams could embark from Boston, "provided he carry himself inoffensively according to his promise." Williams and Clarke sailed in November 1651 to an England still in throes of crisis – now a commonwealth under control of the rump Parliament (before being disbanded by Cromwell in 1653), but with nervous gentry and clergy pushing to establish again a state church to resist the "spiritual bolshevism" of the Levellers and others who were forcefully advocating libertarianism in politics and religion. The two men went about their business of informing the key individuals (Williams communicated with Cromwell, Vane, and the poet John Milton, among others) of the fraudulent nature of Coddington's claim to Aquidneck.[88]

It soon became clear that, because of opposition from the United Colonies and England's escalating conflicts with the Dutch, final action would not be forthcoming anytime soon. "I see now the mind of the Lord to hold me here one year longer," Williams wrote to his printer, Gregory Dexter, in September. "[This is] a work of time." But Williams and Clarke enjoyed substantial success more quickly than expected, when their efforts to show the fraudulent nature of Coddington's grant persuaded sufficient numbers of the Council of State to vote on October 2, 1652, to effectively nullify Coddington's charter. Having accomplished half their task, they continued lobbying to have the council expressly ratify Williams's earlier 1644 charter or to grant a new charter entirely, so as to foreclose claims by representatives of Connecticut and Plymouth of the United Colonies to the Narragansett country.[89]

During this time, Williams heard from the towns that, because of "internal distractions," they would not be able to pay him but would try to look after his family while he was gone. Williams missed his family, writing to the towns of Providence and Warwick in early 1653 once it became clear the months away were turning into years, "Remember, I am a father and a husband," and telling his wife "how joyful I should be of her being here with me until our affairs were ended." In early 1654, though, short of funds and concerned about the growing unrest in Rhode Island, he decided to return to New England, even though he and Clarke had not yet succeeded in having the council reauthorize the 1644 charter. Once again, he carried a letter from Oliver Cromwell and the council asking Massachusetts for his safe passage. Good word came at the eleventh hour, just as Williams was ready to depart from Portsmouth, that the council had decided tentatively in favor of Rhode Island – so he was able to carry back to New England three letters affirming the legitimacy of Providence Plantations under the 1644 charter. John Clarke stayed on in England to seal the deal.[90]

Once again, while in England, Williams entered the fray with published pieces seeking to rebut the increasing calls among fundamentalists for intolerance in England in the face of the burgeoning diversity of religious sects. For example, he urged in the preface to *The Fourth Paper Presented by Major Butler* (a collaboration with Vane and Milton published in March 1652) that freedom of conscience required total abandonment of any national church program. In his 1652 *The Bloody Tenent Yet More Bloody: By Mr. Cottons Endevour to Wash It White* (ostensibly a response to Cotton's 1647 *The Bloody Tenent Washed White in the Blood of the Lambe*), he again "skirmish[ed] against the priests." Whereas his earlier version had been ordered burned by Parliament, this effort was welcomed "with applause and thanks by the army" and by a parliament that understood that toleration was a necessary attribute for those interested in peacefully "living together."

In *The Bloody Tenent Yet More Bloody*, Williams countered Cotton's "Fig-leave Evasions and Distinctions" with a rat-a-tat of biting charges and observations, including that New England ministers demand compulsory church attendance because they are afraid of otherwise "thin" congregations and that churches that force tithing tend to become intellectually stagnant, "rich and lordly, pompous and princely." Moreover, he reasoned, toleration is good for the government's reputation and business – Holland, for example, with its tolerant government, became a "confluence of the persecuted... so mightily in so short a time, that Shipping, Trading, wealth, Greatness, Honour" descended on the country much like a garland from heaven. Williams emphasized the importance of liberty of conscience, querying why Irish Catholics who acknowledged the pope in spiritual affairs but had promised civil obedience should be more oppressed than others. With these "Laws against their Consciences and Worships," no wonder the Catholics in Ireland are "so enraged and desperate," he declared.

Moreover, he argued, tolerance extends well beyond the Christian faith. The "best Historians and Cosmographers," Williams explained, had shown that only five of the world's thirty parts were "acquainted" with "the sound of Christ Jesus," so it is clear God intended to leave different peoples free to choose how to arrange their own civil affairs. Government is secular, and its proper role is to serve the people and protect each person in the "natural and Civil Rights and Liberties... due to him as a Man, a Subject, a Citizen." A ruler, "whether succeeding or elective," is "but a Minister or servant of the people" who "make the laws, and give the Magistrate his commission and power," he wrote, in language previewing that of Thomas Paine in *Common Sense* and *Rights of Man* some 130–40 years later. The people are "the Original of all free Power and Agreements . . . according to their several Natures, Dispositions and constitutions, and their common peace and welfare."[91]

In April 1652, Williams published a couple of other pamphlets, as well: *Hireling Ministry None of Christ* and *Experiments of Spiritual Life and Health. Hireling Ministry* repeated his plea to allow Jews to be readmitted to England, urging the government to dispense with the "superstitious wall of separation (as to civil things) between us Gentiles and the Jews"; *Experiments*, dedicated to Lady Vane and sent to Williams's wife, Mary, as she convalesced from an illness, emphasized the importance of "doing good to men" and being compassionate for the "affected or miserable." During this time, he also attempted to renew contacts with his old mentor Edward Coke's daughter, Mrs. Anne Sadleir, by successively sending her copies of his *Experiments* and *Bloody Tenent More Bloody,* but she was uninterested. First, on receiving "Experiments" from Williams, she replied that she restricted her reading to the Bible, "the late King's book," and mainstream Anglican works. Then, after receiving *Bloody Tenent*, she responded, "When I . . . saw it entitled 'The Bloody Tenent,' I did not adventure to look into it," and asked to be contacted "no more in this kind." Finally, exasperated after reading Williams's letter suggesting the wisdom of being open to new ideas, she spat, "Mr. Williams, – I thought my first letter would have given you much satisfaction, that, in that kind, I should never have heard of you anymore; but it seems you have a face of brass, so that you cannot blush," and she wished him back "in the place from whence you came" from across the ocean.[92]

Williams returned in 1654 after two and a half years away to a disorganized, fractious colony. On top of the relentless bickering among residents, Coddington showed no signs of relinquishing authority, despite the nullification of his 1651 charter, and William Arnold was proceeding with plans to annex Pawtuxet to Massachusetts Bay. The last straw for Williams was when the recriminations were directed against him personally, at which point he responded with a piqued letter to the town of Providence. "I am like a man in a great fog," he lamented, who does "not [know] well how to steer. . . . I have been charged with folly for that freedom and liberty which I have always stood for." "[I have never given] to myself a foot of land or an inch of voice in any matter [and was taken away] from my employment and sent so vast a distance from my family, to do your work, of a costly and high nature, for so many days and weeks and months together, and there left to starve or steal, or beg or borrow[.]" If not for his efforts, he continued, the colony would still be "enslaved to the bondages ... of ... soul and body oppressions of the English and the barbarians about us."[93]

The letter seemed to have its desired calming effect; and letters from some of Williams's friends in high places helped as well. In April 1655, for example, Cromwell wrote to urge Rhode Islanders to avoid "any intestine commotions or foreign invasions," which would bring "any detriment or dishonor to the Commonwealth or yourselves as far as you by your care and diligence can prevent." A few months after Williams's return, Providence voted to name him president of Providence Plantations, a position he held from 1654 to 1657 (his last stint of formal public service).[94]

During the three years of his presidency, Williams put into practice his governance theory of combining respect for liberty of conscience with concern for the government's responsibility to maintain law and order. During Williams's time as president, the colony became stronger and the towns became more unified. Even William Coddington came around, pledging in 1656 "to adhere to the authority ... in the Colony as it is now united," and the Arnolds dropped their efforts to secede to Massachusetts Bay.[95]

Six years after concluding his turn in the presidency, and nearly ten years after Williams's return home from England, he and John Clarke finally got a new charter on July 8, 1663, for the Rhode Island and Providence Plantations. And this time it was a royal charter, from Charles II, who had assumed the throne with the 1660 Restoration of the monarchy. The most remarkable aspect of the 1663 charter (besides the fact that Williams and Clarke were able to secure it at all, given their past criticisms of the monarchy – Charles II had his own reasons for opposing the dour, intolerant Bay Puritans) was its assertion that "a most flourishing civil state may stand and best be maintained ... with a full liberty in religious concernments":

> Our royal will and pleasure is that no person within the said colony, at any time hereafter, shall be any wise molested, punished, disquieted, or called in question, for difference in opinion in matters of religion, [that] do not actually disturb the civil peace of our said colony; but that all and every person and persons may, from time to time, and at all time hereafter, freely

> and fully have and enjoy his and their own judgments and consciences in matters of religious concernments.

When it came to ensuring liberty of conscience from government interference, Roger Williams could not have asked for anything more.

The 1663 charter was not the panacea for all of Rhode Island's ills, however. Because the 1663 charter essentially technically amended a 1662 royal charter granting some of the Narragansett lands to Connecticut's Governor Winthrop, the conflicting claims led to a half century and more of conflicts between Rhode Island and its neighbors. Incessant attempted landgrabs by the New England Confederation of portions of southern Rhode Island led Williams in 1670 to pointedly write his old friend from the Pequot War, Major Mason of offending Connecticut, that the bids for "great portions of land, land in this wilderness... [represent] a depraved appetite after the great vanities, dreams and shadows of this vanishing life." And internally, as well, the insatiable quest for land, combined with Rhode Island's own laws and policies as they developed throughout the rest of the seventeenth and eighteenth centuries tying suffrage to land ownership (when sufficient land was virtually impossible for newcomers to obtain), substantially diminished Rhode Island's democracy.[96]

But solely in terms of effective governance, after the 1663 charter, the colony government was able to assert for the first time a measurable degree of control over the towns by legally threatening noncomplying town officials with "contempt" and by authorizing members of the governor's council to address "necessary town affairs" in specially convened town meetings. And – of course – the charter ensured that religious freedom would always remain sacrosanct, forever beyond reach of any civil authority.[97]

For the remaining twenty years of his life, Williams would remain civically involved – participating at various times, for example, as assistant deputy, councilor, commissioner, and clerk. When called on to assist with the government created under the 1663 charter, he commented to Winthrop: "I have since been occasioned and drawn... from my beloved privacy; my humble desires are to contribute my poor [efforts]... to preserve plantation and public interest of the whole New England and not interest of this or that town, colony, [or] opinion." Williams's selfless virtue reminds one strikingly of another reluctant leader, a talented yet reticent Virginian coaxed out of his Mount Vernon retirement to assume the presidency of the newly constituted United States some 125 years later.

As was George Washington, Roger Williams, too, was above all a patriot who sought to protect the liberty of his fellow citizens. When all was said and done, the 1663 royal charter establishing the Rhode Island and Providence Plantations, with its triumphant commitment to "full liberty in religious concernments" – which flew in the face of a powerful Puritan orthodoxy of much greater numbers deeply committed to systematically repressing and persecuting nonconformers – was Williams's crowning achievement, a fitting tribute to a lifetime of struggle for religious liberty and equal justice.[98]

Legacy

Roger Williams was the first American radical. Before him, there was no liberty of conscience anywhere in New England – not to mention England and the vast majority of the rest of Europe and world. Instead, intolerance was the express rule – among clergy and government alike. "Tis Satan's policy," said minister Thomas Shepard in a 1672 sermon, "to plead for an indefinite and boundless toleration." Harvard President Urian Oakes said in a 1673 sermon, "I look upon toleration as the first born of all abominations." Increase Mather added, in 1677, "I believe that Antichrist hath no, at this day, a more probable way to advance his kingdom of darkness than by toleration of all religions and persuasions." And Williams's longtime adversary John Cotton opined that it is "toleration that made the world antichristian, and the church never took hurt by the punishment of heretics."[99]

Intolerance was not only a theoretical principle for the Puritans – they extended its reach into the coercive power of the state to severely persecute nonconformists, sometimes even to the death. "The arm of civil government was constantly employed in support of the denunciations of the [unapproved] church," recounts Supreme Court Justice Joseph Story. In Massachusetts Bay, "the Inquisition existed in substance with a full show of its terrors and violence."[100]

Roger Williams stood up to all of that, arguing instead for the revolutionary concept of perfect liberty of conscience – government must tolerate all religions and nonreligion. For Williams, government simply has no moral authority to be involved at any level, at any time, in someone's own personal relationship with God.

Ultimately, Williams's ideas prevailed, and for most of the more than 350 years since, he has been remembered for his role in creating an America where religious freedom is guaranteed. As Daniel Eddy wrote in 1860, "[There has been] no exhibition of moral heroism grander than the spectacle presented by Roger Williams, casting himself, for a principle, upon the charity of savages; meeting the rigors of banishment in midwinter... and founding a commonwealth the law of which should be 'Toleration.'" Justice Story said of Williams's legacy, "We read, for the first time since Christianity ascended the throne of the Caesars, the declaration 'that conscience should be free, and men should not be punished for worshipping God in the way they were persuaded he required.'"[101]

Toleration – the deep commitment to official noninterference in others' differences on core matters involving natural human dignity – is the first of two attributes shared among all of the radicals profiled in this book. On the matter of toleration, Roger Williams set the trend for all the others to follow. Specifically, Williams demanded liberty of conscience – that is, an official hands-off policy for government on matters involving religion. Given his views that God had bestowed on no people a covenant since Christ's birth, it was inappropriate for any government "to set up a civil and temporal Israel, to bound out new Earthly holy Lands of Canaan" and to regulate religion in the name of God. To Williams, "there was nothing special in God's mind about England or New England or any other people or place in the world." Moreover, although he was himself a devout Christian, he recognized that one's religion or conscience had nothing to do with one's earthly pursuits. "A Christian Captain, Christian Merchant, Physician, Lawyer, Pilot, Father, Master, and... Magistrate," he reasoned, "is no more a Captain, Merchant... [and so on] then a Captain, Merchant, etc. of any other Conscience or Religion."[102]

The second common attribute of all the profiled radicals is that Christian religious orthodoxy was a major source of trouble for each. Roger Williams dared to confront an established Puritan church in Massachusetts Bay out of a "basic disgust for official orthodoxy," and his life was forever altered when he was cast out of the colony to fend for himself. Unable to return to England for fear of persecution at the hands of the prevailing orthodoxy of the Church of England and Archbishop Laud, he was forced to carve a new life for himself and his family out of the New England wilderness. In a world where for thousands of years people have been harassed or persecuted for their views on religion, including Jesus Christ himself, Roger Williams was certainly not the first to have suffered at the hands of the religious establishment. He was, however, among the first Americans to have been so beleaguered – but he would hardly be the last.[103]

For a person derided by his chief adversary, John Cotton, as "A Haberdasher of small Questions against the Power [of the state]," Roger

Williams and his "small Questions" have had a remarkable and lasting impact in America. Indeed, if it is so that the best innovations eventually prevail in the marketplace of ideas, Williams's conceptions of government and religious freedom began prevailing in relatively short order. Starting immediately in the years following the 1663 grant, charters from Charles II to New Jersey and Carolina followed from Williams's earlier demands, providing, respectively, that no person would be "molested, punished, disquieted, or called in question" for their religious views and that no person would be "molested, punished, disquieted, or called in question for any differences of opinion or practice in matters of religious concernments." Guided by William Penn's 1670 work *The Great Case of Liberty of Conscience*, Pennsylvania was founded in the early 1680s on core principles of religious freedom, ensuring that nobody living "peaceably and quietly under the civil government shall in any case be molested or prejudiced for his or her conscientious persuasion or practice."[104]

John Locke, the great English Enlightenment thinker whose writings so profoundly influenced America's revolutionary generation, began writing on topics near and dear to Roger Williams shortly after Williams's 1683 death. (Locke, born in 1632 and coming of age during and after Williams's 1643–4 and 1651–4 visits to London, would have been exposed to Williams's contributions to the intellectual debates during that seminal period in English history.) Writing in his 1689 *Letters on Toleration*, for example, Locke commented, "I regard it as necessary above all to distinguish between the business of civil government and that of religion.... It does not appear that God ever gave any such authority to one man over another as to compel other men to embrace his religion." Echoing Williams's condemnation of the sorry history of Christian Crusades and other pogroms, Locke observed "what limitless occasions for discords and wars, how powerful a provocation to rapines, slaughters, and endless hatreds."[105]

Following the American Revolution, citizens of the new nation debated what should be the nature of government's involvement in religion. Opposing the esteemed orator Patrick Henry's suggestion in the Virginia Assembly that Christianity should be Virginia's official religion, James Madison argued in his 1785 *Memorial and Remonstrance* in terms that could have come from Roger Williams, as channeled through John Locke:

> The Religion... of every man must be left to the conviction and conscience of every man; and it is the right of every man to exercise it as these may dictate. This right is in its nature an unalienable right. It is unalienable,

> because the opinions of men, depending only on the evidence contemplated by their own minds cannot follow the dictates of other men: It is unalienable also, because what is here a right towards men, is a duty towards the Creator. It is the duty of every man to render to the Creator such homage and such only as he believes to be acceptable to him. This duty is precedent, both in order of time and in degree of obligation, to the claims of Civil Society.... [I]f Religion be exempt from the authority of the Society at large, still less can it be subject to that of the Legislative Body. The latter are but the creatures and vicegerents of the former.

Madison added, nodding to the sum total of Williams's contributions, "The American Theatre has exhibited proofs that equal and complete liberty [has most] salutary effects." Madison's views ultimately prevailed in the Virginia Assembly in the form of Thomas Jefferson's 1786 Bill for Establishing Religious Freedom, which incorporated words reminiscent of Rhode Island's 1663 charter: "[N]o man shall be compelled to frequent or support any religious worship, place, or ministry whatsoever, nor shall be enforced, restrained, molested or burdened in his body or goods, nor shall otherwise suffer on account of his religious opinions or beliefs."[106]

A primary goal of the delegates to the 1787 Constitutional Convention in Philadelphia was to ensure that any newly empowered federal government would have nothing to do with religion and vice versa. Accordingly, aside from providing in article 6 that "no religious test shall ever be required as a qualification to any office or public trust under the United States," the Constitution included no mention of religion.[107]

Many Americans, however, including Thomas Jefferson, believed the Constitution's silence unacceptably left open the door for subsequent rulers to infringe on citizens' liberties, including religious freedom, and sought to amend the newly ratified Constitution to include greater protections. Ten such amendments (of the twelve proposed by Congress in 1789), afterward known as the Bill of Rights, were ratified by the requisite three-fourths of the states in 1791. The very first two provisions of the First Amendment deal with religious freedom: "Congress shall make no law regarding the establishment of religion, or prohibiting the free exercise thereof." The establishment clause thus guarantees that there would be no government support of religion (including no official national church); the free-exercise clause protects liberty of conscience from government interference. Of course, it has not been as simple as that, and much of the U.S. Supreme Court's jurisprudence over the past two centuries has involved questions involving the extent and scope of the First Amendment. Overall, the religion clauses – a direct legacy of the courageous work of Roger Williams and others – have done a remarkably good job of protecting Americans' religious freedoms.

Ola Winslow plays an intriguing game of might-have-beens with Roger Williams. "[If he would] have remained in Salem, or wherever else he might have found a brief hospitality, with his individual thought throttled at every new birth," she speculates, "he might presently have become no more than a perennial rebel, increasingly aggressive, and futilely spending his force in embattled opposition." But instead, he said "no more" to a life of hypocrisy, of preaching in a church whose authenticity he could not support in a community he believed dishonored God's commands.[108]

Something changed for Roger Williams between early 1634 and the autumn of 1635 – from the time he "submissively" and "penitently" sought forgiveness from Bay authorities for his indiscretions in pointing out for William Bradford the bankruptcy of the king's actions in granting land he did not own to English colonists to the time of his banishment in refusing the court's offer to postpone his sentencing for further counseling. There were glimmers in his earlier life foretelling this radical turn, such as his recollection of being "persecuted even in and out of my father's house these 20 years" during his childhood and young adulthood, and his first apparent push-back against authority in dropping out of graduate school at Cambridge. In true radical fashion, however, there came a point when Williams could not compromise his dearest principles to stay in the man's good graces. Better to suffer the consequences – whatever they may be – and retain a clear conscience than to continue to submit to hated dogma.

Given his hardening resolve, it was probably fortunate for Williams's long-term health that he did not return to England in 1635. "One might conjecture also that had Captain Underhill and his pinnace caught up with him before the three day head-start through the snow, and carried him off to England in his 1635 frame of thinking," Winslow speculates, "he might one day have shared a scaffold on Tower Hill with impetuous, high-thinking Sir Harry Vane." (Vane, Williams's great ally for religious tolerance during his 1643–4 and 1651–4 visits to England, was executed for treason in 1662 after the restoration of Charles II to the throne.) "Instead," Winslow concludes, "[Williams] was given a chance, first to learn, and then to throw his weight for nearly a half century against controlled thinking, and to do so on the affirmative side of rebellion."

Indeed, had Williams not gone on to found Providence, which for the first time in human history institutionalized the principles protecting liberty of conscience from government interference, he might be little more remembered than any of the other twenty individuals previously banished from the colony. And who knows – might Massachusetts Bay, in fulfilling John Cotton's grand vision for the Bay as God's model for civil-religious governance, have succeeded in spreading its model throughout the other colonies and England?[109]

It is true that Roger Williams's view of government's role vis-à-vis the individual falls short when compared with modern progressive, libertarian expectations, in the sense that he believed it was government's duty and role to regulate morality. More than 350 years later, liberal thought firmly resists the notion that the government possesses the authority to interfere with people's private lives (although government still incessantly violates this fundamental maxim). The toleration principle has undergone an evolution from Williams – he was a crucial, indispensable step along the way, but it has been left to later radicals to push beyond Williams's own boundaries.

Williams's ideas, like those of his seventeenth-century contemporary René Descartes, foreshadowed the age of Enlightenment. Williams possessed "a quality that always seems to lift a man above his time: intellectual courage, the willingness to go where the mind leads," Morgan explains. "His greatness was simple.... He dared to think."[110]

Indeed. And Roger Williams's radical thinking gave birth to a colony, Rhode Island, which provided a laboratory of experimentation for the novel idea of government protection of religious freedom, an idea that took hold and changed the world.

2

Thomas Paine (1737–1809)

Revolution

> *When it shall be said in any country ... "my poor are happy, neither ignorance nor distress is to be found among them; my jails are empty of prisoners, my streets of beggars; the aged are not in want; the taxes are not oppressive ..."; when these things can be said, then may that country boast its constitution and its government.*[1]
>
> – Thomas Paine, 1792

I. England

The boy had an odd, unpleasant feeling as he exited the sanctuary. He could not quite put his finger on it – recently he had been experiencing the feeling more regularly when attending his mother's Anglican church.

Picking his way carefully down the churchyard steps, the boy was struck by an insight of such crystalline clarity that it stopped him in his tracks.

"The preacher says God Almighty is passionate and good," he puzzled to himself. "And they say he killed his son to teach the people a lesson. But I am certain a man would be hanged if he did such a thing... So, it must be impossible that God, who is good, would have killed his son."

For all his effort, young Thomas Paine could not imagine why ministers preached such frightening sermons, and at that moment on the garden steps, he decided that "any system of religion that has anything in it that shocks the mind of a child, cannot be a true system" – a conviction Paine held for the rest of his days.[2]

The words of Thomas Paine played a pivotal role in the histories of no fewer than three nations and two revolutions. *Common Sense*, first published on January 9, 1776, instantly transformed the debate from a question of *if* the American colonies would declare independence from England to a matter of when they would make the break. The pamphlet had an astounding immediate impact, going through twenty-five editions and selling as many as 150,000 copies in 1776 alone – with countless other people in the thirteen colonies reading borrowed copies.[3]

Paine's *American Crisis* series, published in eighteen papers during the Revolutionary War, from 1776 until 1783, focused on the practical challenges facing Americans during wartime. The first installment, commiserating, "These are the times that try men's souls," contains some of the most immortal words in the English language. By war's end, Paine – himself now known as Common Sense – had become a popular American hero.[4]

Years later, after Paine had essentially retired to a quieter life of scientist-inventor, events in Europe led him to write *The Rights of Man* in 1791 and 1792 (part 2). With those volumes, Paine altered the course of history in England and France, becoming a hero to many and bitter villain to others. The book encouraged and emboldened the French citizenry during the Revolution, prompting Paine's election to the Revolutionary French National Constitutional Convention. In England, *The Rights of Man* spurred a massive reform movement that, though effectively squashed by the ruling regime, persisted underground for decades and more before emerging in the form of empowered working classes in the nineteenth and twentieth centuries.

Published in 1794 and 1795 (part 2), *The Age of Reason* harshly criticized Christian orthodoxy even while expressing great admiration for Jesus Christ the man and maintaining that God's divinity touched everything on Earth. Like *Common Sense* and *The Rights of Man* before it, *The Age of Reason* was a blockbuster bestseller, going through seventeen editions and selling tens of thousands of copies in America and many more abroad. Paine's words inspired many for decades and centuries afterward (including, among others, Abraham Lincoln, Mark Twain, Thomas Edison, and more). Finally, *Agrarian Justice*, published in 1796, continued the case Paine had been making elsewhere for

PHOTO 1. Thomas Paine (William Sharp Engraving), 1792. Courtesy of Library of Congress.

government's affirmative responsibility in guaranteeing the welfare of all citizens.[5]

With such a remarkable record of influential writings, one would expect a spot in the pantheon of history's greats – with the attendant plaudits, statues, and riches – would be ensured for Thomas Paine. Yet Paine died in disgrace and, for well more than a century, the memory of his contributions was forgotten by all but a relative few devotees.

Why the massive societal denigration? The answer depends, in part, on which side of the Atlantic the question is asked. In England, once it became clear that the ideas Paine had espoused in *The Rights of Man* were stirring up the working classes, William Pitt the Younger initiated a comprehensive – and brutally effective – anti-Paine campaign in 1792.

In America, by contrast, everything changed when Paine published *The Age of Reason*. Paine's direct repudiation of Christianity's core tenets enraged the Christian establishment – which, especially in light of reports from around the country of increased infidelity to God, viewed the work as a major threat. From that point forward, any self-respecting, devout American was simply not permitted to tolerate Thomas Paine.[6]

The story of Thomas Paine's fall from grace is a potent reminder that one challenges dominant Christian religious orthodoxy only at considerable risk in America – a lesson Paine's fellow radicals Roger Williams, Elizabeth Cady Stanton, W. E. B. Du Bois, and Vine Deloria Jr. learned as well.

Thomas Paine was born in Thetford, England, the only child of Joseph Pain (the *e* was added after Thomas moved to America), a maker of whalebone stays for women's corsets who also owned a small farm in the country, and Frances Cocke, who was nearly forty when Thomas was born. The couple was solidly lower middle class – humble but not impoverished.[7]

As in other parts of eighteenth-century England, a popular form of entertainment in Thetford (located about seventy miles northeast of London) on the only public holidays for workers besides Christmas and Easter were the public hangings for transgression of one of the two hundred capital offenses, including theft of such items as a handkerchief or a box of tea. Paine's family – like Williams's before him and Stanton's after – lived within close distance of Gallows Hill.[8]

Paine's father was a Quaker and his mother an Anglican. Although Paine was baptized in the Church of England and nominally identified himself as Anglican into his late thirties, even as a boy he was troubled by much of the church's doctrine, as dramatized earlier. He also regularly attended Quaker meetings with his father, later crediting his exposure to Quaker principles for his "exceedingly good moral education and . . . tolerable stock of useful learning." Paine's Quaker background, then, was the more influential in forming his aversion to hierarchy and his passion for social reform. He was not above criticizing the Friends, however (especially the loyalist Pennsylvania Quakers during the American Revolution) for their passivity and general affect: "[I]f the taste of a Quaker could have been consulted at the Creation, what a silent and drab-colored Creation it would have been!" "Not a flower would have blossomed its gayeties, nor a bird been permitted to sing."[9]

Paine spent seven years studying at Thetford Grammar School (at no small financial sacrifice by his parents), where "the natural bent of my mind was to science" and poetry – here reflecting, for example, on the death of a pet bird he buried in his yard:

> Here lies the body of John Crow,
> Who once was high but now is low;
> Ye brother Crows take warning all
> For as you rise, so must you fall.[10]

In school, Paine obstinately failed to learn Latin, which would have qualified him for higher education and a way out of the craftsman's life to a more lucrative career in law, medicine, or theology. Latin was frowned on by the Quakers; plus, Paine later explained in *The Age of Reason*, it "smacks of popery."[11]

Bereft of additional educational options, Paine left school in 1750 at the age of thirteen to become an apprentice in his father's stay-making shop – a profession in which he would spend most of the following twelve years pursuing the typical path of advancing from apprentice to journeyman (day worker for a master craftsman) to master stay maker. After six years with his father, he joined the shop of Mr. John Morris, "a very noted stay-maker," as a journeyman in 1756.[12]

Paine never much cared for the trade, with its considerable physical demands and its requirement for "a tolerable share of assurance" with women. So, feeling "raw and adventurous" and "heated with the false heroism of a [ship's] master," he ran off one day in 1756 at the outset of the Seven Years' War with France to crew on the privateer *Terrible*, captained by the aptly named William Death. "All gentlemen sailors, and able-bodied landmen, who are inclinable to try their fortune, as well as serve their King and country are desired to repair on board the said ship," the *Terrible*'s fliers had enticed. Before Paine could set off, however, his father Joseph intervened and prevailed on him not to go. Good thing, too, for within days out of port, the *Terrible* was set on by a French privateer, the *Vengeance*, and all but 17 men, of more than 165 on board, perished.[13]

Undeterred, Paine returned to the docks and signed on with the *King of Prussia* – this time, his father was unable to stop him. Fortunately for Paine, the *King of Prussia* was more successful than the *Terrible*; in his eight months "between the devil and the deep blue sea," Paine assisted in the taking of a number of merchant vessels and their cargoes. Paine was not enough enamored of life at sea to sign up for another cruise, so he remained ashore, thirty pounds richer (a small fortune for a young man of Paine's standing) and wiser for the experience.[14]

Twenty years old when he left the *King of Prussia*, Thomas Paine as a young man was broad shouldered; about five feet, ten inches tall; and medium athletic build – with blue eyes being his most distinguishing physical characteristic. His longtime friend and eventual biographer, Thomas Clio Rickman, commented: "His eye, of which the painter could not convey the exquisite meaning, was full, brilliant, and singularly piercing. He had in it the 'muse of fire.'" A historian described his eyes as "full of fire, the eyes of an apostle."[15]

Paine then spent about the next year (1757–8) in London. For seemingly the first time in his life, Paine fully indulged his intellectual interests, thoroughly immersing himself in the offerings of London – a city of six hundred thousand, with riches of lectures, bookstores, theaters, and debating clubs. On this and later visits, he reveled in learning about the nuances of a Newtonian-ordered universe, and he especially enjoyed the lectures of the painter-astronomer James Ferguson and the mathematician–spectacle maker Benjamin Martin, befriending both. It was during his time in London that Paine first began seriously considering the ideas of London's artisan-intellectual community – including those of commonwealthmen who looked back to Cromwell's republican-inspired reign with fondness, and of John Locke, who discounted divine right in favor of natural rights and consent-of-the-governed forms of governance.[16]

When his money ran out, Paine moved first to Dover in 1758 to resume his trade as a journeyman stay maker; then, with a ten-pound loan from his master, Mr. Grace, he opened his own stay-making business in Sandwich in 1759. Despite his skepticism about religion, he attended and occasionally preached in gatherings of Methodists. It may have been at a Methodist gathering where he met and fell in love with Mary Lambert, whom he married in September 1759.[17]

Paine's attempt to open his own stay-making business was short lived; indeed, he and his pregnant wife, Mary, were forced to sneak out of their home in Sandwich one night in early 1760 with creditors literally banging on the door. Thereafter, they settled in Margate, but soon afterward, Mary died during childbirth, an all-too-common occurrence in those days. Paine, maintaining a stiff British upper lip, wrote, "[T]here is neither manhood nor policy in grief" – then he returned, broke and alone, to his parents' home in Thetford.[18]

He stayed in Thetford for the next couple of years, spending a good portion of his time studying, at Mary's father's recommendation, for the excise officers' exam given by the customs service. By virtue of his ability to write clearly and calculate math reasonably well, together with the favorable recommendation of the Duke of Grafton and Mary's father (himself an excise officer), Paine passed the exam and was accepted into the customs service in December 1762. The following August he began at the low-level position of excise tax collector in Alford, along the North Sea coast.[19]

It was not an easy job. In addition to collecting duties on legitimately imported goods, Paine patrolled the firm sand shoreline on horseback looking for smugglers. He enjoyed the work but was fired little more than a year later for the not-uncommon offense of "stamping his ride" (taking the importer's word and stamping the goods without actually inspecting them).[20]

After failed attempts in 1765–6 to resume stay making both in Diss, near Thetford, and then Lincolnshire, Paine taught English at two different schools in London and then Kensington for the "poverty-level" amount of twenty-five pounds per year, about half his customs service salary. He lived for a time in the Covent Garden area of London, one of the city's "dreadful places" of crime and wretchedness.[21]

Though nearly destitute, Paine resumed his pursuit of knowledge in London, attending lectures on the wonders of science and voraciously reading the newest scientific journals. Paine was influenced deeply by the work of Sir Isaac Newton, who had commented in *Principia* in 1687: "This most beautiful system of the sun, planets and comets, could only proceed from the counsel and domination of an intelligent and powerful Being . . . eternal and infinite, omnipotent and omniscient; that is, his duration reaches from eternity to eternity." Ironically, for making essentially the same religious arguments in *The Age of Reason*, Paine was vilified for nearly two centuries.[22]

In July 1767, two years after being sacked from the excise officer post, Paine filed a contrite petition with the customs service asking to be reinstated. His petition was granted and, in February 1768, he accepted a posting as an exciseman to Lewes, a town of five thousand residents fifty miles south of London, where he would live for most of the following six years until his move to America. In Lewes, he lodged with Samuel Ollive, a prominent local tobacconist and grocer, and he happily fit into the life of the community, being elected to the town council and working on the local Anglican Church's parish committee responsible for disbursing aid to the poor. Lewes, a center of political dissent dating back to the thirteenth century, provided fertile ground for Paine's radical development and provided him with an altogether new perspective on England's history.[23]

He also was an enthusiastic participant in the Headstrong Club that met at the White Hart Inn for drinking, dining, and debating. Paine started expressing his political views at Headstrong – he was "at this time a Whig, and notorious for that quality which has been defined perserverance in a good cause and obstinacy in a bad one," according to his friend Thomas Clio Rickman, whom he first met around this time in Lewes. "He was tenacious of his opinions, which were bold, acute, and independent, and which he maintained with ardour, elegance, and argument" – and he honed his debating skills, frequently winning the Headstrong's competitions.[24]

Paine moved out of Ollive's home when Ollive died in 1769; then, two years later in 1771, at the urging of Ollive's widow, he married Ollive's daughter Elizabeth and helped operate the store in addition to continuing his excise work. Although Paine was quite happy with his life in Lewes, he and Elizabeth were poor, even with his excise salary of fifty pounds per year (out of which came his considerable travel expenses).[25]

So Paine was well disposed when his fellow Sussex excise officers, resentful of their poverty, nominated him in 1772 to draft a formal request to the government for higher salaries. He took this task seriously, writing a thoughtful petition titled *The Case of the Officers of Excise*. The letter displayed some of the themes that Paine would more fully develop in his subsequent works, such as compassion for the poor and criticism of excessive wealth. Caring for the poor was actually good policy, he argued, as it would have the meritorious effect of lowering crime rates: "Poverty, in defiance of principle, begets a degree of meanness that will stoop to almost anything.... He who never was [hungry] may argue finely on the subjection of his appetite," Paine reasoned. "But poverty, like grief, has an incurable deafness, which never hears; the oration loses all its edge; and '*To be, or not to be*' becomes the only question."[26]

Nearly every excise officer in the country signed the petition and contributed a small amount to send Paine to London, where he stayed for a number of months over the winter of 1772–3 attempting to make the case to Parliament. While in London, he befriended a number of influential people, including George Lewis Scott; the historian Edward Gibbon

(*The Rise and Fall of the Roman Empire*); the author Samuel Johnson; and Benjamin Franklin, who himself later invited Paine to join his "Club of Honest Whigs" in London, which included among its numbers the influential Dissenting authors James Burgh, Richard Price, and Joseph Priestley.[27]

Paine's efforts on behalf of the excisemen ultimately failed. Adding insult to injury, the Excise Commission fired Paine on April 8, 1774, for abandoning his post in Lewes, thus exposing him to immediate arrest for debt. A week later, a notice appeared in the *Sussex Weekly Advertiser*: "To be sold . . . all the Household Furniture, Stock in Trade and other Effects of Thomas Pain, Grocer and Tobacconist." By June, Elizabeth and Paine had separated.[28]

It is uncertain whether the financial difficulties were a cause of the separation, for as Paine told Clio Rickman: "it is nobody's business but my own; I had cause for it, but I will name it to no one." Neither Paine nor Elizabeth ever requested a final divorce or remarried, even though they both lived nearly another four decades and died just eight months apart. For the rest of their days, they clearly felt respect, if not affection, for the other – with Paine anonymously sending Elizabeth money when he learned years later that the Ollives were having financial difficulty and Elizabeth categorically refusing the British government's offers to pay her to participate in its 1790s efforts to defame her ex-husband.[29]

After the disintegration of his life in Lewes, Paine returned to London in June 1774, renewing former acquaintances and immersing himself once again in the intellectual life of the city. Despite his own lack of education and breeding, Paine – with a natural charm and pleasant disposition, together with a straightforward, comfortable way of speaking – once again made his way remarkably well in the crowd of London sophisticates including Franklin (who was now Pennsylvania's agent in London).[30]

Franklin was especially taken with Paine – perhaps seeing something of himself in this nervy, loquacious (no longer "young," at thirty-seven years of age) man. Despite their thirty-one year difference in age, the men complemented each other well. Both were born into the lower classes of English society; both, while lacking in formal education, were committed autodidacts who ended up ranking among the foremost thinkers of their own and succeeding generations; both were fascinated with science and invented various useful devices; both shared a healthy skepticism of Christian orthodoxy; and both were deeply committed to the principle of virtue, work for the public good, as a key attribute for good governance and self-development alike. Indeed, Franklin steadfastly chose

PHOTO 2. Benjamin Franklin. Courtesy of National Archives.

not to patent inventions such as the lightning rod and stove, and Paine scrupulously declined to copyright even his most successful writings – both so their intellectual property could be more widely distributed and prove useful to greater numbers of people.

In short, the two men were kindred spirits. After Franklin encouraged Paine – who had completely depleted his options in England – to consider resettling in America, he wrote a strong letter of introduction to his son-in-law Richard Bache and son, William Franklin (royal governor of New Jersey), to help get Paine started:

> The bearer, Mr. Thomas Pain, is very well recommended to me as an ingenious worthy young man. He goes to Pennsylvania with a view of settling there. I request you to give him your best advice and countenance, as he is quite a stranger there. If you can put him in a way of obtaining employment as a clerk, or assistant tutor in a school, or assistant surveyor (of all which I think him very capable) so that he may procure a subsistence at least, till he can make acquaintance and obtain a knowledge of the country, you will do well, and much oblige your affectionate father.[31]

Franklin's letter for Paine marked the start of a lifelong friendship. Franklin adopted Thomas Paine as a kind of "political son" – and Paine, consulting Franklin on everything he wrote and invented, would "reinvent himself" in America "and become Benjamin Franklin unleashed." Neither man, even in his wildest dreams, could have imagined the sort of momentous impact Paine would have in America less than a year and a half later.[32]

II. America

> *These are the times that try men's souls. The summer soldier and the sunshine patriot will, in this crisis, shrink from the service of their country; but he that stands it now, deserves the love and thanks of man and woman. Tyranny, like hell, is not easily conquered; yet we have this consolation with us; that the harder the conflict, the more glorious the triumph.*
>
> – Thomas Paine, 1776

The weary soldiers huddled close to the fires in the cold December night. After months of defeats and retreats, the men were exhausted and discouraged.

Morale was exceedingly low – indeed, most of the men were counting the hours until they would fulfill their service obligation and return home to their loved ones. Suffering miserable conditions for a seemingly futile cause, many were straggling away from the army.

The general pondered the woeful scene. Having made the decision to engage in a highly risky surprise attack against a better-equipped, more rested enemy, he knew he had to do something special to motivate his demoralized men.

So he turned to the words of an unlikely person – a man new to America who had himself endured his share of failure and hardship but who, having only recently experienced a meteoric midlife rise as a writer, understood the importance and power of maintaining hope when all seemed lost.

Assembling his men in every military encampment shortly before his fool's errand, then, the general and his officers read aloud Thomas Paine's now-immortal words:

> *These are the times that try men's souls.... What we obtain too cheap, we esteem too lightly: it is dearness only that gives everything its value.*

Inspired by these words, General George Washington and his Continental Army, after crossing the Delaware River in the dead of night, successfully executed their surprise attack on the Hessian troops at Trenton on Christmas Day, 1776, proving to the world, and themselves, that they were for real.[33]

Thomas Paine's physical entry onto the American stage could hardly have been less auspicious. On his arrival in Philadelphia on November 30, 1774, after a brutal nine-week sea journey on which 5 passengers died and most of the remaining 115 on board became ill with typhus, Paine himself was so afflicted that he had to be carried off the *London Packet* in a blanket by two men. The men had been dispatched by Dr. John Kearsley, who had heard that Paine was a friend of Benjamin Franklin. Kearsley also provided room and board and cared for Paine through six weeks of convalescence when he would need help even turning over in bed.[34]

Finally, by mid-January 1775, Paine had recovered sufficiently that he could find his own accommodations and present his priceless letters of introduction. Franklin's son-in-law Richard Bache, on hearing of Paine's intent to set up an academy for educating young women modeled "on the plan they are conducted in and about London," introduced Paine around town and arranged for him to tutor the sons of several of his friends.[35]

What Paine would have found upon exploring Philadelphia – "sharp-featured and dressed in a plain brown coat, soon bec[oming] a familiar figure as he tramped the city's cobblestone streets" – was a city of thirty thousand (the largest in the colonies), covering a bit less than one square mile. Founded in 1682 by the Quaker William Penn, it had a heavy Quaker influence – although people of many other religions lived there as well. By the time of Paine's 1774 arrival, the city was the continent's commercial center, where as many as one hundred ships could be accommodated during high tide, and it was its political center as well, with the Continental Congress having recently begun meeting there. "Nothing there recalled the miserable London hovels and other abominations of the English capital," recalls the French biographer Bernard Vincent.[36]

Among the people Paine met through Bache was Robert Aitken, a Philadelphia printer who had just begun publishing the *Pennsylvania Magazine*. Aitken needed help and hired Paine as editor (and author of most of the articles) of the new monthly. Paine described to Franklin the progress of his early months in America in early 1775:

> [Y]our countenancing me has obtained me many friends and much reputation, for which, please to accept my sincere thanks. I have been applied to by several gentlemen to instruct their sons, on very advantageous terms

> to myself, and a printer and bookseller here, a man of reputation, and property a Robert Aitken, has lately attempted a magazine, but having little or no turn that way himself, has applied to me for assistance. He had not about 800 subscribers, when I first assisted him. We have now upwards of 1500 and daily increasing. I have not yet entered into [salary negotiations] with him. This is only the second number, the first I was not concerned in.[37]

Paine's relationship with Aitken would turn acrimonious by the end of 1775 as a result of disagreements over what Aitken would pay him, but the ten- or eleven-month period during which he wrote for the *Pennsylvania Magazine* provided Paine with a priceless outlet for his ideas (not unlike Stanton, Du Bois, and Deloria with, respectively, the *Revolution*, the *Crisis*, and the *Sentinel*).[38]

Paine needed only to look outside his own window to find the topic of one of his first essays – and he was repulsed with what he saw. The slave auctions of Philadelphia were conducted in a shed in front of the London Coffee House, adjacent to Paine's quarters – he characterized the activities as "monstrous," a "barbarous usage,... [with] many evils attending the practice; as selling husbands away from wives, children from parents, and from each other, in violation of sacred and natural ties." "With what consistency or decency," he demanded, do American slaveholders "complain so loudly of attempts to enslave them, while they hold so many hundred thousand in slavery?" Slave owners are thieves, he argued, and the "the slave, who is the proper owner of his freedom, has a right to reclaim it." "I consider freedom as personal property," he added in 1778.[39]

From early 1775 forward, Thomas Paine, this newcomer just three months off the boat (and carried off, at that), found himself as a leading public voice for a group of radical Quakers and others, including Benjamin Franklin, Benjamin Rush, and David Rittenhouse, for the total abolition of slavery in America – even while Franklin, Rush, and others continued to hold slaves themselves. Shortly after the publication of Paine's "African Slavery in America" in *Pennsylvania Magazine* on April 14, 1775, these and other men organized the Pennsylvania Society for the Relief of Negroes Unlawfully Held in Bondage, North America's first abolitionist group.[40]

Paine's early criticisms were not limited to slavery alone. More generally, he wrote about tolerance and of the liberty of the poor, downtrodden, and entrapped from their oppressors, whomever they might be. "But what singular obligations are we under to these injured people!" he

PHOTO 3. Philadelphia Slave Market at the London Coffee House, 1770s. Courtesy of Michigan State University Library.

lamented – people including those of the Indian subcontinent, who suffered "the horrid cruelties" of the British; women, who were subject to breathtakingly unjust laws regarding marriage, child rearing, and property; and American Indians, who should be freed from the white man's "treachery and murder."[41]

After the "shot heard 'round the world" on April 19, 1775 triggered the battles of Lexington and Concord, Paine became an even more staunch supporter of the Americans' cause. "When the country, into which I had just set my foot, was set on fire about my ears," he wrote, "it was time to stir. It was time for every man to stir.... Those who had been long settled had something to defend; those who had just come had something to pursue; and the call and the concern was equal and universal." In taking leave of the pacifism of his Quaker roots, he explained: "Whoever considers the unprincipled enemy we have to cope with, will not hesitate to declare that nothing but arms or miracles can reduce them to reason and moderation. They have lost sight of the limits of humanity."[42]

Common Sense

Thomas Paine began writing the pamphlet *Common Sense* around November 1, 1775, after Benjamin Rush, a Philadelphia doctor-writer who later signed the Declaration of Independence, suggested that he write a pamphlet discussing independence from England. Paine shared drafts with Benjamin Franklin, David Rittenhouse, Samuel Adams, and Rush, incorporating some suggestions (including Rush's suggested title) and disregarding others (Rush's advice, for example, to avoid using the actual words *independence* and *republicanism*). Paine admitted that the book had "no plan ... to support it" but "was turned upon the world like an orphan to shift for itself."[43]

Rush, acting as Paine's agent, at first could find no printer willing to publish the pamphlet. Finally, Robert Bell, a "republican printer," agreed – what resulted was "the most brilliant pamphlet written during the American Revolution, and one of the most brilliant pamphlets ever written in the English language," the historian Eric Foner suggests.[44]

Common Sense arrived in the Philadelphia booksellers on January 9, 1776, with the simple anonymous byline "written by an Englishman." The reaction was breathtaking, creating "an effect which has rarely been produced by types and paper in any age or country," Rush observed. Within the first year, 150,000–250,000 copies were sold in America. Its appeal reached beyond America as well. John Adams reported the pamphlet was "received in France and all of Europe with rapture," including London, Edinburgh, and Newcastle, with translated versions in Warsaw, Rotterdam, Copenhagen, Berlin, Dubrovnik, and Moscow.[45]

At first there was much speculation as to the author's identity – John Adams, for one, shared a rumor that the author's "name is Paine, a gentleman about two years from England – a man who, General [Charles] Lee says, has genius in his eyes." Any mystery was dispelled when the Bradford second edition was published a month later in February; it carried the words "by Thomas Paine" on the cover.

"You have declared the sentiments of millions," one Connecticut man declared in a missive to Paine. "We were blind, but on reading these enlightening words the scales have fallen from our eyes; even deep-rooted prejudices take to themselves wings and flee away.... The doctrine of independence hath been in times past, greatly disgustful; we abhorred the principle – it is now become our delightful theme, and commands our purest affections." A Massachusetts man, Joseph Hawley, added, "Every sentiment has sunk into my well prepared heart." Another from Boston opined, "[I]ndependence a year ago could not have been publickly [*sic*] mentioned with impunity.... Nothing else is now talked of, and I know not what can be done by Great Britain to prevent it."[46]

"Have you seen the pamphlet *Common Sense*?" General Lee wrote to ask General George Washington. "I never saw such a masterly irresistible

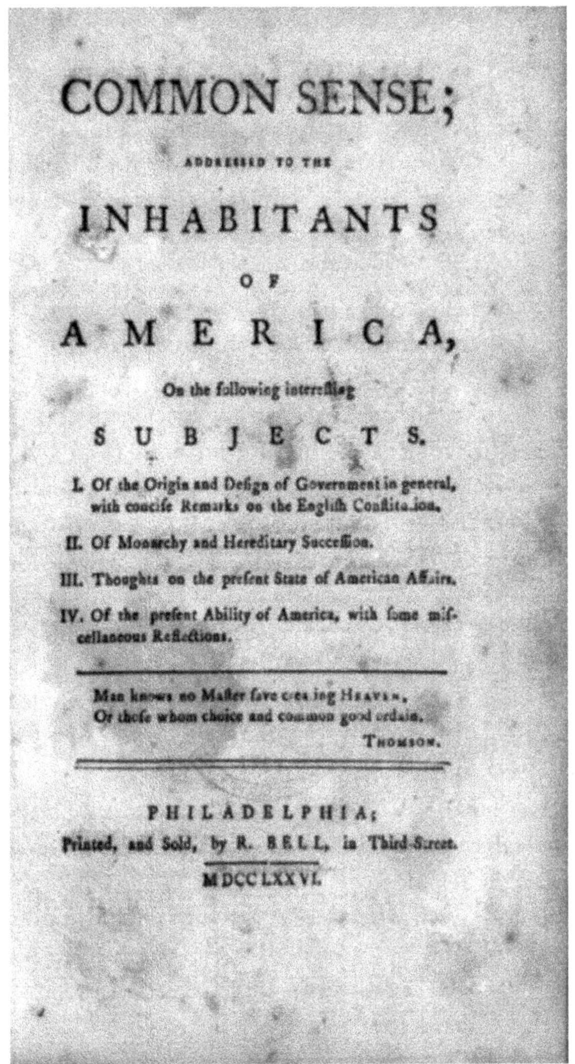

COMMON SENSE;

ADDRESSED TO THE

INHABITANTS

OF

AMERICA,

On the following interesting

SUBJECTS.

I. Of the Origin and Design of Government in general, with concise Remarks on the English Constitution.

II. Of Monarchy and Hereditary Succession.

III. Thoughts on the present State of American Affairs.

IV. Of the present Ability of America, with some miscellaneous Reflections.

Man knows no Master save creating Heaven,
Or those whom choice and common good ordain.
THOMSON.

PHILADELPHIA;
Printed, and Sold, by R. BELL, in Third-Street.
MDCCLXXVI.

PHOTO 4. *Common Sense* Title page, 1776. Courtesy of Library of Congress.

performance. It will, if I mistake not, in concurrence with the transcendent folly and wickedness of the Ministry, give the *coup-de-grace* to Great Britain. In short, I own myself convinced, by the arguments, of the necessity of separation." Washington agreed, commenting, "[It is] working a wonderful change in the minds of many men." "A few more of such flaming arguments as were exhibited [on the battlefield]," Washington continued, "added to the sound doctrine and unanswerable reasoning contained in the pamphlet *Common Sense*, will not leave members [of Congress] at a loss to decide up on the propriety of separation." John Adams, ever jealous of credit being given to anyone other than John Adams, called the pamphlet "a tolerable summary of the arguments which I had been repeating again and again in Congress for nine months," later writing Thomas Jefferson rather wistfully that "every post and every day rolls upon us independence like a torrent.... History is to ascribe the American Revolution to Thomas Paine." "No writer," Jefferson later opined, "has exceeded Paine in ease and familiarity of style, in perspicuity of expression, happiness of elucidation, and in simple and unassuming language."[47]

What did Paine say in *Common Sense* that created such a stir? First, it was *how* he said it that accounted for much of its appeal. Written in simple terms (in contrast to the typical turgid political writings of the day), the pamphlet rang true to common people. "As it is my design to make those that can scarcely read understand," Paine once explained, "I shall therefore avoid every literary ornament and put it in language as plain as the alphabet." "Every farmer and field laborer could understand what Paine meant when he called William the Conqueror 'a French bastard' who made 'himself king of England against the consent of the natives,' or pilloried George III 'The royal brute of Great Britain,'" Gary Nash suggests. Moreover, it was written in palpable tones of outrage: After Lexington and Concord, Paine explained, "I rejected the hardened, sullen-tempered Pharoah of England for ever; and disdain the wretch, that with the pretended title of Father of his People can unfeelingly hear of their slaughter, and composedly sleep with their blood upon his soul."[48]

As for substance, Paine cast the colonies' grievances as possessing universal significance. "The sun never shined on a cause of greater worth," he rhapsodized. "'Tis not the concern of a day, a year, or an age; posterity are virtually involved in the contest, and will be more or less affected even to the end of time, but the proceedings now." To the criticism that adolescent America should not rebel against parent England, Paine rejoined: "The more shame upon her conduct. 'Even brutes do not devour their young, nor savages make war upon their own families.'"[49]

The English monarchy, moreover, was fraudulently obtained in 1066 by William the Conqueror: "A French bastard landing with an armed banditti and establishing himself king of England against the consent of the natives, is in plain terms a very paltry rascally original," Paine charged. "The plain truth is that the antiquity of the English monarchy will not bear looking into." Moreover, he quipped, "One of the strongest natural proofs of the folly of hereditary right in kings, is that nature disproves it, otherwise she would not so frequently turn it into ridicule, by giving mankind *an ass for a lion*."[50]

"My motive and object in all my political works, beginning with *Common Sense*," Paine much later recalled, was "to rescue man from tyranny and false systems and false principles of government, and enable him to be free" – regardless of where such false systems and principles may exist. Accordingly, "[t]he mere independence of America, were it to have been followed by a system of government modeled after the corrupt system of English Government, would not have interested me with the unabated ardor it did," he revealed. "It was to bring forward and establish the representative system of government, as the work itself will show, that was the leading principle with me in writing."[51]

Early in *Common Sense*, Paine enunciated his classic distillation of the role of government in any society: "Society is produced by our wants, and government by our wickedness. The former promotes our happiness *positively* by uniting our affections, the latter *negatively* by restraining our vices. The first is a patron," Paine explained, "the last a punisher. Society in every state is a blessing, but government even in its best state is but a necessary evil; in its worst state an intolerable one.... Government, like dress, is the badge of lost innocence." Paine posed an elegantly intuitive thought experiment to illustrate the proper relationship of the people to their government:

> In order to gain a clear and just idea of the design and end of government, let us suppose a small number of persons settled in some sequestered part of the earth, unconnected with the rest, they well then represent the first peopling of any country, or of the world. In this natural liberty, society will be their first thought. A thousand motives will excite them thereto, the strength of one man is so unequal to his wants, and his mind so unfitted for perpetual solitude, that he is soon obliged to seek assistance and relief of another, who in his turn requires the same....

Society, in other words, is an arrangement into which people enter voluntarily for their own convenience and security. And but for the tendency of human beings not to respect one another's rights, society would not even need to form into government:

> Thus necessity, like a gravitating power, would soon form our newly arrived emigrants into society, the reciprocal blessings of which, would supersede, and render the obligations of law and government unnecessary while they

> remained perfectly just to each other; but as nothing but heaven is impregnable to vice, it will unavoidably happen, that . . . they will begin to relax in their duty and attachment to each other; and this remissness will point out the necessity of establishing some form of government to supply the defect of moral virtue.[52]

This view of government as necessary evil was widely shared among the other founders and framers. As James Madison, the primary architect of the Constitution, stated in *The Federalist Papers*: "If men were angels, no government would be necessary. If angels were to govern men, neither external nor internal controls on government would be necessary."[53]

To maintain its legitimacy, then, any government must strive to reach its "best state." To the founders, Enlightenment educated as they were, this meant that government officials must above all else follow the axiomatic guiding principle of *Virtue* – without which, Madison declared, "*no* form of government can render us secure."[54]

Virtue, translated, means "public spirit." As Paine later insisted in *Dissertations on Government* (1786), "Public good is not a term opposed to the good of individuals."

"On the contrary, it is the good of every individual collected. It is the good of all, because it is the good of every one." All the key founding fathers were committed to the classic value of virtue; nearly all came to believe, however, that those qualities had been lost among Americans and their leaders as the nation moved into the nineteenth century, and they were accordingly deeply disillusioned in their later years.[55]

Not everyone was enamored of *Common Sense*. Certainly British Loyalists were offended by Paine's characterizations of the monarchy and of British rule, but conservative Whig revolutionaries also objected to Paine's radical visions of republican government. John Adams, for one, criticized Paine's call for a unicameral legislature as "so democratical, without any restraint or even an attempt at any equilibrium or counterpoise, that it must produce confusion and every evil work." Popularly elected legislatures were "productive of hasty results and absurd judgments."[56]

Adams was concerned that mob rule might result from a system such as that proposed by Paine, so he responded with a pamphlet entitled *Thoughts on Government*, which advocated a bicameral legislature, an executive (selected by the legislatures) who could veto legislative acts, and an independent judiciary, all to combat both "democratic tyranny" of the sort opened up by Paine's suggestions and the tyranny of concentrated governmental power. (On this point, at least, Adams's view was vindicated by the creation of just this sort of separated government in the new American Constitution a little more than a decade later – not to mention the mayhem caused by a unicameral legislative body during the French Revolution). Adams espoused the distinctly elitist view that government should be run by "a few of the most wise and good." A staunch supporter of limiting the vote to property owners, Adams declared that "one thing" must exist in any new republican government: "a decency, and respect, and veneration introduced for persons in authority."[57]

Paine's major gripe with Adams was that *Thoughts on Government* would tend to undermine the revolutionary cause by demonstrating a division in the revolutionary ranks. "Mr. Thomas Paine was so highly offended with [*Thoughts*] that he came to visit me at my chamber," Adams wrote, "to remonstrate and even scold me for it, which he did in very ungenteel terms." Although the two men fundamentally differed on what a postindependence American government should look like, they agreed on the larger prize: American independence – and that common goal allowed them to work past their personal enmities at least until the end of the Revolutionary War.[58]

In addition to Adams's criticisms, another attack on *Common Sense* came from *Plain Truth*, a pamphlet published anonymously by the Maryland Loyalist James Chalmers in March 1776. *Plain Truth* did not gain much traction, but a far more serious attack came from eight letters published in the *Pennsylvania Gazette* and other newspapers by "Cato," likely the Reverend Dr. William Smith, provost of the College of Philadelphia. Cato warned Americans against advancing into the "the dark and untrodden way of independence and republicanism" and accused Paine and other colonials of grossly overstating the seriousness of the dispute between America and England for their own purposes. When it became evident that Cato's arguments were having a significant effect on public opinion, Franklin and other allies convinced Paine to return to Philadelphia from a New York visit posthaste, to offer a direct response.[59]

Paine replied to Cato, under the name "The Forester," in a series of articles defending independence and the principles of republican government in the April and May 1776 editions of the *Pennsylvania Journal*. America "hath a blank sheet to write upon" regarding its form of government, Paine observed, adding that republican government, where "the power of kings is shut out," is much to be preferred.[60]

In the Forester letters, as in virtually all of his responses to critics over the years, Paine displayed a thin-skinned sensitivity and tendency to resort to ad hominem attacks. Addressing Cato, he wrote, "Sir, you must content yourself with being ranked among the rankest of the writing Tories"; regarding Cato's admiration of King George, Paine added, "It suits not Cato to speak the truth. It is his interest to dress up the sceptered savage in the mildest colors."[61]

Independence

On June 7, 1776, the Virginian Richard Henry Lee introduced a motion in Congress that took the first steps toward creating the manifesto Paine had called for in *Common Sense*: "Resolved, That these United Colonies are, and of right ought to be, free and independent states, that they are absolved from all allegiance to the British Crown, and that all political connection between them and the state of Great Britain is, and ought to be, totally dissolved." The proposed resolution was referred to the Committee of Five on June 11 (Thomas Jefferson, John Adams, Benjamin Franklin, Robert Livingston, and Roger Sherman), which late in June produced the Declaration of Independence, which was signed in Congress on July 4, 1776.[62]

The Declaration of Independence was so infused with Paine's ideas from *Common Sense* and his other early American writings that "some historians have claimed that Paine himself secretly wrote it, or that Jefferson copied him so thoroughly that it amounted to the same thing," Craig Nelson reports. Paine and Jefferson, who likely first met during this summer of 1776, remained lifelong friends, although Jefferson distanced himself during his presidency because of Paine's political intemperance. Paine, together with his two closest associates, Jefferson and Franklin, formed a fascinating troika of massively influential American founders. Men of the Enlightenment all, Franklin was the most entirely politically pragmatic; Paine, the most purely idealistic (to his considerable detriment); and Jefferson, the most conflicted, Nelson suggests, with the competing demands of pragmatic politics and lofty ideology. The historian Bernard Bailyn comments, "[Jefferson] remained throughout his long career the clear voice of America's Revolutionary ideology, its purest conscience, its most brilliant expositor, its true poet, while struggling to deal with intractable mass of the developing nation's everyday problems."[63]

Although both Paine and Jefferson were generally optimistic about human nature and shared a keen interest in science, they differed in the sense that Jefferson saw humankind's greatest achievements in the past, whereas Paine cared little for the past and instead viewed the more industrialized future – with its "cotton mills, potteries and steel furnaces" – as the great opportunity for human advancement.[64]

Throughout 1775 and 1776, Paine was active in local politics as well, agitating for a new Pennsylvania constitution – which in final form adopted many of Paine's *Common Sense* recommendations. Paine was not in Philadelphia for the Pennsylvania Convention's actual debates, however – for shortly after the Declaration of Independence was distributed to the states, he volunteered to serve in a military unit and spent the rest of the summer in Perth Amboy. Then in September, after the Continental Army had been in nearly constant retreat across first the Hudson and then the Delaware River, Paine went to Fort Lee to serve as General Nathanael Greene's aide-de-camp. Through Greene, Paine met many people involved in the Revolution, including George Washington, with whom Paine would share a long personal and professional friendship before it dissolved in acrimony (mostly Paine's) in later years.[65]

Paine was not a natural soldier. "Common Sense and Colonel Snarl [Cornwell] are perpetually wrangling about mathematical problems," General Greene wrote his wife, and other soldiers swapped amusing stories of Paine's "less-than-military bearing." What he did do well, however, was write favorable reports of the Americans' activities from the field for the Philadelphia newspapers – even in the midst of the army's many retreats.[66]

Things only got worse for the Americans as October turned into November and then a cold and rainy December. Paine watched with Generals Greene and Washington from a hilltop as the British took Fort Washington on the Hudson, along with its 2,858 men – nearly half the colonial troops in the New York area. Washington then ordered the retreat to Hackensack from a besieged Fort Lee, which Greene and his men (including Paine) abandoned with cooking pots still on the fires. Morale was exceedingly low, and the men were sick, hungry, and cold. Two thousand of them from Maryland and New Jersey left on December 1, when their enlistment contract was up, and the rest of the contracts would expire on December 31.[67]

The British continued to gain territory, capturing Newport, Rhode Island, on December 3 and Trenton, New Jersey, on December 8. They did not, however, press an all-out attack. Had they done so, very possibly the British could have won the war then and there (given the Americans' miserable circumstances without adequate shoes, food and water, and ammunition). Paine, too, was demoralized with the retreats, but he spun them in positive terms, writing (reportedly on a drumhead by candlelight) for a Philadelphia paper: "[If critics only knew] that our army was at [the] time less than a thousand effective men, . . . that the number of the enemy was at least 8000, [and that it] retreated *slowly* above 80 miles with losing a dozen men, . . . they would never have censured it at all." Rather, "they would have called it prudent – posterity [will] call it glorious – and the names of Washington and Fabius will run parallel to eternity."[68]

Washington and the army retreated again on December 13 to the west bank of the Delaware River, across from Trenton, at which time Washington advised Congress to evacuate Philadelphia immediately (which it did, to Baltimore). Learning of the capture of General Charles Lee that same day, on whose three thousand men Washington had been anxiously awaiting, Washington wrote his cousin Lund at Mount Vernon to express his deep concern. "Your imagination can scarce extend to a situation more distressing than mine," he wrote. "Our only dependence now is upon the speedy enlistment of a new army. If this fails, I think the game will be pretty well up."[69]

Times were dire indeed. Although Washington in the following days ordered a series of guerrilla attacks by small parties of soldiers on the mercenary Hessian troops in Trenton, Paine, after being told by senior officers (and maybe Washington) that he could better serve the country by writing than by staying in camp, walked the thirty-five miles back to Philadelphia on December 13, wondering all the while whether he might be captured by British forces, who "knew all too well who 'Common Sense' was."[70]

The American Crisis

Philadelphia was in a state of panic when Paine arrived after his eleven-hour walk. Most residents were fleeing on news of the Continental Army's demoralizing string of defeats, and Paine witnessed "the deplorable and melancholy condition the people were in, afraid to speak and almost to think, the public presses stopped, and nothing in circulation but fears and falsehoods." Unknown to Paine, Washington, and other Americans, however, was the fateful decision by British commander William Howe at his Trenton headquarters (on that very same December 13 of Paine's long walk) to suspend military operations until spring – "the weather having become too severe to keep the field." The British would immediately withdraw to more comfortable winter quarters in New York City and northern New Jersey, leaving the defense of Trenton to the 1,500 Hessian troops under the command of Colonel Johann Rall. So, the British would not be marching on Philadelphia – yet.[71]

In Philadelphia, Paine, not knowing what else to do, did what he did best – he began writing, hastily putting pen to paper in an effort to bolster flagging morale during these uncertain, dangerous times of unvarnished American crisis. "In what I may call a passion of patriotism," Paine later recounted, "[I] wrote the first number of the *Crisis*. It was published on the 19th of December, which was the very blackest of times."[72]

The *Pennsylvania Journal* published this first of what would be a series of *American Crisis* articles, and eighteen thousand copies were hurriedly distributed in the streets. Paine again forswore royalties and copyrights, so the pamphlet's cost was minimal, and other printers throughout the colonies eagerly published this latest offering from America's best-selling author.[73]

What readers received was an eight-page pamphlet promising to "bring reason to your ears, and, in language as plain as A, B, C, hold up truth to your eyes." Paine urged Americans to confront their fears, appealing to their sense of dignity and destiny in order to stand heroically strong, and to maintain hope – while pursuing, against seemingly overwhelming odds, the higher values of liberty and justice.[74]

Meanwhile, a few days later, Washington wrote his adjutant, Joseph Reed, to confirm that the Continental Army – which in nearly two years of fighting had yet to register an important victory – would be mounting a bold attack: "Christmas Day at night, one hour before day, is the time fixed for our attempt on Trenton. For Heaven's sake, keep this to yourself, as the discovery of it may prove fatal to us; our numbers, sorry I am to say, being less than I had any conception of: but necessity, dire necessity, will – nay, must – justify any attempt." Around this same time, Washington must have been pleased, as he sorted through his daily briefings and found a copy of *American Crisis*, to see that the erstwhile soldier Thomas Paine had so quickly and effectively managed to capture the exact sentiments that he wished to impart to his soldiers as they embarked on this most important, dangerous effort.[75]

And now it was nearly time. On the night of December 23, Washington ordered his officers in every American encampment spread out over twenty-five miles on the Delaware River's western bank to gather the men into small groups and to read aloud Paine's *American Crisis*:

> These are the times that try men's souls. The summer soldier and the sunshine patriot will, in this crisis, shrink from the service of their country; but he that stands it now, deserves the love and thanks of man and woman.
>
> Tyranny, like hell, is not easily conquered; yet we have this consolation with us, that the harder the conflict, the more glorious the triumph. What we obtain too cheap, we esteem too lightly: it is dearness only that gives

> every thing its value. Heaven knows how to put a proper price upon its goods; and it would be strange indeed if so celestian an article as Freedom should not be highly rated....
>
> Let it be told to the future world, that in the depth of winter, when nothing but hope and virtue could survive, that the city and the country, alarmed at one common danger, came forth to meet and to repulse it.[76]

At two in the afternoon on Christmas Day, the men set off for the river in the face of an approaching nor'easter. Once there, they moved onto big flat-bottomed, high-sided Durham boats to cross the river (as later memorialized in Emanuel Leutze's familiar painting *Washington Crossing the Delaware*). The logistics of moving 2,400 men, eighteen field cannon, and fifty horses across an ice-choked river during a strengthening storm were massive – and the last crossing did not occur until around three in the morning, three hours behind schedule, which would make it difficult to reach Trenton before daylight as planned. As the men marched south – with "none but the first officers kn[owing] where we were going" – the conditions were miserable, with rain, sleet, snow, and violent hail. Two men froze to death during the march. Finally, they reached their positions outside Trenton an hour after daybreak, just before eight o'clock.[77]

Shortly after eight, the attack began, and each man "seemed to vie with the other in pressing forward," Washington wrote. After General Henry Knox's artillery cleared the streets "in the twinkling of an eye," they rushed into town shouting "*These* are the times that try men's souls!" Colonel Rall and the Hessians, thoroughly surprised (and perhaps affected in the aftermath of their Christmas libations), put up a fierce, though brief, defense. It was all over in fewer than ninety minutes – with the Americans taking more than nine hundred prisoners and, remarkably for an attack of such intensity, suffering only a handful of casualties.[78]

News of the Continental Army's surprising success at Trenton had immeasurable positive effects on the Americans' spirits. Washington had earlier believed that a "lucky blow" could "rouse the spirits of the people," but as the popular author David McCullough explains, "he could hardly have imagined how stunning the effect of the news of Trenton would be on the morale of the country. In a matter of days, newspapers were filled with accounts of Washington's crossing of the Delaware, the night march and the overwhelming success of the surprise attack," and word of mouth spread the news even more quickly. One soldier, John Adlum, who had been captured at Fort Washington and was confined by the British in New York, later wrote of how the news of Trenton had

PHOTO 5. *Washington Crossing the Delaware* (Emanuel Leutze, 1851). © The Metropolitan Museum of Art. Used with permission.

reached him: "The owner of a grocery store had pulled him into a back room and kept shaking his hand and trembling with such emotion he was unable to speak. 'I looked at him and thought him crazy or mad,' Adlum wrote, 'but as soon as he could give utterance to his word he says to me, 'General Washington has defeated the Hessians at Trenton this morning and has taken 900 prisoners and six pieces of artillery!'"[79]

The night crossing of the Delaware and the stunning success at Trenton gave Americans comfort that all was not lost and provided a glimmer of hope that maybe, just maybe, they could prevail. In her history of the Revolution, the contemporaneous writer Mary Warren wrote, "The energetic operation of [Americans'] sanguine temper was never more remarkably exhibited than in the change instantaneously wrought in the minds of men, by the capture of Trenton at so unexpected a moment. From the state of mind bordering on despair, courage was invigorated, every countenance brightened." "It may be doubted," the historian Sir George Otto Trevelyan added in the next century, "whether so small a number of men ever employed so short a space of time with greater and more lasting effects upon the history of the world." Frederick the Great of Prussia considered "the achievements of Washington and his little bank of compatriots the most brilliant of any recorded in the history of military achievements."[80]

Speaking on behalf of the entire Congress at Baltimore, John Hancock told Washington the achievement was "extraordinary," especially because the men were "broken by fatigue": "But troops properly inspired, and animated by a just confidence in their leader will often exceed expectation, or the limits of probability." With his rousing message "These are the times that try men's souls," Thomas Paine had played no small part in inspiring those troops toward their greatest triumph.[81]

Most crucially, looking forward, the combination of the financier Robert Morris's ten-dollar bonus, Paine's inspiring words, and George Washington's pleas prompted 1,400 men to reenlist, thus ensuring that the Continental Army would live to fight another day. And "in the mouths of everyone going to join the army," one contemporary observed, was "These are the times that try men's souls." Even James Cheetham (who published a scurrilous biography shortly after Paine's death), acknowledged the importance of Paine's first *American Crisis* article: "Militiamen who, already tired of the war, were straggling from the army, returned. Hope succeeded to despair, cheerfulness to gloom, and firmness to irresolution."[82]

Although the Continental Army would face many more challenges in the coming years (including a brutal next winter in Valley Forge while the British enjoyed the comforts of Philadelphia), after Trenton, Americans never again doubted that they had at least a fighting chance.[83]

III. Europe – Revolution Redux

> *Man did not enter into society to become worse than he was before, nor to have fewer rights than he had before, but to have those rights better secured.... Society grants him nothing. Every man is a proprietor in society, and draws on the capital as a matter of right.*[84]
>
> – Thomas Paine, 1792

The three Belgian prisoners did what they could to keep their sick American cellmate comfortable.

"May we leave the celldoor open during the day?" they asked the guards. "His fever is very high, and the fresh air will help."

The guards granted the request, as the prisoners were unlikely to escape in any event.

A bit later, unknown to the four prisoners inside, a man marked the number 4 in chalk on the open door resting flat against the hallway wall.

That night, a few hours after the men had closed the cell door, a special detail of government officials made their way through the prison.

Stopping at each cell with a number marked in chalk on the door, they collected that number of poor souls for their last walk among the living – to the guillotine.

Approaching the cell holding the four men, the "destroying-angel" looked at the door and, seeing no chalk mark – which "came on the inside when we shut it at night" – passed on by.

Thus were spared the lives of one very lucky Thomas Paine and his equally lucky Belgian cellmates in Revolutionary Paris in July 1794.[85]

The following ten years in Thomas Paine's life after Trenton more than not resembled his career in England – never quite seeming able to stick long in any one setting, instead mostly stumbling through a series of false steps and misunderstandings. There was one major difference, however, between America and England – Thomas Paine in 1777 was a famous author whose words had played a vital role in the new nation's move to independence. So, although his personal and professional circumstances were rocky, during those years, he continued to write and to prominently influence American politics and policy, for which he was for a time widely admired and much beloved. Although nothing he wrote matched the colossal magnitude of *Common Sense* and the first *American Crisis*, he did produce a number of notable works.[86]

During the war years, Paine would write a total of eighteen articles in the *American Crisis* series. During that time also, his views shifted toward a more laissez-faire economic approach and an appreciation of Adam Smith and his 1776 *Wealth of Nations*. As he would write in *The Rights of Man* a decade later criticizing wage regulations, "Why not leave [workingmen] as free to make their own bargains, as the law-makers are to let their farms and houses? Personal labor is all the property they have." Paine's newfound free-market view lined up with the 1780 economic program of the influential Philadelphian Robert Morris, which led to an alliance between the two men over the coming years.[87]

In 1782, Paine wrote *Letter to the Abbé Reynal, on the Affairs of North America in which the Mistakes in the Abbé's Account of the Revolution of America are Corrected and Cleared Up*, which sought to achieve two purposes – one, to explain to Europeans that America's struggle with England was much more than a minor dispute over tea and tariffs, and two, more subversively, to begin exporting America's revolutionary ideas back to Europe. The *Letter* was highly successful – as one American in Europe reported, "I have lately traveled much, and find him everywhere.

His letter to the Abbe Reynal has sealed his fame.... Even those who are jealous of, and envy him, acknowledge that the point of his pen has been as formidable in politics as the point of the sword in the field."[88]

In 1785, Paine, following from his lifelong interest in the sciences, decided to forsake his writing career for the entirely different dream of designing and manufacturing an iron bridge based on models he had seen in France a few years earlier. When in 1787 Franklin suggested that Paine present the design to the French Academy of Sciences (having had no takers in Philadelphia), Paine enthusiastically agreed.

As he sailed for Europe on April 26, 1787, with the intent of staying no longer than a year before returning to America, fifty-year-old Thomas Paine considered his political career "closed" – he intended instead to spend the rest of his years toiling contentedly in "the quiet field of science." Little could he know that both intentions would go wildly awry: rather than returning the next year to America, he would not again cross the Atlantic for another fifteen years, and rather than living the quiet life of a scientist, he would instead play a crucial role in the political upheavals of both England and France.[89]

Paine's first years back in Europe were mostly a pleasure, and he shuttled between Paris and London for several months at a time. Shortly after his first arrival in Paris, Paine dined with Thomas Jefferson in July 1787, and through another set of generous letters of introduction from Benjamin Franklin, he was able to meet important Parisians such as Marquis de Condorcet and the publisher Jacques-Pierre Brissot and to become reacquainted with the Marquis de Lafayette. The French were enamored of all things American after their successful break from the reviled England, and to them, the presence of *Common Sense*'s author in their midst was a great pleasure.[90]

Late in the summer, Paine was delighted when the French Academy gave his iron-bridge design a favorable review, so he amplified his efforts over the next few years to secure funding and builders for the bridge both in France and England. He spent a fair amount of time in Yorkshire overseeing the building of a model of the iron bridge, but he also found time to meet and socialize with leading English figures, including Edmund Burke and the reformer Mary Wollstonecraft (whose writings, like Paine's, would later influence Elizabeth Cady Stanton).[91]

Paine became especially close to Burke, the author and influential member of Parliament who today is considered a high priest of conservatism but who actually publicly supported the American revolutionaries in 1776. Burke also opposed slavery and was highly critical of British corruption in India. Paine frequently visited Burke's estate at Beaconsfield, from where Paine visited nearby ironworks and other factories of the day.[92]

The French Revolution, which began in May 1789, quickly escalated with the people's storming of the Bastille royal prison on July 14, 1789, and then to the countryside when peasants attacked their landlords' properties. The National Assembly adopted the Declaration of Rights of Man on August 26, 1789.[93]

The escalation of events in France eventually forced the English to take sides. The great majority of Paine's new associates (and Paine himself) strongly supported the developments in France. Paine believed that if republicanism could blossom in such an environment, it could blossom elsewhere across Europe and the rest of the world as well. As he shared in a January 1790 letter to Burke: "The Revolution in France is certainly a forerunner to other revolutions in Europe."[94]

The Paris city government voted later that summer, on August 26, 1790, to bestow the honor of citizenship on Paine and sixteen others, including Madison, Hamilton, and Washington, "who, by their writings and by their courage, have served the cause of liberty and prepared the freedom of the people." Meanwhile, Edmund Burke continued working on an essay, originally addressed to the deputy of the French Assembly, which would detail his views on the events in France over the previous year.[95]

At first, Paine thought Burke mostly sympathized with the French Revolution. As time went on, however, it became more and more apparent to Paine that he and Burke viewed the matter entirely differently.[96]

Burke's and Paine's differences finally exploded into public view over the next several months, in one of the more remarkable pair of books to emerge from the eighteenth, or any, century. On November 1, 1790, Burke published *Reflections on the Revolution in France*, which not only harshly criticized the French Revolution but also attacked the very foundational premises of equality and natural rights. The book explained that stable institutions and long-standing traditions provide far superior guideposts for government than does abstract "prattling about the rights of men," which tends to undermine "principles of natural subordination" by "the body of the people." In short, to Burke, the Glorious Revolution of 1688 had saved English history, traditions, and laws, whereas the

French Revolution had, overnight, decimated a thousand years of French history. Let the so-called rights of man prevail, Burke warned, and "learning will be cast into the mire, and trodden down under the hoofs of the swinish multitude."[97]

Reflections met with widespread approval in England. Prime minister Horace Walpole, for example, wrote, "[It is] far superior to what was expected even by [Burke's] warmest admirers. I have read it twice, and though of 350 pages, I wish I could repeat every page by heart."

It also had its share of detractors, prompting more than forty-five responses over the following few years, including that of thirty-one-year-old Mary Wollstonecraft, the early women's rights activist, in *Vindication of the Rights of Man.*

As for Thomas Paine, he felt betrayed. After all of their conversations about Enlightenment political theory and other topics, a "loyal" Paine believed Burke had abandoned him. Burke's *Reflections* had the positive effect, however, of sharpening Paine's focus for an essay he had begun the year earlier in praise of Lafayette's new government in France. He could use Burke's arguments to highlight just how out of step the British establishment was with the principles of liberty promoted by Enlightenment thinkers.

The Rights of Man

The essay that Paine had been working on turned out to be *The Rights of Man*, which was published and released to booksellers on March 13, 1791. Like two of his previous pamphlets – *Common Sense* and the first *American Crisis* – *Rights* had an immediate, stunning impact – selling fifty thousand official copies in England in the first three months after its release.[98]

The Rights of Man both defended the French Revolution and set forth the basics of republican government in clear, cogent terms; as compared, Paine suggested, to Burke's affected style of writing in *Reflections*: "As the wondering audience, whom Mr. Burke supposes himself talking to, may not understand all this learned jargon, I will undertake to be its interpreter." And here, Paine says, is what Burke is suggesting: "That government is governed by no principle whatever; that it can make evil good, or good evil, just as it pleases. In short, that government is arbitrary power." Paine replies that such government is without authority: "In short, it is usurpation."[99]

Paine argued vehemently against government's reliance on precedent and tradition: "Every age and generation must be as free to act for itself, *in all cases*, as the ages and generations which preceded it. The vanity and presumption of governing beyond the grave, is the most ridiculous and insolent of all tyrannies. Man has no property in man," he emphasized; "neither has any generation a property in the generations which are to follow.... I am contending for the rights of the *living*." As he had previously averred in *Common Sense*, the people have the power to begin the world anew: "[N]othing of reform in the political world ought to be held improbable," he stressed. "It is an age of Revolutions, in which everything may be looked for."[100]

Paine was incredulous that Burke was entirely unempathetic to the fate of the many struggling poor (as compared to that of the French queen, Marie Antoinette): "Not one glance of compassion, not one commiserating reflection that I can find throughout his book, has he bestowed on those who lingered out the most wretched of lives, a life without hope in the most miserable of prisons," Paine charged.[101]

Whereas in *Common Sense* Paine had attacked monarchy, in *The Rights of Man* he focused his ire more on the nobility (or "no ability"). France's King Louis XVI was "a man of good heart" – in a sense, a victim of circumstances – and it was actually the aristocracy that oppressed the people in France and elsewhere. They were just "a band of interested men," Paine charged, "Lords of the bed-chamber, Lords of the kitchen, Lords of the necessary-house, and the Lord knows what besides." It was time, he concluded, for the people to assert their own rights against this tyranny of the aristocracy.[102]

In explaining these rights, Paine referred to the French Declaration of the Rights of Man and Citizen (adopted by the National Assembly in 1789), and he further developed his elucidation, begun in *Common Sense*, of the nature of the relationship of the individual vis-à-vis society and government. In particular, he discussed in greater detail "that class of natural rights which man retains after entering into society and those which he throws into the common stock as a member of society" ("civil rights"):

> Man did not enter into society to become *worse* than he was before, nor to have fewer rights than he had before, but to have those rights better secured. His natural rights are the foundation of all his civil rights....
>
> The natural rights which are not retained, are all those in which, though the right is perfect in the individual, the power to execute them is defective....

> He therefore deposits [civil] right[s] in the common stock of society, and takes the arm of society, of which he is a part, in preference and in addition to his own. Society *grants* him nothing. Every man is a proprietor in society, and draws on the capital as a matter of right.[103]

By contrast, "the natural rights which he retains are all those in which the *power* to execute it is as perfect in the individual as the right itself." For these last sorts of rights, government has no authority to interfere – period.[104]

By the time Paine returned to London in July 1791, a few months after the release of *The Rights of Man*, papers were attributing almost-supernatural power to his writings. One breathlessly reported, for example, "Paine is writing a new pamphlet to be entitled *Kingship* and its subject is to demonstrate the inutility of kings. It is to appear in November, in French, German, Spanish, Italian, and English at the same time, as persons are translating it into the four first languages as he advances in writing it. Such is the range for disseminating democratic principles!"[105]

But for the first time, there also started to emerge a serious push against the principles underlying Paine's work. When supporters of the Revolution rallied in Birmingham on the second anniversary of the fall of the Bastille, for example, Tory opponents rioted for two days, destroying the home and laboratory of the religious philosopher Joseph Priestley. Several critiques of *The Rights of Man* also appeared – one by Burke himself in which he charged Paine with seeking "to destroy in six or seven days . . . all [that] the boasted wisdom of our ancestors has labored to bring to perfection for six or seven centuries."[106]

In America, *The Rights of Man* was extremely popular as well, despite attacks on the book by John Adams and his son John Quincy, selling more than one hundred thousand copies. As Jefferson wrote Paine: "[O]ur people, my good friend, are firm and unanimous in their principles of republicanism, and there is no better proof of it than that they love what you write and read it with delight. The printers season every newspaper with extracts from your last, as they did before." Jefferson encouraged Paine to "[g]o on then in doing with your pen what in other times was done with the sword."[107]

Meanwhile in France, in the year and months since the fall of the Bastille in July 1789, the movement led by Lafayette and Jacques Necker (the Fayettistes) created a constitutional monarchy, with the unicameral National Assembly, elected by voters, and with a much reduced role for the executive (monarchy). Fractures eventually began appearing among the assembly's leaders, however, resulting in factions of Jacobins, Cordeliers, and Brissotins (or Girondins), all of whom criticized the Fayettistes for their perceived mismanagement of the Revolution.[108]

In the summer of 1791, the morning after the royal family failed in an escape attempt to the Austrian Netherlands, angry crowds gathered near their quarters in the Tuileries Palace. After an assembly spokesperson reassured a crowd near the Tuileries that the government would continue to operate well even without a king, Paine and the other men in attendance replaced their hats on their heads – except Paine had forgotten to place his tricolor ribbon on his hat that morning, and the crowd turned on him. One pointed his finger and accused, "Aristocrat!" (a most ironic charge, in light of Paine's bitter denunciations of aristocracy in *The Rights of Man*); and he was punched in the face and kicked in the leg as the crowd started chanting, "Aristocrat! A la lantern! Aristocrat! A la lantern!" urging he be hanged from the lantern and disemboweled. Paine was fortunate, however – a legislator or another person able to command the crowd's attention shouted that Paine was an American who had merely left behind his hat ribbon, and he was released, rattled but unharmed.[109]

The hat-ribbon incident did not dissuade Paine from his activism, however; indeed, he soon joined an audacious campaign to move France toward a democratic republic. In making this move, Paine was more radical in the summer of 1792 than virtually any other French leader, most of whom believed it would be a mistake to dispense with the monarchy entirely.[110]

"The Republican Proclamation" was then attached to the assembly doors on July 1, announcing the formation of the Societé des Republicains and boldly disclaiming the monarchy with the words, "The reciprocal obligation which subsisted between [the king and the people] is dissolved. He holds no longer any authority. We owe him no longer obedience. We see in him no more than an indifferent person; we can regard him only as Louis Capet."[111]

Paine traveled back to London in early July 1791, not to return to Paris until September 1792. While he was gone, the Fayettistes lost power, and as of September 1791, Paine's Societé des Republicains controlled the assembly.[112]

Paine spent a pleasant fall of 1791 and early 1792 living at the home of his friend, the corpulent poet, writer, and bookseller Clio Rickman in London. He had his portrait painted by the famous artist George Romney, and he enjoyed writing and visiting friends. He was extremely popular among the working classes and groups like the London Corresponding Society (a group of radical artisans and laborers), the Society for Constitutional Information, and dozens of other groups dedicated to convening a national convention to draft a new written constitution for England.[113]

Around the time one hundred thousand French volunteers began waging war at the borders, Paine published *The Rights of Man* (part 2) in March 1792, both to respond to Burke's and others' criticisms of *The Rights of Man* and to offer his support for his compatriot Girondin *republicains* in France. "I speak an open and disinterested language, dictated by no passion but that of humanity," he declared. "Independence is my happiness, and I view things as they are, without regard to place or person; my country is the world and my religion is to do good."[114]

Dedicated to his friend the Marquis de Lafayette, who in early 1792 was serving as commander in chief of the army in France's efforts against the Austrians and Prussians, part 2 proposed nothing less than revolution around the world. "The iron is becoming hot all over Europe. The insulted German and the enslaved Spaniard, the Russ and the Pole are beginning to think. The present age will hereafter merit to be called the age of reason," he predicted, "and the present generation will appear to the future as the Adam of a new world." America has "made a stand, not for herself only, but for the world," and "it is natural to expect that other revolutions will follow," resulting in "universal peace, civilization, and commerce . . . the happy lot of man." Once revolution has begun, Paine concluded, further revolution is inevitable.[115]

A continuing theme in the book was that America offered a template on which other nations' governments could be modeled – in America, the republic was "no other than government established and conducted for the interest of the public, as well individually as collectively." "[B]y the simple operation of constructing government on the principles of society and the rights of man, every difficulty retires, and all the parts are brought into cordial unison. . . . There," moreover, "the poor are not oppressed, the rich are not privileged. Industry is not mortified by the splendid extravagance of a court rioting at its expense. Their taxes are few, because their government is just; and as there is nothing to render them wretched, there is nothing to engender riots and tumults."[116]

Paine then shifted into a higher gear, arguing for social as well as political transformation. Government has a responsibility, he insisted, to provide assistance for citizens who struggle to make ends meet (such as his own parents when he was a boy). Elements of such government programs would include progressive taxation on property, money to the poor to educate children, and a social security system allowing retirement at sixty. Then, as now, there was concerted resistance to a government-provided social safety net. Reverend Christopher Wydell, for example, liked the idea of some parliamentary reform but found it "unfortunate for the public cause, that Mr. Paine took such unconstitutional ground, and has formed a party...among the lower classes of the people, by holding out to them the prospect of plundering the rich."[117]

The response to part 2 of *The Rights of Man* was simply overwhelming, with two hundred thousand copies sold or given away by the end of 1793 – the biggest best seller in English history after the Bible. The *Annual Register* observed, "The avidity with which this work...was read by the middle and lower classes of the people,...particularly in the great manufacturing towns both in England and Scotland, is incredible." By the time of Paine's death in 1809, something more than 1.5 million copies of *The Rights of Man* had sold in Europe.[118]

Beyond the boffo sales figures, *Rights of Man* transformed English radicalism, with vastly greater numbers thereafter participating in radical causes. In 1792, a worried Sheffield government official fretted that "[t]he seditious doctrines of Paine" spread among the people "to a great degree very much beyond my conception." The Sheffield group, which numbered more than two thousand in mid-1792, met to vent about "the enormous high price of provisions," the "luxury and debauchery" of the monarchy, Parliament's "mock representation of the people," and more.[119]

By 1792, groups modeled on the Sheffield society had sprung up throughout Britain, including the London Corresponding Society, led by the master shoemaker Thomas Hardy, which went from only eight members at its early 1792 inception to several thousand by the end of the year. The groups, one member remembered, had intangible benefits: "The moral effects of the Society were considerable. It induced men to read books, instead of wasting their time in public houses, it taught them to respect themselves.... The discussions...opened to them views which they had never before taken."[120]

And more than anyone else, the person most revered in these groups was Thomas Paine. One Sheffield group modified the words of "God Save the Queen":

> God save great Thomas Paine,
> His "Rights of Man" to explain – To every soul.
> He makes the blind to see
> What dupes and slaves they be
> And points out liberty – From pole to pole.[121]

Paine's vocabulary – "worm-eaten volumes," "musty roll of parchment," "Him whom all nature obeys – Reason" – found its way into the writings of many, and the philosophy promoted in *The Rights of Man* infused the societies as they reconstructed their own understandings of the world.

As much as Paine and most of the radical groups believed the government owed the people a form of welfare state, they were not Levellers who wished to make all property common. What they wanted was "Equality of Rights, not an Equality of Property," explained a broadside posted in Leeds.[122]

Although Paine's thinking on social equality had many adherents, it also had powerful detractors – including the British government itself. Indeed, the "social chapter" was considered mostly unremarkable in America, but Paine believed the chapter – more than anything else – was responsible for the British government's later sedition charges against him.[123]

Prime minister William Pitt at first thought Paine's *Rights of Man* was harmless, commenting to an associate, "Paine is quite right, but what am I to do? As things are, if I were to encourage Tom Paine's opinions I should have a bloody revolution." As we shall see, Pitt dramatically reformed his opinion and approach within the next year and more, when paranoia in the government about American- and French-inspired revolts reached a fever pitch and Thomas Paine became a prime scapegoat in Pitt's "reign of terror" – which was extremely effective in stamping out public support for Paine. Pitt came to believe the French Revolution was "the severest trial which the visitation of providence has ever yet inflicted upon the nations of the earth" because it encouraged the masses "to abandon the system which practice has explained and experience has confirmed, for the visionary advantages of a crude, untried theory" – and Thomas Paine's writings were fomenting just that kind of thinking.[124]

The attorney general explained that *The Rights of Man* (part 2) was much more threatening to the government than part 1 because it was "ushered into the world in all shapes and sizes, thrust into the hands of subjects of every descriptions, even children's sweetmeats being wrapped in it" – that is, it was being read by the threatening masses.[125]

On May 21, 1792, Paine was issued a forty-one-page summons at Clio Rickman's house, charging him with "being a wicked, seditious, and ill-disposed person, and wickedly, seditiously, and maliciously intending to scandalize, traduce, and vilify the character of the said late Sovereign Lord, King William the Third, and the said late Happy Revolution, and the Parliament of England and to bring the constitution, legislation, and government of this kingdom into hatred and contempt with his Majesty's subjects." Paine's writings, Pitt asserted, "struck at hereditary nobility ... the destruction of monarchy and religion and the total subversion of the established form of government."[126]

That same May 21, the king issued a proclamation against "wicked and seditious writings," which prompted, paradoxically, even greater sales of *The Rights of Man.* Thereafter, government spies shadowed Paine wherever he went, and taverns and coffeehouses that regularly hosted gatherings of Paine followers were so besieged by the government that a couple hundred of them grouped together to declare they would no longer offer their facilities for meetings of groups advocating "the destruction of this country." The government organized riots and public demonstrations (sanctioned also by elite institutions like Cambridge University), where Paine's books and effigies were burned to cries of "God Save the King!" A drinking song of the time chanted: "Up with the cause of old England; And down with the tricks of Tom Paine!" Another rhymed:

> Old Satan had a darling boy
> Full equal he to Cain
> Born peace and order to destroy
> His name was – Thomas Paine.[127]

The literal demonization of Paine continued in coming years, with the Association for Preserving Liberty and Property against Republicans and Levellers organizing anti-*Rights of Man* protests in three hundred towns, such as one in Leeds where "an image of Tom Paine [was hung] upon a pole, with a rope round his neck which was held by a man behind, who continually lashed the effigy with a carter's whip. The effigy was at last burned in the market place, the market-bell tolling slowly."[128]

Not everyone in England was cowed by the government blitzkrieg, however. Paine still had massive public support – it had just been pushed underground. During and long after Pitt's reign of terror, many thousands of English men and women kept and read – and reread – their copies of *The Rights of Man* (and many long kept a print of William Sharp's engraving of Paine, pictured on this book's cover, in their homes). Indeed, the events in England during the 1790s made *Rights* a "foundation-text of the English working-class movement" and elevated Paine to icon status for generations of English leftists and radicals.[129]

The resistance bubbled to the surface about four decades later, when more than one hundred thousand protestors came out in Birmingham, London, Bristol, Derby, and Nottingham, demanding reforms for

PHOTO 6. Thomas Paine – *Fitting Brittania into an Ill-Fitting Corset*, 1793. Courtesy of Library of Congress.

universal suffrage, more frequent elections, and ballot voting. Appended to the list of demands was *The Rights of Man*. The manifesto from one of the groups, from East London, declared its plan to support the working classes "by disseminating the principles propagated by that great philosopher and redeemer of mankind, the Immortal Thomas Paine." Even into the late-twentieth-century, Labour Party leader Michael Foot gave tribute to Paine's influence on the party's history and ideas, commenting, "International arbitration, family allowances, maternity benefits, free education, prison reform, full employment; much of the future later offered by the British Labour Party was previously on offer, in better English, from Thomas Paine." It seemed that John Thelwall's 1790s prophecy was coming true: "So long as the tongue of man can articulate the names of those heroes who have benefitted mankind, so long, in defiance of persecution, will the name of Thomas Paine resound throughout the world."[130]

But for now, the best thing for the English government would have been for Paine to just go away – out of sight, out of mind, in true British fashion. As the *London Times* suggested, "It is earnestly recommended to Mad Tom that he should embark for France and there be naturalized into the regular confusion of democracy."[131]

And that is exactly what Paine did in September 1792 – though not to escape prosecution; rather, he was responding to a charm offensive from the French. First, on August 26, 1792, the National Assembly made Paine and several other foreigners full citizens of France. Very soon after, Paine was elected to the National Constitutional Convention by no fewer than four French districts. Paine chose to represent Pas-de-Calais, as it was the first to elect him and the only one to send a representative, Achille Audibert, to London to inform him of the good news.[132]

Paine left for Paris on September 13, 1792, accompanied by Audibert and a lawyer friend and supporter, John Frost. Stopping in Dover for the night before the Channel crossing, they were accosted by government agents who searched for incriminating letters or other treasonable works and confiscated a recently written pamphlet that criticized the king. After being searched again in the morning, a large crowd gathered on the dock as they boarded the ship for France to "stare at Tom Paine.... He was hissed a great deal, and many ridiculous speeches were made relative to his trade [stay maker]," a government eyewitness reported. "The crowd increased very much: the wind being slack the packet was obliged to be towed out. I believe had we remained much longer they would have pelted him with stones from the beach." As the ship departed, the crowd shouted "down with Tom Paine," "death to the corsetmaker," and "down with the traitor" – an ignominious final farewell for Thomas Paine from the land of his birth.[133]

A far different scene awaited Paine a couple of days later on his arrival in Calais, where he was welcomed with a salute from the battery, crowds lining his route shouting "Vive Thomas Paine! Vive la nation!" and an official public welcome from the mayor and other dignitaries. Arriving then in Paris from Calais on September 19, 1792, as a national hero, Paine was ready to attempt to help his newly adopted nation find its way during turbulent times.[134]

The France to which Paine returned was much changed from when he had last departed in July 1791. Several months before his arrival, on June

20, 1792, the Cordeliers and sansculottes (armed working-class radicals, led by Cordeliers leaders, who distinguished themselves by wearing red bonnets and long pants instead of the knee breeches favored by nobility) were mistakenly let into the royal quarters of the Tuileries Palace in Paris, where they spent hours berating and threatening the king and queen before the mayor arrived and managed to disperse the protesters. Six weeks later, a crowd attacked the Tuileries Palace again, this time killing and mutilating six hundred Swiss Guards. The royal family managed to hide, but it was clear the monarchy was on its last legs.[135]

Paine took his seat in the Constitutional Convention on September 21, 1792, and one of its first acts was to end France's centuries-long monarchy and announce France as a republic. On September 25, Paine optimistically addressed France's citizens: "It is the peculiar honor of France that she now raises the standard of liberty for all nations; and in fighting her own battles, contends for the rights of all mankind." He urged the people not to fight among themselves – sadly ironic advice, given the bloodshed at the Tuileries Palace over the summer and another bloody event only weeks before on September 2 and 3, when marauding mobs of sansculottes broke into prisons all over France and gruesomely murdered more than 1,300 prisoners suspected of being loyal to the monarchy.[136]

While Paine had been away, the factions in the convention had consolidated and hardened. The Cordeliers united with the Jacobins, forming what came to be known as the radical "Mountain" for the fact that they sat on raised chairs in the convention. To the political right of the Jacobins and Cordeliers were the more worldly, moderate Girondins, led by Paine's friends Brissot, Antoine-Nicolas de Condorcet and Manon, and Jean-Marie Roland. Paine and the Girondins believed a republican constitution would unite the country: "Had a Constitution been established, the nation would then have had a bond of union, and every individual would have known the line of conduct he was to follow," Paine later lamented. "But instead of this, a revolutionary government, a thing without either principle or authority, was substituted in his place."[137]

Physically and philosophically situated between the Girondin and the Mountain in the convention was the "Plain" – the independents who sat on the lower seats in the convention. Because it possessed the controlling votes, the Plain had considerable power for a time, until Maximilien Robespierre and Louis-Antoine de St.-Just took control of the Committee of Public Safety (essentially an executive committee) in mid-1793.[138]

In late 1792 and early 1793, the convention was consumed with what to do with King Louis XVI. Delegates were divided. The radicals charged that those who argued for moderation were simply royalist tools seeking to restore the monarchy. A new tone of paranoia began taking over the convention – enemies of the Revolution were everywhere, even in the convention itself. Soon enough, to protect the Revolution, those enemies would need to meet the guillotine.[139]

The trial of Louis Capet began on December 11, with the Mountain arguing for execution and the Girondins (and Paine) for banishment from France. Paine argued that Louis, as a man of some virtue who had demonstrated that he understood liberty, should be acquitted and deported. "It is to France alone, I know, that the United States of America owe that support which enabled them to shake off the unjust and tyrannical yoke of Britain," he said through a translator on January 15, 1793. "Let then those United States be the safeguard and asylum of Louis Capet. There, hereafter, far removed from the miseries and crimes of royalty, he may learn, from the constant aspect of public prosperity, that the true system of government consists not in kings, but in fair, equal and honourable representation." The convention disagreed, however, voting overwhelmingly "guilty."[140]

The question of punishment was next, and after twenty-four hours of deliberation, on January 17, the vote came back 387 to 334 in favor of death. With the support of Brissot and Condorcet, on January 19, 1793, Paine again pleaded for Louis's life before the convention. Paine's last appeals were to no avail; on January 21, 1793, after a final statement declaring, "I die innocent of all the crimes of which I have been charged. I pardon those who have brought about my death and I pray that the blood you are about to shed may never be required of France. I hope that my blood may secure the happiness of the French people," the last king of France was beheaded in Place de la Révolution before a crowd of twenty thousand.[141]

From there, things spun quickly out of control in France. In April 1793, the convention formed the Committee of Public Safety to replace the executive council. In July, the Committee of Public Safety was given almost total authority as the "emergency government" to run the country and maintain the purity of the Revolution. Over time, this committee of twelve, eventually led by Robespierre, sent many thousands to increasingly gruesome deaths with little due process during the Reign of Terror.

Coupled with French military successes, which in a sense legitimated the leadership, the new French Republic executed well more than sixteen thousand (with some estimates as high as forty thousand) dangerous citizens in 1793–4.[142]

The Girondins were among the first to fall, starting in June 1793 and culminating in trials in October in which every one of twenty-one defendants was unanimously found guilty, sentenced to death, and executed, along with a procession of other founding fathers and mothers of the Revolution, including Paine's friend Brissot on October 31.[143]

During the second half of 1793, Paine withdrew from his public activities rather than either favoring the Jacobins, who were imprisoning and executing his friends, or opposing them and putting himself at grave risk. "I appeared to myself to be on my death-bed, for death was on every side of me." Of this period, Paine later wrote:

> I used to find some relief by walking alone in the garden after dark, and cursing with hearty good will the authors of that terrible system that had turned the character of the Revolution I had been so proud to defend.... [M]y heart was in distress at the fate of my friends, and my harp hung upon the weeping willows.[144]

Paine's dreams in France were fast turning into a nightmare. As early as April 1793, he had written Jefferson, "Had this revolution been conducted consistently with its principles, there was once a good prospect of extending liberty through the greatest part of Europe; but I now relinquish that hope." Thereafter, Paine fell into depression and drinking. "Borne down by public and private affliction, [I was] driven to excesses in Paris," he later confided to Clio Rickman. Even so, Paine was not entirely paralyzed; indeed, he looked to a familiar place for solace – in writing, as he put pen to paper on some ideas about religion he had long been working through.[145]

By late 1793, the Jacobins had managed to jail, exile, or execute most of their enemies. Soon it was Paine's turn. In October, he had been included in the indictment of Brissot and other Girondins for opposing the king's execution. Then, in the early morning of December 28, 1793, Paine was arrested in his room by five police officers and two Committee for General Security agents. After allowing Paine to drop off the manuscript he had been working on with his friend Joel Barlow, he was taken away to Luxembourg Prison, where he would remain for the next 315 days.[146]

The only possible help for Paine would have come from official American action in the person of the U.S. minister to France Gouverneur Morris.

Morris, however, though he had spent much time with Paine over the years, harbored a great enmity for him. "Lest I should forget it, I must mention," he told Jefferson, "that Thomas Paine is in prison, where he amuses himself with publishing a pamphlet against Jesus Christ," Morris informed Jefferson in a letter. Morris was little help in response to Paine's pleas for assistance, duplicitously telling him he was doing all he could while telling half-truths all around. Morris's preference, in short, "was to see Paine liberated in only one way," the Paine biographer Jack Fruchtman Jr. suggests: "headless and feet first."[147]

During his first months in Luxembourg Prison, Paine became ill with a very high fever, which, he later recalled, "almost terminated my existence." He was moved into a larger room with three Belgians, who did what they could to care for him, including successfully requesting that the guards leave open the cell door during the day for better air circulation. Paine never knew when it would be his turn to die: "There was no time when I could think my life worth twenty-four hours, and my mind was made up to meet my fate."[148]

As dramatized earlier in this chapter, only a stroke of good fortune – in the form of that open door that hid the chalk mark when closed – saved Paine from execution. Paine later wrote, "One hundred and sixty-eight persons were taken out of the Luxembourg [that] one night, and a hundred and sixty of them guillotined the next day, of which I now know I was to have been one."[149]

Meanwhile, outside, the Terror accelerated throughout the first six months of Paine's imprisonment, until finally Robespierre went too far. When he demanded on July 26, 1794, that even the Committee for Public Safety be purged, one in the convention dared to confront the tyrant: "It is time to tell the whole truth," Pierre Cambon cried. "One man alone paralyzes the will of the Convention. That man is Robespierre!"[150]

The dam, once cracked, burst. Over a tense few days, the Plain was able to wrest control from Robespierre and send him, together with St.-Just and a number of others, as he had sent so many others, to the guillotine to meet his own fate. "To an inured nation," Jay Winik comments, "one more death would hardly have been noticed. But . . . all of Paris felt that this one had a special meaning – that its national nightmare might, at long last, have come to a close."[151]

Yet Thomas Paine remained in jail, even after the perfidious Gouverneur Morris was replaced by James Monroe in August 1794. Frustrations abounded – when his friend Peter Whiteside met with Monroe on his behalf, Whiteside returned ten days with a sobering report. "Mr. Monroe has told me that he has no order [from President Washington] respecting you, but that he [Mr. Monroe] will do everything in his power to liberate you," Whiteside related. "From what I learn . . . you are not considered, either by their American Government, or by the individuals, as an American citizen." In a September 18 letter, however, Monroe told Paine he believed he was still an American citizen, as did the American people and president, and he would continue to work to free him as soon as possible.[152]

Finally, after additional efforts by Monroe on his behalf, Thomas Paine was released from Luxembourg Prison on November 6, 1794. He was, however, never again the same man.[153]

IV. Religion and Purgatory: Legacy

> *I believe in one God, and no more; and I hope for happiness beyond this life. I believe [in] the equality of man, and I believe that religious duties consist in doing justice, loving mercy, and endeavoring to make our fellow-creatures happy.*[154]
>
> – Thomas Paine, 1794

On his way from Philadelphia to New York City to see an old friend, the sixty-five-year-old man stopped in Trenton to arrange passage on a longer-distance carriage.

"May I purchase a seat on the express coach?" he asked the owner.

"I'll be damned if you shall go in my stage," the owner coldly replied, turning on his heel and walking away.

Undeterred, the man asked a second driver for a ticket.

"My stage and horses were once struck by lightning," the second answered a bit more sympathetically, "but I don't want them to suffer again – so no, you may not."

Finally, a third driver agreed to take the man.

By now, though, a crowd of locals had learned of the man's presence in their town and wanted to let him know exactly what they thought of him. One man tried to scare the horses by beating a drum. The rest of the mob started throwing rocks at the coach's windows.

Displaying not the least emotion of fear or anger, the man emerged from the carriage to address the crowd.

"Do what you will," he calmly announced, surveying the crowd. "Your conduct will have no tendency to hurt my feelings or injure my fame."

With that, Thomas Paine got back into the carriage, closed the door, and was on his way to New York.

The manuscript that Thomas Paine was able to leave with his friend Joel Barlow as he was being hauled off to Luxembourg Prison in December 1793 was in fact his third, and most controversial yet, blockbuster, *The Age of Reason.* As Paine sat in prison, the manuscript was translated and first published in France in 1794 and then England shortly thereafter.

Planted perhaps by his boyhood churchyard epiphany, Paine had long nurtured the seeds of an idea to write a book about his views on religion. As he observed and endured the unraveling of the French Revolution in Paris in 1793, the opportunity presented itself:

> My friends were falling as fast as the guillotine could cut their heads off, and as I expected, every day, the same fate, I resolved to begin my work.... I had no time to lose. This accounts for my writing at the time I did, and so nicely did the time and intention meet, that I had not finished the first part of the work more than six hours before I was arrested and taken to prison. The people of France were running headlong into atheism, and I had the work translated in their own language, to stop them in that career, and fix them to the first article of every man's creed, who has any creed at all – believe in God.[155]

It is most ironic – given Paine's stated purpose of diverting the French from atheism in a time of fanatical official dechristianization, and his own "I believe in one God and no more" pledge of fidelity to God at the beginning of *The Age of Reason* – that Paine for decades and centuries was lambasted, denigrated, and ostracized for the book's supposed expressions of infidelity.[156]

In fact, *The Age of Reason* did accept the idea of a Supreme Being, and Paine made clear that he admired Jesus Christ as "a virtuous and amiable man. The morality that he preached and practiced was of the most benevolent kind." Paine conceded, moreover, how the ancients, who lived during eras of superstition and mythology, not reason, could have believed the miraculous stories about Jesus' life and death, and he believed like most deists that one loses moral grounding, compassion, and virtue without faith in God.[157]

Where Paine began to get in trouble with the religious orthodoxy was in the next few paragraphs after he professed his belief in God: " I do not believe in the creed professed by the Jewish church, by the Roman church, by the Greek church, by the Turkish church, by the Protestant church, nor by any church that I know of. My own mind is my own church." But that was not all. Paine went on to impute less than noble motivations on churches. "All national institutions of churches, whether Jewish, Christian, or Turkish," he explained, "appear to me no other than human inventions set up to terrify and enslave mankind, and monopolize power and profit. It defies reason, moreover, that there should be only one path to God:

> Every national church or religion has established itself by pretending some special mission from God, communicated to certain individuals. The Jews have their Moses; the Christians their Jesus Christ, their apostles and saints; and the Turks their Mahomet; as if the way to God was not open to every man alike.[158]

Finally, Paine charged that the holy books of each of the religions had perpetuated the deception:

> Each of those churches shows certain books, which they call revelation, or the Word of God. The Jews say that their Word of God was given by God to Moses face to face; the Christians say, that their Word of God came by divine inspiration; and the Turks say, that their Word of God (the Koran) was brought by an angel from heaven. Each of those churches accuses the other of unbelief; and, for my own part, I disbelieve them all.[159]

Paine advanced instead the deist conception of the Creator as a "watchmaker God," who created the universe, "but does not interfere in the operation of its laws." "The word of God," moreover, "is the creation we behold, and it is in *this word,* which no human invention can counterfeit or alter, that God speaketh universally to man," Paine argued. Moreover, it is only in science that may one find the "true theology" of a God so powerful as to form "the immensity of the creation," so benevolent as to bequeath "the abundance with which He fills the earth," and so wise as create the universe's "unchangeable order."[160]

These were the deist ideas of the likes of Voltaire, Montesquieu, Rousseau, and Hume in Europe, and Jefferson, Franklin, Hamilton, and Washington in America. Deism's core principles included "the belief in a supreme being, the worship of that being through a life of virtue and goodness, the repenting of sin, and the hope of a benevolent afterlife," said Lord Herbert of Cherbury in 1645. "[These] were the underpinnings of all worthy religions, and were so innate that they must have originated with the first thinking human creatures." To deists, the prophets of every religion were actually working toward a common goal: "Socrates, Jesus, the Buddha, and Mohammed were each attempting to return his society's corrupt religion back to its natural state – the state of deism."[161]

In 1795, Paine published part 2 of *The Age of Reason*, replacing the relatively measured tones of part 1 with a more heated rhetoric that focused its ire on one particular established church – Christianity. "Of all the systems of religion that ever were invented, there is none more derogatory to the Almighty, more unedifying to man, more repugnant to reason, and more contradictory in itself, than this story is," he flamed. "Too absurd for belief, too impossible to convince, and too inconsistent for practice, it renders the heart torpid, or produces only atheists and fanatics."[162]

In part 2, Paine focused on specific scriptural stories. "Were any girl that is now with child to say, and even to swear to it, that she was gotten with child by a ghost, and that an angel told her so, would she be believed?" he implored. The tale of the whale and Jonah was "a fit story for ridicule, if it was written to be believed; or of laughter, if it was intended to try what credulity could swallow; for if it could swallow Jonah and the whale, it could swallow anything."[163]

In addition, Paine continued flinging relentless barbs at Christian "mythologists," "calling themselves the Christian Church, [who] have erected their fable, which for absurdity and extravagance is not exceeded by any thing that is to be found in the mythology of the ancients." "Whenever we read the obscene stories, the voluptuous debaucheries, the cruel and torturous executions, the unrelenting vindictiveness, with which more than half the Bible is filled," he added, "it would be more consistent that we called the word of a demon than the Word of God. It is a history of wickedness that has served to corrupt and brutalize mankind; and, for my part, I sincerely detest it as I detest everything that is cruel." Regardless of whether they were Christian, Hebrew, or Muslim, the second-generation prophets – those who claimed to speak for God after having received divine messages – were "useless and unnecessary," Paine argued, because they ignored God's "choicest gift to man, the gift of reason."[164]

Once again, the public loved *The Age of Reason*, with sales eventually exceeding even those of Paine's earlier blockbusters, *Common Sense* and *The Rights of Man*. Published in America by Benjamin Franklin's favorite grandson, Benjamin Franklin ("Benny") Bache, *Age* sold one hundred thousand copies in 1797 and went through seventeen editions.[165]

And yet, not surprisingly, the reaction to *The Age of Reason* among the Christian church establishment in America and England was extremely negative – and it would continue to be for nearly the next two hundred years. Within just a few years, authors in England published more than thirty pieces criticizing, among other things, Paine's imprecise Bible scholarship; his failure to accurately interpret Christian philosophy; and his advocacy of deism – a theology, they claimed, that was devoid of ritual, justice, and moral inspiration. The British government wasted no time in finding the book blasphemous and in punishing anyone who sold or printed it – eventually arresting more than 150 for trafficking in contraband.[166]

In America, it was little surprise that John Adams, who so disliked Paine (once referring to him as "a mongrel between pig and puppy, begotten by a wild boar on a bitch wolf"), was offended by *The Age of Reason*, commenting: "The Christian religion is, above all the religions that ever prevailed or existed in ancient or modern times, the religion of wisdom, virtue, equity and humanity, let the Blackguard Paine say what he will."[167]

It is precisely the bluntness of *The Age of Reason* that explains why Paine has been both lionized and vilified for the past two hundred years. The deist leader Elihu Palmer, a former Methodist minister, described Paine as "the undaunted champion of reason, and the resolute enemy of tyranny, bigotry and prejudice... probably the most useful man that ever existed on the face of the earth." Although earlier deists had kept their beliefs mostly to themselves, the deist organizations, prompted by Paine, became more aggressive in challenging Christianity, with pamphlets, lectures, and the like. Deism started becoming a popular movement, and reports of infidelity increased markedly. Of course, the religious establishment and the devout viewed this as a major threat. It also aroused hostility even among some religious liberals and dissenters who agreed with much of Paine's message but objected to his sweeping criticisms of all churches and his failure to acknowledge the Bible's positive mythic and symbolic qualities.[168]

Although Republicans in the mid-1790s still regarded Paine as "a near saint," after the *Age of Reason*, they began distancing themselves. Said one Republican, "[*Common Sense* was the] the Bible of the American Revolution," but "Mr. Paine's attack upon our most sacred religion" is unacceptable. "May [Paine's] *Rights of Man* be handed down to our latest posterity, but may his *Age of Reason* never live to see the rising generation," resolved a New York Jeffersonian society of the day.[169]

More surprising was the reaction of many of Paine's old revolutionary compatriots in America, including Samuel Adams, Benjamin Rush, John Dickinson, Patrick Henry, and John Jay, all of whom bitterly denounced the book. The criticism that most deeply wounded Paine was that of Samuel Adams, now eighty-four years old, with whom Paine had such an affinity during the Revolution. Responding to Adams in a letter published (along with Adams's letter) in the Philadelphia *National Intelligencer*, Paine wrote in unusually conciliatory terms (for Paine): "I endangered [my life] by... opposing atheism; and yet some of your priests... cry out, in the war-whoop of monarchical priestcraft, What an Infidel, what a wicked Man, Is Thomas Paine! They might as well add," he noted ironically, "for he believes in God and is against shedding blood.... [I give] the right hand of fellowship... my dear friend,... to you."[170]

Even the influential Unitarian Joseph Priestley, who was himself considered dangerous for supporting free will and rejecting certain traditional Christian principles, worried that *The Age of Reason* was "much read," and had "made great impression." Like an animal backed into a corner, the religious establishment bared its fangs and lashed out in a bitter defense of the faith – a defense, in the form of attacking Thomas Paine, that endured for well over a hundred years.[171]

After his November 1794 release from prison, Paine moved in with James Monroe and his family, with whom he lived in Paris for the following eighteen months, until June 1796. Almost immediately he was reinstated as a deputy in the National Convention, where he attempted, to no avail, to influence debate on the new constitution that took effect in September 1795. Paine no longer took an active role in French government after that point.[172]

Paine published what would be his last major work, *Agrarian Justice*, in France in 1796 (1797 in English). A logical next step from the "social chapter" of *The Rights of Man* (part 2), *Agrarian Justice* posited that poverty could be explained by the vast inequalities in land ownership and that such unequal distributions violate natural rights because land is "the common property of the human race." It is the role of government to regulate land's use for the common good – to correct the inequities, Paine proposed imposing an estate tax that would assist young adults and the elderly. With such arguments, it is understandable why Paine's work in *Agrarian Justice* and elsewhere has been lauded over the decades by progressive theorists and politicians.[173]

Also in late 1796, Paine published (again with Benny Bache) *Letter to George Washington*, spelling out his grievances against the president for failing to do more to try to get Paine out of prison and ridiculing Washington's military and political skills. "You folded your arms, forgot your friend, and became silent," Paine brooded. "[Y]ou, Sir, treacherous in private friendship (for so you have been to me, and that in the day of danger) and a hypocrite in public life, the world will be puzzled to decide whether you are an apostate or an imposter; whether you have abandoned good principles, or whether you ever had any."[174]

The *Letter* created an uproar and cast a pall over Republicans immediately before the 1796 presidential election. For many Americans, *Letter to George Washington* was the final straw in solidifying their dislike for Paine. As for Washington himself, he "barely responded and certainly not in public."[175]

In May 1797, Paine accepted his French publisher Nicolas de Bonneville's offer to stay for a few days with his family in Paris – and five years later he was still there. "Not a day escaped without his receiving many visits," Bonneville's wife Marguerite recalled. "Many travelers also called on him; and, often, having no other affair, talked to him only of his great reputation and their admiration of his works."[176]

Among Paine's more noteworthy visitors were Tadeusz Kościuszko, the great Polish republican leader, who so impressed Paine that he considered moving to Poland; Robert Fulton, who offered complimentary comments on Paine's iron-bridge design; and Napoléon Bonaparte, who told Paine that "a statue of gold should be erected to you in every city in the universe" and confided that he slept with a copy of *The Rights of Man* under his pillow. For his part, Paine – still bitterly opposed to the British monarchy – advised Napoléon of the firm flat sand at Alford on the North Sea, which Paine had patrolled on horseback those many years before, as a possible invasion landing site.[177]

Final Years

When Thomas Jefferson became president in 1801, he warmly reached out to Paine: "I am in hopes you will find us returned generally to sentiments worthy of former times," Jefferson wrote. "That you may long live to continue your useful labors and to reap the reward in the thankfulness of nations, is my sincere prayer. Accept assurances of my high esteem and affectionate attachment." In light of these improved circumstances, Paine, then sixty-five, resolved to make a change – on September 1, 1802, he boarded a ship to return from Europe to United States for the first time in fifteen years.[178]

Paine and Jefferson may have hoped Paine would receive a uniformly warm welcome on his return to the United States in late October 1802, but it was not to be. Along the full 1,500-mile expanse of the Atlantic seaboard, Paine's arrival was alternately lauded and loathed. Few were neutral – it seemed everyone either loved or, more often, hated Thomas Paine in America.

The very first news articles were mostly positive, and Republican organizations in New York, Washington, and Philadelphia welcomed Paine – as did Jefferson, who invited him to the White House on numerous occasions. There, the "two Toms" resumed their close relationship, often walking the roads near the White House deep in conversation. As one observer reported, "Thomas Paine entered, seated himself by the side of the President, and conversed and behaved towards him with the familiarity of an intimate and an equal!"[179]

The Federalist press, by contrast, fiercely castigated Paine. The Boston *Mercury and New-England Palladium* denounced him as a "lying, drunken brutal infidel, who rejoiced in the opportunity of basking and wallowing in the confusion, devastation, bloodshed, rapine, and murder, in which his soul delights." Philadelphia's *Port Folio* branded him "a drunken atheist, and the scavenger of faction"; the *Baltimore Republican* labeled him "this loathsome reptile." The Federalist *General Advertiser* spat, "[Paine is] "that living opprobrium of humanity . . . the infamous scavenger of all the filth which could be raked from the dirty paths which have been hitherto trodden by all the revilers of Christianity."[180]

Thomas Paine had always been intemperate, and – to his detriment – he was not about to change in his mid-sixties. In composing a series of new hostile letters about John Adams and George Washington, he jeopardized his friendship with his best ally, Jefferson, who was attempting to foster a climate of political reconciliation. William Duane, Paine's friend and the editor of the *Philadelphia Aurora*, tried to warn him against publishing the letters, but to no avail. "I have fairly told him," Duane wrote Jefferson, "that he will be deserted by the only party that respects him or does not hate him – that all his political writings will be rendered useless – and even his fame destroyed." Paine stubbornly ignored the advice; sure enough, Jefferson gently distanced himself, eventually neglecting even to respond to Paine's letters. Only at the very end of his life did Paine finally seem to have learned the lesson of the value of discretion, admitting that "an author might lose the credit he had acquired by writing too much" – but by then, regrettably, it was too late for Thomas Paine.[181]

Following his return to America, Paine had tried to renew the connection to the reading public he had so expertly established with *Common Sense* and *The Rights of Man*, publishing ten articles on politics entitled *To the Citizens of the United States and Particularly to the Leaders of the*

Federal Faction, in several newspapers in late 1802 and early 1803. But the memory of the *Age of Reason*, *Letter to Washington*, and the author's own continuing indiscretions largely prevented the public's embrace.[182]

Thomas Paine died on June 8, 1809 – and the religious establishment antagonized him to the bitter end. When the attending physician, a Dr. Manly, saw that the end was near, he leaned close and slowly asked Paine, "Do you wish to believe that Jesus Christ is the son of God?" To which Paine replied weakly, "I have no wish to believe on that subject."

Denied entry to his preferred burial place, the Quaker cemetery in New York City, Paine was buried instead on his New Rochelle property with six mourners in attendance – Madame Bonneville and her two sons (who had all boarded with Paine for a time) and three others. Instructing her son to stand at the other end of the coffin "as a witness for grateful America" before the earth was filled in, Madame Bonneville declared, "Oh! Mr. Paine! My Son stands here as testimony of the gratitude of America, and I, for France!"[183]

Legacy

Thomas Paine is one of the great enigmas of American history. A best-selling author and polemicist whose publications played a leading role in two revolutions and influenced the course of history in three nations, he inspired countless Americans and others during and after his life.

Shortly after publication of *The Rights of Man* (which was "not less popular in America at this day, than his *Common Sense* was in 1776," according to a 1791 newspaper article), his popularity was at its peak among Americans of every political persuasion, with both Federalist and Jeffersonian papers generously excerpting his newest work. Poet Philip Freneau limned:

> Rous'd by the Reason of his manly page,
> Once more shall Paine a listening world engage;
> From Reason's source, a bold reform he brings,
> By raising up mankind, he pulls down kings.[184]

And yet, less than two decades later, Paine died virtually alone and friendless. Although many of the greatest men of his age admired his work, others found him insufferably contrary, impudent, and self-absorbed – and they worked to undermine him wherever possible. "The name is enough. Every person has ideas of him. Some respect his genius and dread the man," one contemporary revealed. "Some reverence his political, while they hate his religious, opinions. Some love the man, but not his private manners. Indeed he has done nothing which has not extremes in it. He never appears but we love and hate him. He is as great a paradox as ever appeared in human nature."[185]

By the time of his death in 1809, Paine's reputation had become so compromised that when his longtime friend Joel Barlow was asked that same year by James Cheetham for personal information for a biography he was preparing on Paine (which turned out to be a scurrilous book filled with half-truths and lies), Barlow replied, "His own writings are his best life. And these are not read at present. The greater part of readers in the [United States] will not be persuaded, as long as their present feelings last, to consider him in any other light than as a drunkard and deist." In a similar vein, when Thomas Jefferson received a request years later in 1822 for copies of correspondence with Paine, Jefferson replied, "No, my dear sir, not for this world. Into what a hornet's nest would it thrust my head!"[186]

As Jefferson's reaction suggests, the character assassinations did not end with Paine's death – indeed, for many decades afterward, his memory was systematically attacked and demeaned by powerful political interests and religious grandees.

It began with Cheetham's biography, which depicted the "atheist" Paine as vain, unpatriotic, and wretched. Theodore Roosevelt's 1888 biography of Gouverneur Morris referred to Paine as a "filthy little atheist"; nineteenth-century Christians essentially painted Paine as Antichrist.[187]

Although Paine's contributions were ignored in the mainstream historical narrative for well more than a century after his death, many Americans – including several of the nation's greatest presidents – kept his memory alive by integrating his ideas and arguments into their own. By and large, those presidents who drew from his work did so (until the past seventy years or so) without attribution, however – finding it too politically risky to invoke the name of Thomas Paine. Most prominent among this group was Abraham Lincoln.

Lincoln likely first read Paine while in his twenties in New Salem, Illinois, when he devoured *Common Sense* and *The Age of Reason* – after which he identified himself as a "religious liberal" and wrote his own deist article. After having his 1846 bid for Congress nearly derailed by charges of "infidelity," however, he never spoke again in public about Paine or deism.

Nonetheless, Paine may have been Lincoln's favorite author, from whom Lincoln perhaps acquired "his most important literary education."

"[N]o other writer of the eighteenth century, with the exception of Jefferson," Lincoln scholar Roy Basler contends, "parallels more closely the temper or gist of Lincoln's later thought."[188]

As America faced its most severe crisis yet with the secession of the Southern states and the Civil War, Lincoln understood that Thomas Paine's plainspoken articulation of a united America as a land of unparalleled promise was just the sort of message Americans should hear – and he did not hesitate to seed his speeches and writings with Paine's imagery, if not his name.[189]

During his academic career as a history professor and president of Princeton University, Woodrow Wilson complimented Thomas Paine's role in American independence in his five-volume *A History of the American People.* As president he never uttered Paine's name in public, but in 1914, Wilson spoke in familiar terms, commenting, "The United States must be neutral in fact as well as in name during these days that are to try men's souls."[190]

Franklin D. Roosevelt was the first president to publicly invoke Paine's name, as we shall see momentarily; then remarkably, in 1980, a conservative candidate accepted his party's nomination for president by expressly quoting and naming Paine – remarkable because political conservatives, along with religious leaders, had been Paine's primary antagonists both during life and ever since. Ronald Reagan acknowledged that the American people "are concerned, yes, [but] they're not frightened. They're disturbed, but not dismayed":

> They are the kind of men and women Tom Paine had in mind when he wrote, during the darkest days of the American Revolution, "We have it in our power to begin the world over again." . . . Nearly 150 years after Tom Paine wrote those words, an American President told the generation of the Great Depression that it had a "rendezvous with destiny." I believe this generation also has a rendezvous with destiny.[191]

Finally, President Barack Obama prominently featured Thomas Paine's writings throughout his historic presidential campaign; then he closed his inaugural address on January 20, 2009, with Paine's immortal words from *The American Crisis*:

> So let us mark this day with remembrance, of who we are and how far we have traveled. In the year of America's birth, in the coldest of months, a small band of patriots huddled by dying campfires on the shores of an icy river. The capital was abandoned. The enemy was advancing. The snow was stained with blood. At a moment when the outcome of our revolution

> was most in doubt, the father of our nation ordered these words be read to the people: "Let it be told to the future world ... that in the depth of winter, when nothing but hope and virtue could survive ... that the city and the country, alarmed at one common danger, came forth to meet [it]."[192]

Though until relatively recently Paine has been denied a place in "official" commemorations and mainstream tellings of the American Revolution, most Americans never abandoned his memory. Among the enthusiasts whose admiration for Paine remained proud throughout the past two centuries have been various less-powerful, nonmainstream groups of freethinkers, workers and labor activists, deists, abolitionists, women's rights activists, immigrants, authors, religious liberals, atheists, progressives, artists, socialists, and communists. As well, at various times the military and, most recently, some political conservatives, have attached themselves to selective parts of Paine's legacy.[193]

Starting around fifteen years after Paine's death, a group of about forty of his old friends decided to gather in New York City to commemorate his birthday and toast "to the memory of the immortal Thomas Paine, who with his dauntless mind and pen, lit up the brilliant sun of liberty, that kings, tyrants and priests will never be able to extinguish." From this came the formation of numerous freethinking groups, societies, periodicals, and lectures around the country extolling the Enlightenment's twin ideals of science and reason.[194]

One of the leading freethinkers to emerge from these activities was the hugely popular orator Robert Ingersoll, who, beginning in 1871, gave many talks praising Paine:

> He had more brains than books; more sense than education; more courage than politeness; more strength than polish. He had no veneration for old mistakes – no admiration for ancient lies. He loved the truth for truth's sake, and for man's sake. He saw oppression on every hand; injustice everywhere; hypocrisy at the altar; venality on the bench; tyranny on the throne; and with a splendid courage he espoused the causes of the weak against the strong – of the enslaved many against the titled few.[195]

Workers and labor groups were long staunch Paine supporters. To those groups, Paine was "that noble patriot, who did more than any other writer of his day to disenthrall the human mind from the fetters of prejudice and superstition." *The Age of Reason* "[is] a work containing more truth than any volume under the sun," glowed an admirer; the populist Andrew Jackson commented that *The Rights of Man* is "more enduring than all the piles of marble and granite that man can erect.... Thomas

Paine needs no monument by hands; he has erected a monument in the hearts of all who love liberty."[196]

Given that Paine had always fervently opposed slavery, beginning with his very first writings for the *Pennsylvania Magazine* and continuing through his assertions in *The Rights of Man* that "man has no property in man," abolitionist groups drew on Paine's example. But because these groups were often church-related, most abolitionists shunned any express associations with Paine. An exception was William Lloyd Garrison, the dynamic leader of the Boston-based American Anti-Slavery Society and, beginning in 1831, publisher of the highly influential *Liberator* magazine. Acknowledging after 1845 that Paine had enabled his escape from the "thralldom of tradition and authority," Garrison thereafter so enthusiastically trumpeted Paine's ideas that he was accused by the religious establishment of trying to "out-Paine Tom Paine."[197]

Individual radical women drew great strength from Paine's writings. The early activist Lydia Maria Child excerpted parts of *The Age of Reason* in her own *Eclectic Bible*, and the Scotswoman Frances Wright (the first woman in America to speak publicly to mixed audiences of men and women outside of the church setting) admired him as well. For criticizing "a crafty priesthood and a monied aristocracy," and for arguing such progressive points as sexual equality, marriage reform, and universal public secular education in the 1820s, Wright was mercilessly derided by the clergy and conservatives as the "Red Harlot of Infidelity" and a "female Thomas Paine."[198]

Fellow radical Elizabeth Cady Stanton first read Paine and Wollstonecraft at her mentor Lucretia Mott's recommendation. As we shall see in the following chapter, the life experiences of Stanton – a "militant anti-cleric" freethinking housewife who considered Paine a "rational and beautiful writer" – and of Paine are eerily similar. Like Paine, Stanton too wrote a late-in-life manifesto bitterly criticizing organized religion (*The Woman's Bible*); like Paine, Stanton's reputation suffered terribly for doing so, to the point that her name was for many decades essentially written out of the official histories of the women's rights movement.[199]

The Polish Jewish immigrant Ernestine Rose, a less famous feminist of the late eighteenth century, was an unabashed Paine acolyte. She gave tribute at an 1852 Paine birthday event:

> There is no need to eulogize Thomas Paine. His life-long devotion to the cause of freedom; his undaunted, unshrinking advocacy of truth; his deep seated hatred to kingly and priestly despotism, are his best eulogies.... But

> to honor the memory of Thomas Paine... [w]e must endeavor to carry out what he so nobly began, for his principles were not for one age or nation, but for all.[200]

The feminist and suffragist Susan B. Anthony spoke prominently and often of Paine as a "Revolutionary patriot [and] authority on the principles upon which our government is founded," directly quoting him for the proposition that: "The right of voting for representatives is the primary right by which others are protected. To take away this right is to reduce a man to slavery."[201]

Thomas Paine also deeply influenced a number of America's greatest nineteenth-century authors and poets, including Ralph Waldo Emerson, Theodore Parker, and Henry David Thoreau (the New England transcendentalists); George Lippard; Herman Melville; the poet Walt Whitman; and Samuel "Mark Twain" Clemens.[202]

Later in the nineteenth century, progressive-minded clerics and spiritualists began to pay more positive attention to Paine. In his 1904 biography of Paine, the Unitarian minister Moncure D. Conway described Paine's impact in the religious community: "Paine had become more than the founder of a theistic church; he was the standard-bearer and apostle of religious freedom [shades of Roger Williams]; to these freethinkers he was what Fox was to the Quakers and John Wesley to the Methodists."[203]

Turn-of-the-century progressive movements, which arose largely in response to the social Darwinism of the day and to Gilded Age excesses and inequities, were drawn naturally to Paine's work as well (Theodore Roosevelt notwithstanding). Progressives especially identified with Paine's ideas about the public good and the responsibility of government to provide social services elucidated in *The Rights of Man* (part 2) and *Agrarian Justice*.[204]

Socialists and communists also adopted Paine's works. History buff and five-time Socialist Party presidential candidate Eugene Debs commented: "The revolutionary history of the United States and France stirred me deeply and its heroes and martyrs became my idols. Thomas Paine towered above them all. A thousand times since then I have found inspiration and strength in the thrilling words, 'These are the times that try men's souls.'"[205]

Popular books and the press were kinder to Paine in the early twentieth century than they had been in the past. A 1926 sesquicentennial piece in *Better Homes and Gardens* commented, "We as a nation probably owe more to Thomas Paine than to any other human being." The restoration of Paine's reputation continued into and during the 1930s, with the publication of four new biographies and several new editions of his works. The Mexican artist Diego Rivera created historical murals in New York City of Jefferson looking at Franklin, who was pointing to a scroll in Paine's hand that read, "Rights of Man... My country is the world... to do good, my religion."[206]

Then came Pearl Harbor; and in his second fireplace chat after Congress's declaration of war, President Franklin D. Roosevelt prominently invoked Paine's name – the first time since the early 1800s (by Jefferson) a president had publicly and expressly acknowledged his contributions. The president said:

> "These are the times that try men's souls." Tom Paine wrote those words on a drumhead, by the light of a campfire. That was when Washington's little army of ragged, rugged men was retreating across New Jersey, having tasted naught but defeat. And General Washington ordered that these great words written by Tom Paine be read to the men of every regiment in the Continental Army, and this was the assurance given to the first American armed forces: "The summer soldier and the sunshine patriot will, in this crisis, shrink from the service of their country; but he that stands it now, deserves the love and thanks of man and woman. Tyranny, like hell, is not easily conquered; yet we have this consolation with us, that the harder the sacrifice, the more glorious the triumph." So spoke Americans in the year 1776. So speak Americans today![207]

This address – which the *New York Times* termed "one of the greatest of Roosevelt's career" – powerfully conveyed the message that Paine's work still held powerful sway over Americans' sense of themselves and their country in the mid-twentieth century.[208]

Paine continued to inspire into the 1960s. The Students for a Democratic Society president Todd Gitlin recalled reading Paine's collected works and *Citizen Tom Paine* as a boy and being "moved to tears by the fate of the great pamphleteer eventually spurned by the Americans for whom he harbored such hopes." Tom Hayden remembered, "The goal of the sixties was, in a sense, the completion of the vision of the early revolutionaries and the abolitionists, for Tom Paine and Frederick Douglass wanted even more than the Bill of Rights or Emancipation Proclamation. True Democrats, they wanted the fulfillment of the American promise."[209]

To counter the sanitized story of the American Revolution being promulgated by the governing elite at the "Buy-centennial" of 1976, Jeremy Rifkin and others formed the People's Bicentennial Commission.

Although "modern-day Tories will attempt to present themselves and the institutions they control – the corporations, the White House – as the true heirs and defenders of the struggle waged by the first American revolutionaries," the commission declared, "we will be celebrating radical heroes like Jefferson, Paine, and [Samuel] Adams." Popular culture honored Paine as well at the Bicentennial and beyond, with new biographies, anthologies, and articles, together with plays, children's books, a postage stamp in 1973, a *Time* magazine page in "A Prophet Honored," and even a song by folk icon Bob Dylan.[210]

As noted, even conservatives like President Ronald Reagan began praising Paine. Many other conservatives continued to criticize him, however, just as they had done at every stage throughout the prior two hundred years. The neoconservative commentator Irving Kristol, for example, commented, "To perceive the true purposes of the American Revolution, it is wise to ignore some of the more grandiloquent declamations of the moment – Tom Paine, an English radical who never really understood America, is especially worth ignoring."[211]

Even though America's religious and conservative establishment has long denigrated Thomas Paine, his reputation never waned among a committed core group of secularists and freethinkers. As succeeding generations of Americans have themselves decided to look under often-suffocating blankets of received knowledge, they have found in Thomas Paine's writings brilliant pearls of wisdom. One young man in the mid-1800s described the experience: "It took a brave man before the Civil War to confess he had read the *Age of Reason.* I read it first when I was a cub pilot, read it with fear and hesitation, but marveling at its fearlessness and wonderful power." From that date forward, the author and humorist Mark Twain became a committed freethinker; much later, in 1908, he nominated Paine as one of history's "One Hundred Greatest Men" – those with "largest visible influence on the life and activities of the race."[212]

Like fellow radicals Roger Williams, Elizabeth Cady Stanton, W. E. B. Du Bois, and Vine Deloria Jr., Thomas Paine detested dogma and despised hypocrisy – to his own political and personal detriment, he did not hesitate to call them out. His idealistic formulations of tolerance, liberty, and democracy to this day resonate deeply with Americans who want to believe not only in their own better selves but also in the possibilities of an America that counts liberty and equal justice among its truly inalienable principles.[213] His influence has been profound. Perhaps John Adams,

Paine's erstwhile revolutionary compatriot, best described the life and times of Thomas Paine:

> I am willing you should call this the Age of Frivolity as you do, and would not object if you had named it the Age of Folly, Vice, Frenzy, Brutality, Daemons, Buonaparte, Tom Paine, or the Age of the Burning Brand from the Bottomless Pit.... I know not whether any man in the world has had more influence on its inhabitants or affairs for the last thirty years than Tom Paine.... Call it then the Age of Paine.[214]

3

Elizabeth Cady Stanton (1815–1902)

Gender Wars

> *[I] cannot believe that a God of law and order... could have sanctioned a social principle so calamitous in its consequences as investing in one half the race the absolute control of all the rights of the other.*
>
> – Elizabeth Cady Stanton, 1879

I. Context and Formative Years: The Gallows

It was a cold December 1827 day in Johnstown, New York, when the jailer's wife opened the cell door to allow her twelve-year-old friend entry to visit the man inside.

"I've brought you some fruit," the young girl said.

The prisoner surely was grateful for the kind gesture. The girl had been visiting almost daily since his arrival weeks before – some days bringing fruit, other times cakes and candy. Sometimes they talked; other days she read to him. As she had gotten to know him better, she was impressed with how gentle and teachable he was, almost like a child himself.

"How are you today?" she inquired.

Responding to this innocent question must have been difficult – how well can one be when sentenced to die at the gallows within a few short days? But it would have been inappropriate to dwell on the macabre with this young girl who had shown him such kindness.

"Oh, I'm all right," he lied.

The dreadful reality of these somber final days, slipping like sand through an hourglass, went unspoken between the man and his young visitor. The man had occupied all of the girl's thoughts, and though she was but a child, she was deeply troubled. Even if the man was a horrible wretch, as the mobs said he was, should he have the dearest of freedoms – life itself – taken away? He was a living human being like anyone else, after all, with hopes, dreams, and fears of his own. She wondered how it could be that anyone could judge another so severely as to take his life. And it broke the heart of the girl, who would later have seven children of her own, to think of how the man's mother might have felt about the tragic fate of her beloved child.

So she decided she could not let him die. "It seems he can be saved only by some special intervention," she thought to herself as the awful day approached. "And as I'm afraid he is too wicked for Heaven, I must save him myself." She watched the building of the gallows on a distant hill and decided to cut the rope so it would break when he fell. But when she hurried early to the spot on the morning of the day he was to die, there was no rope – and there was nothing she could do.

"Oh! how I wept and prayed and wondered what I could do, on that cold December morning," Elizabeth Cady Stanton recalled years later. "At length I heard the distant music, saw the military surround the gallows, saw the poor man ascend it, heard the prayer, saw the death struggle, and in anguish hurried home, and there I lay many weeks in a terrible fever, and every execution I read of in our public Journals, brings back that terrible memory."[1]

This childhood gallows incident offers a revealing insight into the early character of an activist who would, more than any other single person throughout America's four-hundred-year history, define the terms of equal justice by which moral government must treat women. For more than fifty years, Elizabeth Cady Stanton agitated to cut the rope of unjust orthodoxy from the necks of the women. During her life, she played the leading role in introducing the most controversial, intimate issues to public consciousness in her efforts to promote women's self-sovereignty – the respect for the "individuality of each human soul," independent of "incidental relations of life, such as mother, wife, sister, daughter."

Whether agitating for greater sexual autonomy, revised notions of the marriage relationship, liberalized divorce and child custody laws, greater labor equality, and the right of suffrage, or even exposing Christian orthodoxy's insidious role in the oppression of women, she firmly maintained that anything that served to focus attention on women's rights was desirable. "If I were to draw up a set of rules for the guidance of reformers," she wrote in her diary in 1888, "I should put at the head of the list: Do all you can, *no matter what*, to get people to think on your reform, and then, if the reform is good, it will come about in due season."

As we shall see, Stanton took her own advice to heart – often alienating the more conservative activists and, at times, even her own closest friends and supporters with her aggressive take-no-prisoners approach. When, by the turn of the twentieth century, Gilded Age American culture had moved in a decidedly more conservative direction, Stanton, with her radicalism, had become something of a relic, preaching to a diminished audience. "I am a leader in thought," she admitted in her later years, "not in numbers."[2]

But, of course, Elizabeth Cady Stanton would not have had it any other way. In the long term, it was always better to stand on principle than to yield to political expediency – she would no more permanently compromise her principles than voluntarily stop breathing. It simply was not part of her DNA to accept injustice where it existed – even if accepting such injustice seemed a necessary price to pay for progress elsewhere.

Noises had only recently begun to be heard in America about women's rights when young Elizabeth Cady befriended the prisoner at the Fulton County jail in 1827, an age when women were still subjected to breathtakingly inequitable laws. During this era, women were unable to vote, forbidden from serving on juries, banned from testifying in court, powerless to sign contracts or to keep and invest earnings, barred from owning or inheriting property, possessed of no rights in divorce including child custody, and considered the legal property of their husbands who were entitled by law to their bodies and wages.[3]

In the decades immediately following the American Revolution, the prevailing view was that women fulfilled a "republican motherhood" role – to be kept in a "separate sphere" outside of the political process so as to be better able to provide bias-free moral guidance on voting and other political issues. "Mothers do, in a sense, hold the reins of government and sway the ensigns of national prosperity and glory," wrote one author in Cott's *The Bonds of Womanhood* in 1802. "Yea, they give direction to the moral sentiments of our rising hopes." Such sentiments were pervasive and no doubt motivated women's work in various benevolent societies throughout the era.[4]

In hindsight, one cannot help but view such obsequious rationale for denying political rights to an entire class of people as so much self-serving apologia or at least with a healthy dose of skepticism. Indeed, starting in the 1820s and 1830s, a more egalitarian "feminism of equal rights" began emerging to challenge the notion of woman's separate sphere. This new egalitarianism was based on the "self-evident Truth" identified in the Declaration of Independence that "all [humans] are created equal" and are thus possessed of certain "unalienable Rights" – decidedly not the prevailing notion of equality of the sort expressed by one Reverend John Cosens Ogden in the 1793 *Female Guide*: "Every man, by the Constitution, is born with an equal right to be elected to the highest office, And [sic] every woman, is born with an equal right to be the wife of the most eminent man."[5]

One of the first persons to challenge women's status quo in America was the Scotswoman Frances Wright, who visited the United States at age twenty-two in 1820 and published *Views of Society and Manners in America* a year later. Among this trailblazing pioneer's observations was that "the education of women has been but slightly attended to."[6]

Accordingly, improving education for girls and women became a major focus for many in the first half of the nineteenth century. Although the moral imperative of improving literacy for its own sake was no doubt a major motivator in improving educational opportunities for girls and women, another factor arguing for a more educated female workforce was the economic necessity of staffing the rapid expansion of textile mills throughout New England between 1814 (when Francis Cabot Lowell opened the first power-loom factory in the United States in Waltham, Massachusetts) and 1840.[7]

The autonomy that young single women were able to achieve by working in the mills enabled them a greater degree of choice in whether to enter the institution of marriage – which, in the early nineteenth century, carried with it oppressive legal inequities for women. Although a single woman (*feme sole*) had the legal rights of a man (except for voting and jury duty) under the common law, once married, she became "overshadowed" (*feme covert*) and ceded all of her personal and property rights to her husband. Under the *feme covert* doctrine, the husband owned all of his wife's wages and labor, for women were considered incapable of managing or spending money. Everything – her household goods, clothing, dowry, and inheritance – was his. "The subordinate and dependent condition of the wife, opens the husband such an unbounded field to practice on her natural timidity, or to abuse a confidence . . . that there is nothing, however unreasonable or unjust, to which he cannot procure her consent," wrote a disapproving Pennsylvania court in *Watson v. Mercer* in 1820. "[H]ere he has the power to obtain her personal estate, not only without condition, but in some instances . . . even to turn real property into [his] personal estate, *against* her consent."[8]

Neither could she sue, enter into contracts, or make a will on her own. "It excited my towering indignation to think it was necessary for [my husband David] to sign [my will]," exclaimed the early activist Lydia Child in the 1830s. "I was indignant for womankind made chattel personal from the beginning of time, perpetually insulted by literature, law, and custom. The very phrases used with regard to us are abominable. 'Dead in the law.' 'Femme Couvert.' How I detest such language!"[9]

Moreover, the husband owned his wife's person in terms of sexual and parenting rights. "The right of a husband to the person of his wife is a right guarded by the law with the utmost solicitude," commented an 1816 book on domestic relations. Beginning in 1819, women lost their legal right to choose to end a pregnancy, and fathers at any time could apprentice children without their mother's knowledge or turn them over to guardians without her permission. Divorcing was extremely difficult as well. Courts only rarely granted divorce – only for extreme cruelty, adultery, desertion, or nonsupport – and once divorced, the woman lost custody of her own children. In short, observes the author Ellen Carol DuBois, "no people, with the exception of chattel slaves, had less proprietary rights over themselves in eighteenth-century and early nineteenth-century America than married women."[10]

No less an incisive observer than Alexis de Tocqueville commented in his 1831 masterpiece, *Democracy in America*, that "[i]n America the independence of women is irrevocably lost in the bonds of matrimony." Tocqueville pointed to two factors for the near-complete subjugation of women in the marriage institution: one, America's religious nature, and two, its mercantile focus. "Religious peoples and trading nations entertain peculiarly serious notions of marriage," he explained. "[T]he former consider the regularity of woman's life as the best pledge and most certain sign of the purity of her morals; the latter regard it as the highest security for the order and prosperity of the household. The Americans are at the same time a puritanical people and a commercial nation: their religious opinions, as well as their trading habits, consequently lead them to require much abnegation on the part of woman, and a constant sacrifice of her pleasures to her duties which is seldom demanded of her in Europe."

Tocqueville's observation of Christian orthodoxy's effect on women is epitomized in an 1832 comment of one American preacher: "The wife who possesses a mind of superior cultivation and power to her husband's [should] be in subjection to his authority ... because this is conformable to the general order God has established.... Subordination to principles and laws of order is absolutely essential to the existence of the social state. Break up the order of the social state," he concluded, "and woman must become the most abject and helpless of all slaves."[11]

It is impossible to discuss the early days of American feminism without including the movement to abolish slavery, for it was from the abolitionist movement that women received early political training, support, and constituency. The roots of the movement can be traced to young William Lloyd Garrison.[12]

Employing an absolutist natural rights doctrine that demanded liberty and equal rights of the sort claimed by America's founders and framers (whom he labeled as hypocrites, with their failure to practice what they preached in the Declaration of Independence, and for enacting a pro-slavery Constitution), Garrison welcomed women's participation in his American Anti-Slavery Society, capitalizing on the republican-motherhood tradition to further his abolitionist goals. "You cannot be ignorant of the victorious influence which you possess over the minds of men," Garrison wrote an early colleague, Sarah M. Douglass, a free black Quaker woman in Philadelphia. "There is not a glance of your eye," he continued, "not a tone of your voice – however seemingly the look of remonstrance or entreaty be disregarded, or the word of admonition or advice be slighted – but has a direct connexion with the results of masculine actions and pursuits."[13]

Emphasizing the cruelties suffered by slaves, Garrison tapped into the complex network of (mostly New England) female benevolent associations, which had arisen as a respectable nonpolitical means for women to participate in issues outside the home. "Garrison's invitation was special," says Professor Suzanne Marilley, "because by publicly including women as a key constituency along with the clergy and newspaper editors, he effectively asked women to deny the traditional separation of the public and domestic spheres."[14]

Although they were initially drawn to the abolitionist cause to abolish slavery, women began extending Garrison's universal equal rights doctrine to apply to women's rights as well, often through a scripturally based moral equality approach (years later, Stanton herself employed this appeal-to-religious-morality approach before becoming so soured on religious orthodoxy that she could no longer make such appeals). In 1833, for example, the free black woman Maria W. Stewart wrote, in defending herself against criticisms for speaking out in public, "What if I am a woman; is not the God of ancient times the God of these modern days? . . . [H]oly women ministered unto Christ and the apostles; and women of refinement in all ages, more or less, have had a voice in moral, religious and political subjects." Angelina Grimké added in 1836, "*Women* as well as men were to be living stones in the temple of grace, and therefore *their* heads were consecrated by the descent of the Holy Ghost as well as those of men"; and her sister Sarah Grimké wrote, "The Lord Jesus defines the duties of his followers in his Sermon on the Mount. . . . I follow him through all his precepts, and find him giving the same direction to women as to men, never even referring to the distinction now so strenuously insisted upon between masculine and feminine virtues. Men and women were CREATED EQUAL!"[15]

Throughout these years, the abolitionist movement's radical message of change, and the fact that women were active participants, created a backlash – some of it violent, despite the Garrisonians' avowedly pacifist approach. In 1834, the homes of forty-five free African Americans were destroyed in Philadelphia, and throughout 1835, abolitionist speakers were jeered and sometimes beaten. When Angelina Grimké's *Appeal to the Christian Women of the South* reached Charleston in 1836, the postmaster publicly burned all copies, and the police warned the Grimké family that Angelina should not return to the city. In 1838, when Lucretia Mott and other organizers of the Second National Anti-Slavery Convention of the American Women refused the requests of the Philadelphia mayor and others to "ask the black women to stop attending the meeting" and persisted nonetheless in their activities, a mob of seventeen thousand (many of them visitors from the South) burned the newly constructed Pennsylvania Hall to the ground at the end of the three-day convention.[16]

Many men, and some women, objected specifically to the increased role of women in the movement. When women brought numerous petitions calling for the end of slavery in the District of Columbia to the House of Representatives in 1834, a group of Southern congressmen prevailed in passing the Pinckney "gag rule" to block them, thus prompting representative and former president John Quincy Adams to actively defend citizens' right to petition (and thus triggering the first discussions in Congress on the woman's rights issue).

The clergy in particular mounted attacks condemning women's participation in antislavery activities as "unfeminine" and urging women to restrict their activities to the "separate sphere" of the household and less controversial issues. In an 1837 pastoral letter, the Council of Congregationalist Ministers of Massachusetts argued that when a woman "assumes the place and tone of man as public reformer[,] ... her character becomes unnatural" and criticized the Grimkés for "threaten[ing] the female character with wide-spread and permanent injury." To which Sarah Grimké responded with a series of letters for the *Spectator* demanding educational reform, equal wages, and an end to other forms of discrimination against women. "I ask no favors for my sex. I surrender not our claim to equality," she explained, and she added the memorable riposte: "All I ask our brethren is that they will take their feet from off our necks and permit us to stand upright on that ground which God designed us to occupy."[17]

Besides offering cover for these early pioneers, Garrison's Anti-Slavery Society continued to be important for the following several decades. Most who joined the women's rights movement before the Civil War began their activism with antislavery efforts, and their participation in the abolitionist cause seasoned them. "[T]heir antislavery activity put them outside the pale of respectable womanhood," DuBois explains. "Already branded as abolitionist extremists, they were not frightened by public hostility or press indictments of long-haired men and short-haired women." Through the abolitionist movement, they were able to advance their arguments that Article 4 of the Constitution (specifying that Congress "shall guarantee to every State in this Union a Republican form of government") mandates equal treatment for all people in every state. Republicanism, they reasoned, admits of no class boundaries between citizens.[18]

With all of these controversies, by the end of the 1830s, many abolitionist men had concluded that the prominent leadership of women in the antislavery movement was counterproductive, at the very least, or that "equality of the sexes" was "not God's will." Some even challenged women's constitutional right to petition.

Garrison stood with the women, however, staunchly defending them on the universalist egalitarian grounds that, just as first principles of absolute human equality ignored physical, cultural, and historical characteristics that might distinguish blacks from whites, so, too, should they ignore differences based on sex. The basic disagreements among the abolitionists led to a contentious split in the abolitionist movement, when James G. Birney, the 1840 Liberty Party candidate for president, spearheaded the formation of a new group in April 1840 to rival Garrison's American Anti-Slavery Society – the American and Foreign Anti-Slavery Society, which opposed the "insane innovation" of allowing women to be speakers and officers and favored the gradual emancipation of slaves through political solutions.[19]

It was into this cauldron of social upheaval that twenty-four-year-old Elizabeth Cady found herself drawn in 1839 and 1840. She had not gravitated naturally to activism from an early age, notwithstanding her girlhood efforts to save a prisoner from the hangman's noose. She was a child of relative privilege – born in Johnstown, New York, in 1815 of a father, Daniel Cady, a successful lawyer and later judge, who, according to a guest, was a tough-minded "John Quincy Adams type of man," and a mother, Margaret, from the prominent local Livingston family, a "very refined, lady-like, loving, spirited woman." Servants and private schools were part of her childhood life. She was a bright girl, eager to please her father with her mastery of Greek and other intellectual pursuits typically reserved exclusively to males.

But Judge Cady, a socially conservative man in a socially conservative era, could not fully accept her as an individual, ruminating to Elizabeth on at least a couple occasions, "I wish you were a boy!" As hard as she tried, Elizabeth never was able to fill the space of a son in her father's life. Much later, even once she had amassed considerable recognition and plaudits as the erudite leader of a worthy cause, her father continued to disparage her efforts. After one demoralizing visit with him in 1852, for example, she confided bitterly to her longtime coadjutor Susan B. Anthony (on whom more later), "To think that all in me of which my father would have felt a proper pride had I been a man, is deeply mortifying to him because I am a woman.... I never felt more keenly the degradation of my sex."[20]

Elizabeth attended Emma Willard's Troy Female Seminary (one of the twelve thousand young women educated there between 1821 and 1872) because, at the time of her 1830 enrollment, the opportunity to attend college simply did not yet exist for women. Her earlier experience at the coeducational Johnstown Academy had been happy. "[Although I] was the only girl in the higher classes of mathematics and the languages," she recalled, "in our [play] all the girls and boys mingled freely together. In running, sliding downhill, and snowballing we made no distinction of sex.... Equality was the general basis of our school relations." She was uninspired, by contrast, with her experience at the Troy Seminary, commenting, "the isolation of the sexes breeds all this sickly sentimentality, romantic reveries, morbid appetites, listlessness and lassitude." Coeducation, she believed, was the better way to go, as it allows "girls [to] acquire strength, courage and self-assertion and boys courtesy, refinement and

PHOTO 1. Elizabeth Cady Stanton, with Infant Daughter Harriot, 1856. Courtesy of Library of Congress.

self-control." She graduated in 1833; then, in "the most pleasant years of my girlhood... enjoy[ed] a period of irrepressible joy and freedom" riding horses, attending dances and hayrides, visiting relatives, and singing along while playing the guitar and piano.[21]

By 1839, Elizabeth was meeting a fascinating array of people in her frequent visits to the home of favorite cousin Gerrit Smith in nearby Peterboro, New York. Intrigued and intellectually stimulated by the changing cast of fugitive slaves, male and female abolitionists, Oneida Indians, politicians, and other reformers of all shapes and descriptions who passed through Smith's home, she found there "new inspiration in life and... new ideas of individual rights." One of the people she met there in October 1839 was the abolitionist speaker Henry Stanton. Henry, ten years older than Elizabeth, was smitten with Elizabeth's intellect and spirit, and she with his intellectual commitment to the antislavery movement, as well as his dancing skill and good looks. They began courting, and less than a month later, in "one of those charming revelations of human feeling which brave knights have always found eloquent words to utter and to which fair ladies have always listened with mingled emotions," Henry asked her to marry him, and Elizabeth, in a moment of "pleasure and astonishment," accepted his proposal.

After a brief break in the engagement because of Elizabeth's father's objection to the match, they were married in a private ceremony on May 1, 1840 – in which Elizabeth persuaded the reluctant minister not to include the promise that she would "obey" her husband. Then they boarded the steamer *Montreal* on May 12 to London, where Henry was to participate as a delegate to the 1840 World Anti-Slavery Convention. She had decided to take Stanton's name but not "Mrs. Henry Stanton," commenting, "The custom of calling women Mrs. John This and Mrs. Tom That and colored men Sambo and Zip Coon, is founded on the principle that white men are lords of all."[22]

During the *Montreal*'s journey from New York to London, she was surprised by the narrow views of many of the antislavery delegates on the issue of women's roles in the abolition movement. At sea, she listened as 1840 Liberty Party presidential candidate James G. Birney criticized Lucretia Coffin Mott (the forty-six-year-old Quaker minister, abolitionist, and feminist) and other female delegates for "demoralizing" the antislavery movement by insisting on attending the convention. Birney's comments reflected the split of Birney's American and Foreign Anti-Slavery Society from William Lloyd Garrison's more radical American Anti-Slavery Society just a month earlier.[23]

To Elizabeth's regret, Henry Stanton was associated with Birney's new group. As "the only lady present who represented the 'Birney faction,'" she was embarrassed when introduced to delegate Lucretia Mott, who was decidedly in the Garrison camp, while checking into the London Hotel on Great Queen Street. She managed to redeem herself at dinner later that evening, however, when, despite Henry's nudgings under the table, she "found myself in full accord with the other ladies, combating most of the gentlemen at the table" on the matter of women's empowerment – thereby earning the respect of Mott and others. "I shall never forget the look of recognition [Mott] gave me when she saw by my remarks that I fully comprehended the problem of woman's rights and wrongs," Elizabeth later recalled.[24]

Once at the convention, before talk of slavery even commenced, the delegates argued for hours about whether women would be allowed to participate in the proceedings. The debate was pitched, but in the end, most delegates sided with the Birney faction, arguing not to seat the women, so they were made to sit behind a screen out of view of the delegates. The women were furious. "The crucifixion of their pride and self-respect, the humiliation of the spirit was treated by the men as a most trifling matter," Stanton remembered. "It was really pitiful to hear narrow-minded bigots, pretending to be teachers and leaders of men, so cruelly remanding their own mothers, with the rest of womankind, to absolute subjection to the ordinary masculine type of humanity."

William Lloyd Garrison again showed solidarity with the women by sitting with them behind the screen, explaining, "After battling so many long years for the liberation of African slaves... I can take no part in a convention that strikes down the most sacred rights of all women." Elizabeth was deeply influenced by Garrison's stalwart commitment to principle on this (and other) occasions, commenting, "It was a great act of self-sacrifice that should never be forgotten by women." A major disappointment for Elizabeth, however, was that Henry Stanton, although he had earlier said he supported women's participation and made a show at the convention in support of seating the women, ultimately sided privately with the majority and sat with the rest of the delegates on the floor. "I soon found that the pending battle was on women's rights," Stanton recalled, "and that unwittingly, I was by marriage on the wrong side." Throughout their marriage, Henry rarely publicly supported women's rights, leading Elizabeth to lament, "Henry sides with my friends who oppose me in all that is dearest in my heart." As Susan B. Anthony would much later comment, Stanton was the only one of the leaders of the women's movement who stood "all alone, without Father, Mother, Sister, Brother, or Husband."[25]

Despite (and perhaps because of) the snubbing at the convention, the trip to London and the following five-month tour of Great Britain, Ireland, and France was a transformative experience for Elizabeth, largely due to her many conversations with Lucretia Mott, who to her epitomized "an entire new revelation of womanhood." Much to Henry's irritation, Elizabeth "took possession of Lucretia," eagerly soaking up Mott's wisdom as she accompanied her on visits to London's schools, prisons, and tourist attractions. "When I first heard from her lips that I had the same right to think for myself that Luther, Calvin and John Knox had, and the same right to be guided by my own convictions," Elizabeth recalled, "I felt a new born sense of dignity and freedom." On one memorable day at the British Museum, the two women talked for hours about a meeting they would one day hold in America on the topic of women's rights. "I could not see what to do or where to begin,"

PHOTO 2. William Lloyd Garrison. Courtesy of Library of Congress.

Elizabeth later wrote. "[M]y only thought was a public meeting for protest and discussion."

And she made strong favorable impressions on Mott and others during the trip, despite her relative youth and inexperience. "Elizabeth Stanton gaining daily in our affections," read Mott's diary entry of June 20, 1840. William Lloyd Garrison himself wrote, "Mrs. Stanton is a fearless woman and goes for women's rights with all her soul." "Mrs. Stanton is one in two thousand," the English reformer Richard Webb added. "I have met very few women I consider equal to her." And Webb's wife admired, "Elizabeth Stanton (with whom we were highly delighted) is a brave upholder of woman's rights."[26]

II. Seneca Falls

I consider my right to property, to suffrage, etc., as natural and inalienable as my right to life and to liberty. Man is above all law. The province of law is simply to protect me in what is mine.

– Elizabeth Cady Stanton, 1858

Awaking on Wednesday, July 19, 1848, in her fixer-upper house on an often-muddy road on the outskirts of Seneca Falls, the thirty-two-year-old woman readied herself for a meeting that would provide a welcome break in running a home and raising three young sons largely by herself – a domestic routine that had left her depressed, lonely, angry, and exhausted. Her husband and she had moved their young family the previous year to Seneca Falls, a central New York community of four thousand located not far from the Erie Canal roughly between Syracuse to the east and Rochester to the west.

Elizabeth Cady Stanton muttered a silent curse as she dressed herself that morning in the customary lady's garb of starched shirtwaists, ten pounds of muslin petticoats, and binding corsets made of stiff whalebones. "Take a man," she once said, "and pin three or four large tablecloths about him, fastened back with elastic and looped up with ribbons; drag all his own hair to the middle of his head and tie it tight, and hair pin on about five pounds of other hair with a bow of ribbon . . . pinch his waist into a corset and give him gloves a size too small and shoes ditto, . . . and frill to tickle his chin and little lace veil to bend his eyes whenever he goes out to walk and he will know what woman's dress is."[27]

And she reflected how, since moving to Seneca Falls, "the novelty of housekeeping had passed away, and much that was once attractive in domestic life was now irksome." "My duties," she later recalled, "were too numerous and varied and none sufficiently exhilarating or intellectual to bring into play my higher faculties. I suffered with mental hunger, which, like an empty stomach, is very depressing."[28]

This existence was in rude contrast to the contented life she had left in Boston, where she had lived for three years with her growing family in "a kind of moral museum . . . afford[ing] as many curiosities in [its] way as does the British Museum in its." She "had never lived in such an enthusiastically literary and reform latitude before, and [her] mental powers were kept at the highest tension," with a who's-who group of friends of notable reformers, including Abby Kelley and Stephen Foster, Frederick Douglass, Ralph Waldo Emerson, Nathaniel Hawthorne, William Lloyd

Garrison, and Theodore Parker. In the midst of this intellectual ferment, Stanton was contented enough to operate mainly within the "woman's sphere," commenting, "It is a proud moment in a woman's life to reign supreme within four walls, to be the one to whom all questions . . . are referred."[29]

But that season of contentment was past. Now, the realities of life as small-town housewife weighed on her, and finally the combination of "the wearied, anxious look of the majority of women . . . , all I had read of the legal status of women, and the oppression I saw everywhere, intensified by many personal experiences, together swept across my soul . . . [and] conspired to impel me to some onward step."

Stanton's "onward step" was initiated at a tea she had attended the prior Thursday, July 13, 1848, at the home of Jane Hunt in nearby Waterloo with her old friend Lucretia Mott; Lucretia's sister Martha C. Wright; and another Quaker friend, Mary Ann McClintock. That day, Stanton found a sympathetic audience among the four other women, as she "poured out . . . the torrent of my long-accumulating discontent with such vehemence and indignation that I stirred myself, as well as the rest of the party, to do and dare anything" – to address the pervasive insults against women "in the laws, religion, and literature of the world, and in the invidious and degrading sentiments and customs of all nations." Although none of these women had personally "experienced the coarser forms of tyranny resulting from unjust laws, or avocation with immoral and unscrupulous men, . . . they had souls large enough to feel the wrongs of others" and were resolved collectively to act.[30]

What they settled on was a meeting for the following Wednesday, July 19, and Thursday, July 20 – women only on Wednesday and the public generally on Thursday. Shortly, they had convinced the pastor of the Wesleyan Methodist Chapel in Seneca Falls to allow them to use the church for the meeting and placed an advertisement to run the following day in the *Seneca County Courier* "earnestly invit[ing women] to attend . . . a convention to discuss the social, civil, and religious condition and rights of women."

When the five women – none of whom but Lucretia Mott had any experience as an organizer, delegate, or speaker – met again three days later around Mary Ann McClintock's parlor table to map out the agenda, they "felt as helpless and hopeless as if we had been suddenly asked to construct a steam engine," Stanton later recalled. Although ignorant on the details of organizing a meeting, once started they were not timid.

PHOTO 3. Elizabeth Cady Stanton House, Seneca Falls, New York. Courtesy of National Park Service.

Dismissing the format of "various masculine productions... [as] too tame and pacific for the inauguration of a rebellion," they settled on the mechanism of the Declaration of Rights and Sentiments to advance their demands, using the 1776 Declaration of Independence as benchmark.[31]

As the familiar scenery of Seneca Falls rolled past during the carriage ride from her home to the church on the appointed day, Stanton may have ruminated about the eight years that had elapsed since those innocent early days when she and Lucretia Mott sat on the bench at the British Museum thinking big thoughts and pledging to convene a women's conference. Although Stanton and Mott had continued to correspond by letter, mostly on religious matters to indulge Elizabeth's "hungering, thirsting condition for truth," they had not yet followed through on their plans for a conference because, simply put, family life had intervened.[32]

So she was happy finally to be acting on their earlier plan. At the church, the gathered crowd of more than one hundred women and men streamed in and began filling the pews. Although they had intended that only women would attend the first day, the organizers chose not to exclude the men who had entered; indeed, as the five were not confident in their own ability to run a meeting, they hastily agreed that Lucretia's husband, James Mott, "tall and dignified in Quaker costume," should chair the meeting. Stanton may have thought wistfully then of

Henry, who, while helping to draft some portions of the declaration and accompanying resolutions, had escaped town for a few days to avoid associating himself with his wife's radical call in the ninth paragraph for women's suffrage.[33]

It was soon Stanton's turn to speak – only the second public speaking she had ever done. "We have met here today to discuss our rights and wrongs, civil and political," she began quietly. From the Declaration of Rights and Sentiments, she read, more forcefully: "We hold these truths to be self-evident: that all men *and women* are created equal; that they are endowed by their Creator with certain inalienable rights.... The history of mankind is a history of repeated injuries and usurpations on the part of man toward woman, having in direct object the establishment of an absolute tyranny over her. To prove this, let facts be submitted to a candid world." The declaration then stated a like number of grievances (eighteen) as in the 1776 Declaration of Independence but particular here to women.

Having listed the grievances, the declaration insisted: "[Women must] have immediate admission to all the rights and privileges which belong to them as citizens of the United States." "[W]e shall use every instrumentality within our power to effect our object," it continued. "We shall employ agents, circulate tracts, petition the State and National legislatures, and endeavor to enlist the pulpit and the press in our behalf." It concluded with the expressed "hope [that] this Convention will be followed by a series of Conventions embracing every part of the country." One hundred people signed on in support during the afternoon session.[34]

The next day, the convention took up what the *Seneca County Courier* described as "the spirited and spicey resolutions," demanding remedy for the grievances listed in the Declaration of Rights and Sentiments. After lively debate, the delegates unanimously adopted and signed all of the resolutions except one, the ninth, which stated: "*Resolved,* That it is the duty of the women of this country to secure themselves their sacred right to the elective franchise."

Some, including Lucretia Mott, believed demanding the vote would threaten the other "more rational" resolutions "and make the whole movement ridiculous." To Stanton's way of thinking, however, anything short of simple equality – especially when all men could vote – was ridiculous. "Strange as it may seem to many," she said, "we now demand our right to vote according to the declaration of the government under which we live.... [T]o have drunkards, idiots, horseracing rum-selling rowdies, ignorant foreigners, and silly boys fully recognized, while we ourselves are thrust out from all the rights that belong to citizens, is too grossly insulting to... be longer quietly submitted to." She concluded, "The right is ours. Have it we must. Use it we will."

Stanton's position was supported at the conference by Frederick Douglass, the African American abolitionist, who reasoned that women should have the vote because "the power to choose rulers and make laws was the right by which all others could be secured." "All that distinguishes man as an intelligent and accountable being, is equally true of woman," Douglass elaborated a week later, adding, "[T]here can be no reason in the world for denying to woman the exercise of the elective franchise, or a hand in making and administering the laws of the land."

Thereafter, the ninth resolution passed – barely. In the concluding evening session, Stanton, perhaps recognizing the incendiary tone of her earlier rhetoric, praised men as "lords of creation"; after another resolution and a few more statements, Lucretia Mott gave a final speech, putting to a close eighteen hours of historic discussions.[35]

Elizabeth Cady Stanton could not have known it at the time, but she had indeed helped launch the revolution she had only dreamed of the week before.

The Seneca Falls Convention generated an immediate, mostly negative, public reaction, as predicted in the next day's edition of the *Seneca County Courier*: "The doctrines broached... are startling to those who are wedded to the present usages and laws of society. The resolutions are of the kind called radical.... Some will regard them with respect – others with disapprobation and contempt." The *New York Herald* said dismissively, "[The Declaration of Sentiments is] a most amusing document.... The amusing part is the preamble where they asserted their equality." The *Rochester Democrat* suggested, "The great effort [of the Convention] seemed to be to bring out some new, impracticable, absurd, and ridiculous proposition, and the greater its absurdity the better." The *Public Ledger and Daily Transcript* of Philadelphia bloviated, "Our Philadelphia ladies not only possess beauty, but they are celebrated for discretion, modesty, and unfeigned diffidence, as well as wit, vivacity, and good nature.... But all women are not as reasonable as ours of Philadelphia. The Boston ladies contend for the rights of women. The New York girls aspire to mount the rostrum, to do all the voting, and, we suppose, all the fighting too."[36]

The vitriol of these and other reactions surprised the women, leading even Stanton to initial misgivings. "If I had had the slightest premonition of all that was to follow the convention," she admitted, "I fear I should not have had the courage to risk it." (Indeed, the harsh public condemnations led many of the hundred people who had signed the Declaration of Rights and Sentiments within weeks to withdraw their names.)

It was almost as if even Stanton herself did not yet believe her own bold words in the early days following the Seneca Falls conference. Beginning to wonder if it had all been a big mistake, it was only with "fear and trembling" that she accepted an invitation to speak at a follow-up convention to be held two weeks later at the Unitarian Church in nearby Rochester. Then, when a majority of those in attendance at the Rochester meeting voted with the organizer Amy Post to allow a woman, Abigail Bush, to chair the meeting, Stanton, Lucretia Mott, and Mary Ann McClintock left the stage and considered walking out in opposition. "[N]ow," they asked, "with such feeble voices and timid manners, without the slightest knowledge of *Cushing's Manual*, or the least experience in public meetings, how could a woman preside?"

Once Abigail Bush took the chair, however, "the calm way she assumed the duties of the office, and the admirable manner in which she discharged them, soon reconciled the opposition to the seemingly ridiculous experiment." When members of the audience called out, "Louder, louder" to some of the women speaking, for example, Bush quieted them from the chair, stating, "Friends, we present ourselves here before you, as an oppressed class, with trembling frames and faltering tongues, and we do not expect to be heard by all at first, but we trust we shall have the sympathy of the audience, and that you will bear with our weakness now in the infancy of the movement. Our trust in the omnipotency of right is our only faith that we shall succeed."

Observing the courage and competence of like-minded women such as Abigail Bush, Stanton regained her balance, and it was with renewed assurance she then argued to the Rochester delegates that voting is as essential in a representative government as "air and motion are to life." "[Men know] the advantages of voting, for they all seem very tenacious about the right," she noted, querying: "[Do you think] if woman had a voice in this government, that all those laws affecting her interests would so entirely violate every principle of right and justice?" She emphasized, moreover, the importance of women's independence and self-reliance in the struggle: "Woman herself must do this work – for woman alone can understand the height, and the depth, the length and the breadth of her own degradation and woe. Man cannot speak for us."

In the end, the suffrage resolution passed in Rochester by a greater margin than in Seneca Falls, and additional resolutions were added as well. Moved by Abigail Bush's performance and embarrassed by her own faintness of heart on the chair issue, Stanton wrote Amy Post a month later, "I have so often regretted my foolish conduct. My only excuse is that woman has been so little accustomed to act in a public capacity that she does not always know what is due."[37]

Stanton was looking forward. Writing to Lucretia Mott in September after having weathered the initial tsunami of criticism following the Seneca Falls and Rochester conventions, she enthused, "Imagine the publicity given to our ideas by thus appearing in a widely circulated sheet like the [*New York*] *Herald*. It will start women thinking, and men too; and when men and women think about a new question, the first step in progress is taken. The great fault of mankind is that it will not think."[38]

The convention in Seneca Falls had indeed ignited a flame, and women increasingly began finding their voices in the following years. For many women, it was gratifying, and empowering, finally to know that the "radical" ideas of equality they felt within themselves were shared also with others.

The first National Women's Rights Convention was held in 1850 in Worcester, Massachusetts, and was followed thereafter by national conferences every year (except 1857) through 1860, largely organized by Susan B. Anthony, with many more local events as well. Among their other benefits, the meetings and conventions provided networking opportunities. Stanton met Lucy Stone (born in 1818 and raised in Boston, the first woman not to take her husband's name in marriage and the first woman in Massachusetts to receive a college degree), who would later lead the rival American Woman's Suffrage Association, at the first National Convention in 1850; then she met Susan B. Anthony on a street corner in Seneca Falls in March 1851 after an antislavery meeting organized by William Lloyd Garrison. "There she stood," Stanton recalled, "with her good earnest face and genial smile, dressed in gray delaine, hat and all the same color, relieved with pale blue ribbons, the perfection of neatness and sobriety. I liked her thoroughly, and why I did not at once invite her home with me to dinner I do not know."[39]

Little did Stanton know at the time that this chance street-corner meeting would initiate what surely qualifies as one of the great political partnerships in American history. For fifty years, Stanton and Anthony collaborated, through thick and thin, in advancing a broad range of women's rights, agitating for the cause and setting the stage for the 1920 ratification of the Nineteenth Amendment, which finally constitutionalized the right of women's suffrage. Throughout their association, both acknowledged that Stanton was the "brains" of the organization – the better writer and idea person, whereas Anthony was the "brawn" – the tireless and single-minded worker of legendary good health and stamina. Stanton always remained the "biggest gun" in an arsenal possessed by the army of activists led by their "Napoleon," Susan B. Anthony.[40]

The two women had enormous respect and affection for one another – Anthony keeping a framed picture of Stanton in the center of the mantle over her desk; Stanton always keeping a separate room in her home for Anthony. Stanton's daughter Harriot Blatch offers a compelling portrait of the two women as they labored for six months in 1881 in Stanton's Tenafly, New Jersey, home writing and assembling the first volume of *The History of Woman Suffrage*:

> It is as good as a comedy to watch these souls from day to day. They start off pretty well in the morning, fresh and amiable. They write page after page with alacrity, they laugh and talk, poke the fire by turn, and admire the flowers on their desk.... Everything is harmonious for a season, but after straining their eyes over the most illegible, disorderly manuscripts,... suddenly the whole sky is overspread with dark and threatening clouds, and from the adjoining room I hear a hot dispute about something. The dictionary, the encyclopedia, [newspapers,] ... are overhauled, tossed about in an emphatic manner for some date, fact, or some point of law or constitution. Susan is punctilious on dates, mother on philosophy, but each contends as stoutly in the other's domain as if equally strong on all points. Sometimes these disputes run so high that down go the pens, one sails out of one door and one out the other, walking in opposite directions around the estate, and just as I have made up my mind that this beautiful friendship of forty years has at last terminated, I see them walking down the hill, arm in arm.... When they return they go straight back to work where they left off, as if nothing had ever happened.... They never explain, nor apologize, nor shed tears, nor make up, as other people do.[41]

The Seneca Falls convention had an immediate positive impact on Stanton, allowing her for the first time ever "[t]he opportunity of expressing myself fully and freely on a subject I felt so deeply about." It had provided fertile ground for her budding natural rights philosophy to take root. The core of that natural rights philosophy, which would be more fully expressed over the following decades, was based in the same

PHOTO 4. Elizabeth Cady Stanton and Susan B. Anthony, ca. 1890s. Courtesy of Library of Congress.

Enlightenment-inspired principles of reason, science, and individual natural rights that guided Thomas Paine before and W. E. B. Du Bois after her. The first three Seneca Falls resolutions succinctly stated these principles:

> *Resolved,* That such laws as conflict, in any way, with the true and substantial happiness of woman, are contrary to the great precept of nature and of no validity.
>
> *Resolved,* That all laws which prevent woman from occupying such a station in society as her conscience shall dictate, or which place her in a position inferior to that of man, are contrary to the great precept of nature, and therefore of no force or authority.

> *Resolved,* That woman is man's equal – was intended to be so by the Creator, and the highest good of the race demands that she should be recognized as such.[42]

Stanton's natural rights philosophy owed much to the seventeenth-century English political scientist John Locke, as brought into the current day by the progressive theology of Theodore Parker, the Unitarian minister, whom she found especially inspirational. Parker's emphasis on individual free will gave her permission to think for herself and provided a means of escape from her earlier religious superstitions and fears, thus contributing to improved self-esteem and confidence.[43]

She also read Thomas Paine, who had so captured America's revolutionary generation with his common sense articulations of individual rights, even though (or perhaps, partly because) he had fallen far out of favor during the nineteenth century (as detailed in Chapter 2). "The illuminating and divine principle of the equal rights of man," Paine explained in *Rights of Man*, "[is that] every individual is born equal in rights with his contemporary . . . and with equal natural right[s]." As Stanton wrote Susan B. Anthony in 1858, "I consider my right to property, to suffrage, etc., as natural and inalienable as my right to life and to liberty. Man is above all law. The province of law is simply to protect me in what is mine."[44]

Stanton's sensibilities were also given voice in *The Subjection of Women* in 1869 by the great English philosopher J. S. Mill. Addressing the issue of women's rights directly, Mill argued that women need the vote for purposes of self-protection: "Women require the suffrage, as their guarantee of just and equal consideration." He suggested that women's subordination in modern society is not natural; rather, it originated in the rule of force, in that men are more physically powerful. Because men profit at women's expense, Mill added, it is not surprising that they would view such subordination as "natural" and seek its perpetuation. The fact that women go along as well is simply testimony to the powerful social forces inducing conformity. Mill's work moved Stanton to confide to Mill, "I lay [your] book down with a peace and joy I never felt before, for it is the first response from any man to show that he is capable of seeing and feeling all the nice shades and degrees of woman's wrongs, and the central point of her weakness and degradation."[45]

In the broader scheme, Stanton and her more radical fellow activists (including Matilda Joslyn Gage, who wrote the "Preceding Causes" section in *History of Woman Suffrage* in 1881), identified the women's rights movement as a microcosm within the bigger picture of the entire history of Western civilization. The women identified "[t]he twin barriers to human rights... [as] the Church and the State," explain editors Mari Jo and Paul Buhl. "Both conspire to limit freedom. The Church stifles free inquiry and the State maintains artificial order through a temporal sanction." The radical women thought that progress, by contrast, "was signified by rational thinking and individual self-sufficiency. Thus, their historical narrative focuses on the standard milestones of the West: the Renaissance and Reformation as the first stage, the Enlightenment and American Revolution as the immediate precursors to the final advance toward perfection in the nineteenth century" – to include, of course, full equality for women.[46]

III. War and Reconstruction: The Negro's Hour

> *Those who tell us the republican idea is a failure, do not see the deep gulf between our broad theory and partial legislation; do not see that our Government for the last century has been but the repetition of the old experiments of class and caste. Hence, the failure is not in the principle, but in the lack of virtue on our part to apply it. The question now is, have we the wisdom and conscience, from the present upheavings of our political system, to reconstruct a government on the one enduring basis that has never yet been tried* – "EQUAL RIGHTS TO ALL."
>
> – Elizabeth Cady Stanton, 1866

"Union Victory! Peace!" trumpeted the headline of the *New York Times* on April 10, 1865. "Surrender of General Lee and His Whole Army," it explained in smaller type below. The robust woman with the pleasant smile in the Manhattan brownstone at 464 West Thirty-Fourth Street reflected on the news of that April day. "It's over – finally," Elizabeth Cady Stanton thought with relief.

The Confederacy's surrender in April 1865 at Appomattox after four years of bloody war that tore apart a nation and took half a million lives was cause for widespread celebration – not least of all for Stanton. The end of the war meant she and her fellow activist Susan B. Anthony could once again focus their energies exclusively on advancing the cause of women's rights – efforts they had suspended in 1861 with the onset of the war in favor of the more pressing task of freeing the slaves. For the duration of the Civil War, the two leaders, together with the five thousand women of their wartime organization, the Loyal Women of the

Republic (Women's Loyal League), worked tirelessly for emancipation, eventually presenting petitions with four hundred thousand signatures to Massachusetts Senator Charles Sumner during congressional debates on the Thirteenth Amendment to abolish slavery.

When the Thirteenth Amendment passed both houses of Congress in January 1865 and was ratified by the required three-fourths of the states in December of the same year, America's ignoble chapter in formally supporting the institution of human slavery came to a long-overdue close.[47]

Prior to the Civil War and following the Seneca Falls Convention, Stanton had stayed busy balancing the challenges of playing a leading intellectual role in the nascent women's movement with those of raising a family of eventually seven children largely by herself. Despite her embrace of motherhood, Stanton criticized the man-made institution of marriage as inherently unfair to women (where "[a] man in marrying gives up no right, but a woman, [gives up] every right, even the most sacred of all – the right to her own person"), and the traditional marriage ceremony as "humiliating." "It is in vain to look for the elevation of woman so long as she is degraded in marriage," she wrote to Susan B. Anthony in 1853. "I feel, as never before, that this whole question of woman's rights turns on the pivot of the marriage relation" – which she characterized at various times as "nothing more nor less than legalized prostitution, [where] woman can have no self-respect, and of course man will have none for her"; and as bondage, which "though it differs from that of the Negro slave, frets and chafes her all the same. She too sighs and groans in her chains and lives but in hope of better things to come."[48]

Given her domestic demands during the 1850s, Stanton attended few of the state meetings or national conventions, but she contributed a number of speeches for Susan B. Anthony, who for her part occasionally cared for Stanton's children in Seneca Falls to help Stanton find time to write. One event Stanton did attend was the first meeting of the New York association in Albany in February 1854, during which she and Anthony carried petitions with nearly six thousand signatures to the New York legislature urging woman suffrage, divorce and child custody reform, and protection of women's wages from husbands.

Concurrently, she addressed the legislature – the first woman to do so – on the topic of women's legal disabilities, and sought (unsuccessfully, as it turned out) extension of the Married Woman's Property Act for that year. "[We] are persons, native, free-born citizens, property-holders, taxpayers," she emphasized, "moral, virtuous, and intelligent, and in all respects equal to the proud white man himself, and yet by your laws we are classed with idiots, lunatics and negroes." The speech received a broad audience largely because of the efforts of Anthony, who printed fifty thousand copies and distributed it to the press, women's groups, and reform organizations nationwide, and although the speech received its share of criticism, it was widely praised among the reform minded and gave broader exposure to women's grievances. Following this speech, Horace Greeley, editor of the *New York Tribune* and later presidential candidate, invited Stanton to contribute columns to his paper.[49]

Her admirers did not include her own family, however, which helps explain why she did not deliver another public speech for six years. Judge Daniel Cady was embarrassed and offended by the notoriety brought on by his daughter's public reform activities, and he did not hesitate to tell her about it. After one visit with her father in 1855, Stanton wrote Anthony: "I passed through a terrible scourging when last at my father's. I cannot tell you how deep the iron entered my soul.... I wish that I were as free as you and I would stump the state in a twinkling. But I am not.... The pressure on me just now is too great.... Sometimes, Susan, I struggle in deep waters." So, yielding to her family's opposition to her assuming a more public career, Stanton largely confined herself to her domestic responsibilities for the rest of the decade, apologizing to Anthony, "My whole soul is in the work, but my hands belong to my family."[50]

When finally she resumed public speaking in May 1860, she caused an uproar at the Tenth Annual Women's Rights Convention in New York in insisting that "[p]ersonal freedom is the first right to be proclaimed" in the marriage relationship and that marriage is "a theology which makes her a conscientious victim of another's will, forever subject to the triple bondage of the man, the priest, and the law." She concluded provocatively, commenting, "So long as our present false marriage relation continues, which in most cases is nothing more or less than legalized prostitution, women can [never truly be free.]"[51]

The sharp words led most of the other leaders (including Lucy Stone) to distance themselves from her at the meeting. Stanton was unabashed, insisting, "My reason, my experience, my soul proclaim [I am right]." She took up once again the taboo topic of divorce reform, specifically arguing and offering resolutions to broaden the grounds for divorce beyond adultery to simple incompatibility, despite polite mid-nineteenth-century society's abject terror that easier divorce would lead to unabashed free love.[52]

When late in 1860 a number of Southern states, led by South Carolina in December, followed in close succession by Mississippi, Florida, Alabama, Georgia, Louisiana, and Texas, seceded from the Union within months of Abraham Lincoln's surprise November election, Henry and Elizabeth Stanton, along with many other abolitionists, welcomed the news of the wayward states' departure. "I suppose it is the last time we shall be compelled to insult the Good Father by thanking him that we are a slave holding Republic," she wrote her sons in preparation for Thanksgiving. "I hope and look for dissolution."[53]

As for Henry's political prospects, despite again having backed the wrong horse in William Seward earlier at the Republican National Convention in Chicago but making up for it in his energetic efforts on behalf of Lincoln in the general election, he finally received a long-sought-after patronage job as deputy port inspector, so the Stantons moved to New York City in spring 1862 after their fifteen-year stay in Seneca Falls. Making a home first in Brooklyn, then in a four-story brownstone at 75 West Forty-Fifth Street, Stanton befriended powerful men and women in New York, including Horace Greeley of the *Tribune* and Theodore Tilton of the *Independent*. After the isolation of Seneca Falls, New York City was a most welcome change.[54]

With the Civil War ended and the ratification of the Thirteenth Amendment to abolish slavery close at hand, Elizabeth Cady Stanton again took up the women's cause – starting with a call for universal suffrage. "Where did the privileged few get their power to deprive the masses of their inalienable right to life, liberty and the pursuit of happiness?" she wrote on July 29, 1865. "Now let us try universal suffrage. We cannot tell its dangers and delights until we make the experiment.... At all events let us leave behind us the dead skin of class legislation which, in the progress of civilization, we have, at last, outgrown."[55]

Stanton, Anthony, and their radical colleagues were to be bitterly disappointed by the course of events following the war, however. Very soon they learned they no longer had the support of many of their former allies, who had either stepped back from politics (William Lloyd Garrison) or had dropped the women's cause altogether in favor of freeing black slaves.

"First negro suffrage, then temperance, then the eight-hour movement, then woman suffrage," said one. "One idea for a generation to come up in the order of their importance," said another. "Put women's suffrage in a separate bottle.... It is the Negro's hour," said Stanton's erstwhile friend Wendell Phillips.[56]

Stanton was deeply disappointed by the betrayal of many of her old allies. "I have argued constantly with Phillips and the whole fraternity," she confided in an August 11 letter to Anthony, who had been in Kansas visiting her brother following Congress's February 1865 passage of the Thirteenth Amendment, "but I fear one and all will favor enfranchising the negro without us. Woman's cause is in deep water.... Come back and help," she pleaded. "I seem to stand alone."[57]

With the ominous word over the summer from a divorce-reform ally, Congressman Robert Dale Owen of Indiana, that Congress would soon propose a new fourteenth constitutional amendment to enfranchise the former slaves but not women (and, moreover, qualify states' representation in Congress on not disenfranchising "male" citizens), Anthony returned to join Stanton in mid-October to campaign once again for women's suffrage. When the Thirty-ninth Congress reconvened in early December, several such resolutions were indeed introduced. Stanton's and Anthony's major task now was to counteract those who would interpret "universal suffrage" to include only "all" men.[58]

Writing "This is the Negro's Hour" in the December 26, 1865, issue of the *National Anti-Slavery Standard*, Stanton reflected, "The representative women of the nation have done their uttermost for the last thirty years to secure freedom for the negro, and so long as he was lowest in the scale of being we were willing to press *his* claims; but now, as the celestial gate to civil rights is slowly moving on its hinges, it becomes a serious question whether we had better stand aside and see 'Sambo' walk into the kingdom first.... This is our opportunity to retrieve the errors of the past and mould anew the elements of Democracy," she urged. "The nation is ready for a long step."[59]

Tactically, the women decided once again to agitate through the press and "[to] avail [our]selves of the only right we have in government – the right of petition" guaranteed by the First Amendment. The solicitation letter that went out in December over the names of Stanton, Anthony, and Lucy Stone called on "[w]omen of the Nation now [to] unitedly protest against such a desecration of the Constitution, and [to] petition for that right which is at the foundation of all Government – the right of representation." Petitions with twenty thousand signatures were thereafter delivered to Congress over the following several months.[60]

Maddeningly for the suffragists, however, their efforts were not enthusiastically received – even among usually sympathetic women.

Responding to Anthony's presentation of Stanton's address pleading for support, Lucretia Mott commented, "It is well for your state to revive the question as the time for revising the constitution is near. But as a general move, it would be in vain, while the all-absorbing negro question is up." To Martha Coffin Wright, another of Stanton's Seneca Falls coplotters who wanted not to push immediately for equal suffrage, Stanton wrote, "[Y]our letter... would have been a wet blanket to Susan and me were we not sure that we are right.... Martha, what are you all thinking about that you propose to rest on your oars in such a crisis? I conjure you and Lucretia to be a power at this moment in taking the onward step.... Our time is now." Stanton scolded, "When your granddaughters hear that against such insults you made no protest, they will blush for their ancestry."

The calls were generally met with resistance, however. The *Anti-Slavery Standard*, for example, editorialized, "[Women's suffrage is not] entitled to equal effort at this moment.... Causes have their crises, [and] that of the woman's rights movement has not come." Nevertheless, resistance began to soften somewhat in late 1865, leading Stanton to reflect in early January, "I have so scolded with tongue and pen that really the skies begin to clear." For example, Theodore Tilton, editor of the *New York Independent*, wrote on December 27, "Now, all forward-looking minds know that, sooner or later, the chief public question in this country will be woman's claim to the ballot....To [Congress's proposed] injustice we object totally!" he exclaimed. "[N]o republic is Republican," Tilton concluded, "which denies to half its citizens those rights which the Declaration of Independence, and which a true Christian Democracy make equal to all."[61]

All of which gave Stanton reason to conclude optimistically on January 20, "These are good signs, and the whole question of 'time' is so clear to me that I cannot understand why anyone hesitates."[62]

Alas, Stanton's good feelings were to be fleeting.

Stanton and Anthony had no problem in principle with most of the Fourteenth Amendment as it was finally passed by Congress and sent to the states on June 13, 1866 – especially because Congress postponed making a decision about black suffrage until after the November midterm elections. They agreed with the amendment's overriding purpose of serving as a key component in Republicans' Reconstruction efforts to correct the inherent constitutional flaws and inequities that had allowed slavery to prosper in the nation's first century. One of the leaders of those efforts was the Radical Thaddeus Stevens of Pennsylvania, who viewed Reconstruction as a chance to create a "perfect republic" based on equal rights for all citizens. Stanton agreed. As she said in May at the National Women's Convention, "Those who tell us the republican idea is a failure, do not see the deep gulf between our broad theory and partial legislation; do not see that our Government for the last century has been but the repetition of the old experiments of class and caste. Hence, the failure is not in the principle, but in the lack of virtue on our part to apply it." Key aspects of the proposed Fourteenth Amendment would remedy that deficit.[63]

As proposed (and eventually ratified two years later on July 9, 1868), section 1 – with its citizenship, privileges or immunities, due process, and equal protection clauses, was an epochal event in American history, marking the people's repudiation of eight decades of legalized oppression and providing a template for the way forward. Section 1 radiated with the natural law principles of which Stanton was herself so enamored and on which her philosophy was largely based.

Providing section 1 additional bite against offending states was section 5, which gave Congress the power to pass laws to enforce the provisions of sections 1–4. Section 5 thus represented a fundamental change in the U.S. Constitution's federalist structure by shifting a significant degree of governmental power from the states to the federal government. Stanton and Anthony approved of this shift for by now, they, like many, believed the federal government was better situated to protect liberty than were the states.[64]

Neither did either of them have any serious objection to section 3 (disqualifying individuals previously aiding in insurrection or rebellion from serving in official federal capacity) or section 4 (denying any obligation on the part of the United States or any state to repay debts incurred in supporting rebellion).[65]

Rather, it was the Fourteenth Amendment's section 2 apportionment scheme, specifying that any state's number of representatives to Congress would be reduced proportionally by the number of male adult citizens denied the privilege of voting, that rendered the amendment unacceptable to Stanton and Anthony. With this language, section 2 would become the only constitutional provision (aside from the innocuous article 2 provisions identifying the president as "he") to draw a sex-based distinction – and one that disadvantaged women, to boot. Unsurprisingly, Stanton, Anthony, and their radical colleagues could never accept that.

Once it became clear that Congress would pass the Fourteenth Amendment with the section 2 male language intact (which it eventually did, on

July 9, 1866), Stanton and Anthony began plotting their next steps in refocusing their energies to gaining the vote on an individual state-by-state basis. When New York convened its State Constitutional Convention in June 1867, Stanton, Anthony, and Stone were asked to testify before the Committee on Suffrage.

Chairing the subcommittee was Horace Greeley, with whom Stanton had been friendly during her earlier years in New York and who had published many of her writings in the *Tribune* but with whom her relationship had soured with his postwar opposition to universal suffrage. During the state campaign, Greeley, determinedly maintaining that "this is 'the Negro's hour,'" commanded the women that "your first duty now is to go through the State and plead his claims" and threatened, "If you persevere in your present plan, you need depend on no further help from me or the *Tribune*."

During their June 27 testimony before a very large audience of delegates and the public in the Assembly Chamber, Greeley asked Stanton, "The ballot and bullet go together. If you vote are you ready to fight?" "Yes," she replied, "we are ready to fight, sir, just as you did in the late war, by sending our substitutes."[66]

The sparring was to continue, when a couple of weeks later on July 16 during the delegates' debate on Greeley's report, Stanton's ally, delegate George W. Curtis, at the prior urging of Stanton and Anthony, rose to present one last petition of the many the convention had received in favor of woman suffrage (containing a total of more than twenty thousand signatures) just before Greeley was to make his final comments.

"Mr. President," Curtis intoned, "I hold in my hand a petition signed and headed by Mrs. Horace Greeley and 300 other women of Westchester asking that the word 'male' be stricken from the constitution." Embarrassed and at a loss for words, Greeley simply proceeded to give his report to the delegates, recommending against extending the elective franchise to women – a recommendation the convention adopted a few days later.[67]

Several weeks later, Greeley had not forgotten (nor, by Stanton's account, did he ever forget, up to his death in 1873) Stanton's and Anthony's stunt at the convention. At a Sunday reception in the home of Alice Cary, Greeley purposefully approached Stanton and Anthony as they rested in chairs near a window. "Prepare for a storm," Stanton said as Greeley strode toward them. "Good evening, Mr. Greeley," they said. "You two ladies are about the best maneuverers among the New York politicians," Greeley replied roughly. "You tried to bother me at the convention, and I confess that you succeeded. The way Curtis presented

Mary's petition showed me that you had prepared the plan." Turning then directly to Stanton, he curtly continued, "You are always so desirous in public to appear under your own rather than your husband's name, why did you in this case substitute 'Mrs. Horace Greeley' for 'Mary Cheney Greeley,' which was really on the petition? You know why. Well, I have given strict orders at the *Tribune* office that you and your cause are to be tabooed in the future, and if it is necessary to mention your name, you will be referred to as 'Mrs. Henry B. Stanton!'" At which point Greeley stomped off.

Of one thing we may be certain: Elizabeth Cady Stanton was never one to be cowed – by anybody. As she related in a letter to Emily Howland shortly after the Greeley incident, "Of course this will not deter me from speaking my mind in the future as in the past, though I am sorry for our cause that the *Tribune* will henceforth be lukewarm. This may do something to retard our final triumph; but it will take more than Horace Greeley and the New York *Tribune* to prevent the success of the movement which we both have so much at heart. So, more valiant than ever, I am as always, Your old friend and co-worker, 'Mrs. Henry B. Stanton!'"[68]

The next few years were forgettable at best for the cause and Elizabeth Cady Stanton. First, any chance the movement had of influencing Kansas voters to pass the state's women's suffrage referendum was lost when Stanton and Anthony agreed to accept the wealthy Democrat George Train's offer to travel across the state with Anthony (while Stanton would travel with former Governor Charles Robinson) to champion the women's cause. Train, while an ardent financial supporter of women's suffrage, was also a blatantly racist opponent of Negro suffrage. By associating with Train, Stanton and Anthony were painted with the same broad racism brush. The affiliation with Train also cost Stanton and Anthony the support of many key Republicans and others nationwide, and it opened fissures in the women's movement itself.[69]

Asked at the May 1868 American Equal Rights Association (AERA) meeting why women's suffrage had failed in Kansas, for example, Frederick Douglass exclaimed, "Because of your ally, George Francis Train!" And Stanton's and Anthony's longtime loyal ally William Lloyd Garrison added in a January 4, 1868, letter to Anthony, "In all friendliness, and with the highest regard for the woman's rights movement, I cannot refrain from expressing my regret and astonishment that you and Mrs. Stanton should have taken such leave of good sense as to be traveling companions and associate lecturers with that crack-brained harlequin and semi-lunatic, George Francis Train."[70]

Compounding the damage was Stanton's own increasingly strident antiblack, anti-uneducated, antimale, nativist rhetoric. Garrison now referred to Stanton as "untruthful, unscrupulous and selfishly ambitious." Her closest friends such as Lucretia Mott were concerned with Stanton's racist statements. Yet Stanton was unrepentant, and neither she nor Susan B. Anthony would admit that it had been an error to associate with Train. To the contrary, they deepened their association with him in 1868, when they allowed him to fund their fledgling newspaper, the *Revolution*. As Stanton stubbornly insisted, "We are speaking for the cause of Woman, Mr. Train is doing the same. We are satisfied he is a pure minded noble man who neither smokes chews drinks gambols [*sic*] lies steals or swears.... He lays his talents and wealth at our feet."[71]

At this point in her life, Stanton was furious about the perceived betrayal of virtually all of her old champions – even the pious Garrison himself. In a January 13, 1868, letter to Thomas Wentworth Higginson, the abolitionist preacher who had criticized Stanton's racist associations, she commented, "I know we have shocked our old friends, who were half asleep on the woman question.... Time will show that Miss Anthony and I are neither idiots nor lunatics.... We do care what all good men like you *say*" she assured, "but just now the men who will *do* something to help us are more important. Garrison, Phillips, and Sumner, in their treatment of our question to-day, prove that we must not trust any of you. All these men," she noted ironically, "who have pushed us aside for years, saying, 'This is the negro's hour,' now, when we, dropped by them, find help in other quarters, they turn up the whites of their eye and cry out their curses. No, my dear friend, we are right in our present position."[72]

Adding insult to injury, when Congress returned after the November 1868 elections to the suffrage issue, it guaranteed blacks – but not women – the right to vote in its proposed Fifteenth Amendment. Stanton and Anthony were vehemently opposed to the amendment "not for what it is, but for what it is not; not because it enfranchises black men, but because it does not enfranchise all women, black and white." Despite their objections, the amendment was passed by Congress on February 26, 1869, and ratified in short order by the requisite three-fourths of the states by February 3, 1870. Stanton and her colleagues then lobbied for the second-best choice – a separate Sixteenth Amendment guaranteeing women the right to vote. Adequate support for women's suffrage never materialized in the Forty-first Congress, however, and it would be another forty years before the Sixty-sixth Congress on June 4, 1919, would muster the requisite two-thirds vote to pass the Nineteenth Amendment (providing that "[t]he right of citizens of the United States to vote shall not be denied or abridged by the United States or by any State on account of sex") and send it to the states. The amendment was ratified by the states and became part of the Constitution on August 18, 1920.[73]

In short, the entire postwar turn of events left great bitterness for Stanton: "And thus it ever is," she observed in *Eighty Years and More*: "so long as woman labors to second man's endeavors and exalt his sex above her own, her virtues pass unquestioned; but when she dares to demand rights and privileges for herself, her motives, manners, dress, personal appearance, and character are subjects for ridicule and detraction."[74]

Stanton's and Anthony's paper, the *Revolution*, added to the mounting tensions during these years. First publishing on January 8, 1868, under the motto, "Men, their rights and nothing more; women their rights and nothing less," the *Revolution* was stridently confrontational in approach – printing, for example, many of the angry letters it received from other reformers with point-by-point rebuttals. Stanton's angry voice came through loud and clear. "The male element is a destructive force," she wrote, "selfish, aggrandizing, loving war, violence, conquest, acquisition, breeding in the material and moral world alike discord, disorder, disease, and death. The idea strengthens at every step, that woman was created for no higher purpose than to gratify the lust of man." Moreover, she charged, "Society as organized today is one grand rape of womanhood under the man power."[75]

Such rhetoric led the *New York Times* to comment, "[The *Revolution*] is said to be 'charged to the muzzle with literary nitroglycerin.' If Mrs. Stanton would attend a little more to her domestic duties and a little less to those of the great public, perhaps she would exalt her sex quite as much as she does by Quixotically fighting windmills in their gratuitous behalf, and she might possibly set a notable example of domestic felicity."[76]

By now it was evident that a tipping point had been reached in the women's movement at which the radical and more moderate elements could no longer peacefully coexist. Accordingly, in 1869, they broke into rival groups, the National Woman Suffrage Association (the National, or NWSA) and the American Woman Suffrage Association (AWSA), in a split that would last twenty-one years. The two organizations took fundamentally different approaches in their efforts to advance women's rights. The Boston-based AWSA, led by Lucy Stone (who chose not to participate in any leadership roles with Stanton and declined to join any organization that forbade her husband from voting), sought to revive the historic alliance between the antislavery and woman's rights reformers, and so relied largely on men and focused solely on the suffrage issue.[77]

By contrast, Stanton's and Anthony's New York-based NWSA allowed no male voting members and addressed a full range of women's issues. As the NWSA's statement of purpose explained, "The woman question is more than a demand for suffrage.... [It] is a question covering a whole range of woman's needs and demands... including her work, her wages, her property, her education, her physical training, her social status, her political equalization, her marriage and divorce." In short, the NWSA was concerned with nothing less than women's freedom and equality on all matters, not just suffrage.[78]

For later generations of feminists, this "quest for political equality" by Stanton, Anthony, and other female reformers in claiming their own space free of male influence was of crucial importance "because it represented a direct assault on the 'male monopoly of the public sphere,' an assault that sent 'shockwaves' reverberating through the culture." Previously, women had always proceeded in the political arena with the shared leadership of strong, influential men. After the creation of the *Revolution* and especially with the suffragists' split into rival groups, Stanton and Anthony made conscious efforts to collaborate only with women. This decision to go it alone allowed them to focus entirely on women's needs, free of any male bias that would almost inevitably arise with shared leadership.

The author Vivian Gornick suggests, "It is here, at this exact moment in history, that the meaning of radical feminism in America is established" as separate from liberal feminism. "Throw down *this* gauntlet, it is felt by the liberal, and the world as we know it goes under or changes beyond recognition: either way, a fearful prospect." Lucy Stone (relatively liberal though she was) and AWSA were unwilling to go it alone. Stanton and Anthony, by contrast, took a more radical approach: "*Refuse* to throw down this gauntlet, says the radical feminist, and not only is the true nature of women's rights obscured, but all hope of success is painfully compromised."

Stanton and Anthony simply refused to accept second-class citizenship any longer, even if it meant alienation from their longtime allies. "[W]hen we forsake principle for expediency, all is doubt and bewilderment," Stanton believed.

"In the end, of course," Gornick observes, "the radical prevails only by inching the liberal forward – a generation later." Such certainly describes what has in fact occurred with the painfully slow progress in women's rights in America in the 130 years since Stanton and Anthony split from the mainstream movement – progress had occurred but at a maddeningly slow pace.[79]

For Elizabeth Cady Stanton, the close of the 1860s, with its numerous setbacks, could not have come soon enough. As the Stanton biographer Elisabeth Griffith describes the postwar years, "After five years of fighting, Stanton had lost every battle and most of her allies. She had lost married women's property rights, divorce reform, and limited suffrage for the New York constitutional convention. She had lost woman suffrage in New York, Kansas, the District of Columbia, and the Constitution." And if that were not enough, "[s]he had lost her newspaper and the presidency of the National Association. Even more significant, she had alienated a host of former allies. Her antagonists in 1870 numbered the members of the American Association plus Garrison, Greeley, Higginson, Douglass, Phillips, Foster, and even Gerrit Smith."[80]

Reflecting on the postwar-era years later in *The History of Woman Suffrage*, Stanton herself recalled (in the third person), "The few who insisted on the absolute right [to universal suffrage] stood firmly together under a steady fire of ridicule and reproach even from their lifelong friends most loved and honored.... With all these friends against them... and most of the liberals in the press," she acknowledged that "the position of the women seemed so untenable to the majority that at times a sense of utter loneliness and desertion made the bravest of them doubt the possibility of maintaining the struggle or making themselves fairly understood.... Few only were equal to the emergency."

After these many disappointments, Stanton was ready for a change, so, starting in the 1870s, she largely turned her back on women's organization work and conventions. Throughout the decade, she concentrated instead on preaching the principles of equality and justice as a well-paid lecturer on the lyceum lecture circuit, where for eight months out of the year she would visit about three dozen western cities and towns in roughly six weeks, return briefly to New York, Chicago, or St. Louis, and then start all over again.[81]

Stanton was, as ever, motivated by the idea of stirring women up, and the lyceum circuit allowed her to put to the test her belief that "radical reform must start in our homes, in our nurseries, in ourselves." Notwithstanding criticisms of being too outspoken by some such as Lucy Stone, she was extremely popular with her largely female audiences, shrewdly leveraging her matronly appearance, even as she sought to introduce "radical thoughts . . . into their heads, . . . [so] they feel untrammeled, [and] these thoughts are permanently lodged there!"

In the course of delivering her talks, sometimes she was overwhelmed by the sheer injustice of woman's fate. "When I think of all the wrongs that have been heaped on womankind," she lamented, "I am ashamed that I am not forever in a condition of chronic wrath, stark mad, skin and bone, my eyes a fountain of tears, my lips overflowing with curses, and my hand against every man and brother! Ah, how I do repent me of the male faces I have washed, the mittens I have knit, the trousers mended, the cut fingers and broken toes I have bound up!" And despite her usual optimism, sometimes she could not help but be discouraged. "As I sum up the indignities toward women, as illustrated by recent judicial decisions," she wrote in 1878, "denied the right to vote, denied the right to practice in the Supreme Court, denied jury trial – I feel the degradation of sex more bitterly than I did on that July 19, 1848." But for the most part, she maintained hope, believing that she was playing an important role in "teaching woman her duties to herself."[82]

By the end of 1879, sixty-four years old and exhausted after nearly ten years of relentless travel on the lyceum circuit, Stanton decided to stop touring and to devote her energies instead to writing – in particular to assembling *The History of Woman Suffrage*, mainly together with Susan B. Anthony.[83] She also spent much of the 1880s and 1890s visiting her children and grandchildren, now anxious in her later years for her children to understand why she had often been physically or emotionally absent during those years when she had been traveling.

She sometimes lamented the shortcomings of her own marriage to Henry, which had long been one of parallel, largely separately lived lives – but she mostly accepted it and adapted her own habits to the realities of what had become a civil, if mostly loveless, marriage. When word of Henry's death on January 14, 1887, came to her at her daughter Harriot Blatch's home in Blasingbroke outside of London, she decided to not travel home for a funeral but stayed on in Europe until the following October.[84]

As for her legacy with the women's movement, Stanton had reason to be pleased (though also disappointed, with the slow pace of change), for she knew that her intellectual efforts were making a difference – progress had been made since the early days of Seneca Falls. Whereas in 1848 no state granted women any one of "the rights to speak in public, testify in court and preach from the pulpit, access to equal education, the continuation of civil existence after marriage, control of personal wages and property, legal custody of children, entrance into the professions and suffrage," in her later years "not one state denied them all." She saw her earlier 1870s efforts in lecturing throughout the West vindicated when Colorado granted woman suffrage in 1893, followed by Utah and Idaho in 1896 (Wyoming territory had been the first to grant woman suffrage in 1869). Further evidence of progress was the House Judiciary Committee's 1890 majority report (following testimony from Stanton) favoring a federal suffrage amendment – the first-ever positive congressional report on woman's suffrage.

In summary, Stanton, now in her seventies, was living proof of her essay "The Pleasures of Old Age" that a woman's prime of life comes after the age of fifty: "Then the forces hitherto finding an outlet in flirtations, courtship, conjugal and maternal love, are garnered in the brain to find expression in intellectual achievements, in spiritual friendships and beautiful thoughts, in music, poetry and art."[85]

IV. Taking on Religion: *The Woman's Bible*

> *All through the centuries scholars and scientists have been imprisoned, tortured and burned alive for some discovery which seemed to conflict with a petty text of Scripture. Surely the immutable laws of the universe can teach more impressive and exalted lessons than the holy books of all the religions on earth.*
>
> – Elizabeth Cady Stanton, 1898

As she sat on the New York City Metropolitan Opera House stage on the occasion of her dear friend Elizabeth Cady Stanton's eightieth birthday celebration in November 1895, Susan B. Anthony was more than a little exasperated as she listened to Helen Potter speak.

"Nothing that has ever emanated from the brain of man is too sacred to be revised and corrected," Miss Potter read, from remarks prepared by Stanton. "Our National Constitution has been amended fifteen times, our English system of jurisprudence has been essentially modified in the interest of woman to keep pace with advancing civilization. And now the time has come to amend and modify the canon laws, prayer-books, liturgies and Bibles."

Anthony thought, "Why can Mrs. Stanton not rest her case after describing the wonderful advances made, instead of going on to single out the church and declare it to be especially slow in accepting the doctrine of equality of women?" Although Anthony may have cringed, the obese, matronly looking older woman seated next to her, Elizabeth Cady Stanton, serenely looked out over the six thousand faces in the crowd.

Potter delivered Stanton's punch line: "And now the Woman's imperative duty at this hour, is to demand a thorough revision of creeds and codes Scriptures and constitutions." At that the crowd stirred restlessly. Most would have been familiar with Stanton's radical reputation; many, nonetheless, were uncomfortable with her broaching the topic of religion.

Stanton would have preferred to speak for herself; but because of her obesity and poor health, she had been able to stand only long enough to acknowledge the audience, with unusual humility, "I am well aware that all these public demonstrations are not so much tributes to me as an individual as to the great idea I represent – the enfranchisement of women." She added playfully, "Before I sit down I want to say one word to the men who are present. I fear you think the 'new woman' is going to wipe you off the planet, but be not afraid. All who have mothers, sisters, wives or sweethearts will be very well looked after." The woman of honor then yielded to Miss Potter and sat down amid thundering cheers and waving handkerchiefs in a large thronelike chair festooned with roses in front of a big framework of red carnations spelling her name on a field of white chrysanthemums.

Organized primarily by Anthony, Stanton's birthday party was a big event, covered by the major press. "Elizabeth Cady Stanton – Her Fourscore Years and Services Honored by a Vast Audience – Venerable Suffragist Smiling, Tearful, and Handsome – Susan B. Anthony and Other Notable Women There," read the front-page headline in the *New York Times*. As for Stanton's controversial remarks, those who may have regarded them as mere passing fancy – just another case of "Elizabeth being Elizabeth" – were soon to be disavowed when her sensational revisionist treatment of the Bible's traditional teachings about women, the *Woman's Bible*, was published two weeks later. Elizabeth Cady Stanton was stirring the pot again.[86]

Stanton's ambivalence with religion (like Thomas Paine's) began early in life. "I can truly say," she reflected in *Eighty Years and More*, "that all the cares and anxieties, the trials and disappointments of my whole life, are light, when balanced with my sufferings in childhood and youth from the theological dogmas which I sincerely believed, and the gloom connected with everything associated with the name of religion."

In 1831, when she was sixteen, her stay at Emma Willard's Troy Female Seminary was interrupted when she and many others succumbed

PHOTO 5. Elizabeth Cady Stanton, ca. 1890s. Courtesy of Library of Congress.

to the teachings of Charles Finney and other evangelists relentlessly barnstorming throughout an area of upstate New York along the path of the recently opened Erie Canal (thus earning the region the sobriquet of "burned-over district" for the fire and brimstone to which Finney and the others continually subjected it).

Attending Finney's performances in Troy for six straight weeks in the midst of the Great Revival of 1830–2, Elizabeth became thoroughly confused. "I cannot understand what I am to do," she recalls telling Finney. "If you should tell me to go to the top of the church steeple and jump off, I would readily do it, but I do not know how to go to Jesus." When finally she accepted Finney's advice to confess her sins and convert, "fear of judgment seized my soul. Visions of the lost haunted my dreams. Mental anguish prostrated my health. Dethronement of my reason was apprehended by friends," she recalled. On returning home after dropping out of the seminary for a time, she remembered, "I often at night roused my father from his slumber to pray for me, lest I should be cast into the bottomless pit before morning."

To say the least, Elizabeth's early introduction to evangelical religion was not a positive experience. Her brother-in-law Edward Bayard (who in 1838 asked her to marry him even while married to her older sister Tryphena and with whom she possibly had a romantic affair) rescued her from her religious turmoil during a getaway together with Elizabeth's father and sister to Niagara Falls. Bayard "explained . . . the nature of the delusions we had all experienced, the physical conditions, the mental processes, the church machinery by which such excitements are worked up," Stanton recounted; in fairly short order, "[my] religious superstitions gave place to rational ideas based on scientific facts, and in proportion, as I looked at every thing from a new standpoint, I grew more and more happy."[87]

Not all of Stanton's encounters with religion were negative. One aspect of Christianity that helped shape her character, for example, was its recognition of "the right of individual conscience and judgment. . . . The reason it took such a hold in the hearts of the people," Stanton wrote, "was because it taught that the individual was primary; the state, the church, society, the family secondary." During the first half of the nineteenth century, the church was the one area where women could be active, expanding their horizons beyond the conventional narrow limits of hearth and home.

But for the more radical women, organized religion soon proved too limiting, as clerics reframed the Bible not to teach the "great doctrine" of individual rights, but rather to justify the subjugation of women. "When women understand that government and religions are human inventions," she wrote, "that Bibles, prayerbooks, catechisms and encyclical letters are all emanations from the brain of man, they will no longer be oppressed by the injunctions that came to them with the divine authority of 'Thus Saith the Lord.'" Stanton's biographer Elisabeth Griffith explains, "As a small number of women attempted to act out the pious ideal in tract and mission societies or in temperance or abolition crusades, it became more difficult to sustain the myth of female subordination. Rejection of religious authority and resentment of women's subordinate status were the long-term results for Elizabeth Cady and other nineteenth-century women in revival and reform circles."[88]

For her part, Stanton did not believe that a just God would arbitrarily limit women to a separate, second-class sphere of existence, so when the Bible seemed to contradict her on this point, she responded with appeals to natural law. "The writings of Paul," she wrote in 1855, "like our State Constitutions, are susceptible of various interpretations. But when the human soul is roused with holy indignation against injustice and oppression, it stops not to translate human parchments, but follows out the law of its inner being written by the finger of god in the first hour of its Creation."

Although the tide shifted somewhat by the late 1850s, with more clergy (including the influential Henry Ward Beecher) supporting women's rights, the problem of antiwoman biblical interpretation remained. Later, throughout most of the 1870s, Stanton pressed the attack on Christian orthodoxy on the lyceum circuit, speaking on such topics as the Bible and women's rights and famous women in the Bible, among others. In an 1879 speech in St. Louis, she thundered, "[I] cannot believe that a God of law and order... could have sanctioned a social principle so calamitous in its consequences as investing in one-half the race the absolute control of all the rights of the other."[89]

In the later decades of Stanton's life, a large portion of the women's rights movement was becoming increasingly conservative, as evidenced by the split into rival organizations (the NWSA and AWSA). Led by women such as Frances Willard of the Women's Christian Temperance Union, which operated with the underlying philosophy of women's fundamentally more pious nature and moral superiority to men, the conservative movement sought the vote as means to better accomplish such goals as securing women's place in the home, restricting divorce, and increasing state-sponsored Christian orthodoxy.

These positions stood in polar opposition with those of Stanton and other radicals. As counterpoint to the conservative theological views, the NWSA's annual convention in 1878 passed three resolutions that introduced some of the key elements of the radicals' theology. Proposed by Jocelyn Gage and supported by Stanton presiding as chair, the resolutions stated the following:

> *Resolved,* That as the first duty of every individual is self-development, the lessons of self-sacrifice and obedience taught woman by the Christian church have been fatal not only to her own vital interests, but through her, to those of the race.
>
> *Resolved,* That the great principle of the Protestant Reformation, the right of individual conscience and judgment heretofore exercised by man alone, should now be claimed by woman; that, in the interpretation of scripture,

> she should be guided by her own reason, and not by the authority of the church.
>
> *Resolved,* That it is through the perversion of the religious element in woman – playing upon her hopes and fears of the future, holding this life with all its high duties in abeyance to that which is to come – that she and the children she trained have been so completely subjugated by priestcraft and superstition.[90]

In directly lambasting mainstream Christian orthodoxy as so much superstition and sorcery, the resolutions unsurprisingly met with condemnations from the religious establishment (as well as the AWSA) – resistance that only solidified Stanton's and Gage's resolve.

The radicals continued introducing similar resolutions condemning Christian orthodoxy at NWSA annual meetings between 1880 and 1886. Believing themselves to be the true followers of Christ, Stanton and her allies sought to fundamentally reframe the way Americans interpreted their religion, by going to the source to present contrary claims as to the role of women in God's scheme. In an 1885 article for the *North American Review* titled "What Has Christianity Done for Women?" Stanton "took the ground that woman was not indebted to any form of religion for the liberty she now enjoys, but that, on the contrary, the religious element in her nature had always been perverted for her complete subjection."[91]

A number of events in the early 1880s combined to lead Stanton to undertake the *Woman's Bible* project. First, a revised New Testament was published in 1881, pleasing virtually no one. Conservative and moderate religious leaders objected because the Word, as represented in the King James version, had been inappropriately altered in attempting to create a Bible at least minimally responsive to Darwin, new thought, free thought, and other manifestations of advancing scientific knowledge. By contrast, more radical readers, including Stanton, thought the revision did not go far enough. "There were hopes," Stanton recalled in 1895, "that in the last revision of the New Testament justice might at last be done woman and her equality with man clearly brought out, but they did nothing, and still kept woman in a position that has taken away from her self-respect."[92]

Second, after the many years of traveling on the lyceum circuit during the 1870s, she slowed down and took the time to immerse herself in books and deep thoughts. With this time of contemplation (including a number of months in 1882 when she and daughter Harriot "eloped," as she put it, to the South of France), she came to conclude, "We can make no impression on men who accept the theological view of woman as the author of sin, cursed of God, and all that nonsense. The debris of the centuries must be cleared away before an argument for equality can have the least significance on them."

Stanton thus began to rail more frequently against the clergy for its role in subjugating women. "I have passed from the political to the religious phase of this question," she wrote in 1885, "for I now see more clearly than ever, that the arch enemy to women's freedom skulks behind the altar." She continued, "No class of men [as the clergy] have such power to pervert the religious sentiments and oppress mankind with gloomy superstitions through life and an undefined dread of the unknown after death."[93]

So, believing that "in the sunset of life I feel it to be my special mission to tell people what they are not prepared to hear," during the summer of 1886 Stanton, together with her daughter Harriot and Frances Lord, literally cut the passages mentioning women from several cheap Bibles, pasting them on blank pages with room below for writing commentary. Throughout the rest of 1886 and early 1887, Stanton and Lord solicited interest in forming a "revising committee" comprised of a number of female biblical scholars to interpret anew all of the Bible's passages – going back even to the Hebrew and Greek – involving women. "If we could get twenty-five intelligent well educated good common sense women," Stanton commented, "we could make 'The Woman's Bible' a great feature of the general uprising in this nineteenth century."

Stanton found little enthusiasm for the project from most other women, however. Many begged off with excuses that they were incapable of undertaking such a difficult scholarly task, leading Stanton to drily complain, "The humility of the educated women is quite praiseworthy.... When we get the volume completed I hope they will have sufficient capacity to read and understand it." By spring 1887, only her daughter Harriot was still on the project, and Stanton recalled that soon even Harriot "declared she would go no farther, that [the Pentateuch portion] was the driest history she had ever read and most derogatory to woman." So, the *Woman's Bible* would have to wait.[94]

By the mid-1880s, the positions of many suffragists – even in the more radical NWSA – were moderating. Led primarily by Susan B. Anthony, a group of NWSA pragmatists believed the potential benefit of criticizing religion was ultimately not worth the cost of dividing the movement and thereby jeopardizing gaining the vote.

Counterpoised against their position was that of the still radicals, led by Stanton, who were unwilling to view suffrage as an end in itself but rather as merely one component in a broad array of critical women's issues, including Christian orthodoxy's subjugation of women. The antagonism escalated as the conservatives in the rival AWSA themselves began taking the offensive with resolutions favoring temperance laws and increased state sponsorship of religion (teaching the Bible in schools, constitutional recognition of Christianity, and religious tests for political parties, for example), with a result that the radicals within the NWSA became increasingly marginalized – especially with Anthony's coalition-building compromises with the conservatives.

Anthony finally managed to engineer a merger of the AWSA and NWSA in 1890 into the new National American Woman Suffrage Association (NAWSA), with Anthony as vice president and Lucy Stone chair of the executive committee. Anthony convinced Stanton to serve as president of the newly merged group – much to the disappointment of radicals Matilda Gage and others, who left to form the new Women's Liberal Union, the organizing principles of which included a spirited denunciation of Christian orthodoxy's positions on women. Stanton herself had numerous misgivings of the AWSA's general intolerance, including its failure to include "all types and classes, . . . as well as all races and creeds, . . . [including] Mormon, Indian and Black women," together with its conservative attitudes on such matters as religion and alcohol.

Stanton found the new group's meetings, with their steady diet of singing and praying, insufferable, and disdained the organization's overwrought formalism: "One would think [NAWSA's constitution] was written to hedge in a pack of foxes," she complained. "I ask Susan what is the matter with our little old constitution, which we simple-minded women drew up back I do not know when?" Regarding the new group's decision to allow male officers, she commented, "I would never vote for a man to any office in our societies, not, however, because I am 'down on' men *per se*. Think of an association of black men officered by slave holders!"

Given her ambivalence, Stanton was happy to leave NAWSA's day-to-day operations to Anthony, embarking shortly after her election on an eighteen-month visit to her daughter Harriot and granddaughter Nora Blatch in England. As she had done for many years dating back to the relentless lecture-circuit travel in the 1870s (when she had attended only five of the NWSA's fifteen meetings), she preferred to operate from a distance, participating instead by sending speeches for Susan B. Anthony to deliver.[95]

Given Stanton's reticence about the merger from the very beginning, it was no surprise when two years later she did not stand for reelection to the NAWSA presidency. "I am a leader in thought rather than numbers," she reasoned. "I would rather be a free-lance . . . than to speak as president of an Association." More pointed, she was simply unable to accept the newly merged group's conservative turn and narrow vision. "[The NAWSA] has been growing politic and conservative for some time," she criticized in a letter to a friend, "Lucy and Susan alike see suffrage only. They do not see woman's religious and social bondage, neither do the young women."[96]

Shortly after her departure, Stanton decided to resurrect the dormant *Woman's Bible* project, prompted by the derogatory comments directed by Baptist minister Reverend Hawthorne toward all suffragists and their feebleminded husbands during the 1895 NAWSA annual convention in Atlanta. "[W]hen I read of the ferocious attack of the Baptist clergyman on woman," she told a reporter, "it seemed to me the time had come."

For Stanton, the *Woman's Bible* was to be "the crowning achievement of the nineteenth century . . . the emancipation of women" and the culmination of Stanton's life's work of agitating for women's rights. In taking on Christian orthodoxy, she would be confronting the very core of societal biases against women; if she could make inroads there, America could be truly transformed into a more egalitarian, just society.

Buoyed by the widespread condemnation among suffragists of the Baptist preacher's Atlanta attack, Stanton believed she would now be able to convince others to join her revising committee, so she arranged to have already-completed portions of the *Woman's Bible* printed in weekly columns in Clara Colby's *Woman's Tribune* with a goal of generating interest and momentum for the project. The plan backfired, however, when she published without permission the names of several of her political rivals, including Frances Willard, Isabel Somerset, and Mary Livermore, as members of the revising committee. These women and others vociferously objected to being associated with the project, as did others when approached by Stanton.

Even after three months of weekly excerpts of the *Woman's Bible* in the *Woman's Tribune,* by summer 1895, Stanton still had not managed to form the broad-based revising committee she desired. Instead, she made do with a revising committee of twenty-three collaborators (few of whom actually contributed and who never actually met as a group) from the liberal-radical end of the spectrum.[97]

The *Woman's Bible* was published in 1895. Stanton's introduction set the tone: "The Bible teaches that woman brought sin and death into the world, that she precipitated the fall of the race, that she was arraigned before the judgment seat of Heaven, tried, condemned and sentenced. Marriage for her was to be a condition of bondage," it continued, "maternity a period of suffering and anguish, and in silence and subjection, she was to play the role of a dependent on man's bounty for all her material wants, and for all the information she might desire on the vital questions of the hour, she was commanded to ask her husband at home.... Here," it concluded, "is the Bible position of woman briefly summed up."

Structurally, the book presented biblical passages followed by several strands of parallel commentary from Stanton and other committee members, incorporating a variety of plain English, esoteric, rationalist, spiritual, and faith-based alternative interpretations, united however in their common criticism of traditional Christian orthodoxy as having systematically mistranslated the Bible to the lasting detriment of women. The net effect was somewhat cacophonous, resembling more a disjointed "improvisation spun out of control than a melody sung in unison," according to *Mrs. Stanton's Bible* author Kathi Kern.

Stanton's contributions built on her earlier work, pointing out that, whereas women had in fact assumed strong leadership roles throughout history (especially in ancient Egypt and during early Christianity), the modern Bible ignores those leading roles in favor of elevating the status of men.

Chief among the offending interpretations is Genesis itself, which states in chapter 1, "So God created man in his own image, in the image of God created He him; male and female created He them," but states in chapter 2 that woman was made from Adam's rib. "Why," Stanton asked, "should there be two contradictory accounts in the same book, of the same event?" "If language has any meaning," she said, "we have in these texts a plain declaration of the existence of the feminine element in the Godhead, equal in power and glory with the masculine."

She noted that "the New Testament [as well] echoes back through the centuries the individual sovereignty of woman growing out of this natural fact. Paul, in speaking of equality as the very soul and essence of Christianity, said, 'There is neither Jew nor Greek; for ye are all one in Christ Jesus.'" Why, then, in light of "this recognition of the feminine element in the Godhead in the Old Testament, and this declaration of the equality of the sexes in the New," does woman occupy such "contemptible status... in the Christian Church today"?

Stanton answered: "It is evident some wily writer, seeing the perfect equality of man and woman in the first chapter, felt it important for the dignity and dominion of man to effect woman's subordination in some way," and therefore later inserted the Adam's-rib story as a pretext for the male subordination of woman. So pervasive had these popular biblical interpretations of the Scriptures become, Stanton suggested, that woman herself all too easily accepted them as "the veritable 'The Word of God'"; she lamented the sad irony that "[s]o perverted is the religious element in [woman's] nature, that with faith and works she is the chief support of the church and clergy – the very powers that make her emancipation impossible."[98]

The publication of the *Woman's Bible* caused a sensation – and bitter denunciations from many. Stanton puckishly recalled, "The clergy denounced it as the work of *Satan*, though it really was the work of Ellen Battelle Dietrick, Lillie Devereux Blake, Rev. Phoebe A. Hanaford, Clara Bewick Colby, Ursula N. Gestefeld, Louisa Southworth, Frances Ellen Burr, and myself."

Stanton was circumspect about the criticism. On the one hand, she was delighted with the book's sales, which went through seven printings in six months and was later translated in a number of languages. "My books are selling pretty well," she wrote her son Theodore in September 1898. "Whenever there is a lull in the sale of the *Woman's Bible*, some convention denounces it or some library throws it out, then there is immediately a fresh demand for it. So the bigots promote the sale every time."

What she did not expect, however, was the depth of criticism from her NAWSA colleagues, who passed a resolution at the 1896 convention denouncing the *Woman's Bible*. This NAWSA censure was approved over the objections of Susan B. Anthony, who pleaded, "I pray you, vote for religious liberty, without censorship or inquisition. This resolution adopted will be a vote of censure," she concluded, "upon a woman who is without peer in intellectual and statesmanlike ability; one who has stood for half a century the acknowledged leader of progressive thought . . . in regard to all matters pertaining to absolute freedom of women."

Anthony's protestations were to no avail, however; modern scholars suggest Anthony had mostly herself to blame. "Susan B. Anthony had been far too late in asserting that liberal principles should overshadow political pragmatism," Maureen Fitzgerald points out in the introduction to a 1993 reprint of the *Woman's Bible*. "She had . . . built the very organization, in numbers as well as thought, that turned against Stanton." In any event, thereafter NAWSA no longer invited Stanton to sit on the stage or participate meaningfully in its events, effectively adopting a policy of shunning her to distance itself from Stanton's radical views.[99]

Stanton refused simply to fade away, publishing a second volume of the *Woman's Bible* in 1898. This volume continued the work of the first, offering commentary on additional books of the Bible. It also included in its appendix both the NAWSA's 1896 repudiation of the *Woman's Bible* and a compendium of letters and comments from a number of prominent suffragists responding to two questions: "Have the teachings of the Bible advanced or retarded the emancipation of women?" and "Have they dignified or degraded the Mothers of the Race?"

In the preface to volume 2, Stanton replied to earlier criticism from clergy, commenting, "Another clergyman says: 'It is the work of women, and the devil.' This is a grave mistake. His Satanic Majesty was not invited to join the Revising Committee, which consists of women alone. Moreover," she wickedly added, "he has been so busy of late years attending Synods, General Assemblies and Conferences to prevent the recognition of women delegates that he has had no time to study the languages of 'higher criticism.'"

Stanton also used the second volume to chide her more conservative suffragist sisters for failing to critically examine Christian orthodoxy's role in subjugating women, suggesting the failure is based either in ignorance or in "cowardice" clothed in political pragmatism. "This idea of woman's subordination is reiterated times without number, from Genesis to Revelations; and this is the basis of all church action," she asserted. "Parts I and II of the *Woman's Bible* state these dogmas in plain English.... And yet women meet in convention and denounce the *Woman's Bible*, while clinging to the Church and their Scriptures.... Now, to my mind," she concluded, "the *Woman's Bible*, in denying divine inspiration for such demoralizing ideas, shows a more worshipful reverence for the great Spirit of All Good than does the Church. We have made a fetich [*sic*] of the Bible long enough. The time has come to read it as we do all other books, accepting the good and rejecting the evil it teaches."

Finally, in the concluding words of the introduction to the final volume of what she considered the crowning achievement of a lifetime of agitation, Stanton appealed – as she often did throughout her many decades of advocacy (and with distinct echoes of Thomas Paine's *The Age of Reason*) – to the great Enlightenment principles of reason and science: "All through the centuries scholars and scientists have been imprisoned, tortured and burned alive for some discovery which seemed to conflict with a petty text of Scripture. Surely the immutable laws of the universe can teach more impressive and exalted lessons than the holy books of all the religions on earth."[100]

By now, Stanton the octogenarian was well accustomed to criticism, living by "Michelet's wise motto, 'Let the weal and woe of humanity be everything to you, their praise and blame of no effect; be not puffed up with the one nor cast down with the other.'" She knew once-radical ideas often later become matters of conventional wisdom with the passage of time. As she recalled in *Eighty Years and More*, it had happened before: "[After Seneca Falls] our conservative friends said: 'You have made a great mistake, you will be laughed at from Maine to Texas and beyond the sea; God has set the bounds of Woman's sphere and she should be satisfied with her position. Their prophecy was more than realized," she acknowledged. "We were unsparingly ridiculed by the press and pulpit both in England and America. But now," she added, "many conventions are held each year in both countries to discuss the same ideas; social customs have changed; laws have been modified; municipal suffrage has been granted to women in England and some of the colonies; school suffrage has been granted to women in half of our States, municipal suffrage in Kansas, and full suffrage in four States of the Union.... That first convention, considered a 'grave mistake' in 1848," she observed, "is now referred to as 'a grand step in progress.'"

She believed the same would happen again now, on the matter of Christian orthodoxy's subjugation of women. "When Part I of 'The Woman's Bible' was published," she wrote, "again there was a general disapproval by press and pulpit, and even by women themselves, expressed in resolutions in suffrage and temperance conventions. Like other 'mistakes,'" she predicted, "this too, in due time, will be regarded as 'a step in progress.'"[101]

Nonetheless, in her more honest moments, Stanton could not have been certain about the fate of this final major controversial effort to help release women from their religious bondage. "It requires no courage now to demand the right of suffrage, temperance legislation, liberal divorce laws, or for women to fill church offices. [T]hese battles have been fought and won and the principle governing these demands conceded," she reflected in *Eighty Years and More*. "But it still requires courage to question the divine inspiration of the Hebrew Writings as to the position of woman. Why," she demanded, "should the myths, fables, and allegories of the Hebrews be held more sacred than those of the Assyrians and Egyptians, from whose literature most of them were derived?"[102]

As it turned out, Anthony and other pragmatists had good reason to believe the *Woman's Bible* would politically complicate the movement for women's suffrage. Although the mainstream suffragists tried to bury the

Woman's Bible, it was wielded as a weapon by antisuffragists against the Nineteenth Amendment during its ratification in the states some twenty years later. "This [*Woman's Bible*] is the teaching of the National Suffrage Leaders," read one poster in Tennessee in 1920 after thirty-five states had ratified the amendment leaving just one more for passage. "Are you willing for women who hold these views to become political powers in our country? Every one who believes that the word of God is divinely inspired, who desires to see his State Constitution not violated, and who believes in the purity of the family and the sanctity of marriage would keep women out of politics."

With Tennessee's ratification, women gained the constitutional right to vote – finally, 144 years after the Declaration of Independence proclaimed that "all Men are created equal"; 131 years after We the People created the Constitution to "promote the general Welfare, and secure the Blessings of Liberty to ourselves and our Posterity"; and 52 years after the Fourteenth Amendment explained that "all persons born or naturalized in the United States are citizens of the United States," that "No state shall make or enforce any law which shall abridge the privileges or immunities of citizens of the United States," and that no State shall "deny to any person within its jurisdiction the equal protection of the laws." Regrettably, neither Elizabeth Cady Stanton (who died in 1902) nor Susan B. Anthony (who died in 1906) lived to see the day.[103]

As we have seen, after publishing the *Woman's Bible*, and especially after her death several years later, Stanton was rendered persona non grata by the mainstream women's movement. Griffith notes that "[t]o avoid the Stanton stigma, the younger women intentionally isolated and ignored her. In an effort to appear respectable and politically acceptable, they censured Stanton and canonized Susan B. Anthony." Moreover, "They provided 'Aunt Susan' with a permanent seat on the executive committee, a secretary, and an annuity. After her death they turned her home into a shrine and named the Nineteenth Amendment after her, despite the fact that Stanton had proposed woman suffrage three years before she had met Anthony."

In an omission the equivalent of Thomas Jefferson's name being excised from a celebration honoring the Declaration of Independence, reserving all plaudits instead for Jefferson's later collaborator James Madison, Elizabeth Cady Stanton's name was not included in the printed program at the introduction of the Equal Rights Amendment in 1923 on the seventy-fifth anniversary of the Seneca Falls Convention in Seneca

Falls. Stanton's daughter Harriot Stanton Blatch was the only speaker to mention her name. Even though it was Stanton who had largely drafted and argued on behalf of the Declaration of Rights and Sentiments, she was ignored, whereas Susan B. Anthony's contributions to the movement were honored with a motorcade to her memorial in nearby Rochester, notwithstanding the fact that Anthony herself had not even attended the Seneca Falls Convention.[104]

The neglect extended beyond the women's movement to the general public as well when, for many decades following her death, historians and others failed to adequately chronicle Stanton's contributions – so she was mostly hidden from view for most of the twentieth century. A biography was published in 1940 by Alma Lutz, but it was not until much later that Stanton truly began to receive her due. As Griffith points out in her 1984 Stanton biography, "Later generations, unaware of Stanton's role, put Anthony on a stamp and a coin. As a result, Elizabeth Cady Stanton, both notable and notorious in her own life, is better known as Susan B. Anthony's sidekick than as the instigator and ideologue of the first women's movement." Even as late as 1977, when the beginning of a national conference in Houston celebrating International Women's Year was marked by the arrival of a torch carried from Seneca Falls, Susan B. Anthony's grandniece was seated on the stage – but there was no hint or mention of the denizen of Seneca Falls herself, Elizabeth Stanton.

Things began to change during those same 1970s, however, when a new generation of feminists discovered Stanton and then, in 1984, with Griffith's biography. Finally, when the film editor Paul Barnes (who knew nothing of Stanton until introduced to Griffith's biography) convinced noted filmmaker Ken Burns to produce the 1999 documentary *Not for Ourselves Alone*, about Stanton and Anthony, knowledge of Elizabeth Cady Stanton and her contributions truly began to reach the mainstream.[105]

One may offer any number of explanations for why such an important historical figure as Elizabeth Cady Stanton was ignored by her suffragist successors during the last years of her life and by historians for nearly a century after her death. Possibilities include her misjudgments in associating with racist George Train in the years following the Civil War and certainly her own highly regrettable racist, nativist, and elitist comments during those especially difficult postwar years; the muddled primary sources caused by Stanton's own scattered note keeping; her children's later misguided attempts to resurrect their mother's reputation from being "buried alive" by the younger suffrage leaders by destroying primary materials and rewriting letters and major portions of her autobiography; or perhaps even her abrasive style or "bad karma" from sometimes treating those close to her badly.[106]

But another explanation is worth considering as well: Elizabeth Cady Stanton's shunning is ultimately a cautionary tale of the perils of sharply criticizing America's most sacred cow of all – Christian religious orthodoxy. As developed in the *Woman's Bible* and elsewhere, Stanton's theology of systematically exposing problems in the Bible's fundamentalist teachings was persuasive. At the same time, such efforts were deeply threatening in a nation as thoroughly dominated by the Bible as the United States – still true today, with its official "In God We Trust" proclamations and much more.

One wonders whether twenty-first-century America is ready for serious questions about the role dominant religious orthodoxy plays in official life. Twenty-five years ago, Kevin Phillips commented on the danger of a drift toward "apple-pie authoritarianism" in America, where "the morality of the majority would be upheld and enforced, though with politically convenient lapses; the 'Star Spangled banner' would wave with greater frequency and over many more parades; increased surveillance would crack down on urban outbreaks and extreme political dissidents."

Well, as Phillips notes in his 2006 book *American Theocracy*, "we are seeing it now: church, family, and flag, and more than a few hints of something more." Even with the monumental barriers shattered by the 2008 election of an African American president and the promising 2006 election of the first Muslim to Congress, every would-be politician knows it would still be tactically unwise to claim to be anything other than a God-abiding Judeo-Christian and political suicide to admit to being an atheist. In post-9/11 America, a person posing serious rational criticism of deeply accepted religious conventional wisdom is still considered a threat.[107]

The point is, as pervasive (and oppressive, to nonbelievers) as these religious views are today, they were even more dominant in 1895, when Elizabeth Cady Stanton published the *Woman's Bible*. Stanton took a radical turn in exposing the hypocrisy of conventional Christian views concerning women and their roles in family and society. With that, she went too far, even for her own friends.

In a sense, Stanton met her match when she took on Christian orthodoxy – Victorian America was simply not ready to tolerate such broadsides on the national religious creed. To be sure, other influential people have periodically questioned Christianity's hold on America (Mark Twain wrote, for example, "I am quite sure now that often, very often, in matters concerning religion and politics a man's reasoning powers are not above the monkey's"), but arguably no one attacked Christian orthodoxy quite as systematically and effectively as Stanton.[108]

It is worth noting that Stanton was not lacking in her own theology, notwithstanding the *Woman's Bible* and her other writings attacking Christian orthodoxy. What she and her radical colleagues proposed was itself a religiously based theology but one that fundamentally rejected conventional readings of the Bible that claimed women were merely an "afterthought" in creation, without an independent existence, and whose path to salvation was to subjugate her own interests (and very life, if necessary) to serve man and his children. This deist approach, when coupled with Stanton's civil religion (one shared with Thomas Paine and America's other Founding Fathers) of elevating the Enlightenment's focus on reason, science, and individual rights to fundamental guiding theology, recast feminist theory to recognize women's basic equality with men in all respects. As Stanton said, "[T]he American idea of individual rights [is] more sacred than any civil or ecclesiastical organizations." Equality is a divine idea, "framed into statutes by the Fathers of '76."[109]

One may be forgiven for dreaming that America's national creed can at last be redirected from one based primarily on a religious text, the Bible, to one more properly centered in the tolerant secular Constitution – one to which we the people will devote the same sort of quasi-religious fervor currently reserved for religious Christian orthodoxy. And why not? Why shouldn't the sacred high Enlightenment principles of tolerance, free will, justice, and reason assume sacrosanct status?

Such were the principles, after all, that allowed Europe to emerge during the Renaissance after a thousand years of feudal darkness – a process completed with fifty-eight million deaths in two twentieth-century world wars, events that concentrated the European mind that religious orthodoxy was somehow badly failing the people. Once freed of the strictures of religious convention, European countries like the Netherlands and Czech Republic (not to mention Canada in North America) have become some of the most tolerant, just societies ever known to humankind – approaching the sort envisioned, if not yet realized, by the founders and framers for America itself.[110]

On a most hopeful note, if America with its slaveholding past can elect a black president in the twenty-first century, it can certainly figure out how to move past its excessive official religiosity. To do so, however, will require the brave work of stalwart modern-day radicals in the mold of Elizabeth Cady Stanton and the others profiled in this book.

Elizabeth Cady Stanton was a revolutionary at heart. She sought to "stir[] up women generally to rebellion" by pointing out the many official and unofficial injustices they suffered in a nation supposedly constitutionally committed to principles of freedom, liberty, tolerance, and equal justice. She was unwilling – unable – to compromise on these principles, even when it meant loss of friends and stature. As we have seen, her stubborn refusal to settle resulted in her becoming ostracized during the final years of her life from the movement she had created half a century earlier, and her contributions ignored by history for nearly another century after her death.

Even had she known such slights would occur, it is doubtful she would have changed her approach of speaking truth to power. She understood, in human terms, the sacrifices inherent in her chosen path. "My life has been one long struggle to do and say what I know to be right and true. I would not take back one brave word or deed," she confided to an acquaintance in 1860. "My only regret is that I have not been braver and truer in uttering the honest conviction of my own soul."

A person like Stanton, with firm certitude of the sacred inalienability of the rights of liberty and equal justice identified in the Declaration of Independence and guaranteed in the Constitution, would no more compromise on these basic principles than an ordinary person would submit to slavery.[111]

"Would you do it again?" she might have been asked.

"In a heartbeat," she would have replied. "I couldn't live with myself if I did anything else."

4

W. E. B. Du Bois (1868–1963)

American Apartheid

The Negro race in America, stolen, ravished and degraded, struggling up through difficulties and oppression, needs sympathy and receives criticism; needs help and is given hindrance, needs protection and is given mob-violence, needs justice and is given charity, needs leadership and is given cowardice and apology, needs bread and is given a stone. This nation will never stand justified before God until these things are changed.

– W. E. B. Du Bois, 1905

I. Great Barrington

The ten-year-old boy trembled with excitement as he and his classmates in the small wooden schoolhouse waited to begin exchanging their visiting cards. Glancing around, the boy saw his classmates arranging their cards and whispering to one another in excited tones.

"May I see yours?" one whispered.

"Yes," another replied, offering a gorgeous folded paper creation for inspection. "They were ten cents a package."

"Mine, too!"

When the teacher finally gave permission to begin, the boy and his classmates dashed from boy to girl, girl to boy, merrily collecting and dispensing cards.

Shortly, the boy approached a tall girl who had only recently moved to the school. He reached out his hand. "Here is a card for you," he offered with a shy smile.

The girl looked at him briefly, dismissively refused his card, turned her back, and walked away.

The festive mood rushed out of the room like air from a balloon. Left standing with outstretched arm and burning cheeks, the embarrassed boy felt as if someone had punched him in the gut.

A profound hurt sadness came over young Willie Du Bois in that moment. And with sudden, crystal clarity, he knew. "I am different from them – all of them. And I am shut out of their world, just as surely as if separated by a vast veil."[1]

William Edward Burghardt (W. E. B.) Du Bois would never again be quite as innocent as he had been before this transformative spring 1878 day in the "wee wooden schoolhouse." By his thirteenth birthday a few years later, he had known "days of secret tears" with the growing awareness that some people in his town of Great Barrington, Massachusetts, "actually considered... brown skin a misfortune; [and] some even thought it a crime."

It seems appropriate that Du Bois was born the same year, 1868, as the states ratified the Fourteenth Amendment, which guaranteed due process and equal protection to all persons. This amendment, together with the Fifteenth Amendment that was ratified two years later guaranteeing the franchise to black Americans (albeit men only), was a key piece in the puzzle to reconstruct a shattered Union, which in its brief history had fallen woefully short of honoring the lofty ideals expressed in the Declaration of Independence. During these heady post–Civil War days, African Americans assumed active political roles throughout the South – dominating the state legislature in South Carolina, for example, with more than 600 former slaves elected as legislators during Reconstruction and 265 voting as delegates at state constitutional conventions throughout the South. But alas, the early promise of Reconstruction fell tragically short.[2]

The story of Du Bois's ninety-five-year life can be described, in a sense, as an attempt to resurrect the ideals and gains of the early post–Civil War years. Relentlessly identifying the egregious injustices imposed on African Americans, he stridently demanded liberty and equal justice for all, regardless of color or race. As did this book's other radicals, Du Bois "vigorously opposed any manifestation of human intolerance and social inequality," Manning Marable explains. Moreover, also like the others, Du Bois was harshly critical of Christian orthodoxy, believing it to be the cause of many of society's ills – although he continued throughout his life to champion Christ's own principles of toleration, peace, humility,

PHOTO 1. W. E. B. Du Bois, ca. 1904. Courtesy of Library of Congress.

mercy, and charity – commenting in 1941, for example, "Of course, it is the Churches which are the most discriminatory of all institutions!"[3]

W. E. B. Du Bois ("the pronunciation of my name is *Due Boyss,* with the accent on the last syllable," he often explained) was born in Great Barrington, Massachusetts, on February 23, 1868, to Alfred Du Bois and Mary Silvina Burghardt. Great Barrington, located on the Housatonic River in the far western part of the state between the Berkshires to the east and the Taconic range to the west, was then a town of about four thousand people, of which fewer than thirty families (mostly Burghardts) were African American. In Great Barrington, "[t]he color line was manifest, and yet not absolutely drawn," he later wrote.[4]

Du Bois's great-great-grandfather on his mother's side was onetime slave Tom Burghardt, brought from West Africa and sold by Dutch slavers in New York in the early 1730s. His mother, Mary Silvina, "was dark shining bronze, with smooth skin and lovely eyes; there was a tiny ripple in her black hair, and she had a heavy, kind face." "She gave one the impression of infinite patience," Du Bois recalled many years later, "but a curious determination was concealed in her softness."[5]

Du Bois's father, Alfred, was descended from the wealthy Poughkeepsie, New York, physician James Du Bois of French Huguenot origins, who fathered at least four children with slave mistresses on his Bahamas plantations, including Du Bois's grandfather Alexander, whom he brought back with him to New York around 1812. Alexander fathered Alfred with a Haitian woman during a trip to Haiti sometime before 1833. By the mid-1850s, Alfred was working as a barber, cook, and waiter in upstate New York; around 1867 he moved to Great Barrington, where he met and married Mary Silvina and fathered Du Bois.[6]

Alfred left the young family in 1869 or early 1870, apparently very hastily one night after pistol shots were fired at or near their house by some of Mary Silvina's Burghardt nephews. Thereafter, Alfred worked as a preacher or barber in Connecticut, but it seems Du Bois never saw his father again, inflicting a deep wound from which he never completely recovered. Throughout his life, he rationalized that his father had been forced to leave by the "black Burghardts [who] didn't like [Alfred] because he was too white, and he had a lot of extra manners which they weren't used to." "At any rate, they practically drove him away," the story went, and Alfred expected his wife and new baby to follow.[7]

By Du Bois's seventh year, he was living with his mother and step-brother on Railroad Street, in a very poor part of the community next to the tracks and nearby bars and brothels. Regardless of his surroundings, from an early age Du Bois was highly motivated and excelled academically, advancing through to the upper grades at an age several years younger than his classmates. He indulged his love of books by lingering in Johnny Morgan's bookstore, and it was a proud day when he was able to bring home a full set of Macaulay's five-volume *History of England*, which Morgan allowed him to pay off over time with the twenty-five cents per week he was earning at odd jobs around town. He received special mentoring from Frank Hosmer, the high school principal, who encouraged Du Bois to point toward college and helped him acquire the necessary preparatory textbooks.[8]

When it came to religion, in his youth, Du Bois was a product of his environment, adhering at least superficially to the New England Congregational Church and its rigid Calvinism; into early college, he still "never questioned [his] religious upbringing. Its theory had presented no particular difficulties: God ruled the world, Christ loved it, and men did right, or tried to; otherwise they were rightly punished." This, too, would soon change.[9]

A turning point in young Will Du Bois's life occurred in summer 1883, when he took the train to meet his father's father, Alexander Du Bois, in New Bedford, Massachusetts, before his senior year in high school. Grandfather Alexander gave fatherless Will a much-needed black-adult-male role model, and he soaked in the lessons of this dignified, quiet man. "I suddenly sensed in my grandfather's parlor what manners meant and how people of breeding behaved and were able to express what we in Great Barrington were loath to give act to," he wrote of observing a toast between his grandfather and New Bedford's leading black citizen, Mr. Freedom. "I never forgot that toast," he declared.[10]

As one of thirteen students graduating from Great Barrington High School in the following June 1884, Du Bois gave his commencement talk on the noted abolitionist Wendell Phillips (Elizabeth Cady Stanton's erstwhile ally, who had recently died), "provok[ing] repeated applause" from the enthusiastic audience. Following his mother's death in March, later in 1885, Willie traveled south, enrolling as an advanced-standing sophomore at Fisk University in Nashville, Tennessee, to live among his "own race in the land of the slaves." Fisk, which opened as Fisk Free Colored School on the site of a Union Army hospital in the spring of 1866, less than a year after the end of the Civil War, maintained its ambitious curriculum of Latin, philosophy, science, and history – contrary to the South's emerging orthodoxy that such a liberal arts education was inconsistent with the region's preferences for enforced racial subservience.[11]

At Fisk, Du Bois found "new and exciting and eternal ties" – marveling at the self-assurance of his classmates ("such airs, and colored men at that") and reveling in the comfort of being surrounded by people of like color in a nation where such things mattered:

> Consider, for a moment, how miraculous it all was to a boy of seventeen, just escaped from a narrow valley: I will and lo! My people came dancing about me, – riotous in color, gay in laughter, full of sympathy, need, and pleading; darkly delicious girls – "colored" girls – sat beside me and actually talked to me while I gazed in tongue-tied silence or babbled in boastful dreams. Boys with my own experiences and out of my own world, who knew and understood.[12]

PHOTO 2. Great Barrington High School Graduating Class, 1883. Courtesy W. E. B. Du Bois Library, University of Massachusetts, Amherst.

During the summers after his first and second years at Fisk, he worked teaching in a one-room schoolhouse (actually a log storage barn) just outside tiny Alexandria, Tennessee, fifty miles east of Nashville – where he may as well have stepped back fifty years into antebellum Tennessee. "[I] touched the very shadow of slavery," he recalled; but he treasured nonetheless the camaraderie he developed with his fifteen students (ranging in age from six to twenty), and experienced every teacher's satisfaction in observing "faint and transient glimpses of the dawn in the struggling minds of my pupils."[13]

At this early unformed stage in Du Bois's development, on matters of race relations he was conciliatory, stating in the unpublished "An Open Letter to the Southern People," for example, "Let us, then, recognizing our common interests (for it is unnecessary to speak of our dependence upon you), work for each other's interest, casting behind us unreasonable demands on the one hand, and unreasonable prejudice on the other." His forthrightness in advocating women's rights was decidedly outside of the mainstream, however – stating, for example (in language that Elizabeth Cady Stanton surely would have applauded), that "the Age of Women is surely dawning," in an editorial about a Women's Christian Temperance Union meeting in Nashville.[14]

Just a few months after graduation, Du Bois was on his way to Harvard, thanks to strong recommendations from Fisk professors and his old champion in Great Barrington, Frank Hosmer. Although in his memoirs he speaks of his thrill of "walking beneath the elms of Harvard – the name of allurement, the college of my youngest, wildest visions," he also remembers Harvard as a place too satisfied with itself. Compared to Fisk, he "did not find better teachers at Harvard, but [merely] teachers better known." Among his most influential teachers, philosophy professor William James (brother of Henry James) and history professor Albert Hart stand out as two who especially encouraged Du Bois both during his time at Harvard and for many years afterward.[15]

During his college years, first at Fisk and then Harvard, Du Bois began to question organized religion. He recalls being disillusioned at Fisk by, for example, the Episcopal Church's charges of heresy against a priest whose book was used at the university, the expulsion by the Presbyterians of a minister for heterodoxy, and being "compelled to read" *The Logic of Christian Evidences* (1880) by George Frederick Wright. Having experienced the "Preacher, the Music and the Frenzy" of black Christianity during his summers in Alexandria, orthodox Christian religion now "affronted my logic. It was to my mind, then and since, a cheap piece of special pleading." The combined effect was that he "just stopped and refused to teach Sunday School any more." At Harvard, he harshly criticized white Christianity's "high Episcopal Niocene creed" as a tool for white supremacy. Asked many years later if he believed in God, he replied, "[If] you mean by 'God' a vague Force which, in some uncomprehensible way, dominates all life and change, then I answer, Yes; I recognize such Force, and if you wish to call it God, I do not object."[16]

At Harvard, Du Bois observed a disciplined regimen that would remain a hallmark of his daily routine for the rest of his life. ("Rising at 7:15 and breakfast. Work from 8–12:30. Lunch. Work from 1–4. From 4–5 I go to the gymnasium. 5–5:30 I take a breathing spell. 5:30–7, dinner and daily paper. 7–10:30 study or lectures or social visits, etc."). He graduated cum laude with a concentration in philosophy in June 1890, and he delivered an enthusiastically received ten-minute memorized speech at commencement titled, "Jefferson Davis as Representative of Civilization," in which he called for a new archetype – one committed to coexistence of the races – to replace that of Davis, whose life, represented as "race, or as nation, ... can only logically mean ... the advance of a part of the world at the expense of the whole." His finely balanced language would have been heartily approved by his later arch-antagonist, Booker T. Washington. It pleased the graduation audience, anyway, which burst into applause at the speech's conclusion, and it impressed the critics as well. Said the *Nation,* "[Du Bois approached this] difficult and hazardous subject with absolute good taste, great moderation, and almost contemptuous fairness." Another, *Kate Field's Washington,* anointed Du Bois the "star of the occasion," commenting: "No history of the Civil War will be worth reading, saving as fiction, until . . . the spirit of [Horace] Greeley and Du Bois inspires its writer."[17]

Following his triumphant Harvard commencement address, with scholarship funding for his Harvard doctorate studies secured, he stayed mostly in Boston for the summer, where the affluent "Charles Street" African American community began to assimilate this rising young star. During his second year, he met and fell in love with Maud Cuney, "a tall, imperious brunette, with gold-bronze skin, brilliant eyes and coils of black hair," a student at the New England Conservatory of Music. They socialized happily with others among their elite Charles Street friends, and although she declined his marriage proposal, they remained intimate friends until her death in 1936. During these years, too, he met the dashing Monroe Trotter (the first African American junior Phi Beta Kappa, who made his way in the Cambridge social scene much more easily than the serious-minded Du Bois), with whom Du Bois would maintain a love-hate relationship for decades afterward. Taking time out from his "limited leisure" to speak at the March 1891 meeting of the National Colored League, he urged his audience to "get a liberal education" with this comment: "Never make the mistake of thinking that the object of being a man is to be a carpenter, the object of being a carpenter is to be a man."[18]

The twenty-two-year-old scholar received his master of arts degree in 1892, continuing to impress at Harvard and beyond. His professor Albert Hart thought enough of his master's thesis paper, "The Enforcement of the Slave Trade Laws," to invite him to present the paper to the American Historical Association in December 1891, where it was adjudged by a reporter from the New York *Independent* as one of the conference's three best. "[H]ere was an audience of white men listening to a black man," the reporter marveled, "listening, moreover, to a careful, cool, philosophical history of the laws which have not prevented the enslavement of his race."[19]

The next step in Du Bois's first-rate education would take him to Berlin to study at the esteemed Friedrich-Wilhelm III University (the University of Berlin), supported by the John F. Slater Fund. Sailing for the first time outside of the United States in July 1892, he was "in a trance.... It's not real; I must be dreaming!" He traveled in Germany before starting his studies, thoroughly enjoying the relaxed racial mixing practiced in Germany – often on the arm of Dora Marbach, a pretty young Dutch woman enough taken with Du Bois that she wanted to get married "at once" (which he declined, knowing "this would be unfair to her and fatal for [his] work at home").[20]

He began his Berlin studies in late October, where the demands of an autonomous German program, including a course load of six lectures totaling twenty hours a week, suited the solitary and supremely self-motivated Du Bois well. The sociologist in him observed fairly quickly in Germany "a restlessly pessimistic state founded on obedience," moving at all times at "half military stride," as compared to the "boundlessly optimistic [United States] founded on individual freedom."[21]

During his second year in Berlin, he took a room in the family-style Braun Pension, pugnaciously pleased with "the opportunity to teach an American family [also staying in the pension] what a 'nigger' is," though he "lived more or less regularly" with a young Berlin shopgirl. When classes resumed in October, he committed himself even more to his deep studies, finding particular affinity in Goethe and Hegel. He also began visiting meetings of the German Socialist Party but revealed the lingering elitism that would remain with him for decades in a journal entry commenting that many socialists are part of "that anarchistic, semi-criminal proletariat which always, in all countries, attaches itself to the most radical party."[22]

Although he had hoped to finish his Ph.D. at the conclusion of his second year in Berlin, his plans were thwarted by a technicality requiring that students could not stand for doctoral examination until after the completion of a bare minimum of four semesters in residency; because he had been there only three, he would have needed to stay an extra semester before qualifying to take the exam. The Slater Fund was unwilling to extend its support for the additional semester, instructing him to complete the Ph.D. at Harvard instead (where he would be the first African American to do so). Du Bois swallowed his disappointment and, after final visits to Paris and London, returned to the United States from his magical two years abroad. The contrast was sobering – from learning in Europe to understand white "men and women as [he] had never met before ... [as] not white folks, but folks," to being "dropped suddenly back into 'nigger'-hating America!"[23]

On his return from Europe, Du Bois found his first teaching job (classics) at Wilberforce University. "Life was now begun and I was half happy," he ruminated during the train ride to the Wilberforce campus. "Up through the Berkshire valley with its quiet beauty, then across New York I glided, wrapped in dreams. The lights of Buffalo bade me goodnight, and half asleep, I drifted across Ohio." Wilberforce turned out to be a poor match, however. Discouraged by the autocratic administration of president S. T. Mitchell ("the most perfect realization of what the devil might be in the closing years of the 19th [century]"), the religious evangelism often practiced on campus, and other laments, Du Bois came to conclude that he "had made a mistake" in coming to Wilberforce. "I found myself against a stone wall.... Nothing stirred before [my] impatient pounding!" he later recalled. "Or if it stirred, it soon slept again."[24]

Among the rare strong stirrings were those prompted by the 1895 commencement address visit of seventy-six-year-old African Methodist Episcopal priest Alexander Crummell, who, in his 1877 sermon "The Destined Superiority of the Negro," had written about the way forward for African Americans after the abandonment of Reconstruction and whose feminist and social ideals deeply affected the young scholar. First "politely, then curiously, then eagerly," Du Bois spoke for hours with Crummell apart from the crowd ("where the storming of the lusty young orators could not harm us"), on such matters as Crummell's ideas of a natural Platonic aristocracy that would lead the African American race through troubling times. (Du Bois's later advocacy of a talented tenth leading the African American race owes props to Crummell.) "Instinctively I bowed before this man," Du Bois recalled, "as one bows before the prophets of the world. Some seer he seemed, that came not from the crimson Past or the gray To-come, but from the pulsing Now."[25]

Du Bois completed his twelve-chapter Harvard doctoral dissertation, "The Suppression of the African Slave Trade to the United States of America, 1638–1870," during his first year at Wilberforce, which Harvard (again with the strong recommendation of Professor Hart) arranged to publish the following year. This critically acclaimed book took on a particularly venerable sacred cow – the Constitution's framers – in challenging the conventional wisdom that the constitutional bargain allowing slavery's continuation was inevitable and proper: "It is neither profitable nor in accordance with the scientific truth to consider that whatever the constitutional fathers did was right, or that slavery was a plague sent from God and fated to be eliminated in due time."[26]

Du Bois also met others at Wilberforce, including, most important, the student Nina Gomer – "a slip of a girl," in Du Bois's admiring words, "beautifully dark-eyed and thorough and good as a German housewife." Du Bois and Nina, the well-mannered, well-spoken daughter of a Cedar Rapids hotel chef, were married on May 12, 1896.

During the time Du Bois and Nina were courting early in his second year at Wilberforce, Booker T. Washington, a former slave from Mississippi who had risen to become principal at Tuskegee (Alabama) Institute and an influential public speaker on the education of African Americans, gave what was to be one of the most influential speeches in the history of American race relations before the Cotton States International Expo in Atlanta. "In all things that are purely social [blacks and whites] can be as separate as the fingers, yet one as the hand in all things essential to mutual progress," Washington explained in his speech of September 18, 1895. "The wisest among my race understand that the agitation of questions of social equality is the extremest folly." Washington essentially proposed a bargain: blacks would drop their demands for "social equality" and the right to vote in exchange for the South's ruling white elite allowing parallel vocational, educational, and social progress for blacks and taking steps to reduce violence by Southern bigots.[27]

The editor at Atlanta's influential *Constitution* enthused, "That man's speech is the beginning of a moral revolution in America"; President Grover Cleveland, meeting Washington shortly after his speech, expressed a "new hope" for Negroes. Du Bois too, was among the masses lauding Washington's Atlanta speech, writing him directly, "Let me heartily congratulate you upon your phenomenal success at Atlanta – it was a word fitly spoken," and in a letter to New York *Age*, "[H]ere might be the basis of a real settlement between whites and blacks in the South, if the South opened to the Negroes the doors of economic opportunity and the Negroes cooperated with the white South in political sympathy." Within just a few years, however, Du Bois would emphatically renounce those same words.[28]

II. The Road to Atlanta

The American Negro... wishes neither of [his] older selves to be lost. He would not Africanize America, for America has too much to teach the world and Africa. He would not bleach his Negro soul in a flood of white

Americanism, for he knows that Negro blood has a message for the world. He simply wishes to make it possible for a man to be both a Negro and an American, without being cursed and spit upon by his fellows, without losing the opportunity of self-development, without having the doors of opportunity closed roughly in his face.

–W. E. B. Du Bois, 1903

The two proud men maintained cordial outward appearances but, on closer observation, they were deeply wary of each other – rather like a pair of rival lions positioning themselves to lead the pride. Their correspondence during the summer and fall of 1903 reflected the maneuvering. The subject was the organization of a January 1904 conference in New York City's Carnegie Hall meeting rooms for key African American leaders, and they could not agree on whom to invite.

"We must agree upon certain fundamental principles and see in what way we understand or misunderstand each other," suggested the former slave Booker T. Washington, now principal of the powerful Tuskegee Institute.

"Here are my proposed names," W. E. B. Du Bois, the renowned Atlanta University professor and author of highly regarded scholarly studies and other more provocative works, replied.

"The more I think of it, the more I feel convinced that one should not attend," Washington parried, "but that another be added."

"Very well. Then I think it would be appropriate to add someone else altogether," Du Bois responded.

"But the list should reflect that the bulk of our people are in the South," Washington countered. "Please do try to make a special effort to drop out of consideration all personal feelings."

Disgusted, Du Bois finally threw up his hands and ceased communicating.

After a time, Washington, understanding the importance of Du Bois's attendance, anxiously telegraphed to inquire if he planned to attend.

"I do not think it will be profitable to give further advice which will not be followed," Du Bois announced curtly. "The conference is yours and you will naturally constitute it as you choose." Moreover, he added, "I do not know if I will attend, for I am unsure whether my own presence would be worthwhile."

Coy to the end, Du Bois did finally attend; and he agreed to serve on a postconference planning committee of twelve. But it was not long before Du Bois discovered he could no longer equivocate.

"We should no longer kiss the hands that smite us," he wrote publicly, directly criticizing Washington. "Negros should settle for nothing less than full equal rights, and if they fail, die trying."

All efforts at maintaining even the appearance of cordiality between Du Bois and Washington now ceased; thereafter, "[i]t was war to the knife, and knife to the hilt."[29]

Du Bois's hopes to escape Wilberforce were realized when he accepted a position in June 1896 as assistant instructor in sociology at the University of Pennsylvania, to conduct research for Wharton School Professor Samuel Lindsay in the university's comprehensive study on the Negro population in Philadelphia. The study was intended to identify the scope of the "social wreckage" and how best to manage (i.e., quarantine) it. "We want to know precisely how this class of people live," Penn provost C. C. Harrison instructed. Over the following three months, Du Bois would spend 835 hours collecting data for his report, canvassing nearly 10,000 men, women, and children in 2,500 households in the neighborhood.[30]

Lamenting later that he had made "their first home in the slums of Philadelphia," Du Bois moved with new bride Nina to the heart of the study's subject area at Seventh and Lombard in Philadelphia, a grim area where "kids played intriguing games like 'cops and lady bums' [and where, when at night] pistols popped, you didn't get up lest you find you couldn't." Nina, though, whose "great gift was her singularly honest character, her passion for cleanliness and order and her loyalty" was uncomplaining, and "suddenly, unexpectedly, miraculously," on October 2, 1897, their first child, son Burghardt, was born. After Burghardt's birth, Nina went to stay with the Burghardt relatives in Great Barrington while Du Bois completed work on his Philadelphia project.[31]

The resulting study, *The Philadelphia Negro,* published in the fall of 1899, gave the sponsors what they wanted ("The main results of the inquiry... agree, to a large extent, with general public opinion" that the source of the problems can be traced to the Negro himself: "the Negro is as a rule, willing, honest and good-natured, but he is also, as a rule, careless, unreliable and unsteady") but also offered a forceful critique of the underlying social conditions as an important contributing factor ("In other respects, [conditions are] logically explicable or in accord with historical precedents [of racism and poverty]"). Various mainstream reviewers found the book "[a] very exhaustive study, [useful for] the lesson... of patience and sympathy toward the South, whose difficulties have been far greater than those of the North," and "perfectly frank, laying all necessary stress on the weakness of his people."[32]

Du Bois's ready acknowledgment of the black community's measure of culpability and the responsibility of its elite class to lead the rest (what he would later dub the "Talented Tenth") masked a more subtle and subversive radical message, however: white racism was the exacerbating trigger that made black troubles much worse than they would otherwise be:

> Such discrimination is morally wrong, politically dangerous, industrially wasteful, and socially silly. It is the duty of the whites to stop it, and to do so primarily for their own sakes.... The cost of crime and pauperism, the growth of slums, and the pernicious influences of idleness and lewdness, cost the public far more than would the hurt to the feelings of a carpenter to work beside a black man, or a shopgirl to start beside a darker mate. This does not contemplate the wholesale replacing of white workmen before Negroes out of sympathy or philanthropy; it does mean that talent should be rewarded.[33]

In short, "[h]ow long can a city teach its black children that the road to success is to have a white face?" he asked, concluding, "For thirty years and more Philadelphia has said to its black children: 'Honesty, efficiency and talent have little to do with your success; if you work hard, spend little and are good you may earn your bread and butter at those sorts of work which we frankly confess we despise; if you are dishonest and lazy, the state will furnish your bread free.'"[34]

The insights Du Bois gained while researching and writing *The Philadelphia Negro* proved invaluable to his further development. Following closely the 1896 presidential election, he began to question beliefs he had earlier held as unimpeachable articles of faith, such as the laissez-faire economics he had learned at Harvard, and he began to understand more clearly the connections between politics and economics, leading to his closer alignments with populist or progressive positions.[35]

Perhaps most significant, the more carefully Du Bois considered the ideas set forth by Booker T. Washington (Washington regularly offered apologies for white racism – for example, excusing slavery as a form of citizenship training: "We went into slavery without a language, we came out speaking the proud Anglo-Saxon tongue"; "If in the providence of God the Negro got any good out of slavery, he got the habit of work"), the more he questioned its wisdom. In seconding the nomination of Alexander Crummell (who was among the first to push back against Washington) as president of the American Negro Academy on March 5, 1897, Du Bois framed a difficult question then faced by all African Americans:

> What after all, am I? Am I an American or am I a Negro? Can I be both? Or is it my duty to cease to be a Negro as soon as possible and be an American?... Does my black blood place upon me any more obligation to assert my nationality than German, or Irish or Italian blood would?[36]

Entering the long-standing debate whether the African American must either fully assimilate or fully separate, Du Bois set forth a new hybrid vision:

> We are Americans, not only by birth and by citizenship, but by our political ideals, our language, our religion. Farther than that, our Americanism does not go. At that point, we are Negroes, members of a vast historic race that from the very dawn of creation has slept, but half awakening in the dark forests of its African fatherland. We are the first fruits of this new nation, the harbinger of that black tomorrow which is yet destined to soften the whiteness of the Teutonic today.[37]

Du Bois's breakout *Atlantic Monthly* piece of August 1897, "Strivings of the Negro People," picked up on these themes: first, expressing Du Bois's growing reticence about Washington's vocationally oriented Tuskegee idea ("The training of the schools we need today more than ever," Du Bois argued, "[involves] the training of deft hands, quick eyes and ears and the broader, deeper, higher culture of gifted minds"); second, identifying the conundrum faced by blacks in America:

> [The African American] ever feels his two-ness – an American, a Negro; two souls, two thoughts, two unreconciled strivings. Two warring ideals in one dark body, whose dogged strength alone keeps it from being torn asunder. The history of the American Negro is the history of this strife – this longing to attain self-conscious manhood, to merge his double self into a better and truer self.[38]

With the expiration of his Penn research contract in January 1898, Du Bois moved to Atlanta to begin teaching history and sociology at Atlanta University, an "ivory tower of race," at a salary of $1,000 per year. Committed to providing a broad liberal arts education for blacks, Atlanta University's approach came at a price, with Northern philanthropists fully committed instead to the Tuskegee idea of providing exclusively vocational and industrial curricula. Du Bois was not especially popular at Atlanta. Rather silent and unsocial, he acquired a reputation as something of an enforcer, reporting violators of the smoking code and the like. His major activity at the university, besides teaching, was producing the annual Atlanta Conference of Negro Problems. He established a new vision for the two-year-old series, intending to convene high-level annual meetings designed to make African Americans more familiar to mainstream society and to make the "laws of social living clearer, surer, and more definite."[39]

Du Bois's relationship at the turn of the century with Booker T. Washington (alternately the "Wizard of Tuskegee" or the "Great Accommodator," depending on one's perspective) was on-again, off-again. Du Bois publicly defended Washington at the August 1899 meeting of the influential National Afro-American Council when an angry minority castigated Washington for his equivocations ("[lynching] really indicates progress. There can be no progress without friction"; or "[a black person] will see in [his oppression] a recompense for all that he has suffered if it . . . can be a medium of [Southern whites'] rising into the atmosphere of generous brotherhood and self-forgetfulness") and for not condemning outright the gruesome April 1899 Atlanta lynching of farmer Sam Hose (after which Du Bois, for his part, had concluded that "one could not be a calm, cool, and detached scientist while Negroes were lynched, murdered and starved"). On this occasion, however, Du Bois strongly supported the majority's resolution allowing Washington to be excused from any action "which might be radical in its utterances to the destruction of his usefulness in connection with many causes." In late 1899, Washington formally offered Du Bois a job at Tuskegee at a salary of $1,400 per year, including offices, a "comfortable and convenient house," and printing "wholly at your service." Despite a pleasant-enough February 1900 visit by Du Bois to the impressive Tuskegee campus, the undercurrents of friction between the two men were ultimately too much to overcome, and Du Bois turned down the job.[40]

Their relationship would remain superficially cordial for several more years (the men likely met twice again in 1902–3), but Du Bois was always wary of Washington's potential for duplicity. Even still, he was not "in absolute opposition to the things that Mr. Washington was advocating," and not (yet) ready to issue such harsh judgments as some, like Illinois legislator Edward Morris, who charged that Washington was "largely responsible for the lynching in this country."

Du Bois did not set out to oppose Booker T. Washington per se as much as he sought to criticize the Tuskegee machine's unwillingness to brook dissent. "Things had come to such a pass," Du Bois much later recalled, "that when any Negro complained or advocated a course of

PHOTO 3. Booker T. Washington, ca. 1895. Courtesy of Library of Congress.

action, he was silenced with the remark that Mr. Washington did not agree with this." "Oh, Washington was a politician," Du Bois recollected nearly sixty years later. "He was a man who believed that we should get what we could get. It wasn't a matter of ideals or anything of that sort. He had no faith in white people, not the slightest," he explained, "and he was most popular among them, because if he was talking with a white man he sat there and found out what the white man wanted him to say, and then as soon as possible, he said it."

Around the time Washington's characteristic self-demeaning "darky" jokes were being redirected more frequently against the supposed laziness of highly educated blacks, Washington's autobiography, *Up from Slavery,* was published to great acclaim in February 1901. Du Bois's July review in the *Dial* was muted: "It is as though Nature must needs make men a little narrow to give them force," he noted ironically. Washington's success was not to be found in the substance of his approaches to racial accommodation and industrial education, Du Bois asserted; rather, his contribution was in the "unlimited energy and perfect faith he put into this programme, [changing] a by-path into a Veritable Way of Life." Du

Bois grudgingly observed that none before Washington had demonstrated the "tact and power" to garner "not simply the applause of those who believe in his theories, but also the respect of those who do not." "[But Washington] pictures as the height of absurdity a black boy studying a French grammar in the midst of weeds and dirt. One wonders how Socrates or St. Francis of Assisi would receive this!" With this review, Du Bois sent notice of the stirrings of a loyal opposition – a "large and important group" deeply committed to black self-determination, who believe "in the higher education of Fisk and Atlanta Universities, . . . self-assertion and ambition, and . . . the right of suffrage for blacks on the same terms as whites." Du Bois, though, in his own words "no natural leader of men," recognized his own limitations as a political organizer – in his inability to "slap people on the shoulder, [or to remember] their names."[41]

Du Bois returned to Europe in summer 1900 to participate in the Paris Exposition Universelle, where he won the gold medal for Collaborator as Compiler of Georgia Negro Exhibit. Then it was on to London for the historic Pan-African Meeting in Westminster Town Hall. Organized by Henry Sylvester Williams, a thirty-one-year-old Trinidadian barrister practicing in London, the conference brought together thirty-three women and men of African heritage from around the world, joined by other organizations and spectators. In his closing session address, "To the Nations of the World," Du Bois coined one of his most famous phrases, "The problem of the twentieth century is the problem of the color line," and he called "as soon as practicable [for] the rights of responsible self-government [be given] to the black colonies of Africa and the West Indies." "How far," he asked, "[are] differences of race . . . going to be made hereafter, the basis of denying to over half the world the right of sharing to their utmost ability the opportunities and privileges of modern civilization[?]"[42]

Personal tragedy struck in 1899, when young Burghardt died on May 24, ten days after contracting nasopharyngeal diphtheria. After this devastating blow to both mother ("[i]n the chamber of death writhed the world's most piteous thing – a childless mother") and father ("[i]f one must have gone, why not [me]?"), the marriage was never again the same. "It tore our lives in two," he wrote. Nina's already-negative feelings for the South turned into a visceral loathing. When Burghardt died, Du Bois recalled, "[I]n a sense my wife died too. Never after that was she quite the same in her attitude toward life and the world."[43]

Daughter Yolande was born on October 21, 1900, shortly after Du Bois's return from Europe, providing Nina and Du Bois some emotional closeness after the trauma of Burghardt's death the year before. The couple settled into a comfortable social life at Atlanta University, cultivating friendships with other couples and individuals. Among those Du Bois befriended were professors George Towns and John Hope – each of whom shared Du Bois's passion for liberal arts higher education for African Americans, as well as his growing apprehension about Booker Washington's increasing influence in a South where blacks were fast losing any leverage they once had at the ballot box.[44]

Meanwhile, Du Bois's own academic star continued to rise, with an essay in the January 1899 *Atlantic Monthly* titled "A Negro Schoolmaster in the New South" (recounting his experiences teaching in rural Alexandria while at Fisk) and three more articles elsewhere in close succession. But his authorial coup de grace would be the April 1903 release of *The Souls of Black Folk,* his masterfully executed set of fourteen essays (nine that had been previously published elsewhere). Dedicated "To Burghardt and Yolande: The Lost and the Found," Du Bois rhapsodized: "Leaving . . . the world of the white man, I have stepped within the Veil, raising it that you may view faintly its deeper recesses – the meaning of its religion, the passion of its human sorrow, and the struggle of its greater souls."

The impact of this critically acclaimed collection, which went into its third printing in its first year, was "greater upon and within the Negro race than any other single book published in this country since *Uncle Tom's Cabin*," said James Weldon Johnson. Henry James added this "was the only 'Southern' book of any distinction published in many a year"; Max Weber arranged to publish and write an introduction to this "splendid book" in German. Du Bois's old professor, Albert Hart, claimed for years afterward that the collection was "the only literature published by a Harvard graduate in forty years," and the influential liberal *Independent* wrote that *Souls* was "the best and most logical expression of the clear facts of race hatred yet made by any student of the negro question." In a 2008 book, Jay Parini lists it as one of the thirteen books that changed America. Largely ignored by most of the Southern press (and by much of the African American press, as dictated from Tuskegee), *Souls* was mostly castigated by the few Southern papers that paid it any attention at all: "This book is indeed dangerous for the negro to read," warned the *Nashville American*.[45]

Souls employed the literary device of pairing the music from Negro spirituals with verse from some of the greatest names in the European literary canon (Browning, Tennyson, and Byron, to name a few) as epigraphs at the beginning of each essay, with the culturally subversive intent of placing the two on equal footing. The first essay, "Of Our Spiritual Strivings," for example, paired "Nobody Knows the Trouble I've Seen" with the verse of Arthur Symons ("O water, voice of my heart, crying in the sand, All night long crying with a mournful cry"), in addressing the conundrum of how "it feel[s] to be a problem" to the majority of society.[46]

"Of the Dawn of Freedom," which opened with music of the Negro spiritual "My Lord, What a Mourning!" and verse from James Russell Lowell ("Truth forever on the scaffold, Wrong forever on the throne"), defended the Freedman's Bureau, established by the Thirty-eighth Congress in March 1865 to assist in integrating freed slaves into society, against the prevailing conventional wisdom of the day (advanced by Southern-sympathizer historians at Columbia and Johns Hopkins universities) that the bureau was ill advised, inept, and corrupt. "For some fifteen million dollars, beside the sums spent before 1865, and the dole of benevolent societies," Du Bois countered, "this Bureau set going a system of free labor, established a beginning of peasant proprietorship, secured the recognition of black freedmen before courts of law, and founded the free common school in the South." The irony of the South's all-out pitched battle against the Freedman's Bureau, Du Bois pointed out, was that had the South instead participated in good-faith postwar efforts at reconciliation, "every sensible man, black and white, would have easily chosen... restricted Negro suffrage."[47]

In the withering chapter, "Of Mr. Booker T. Washington and Others" (based on his earlier published review of *Up from Slavery* in the *Dial*), he paired music from Negro spiritual "A Great Camp Meeting in the Promised Land" with Lord Byron ("From birth till death enslaved; in word, in deed, unmanned!"). Here, Du Bois criticized Washington's program of accommodation and vocationalism as "practically accept[ing] the alleged inferiority of the Negro races" rather than placing blame where it properly belonged: on whites' "relentless color-prejudice [that] is more often a cause than a result of the Negro's degradation." The essay (besides "settl[ing] pretty definitely any further question of [my] going to Tuskegee as an employee") served as a manifesto of sorts for the Talented Tenth (a term used in "Of the Training of Black Men," the sixth essay, to denote the educated black elite who would lead the race) – to remember always to speak out, despite Washington's attempts to silence dissent. "So far as [Washington] . . . apologizes for injustice, does not rightly value the privilege and duty of voting[,] . . . and opposes the higher training and ambition of our brighter minds, . . . we must unceasingly and firmly oppose him," Du Bois insisted.[48]

Back in Atlanta, the Atlanta University conferences placed the university in the vanguard of social science research, despite the extremely thin finances exacerbated by the continuing cold shoulder from foundations. With the programs' success came increased attention. The London *Spectator* in 1901 commented on the work "being done with much intelligence, discrimination, and assiduity at the insistence and under the inspiration of Atlanta University"; even the *Outlook,* a stalwart supporter of Washington and the Tuskegee idea, asserted in 1903 that "no student of the race problem, no person who would either think or speak upon it intelligently, can afford to be ignorant of the facts brought out in the Atlanta series." The 1903 visit of a *Chicago Tribune* reporter, who described Du Bois as "one of the most entertaining men I ever talked with," was just one of the increasing numbers of visits to the Atlanta campus from reporters, scholars, and public figures.[49]

Even despite Du Bois's criticism of Washington in *Souls of Black Folk* and the more frequent exposure of chinks in the Tuskegee Machine's armor, Du Bois and Washington still maintained outwardly cordial relations. For example, just months after the release of *Souls,* Du Bois taught a summer class at Tuskegee, and the two men corresponded regularly during the latter part of 1903 while negotiating a list of invitees to a January 1904 New York City conference in the meeting rooms at Carnegie Hall for key African American leaders (although Du Bois, as dramatized earlier in this chapter, exasperated with Washington's quibbling, finally bowed out of the planning but eventually did attend).[50]

At the meeting itself, after wealthy white benefactors Andrew Carnegie and Lymon Abbott began by admonishing the group of the wisdom of Washington's Tuskegee approach to the exclusion of others (leading Du Bois to think, "Even if all they said had been true, it was a wrong note to strike in a conference of conciliation"), over the next couple of days, a tone of compromise was mostly achieved – with the attendees agreeing, among other things, on the idea to appoint the Committee of Twelve to help coordinate future efforts among African American movements and leaders. In further discussions, Du Bois soon recognized that the deck was stacked against him, however; he knew that he could not serve on the committee without seriously compromising his principles.[51]

Du Bois began to seek different ways to tout his own approach as a superior alternative to Washington's Tuskegee idea. His "Credo," initially published in the *Independent* on October 6, 1904, was destined years later to become one of his more effective efforts at reaching a broad cross-section of black and white Americans alike, aided by the wide distribution of playing-card size reprints of its nine paragraphs. African Americans "would hang the 'Credo' on their living room walls after Du Bois included it in [his book] *Darkwater*," reports Lewis, "just as their grandchildren would mount [Martin Luther King's] 'I Have a Dream' on theirs." Carefully written in pious terms in order not to threaten a Judeo-Christian majority, "Credo" explained, "[I believe in] God who made of one blood all races that dwell on earth; [and that] all men, black and brown and white, are brothers, varying through Time and Opportunity, in form and gift and features but differing in no essential particular, and alike in soul and in the possibility of infinite development." Moreover, "Especially do I believe in the Negro Race, in the beauty of its genius, the sweetness of its soul and its strength which shall yet inherit this turbulent earth." Finally, "I believe in Liberty for all men; the space to stretch their arms and souls; the right to breathe and the right to vote, the freedom to choose their friends, enjoy the sunshine and ride on the railroads, uncursed by color; thinking, dreaming, working as they will in a kingdom of God and love."[52]

Du Bois directed part of his considerable energies the next year to organizing a conference of his own, held on July 10–12, 1905, at Niagara Falls (on the Canadian side, ironically, when plans for Buffalo, New York, were undone by American hotel proprietors' race prejudice), to advance two stated goals: one, to encourage "organized determination and aggressive action on the part of men who believe in Negro freedom and growth," and two, to oppose "present methods of strangling honest criticism." This first Niagara Conference brought together a select group of twenty-nine "educated, determined, and unpurchasable" men who "had not bowed the knee to Baal."

The inaugural Niagara meeting issued the Declaration of Principles (notably reminiscent of the Declaration of Rights and Sentiments advanced fifty-seven years earlier by Elizabeth Cady Stanton and Lucretia Mott in nearby Seneca Falls). The document opened by declaring, "We refuse to allow the impression to remain that the Negro American assents to inferiority, [or that he] is submissive under oppression and apologetic before insults." It then singled out for criticism both employers ("importing ignorant Negro American laborers in emergencies, and then affording them neither protection nor permanent employment"), and labor unions ("proscribing and boycotting and oppressing thousands of their fellow-toilers, simply because they are black"), concluding, "These methods have accentuated and will accentuate the war of labor and capital, and they are disgraceful to both sides." Although it acknowledged the help given by many humane white Americans, "our fellow men from the abolitionist down to those who today still stand for equal opportunity and who have given and still give of their wealth and of their poverty for our advancement," the declaration also issued a frank protest decrying the nation's abhorrent treatment of blacks (as quoted in this chapter's opening epigraph). The Niagara Conference received virtually zero coverage from the white press and little in the black press outside of those papers controlled by Niagara attendees.[53]

Things began slipping a bit for Booker Washington in 1904. Early in the year, Edgar Murphy, one of the participants on the Ogden Express (an annual train tour for white philanthropists of favored black vocational colleges, organized by the Tuskegee trustee Robert Ogden), wrote to Ogden in March 1904 of Washington: "Poor fellow! I am glad he does not see – and cannot see – the situation as it is." With the election of Theodore Roosevelt in the presidential election of 1904, Washington lost the influence he had enjoyed in the McKinley administration in having African Americans appointed to federal positions. Then Washington's primary champion, the white philanthropist William Baldwin Jr., died of a brain tumor in early 1905. Washington suffered collateral damage when Roosevelt summarily discharged without honor and without pension 167 of 170 black soldiers (including six Medal of Honor winners and some with twenty-five years of service) in the Twenty-fifth Infantry Regiment (Colored), which had served honorably in battles at home and abroad, after some members of the regiment allegedly killed a white bartender and injured a police officer in Brownsville, Texas. "Politics will yet KILL the great Tuskegee school," exclaimed the Cleveland *Gazette*. "*Mark our prediction!*"[54]

Du Bois did his part as well. Writing "Then and Now" in his own short-lived paper, *The Moon Illustrated Weekly*, in May 1906, Du Bois asked if Frederick Douglass or John Langston would have said, as did Washington, "not to worry over 'Jim Crow' cars but to proceed to buy up railways?" Or whether they would have suggested that ballot fraud "was an encouragement to industry?"

Then, after Atlanta erupted on September 22, 1906, in a race riot with ten thousand white people marauding through streets – where, according to the Atlanta *Constitution,* "in some portions . . . the sidewalks ran red with the blood of dead and dying negroes" – Du Bois essentially blamed the violence on Washington's 1895 Atlanta bargain. "Behold this maimed black man, who toiled and sweated to save a bit from the pittance paid him," he wrote in "Litany of Atlanta" in the October 11 *Independent.* "[Washington] told him: *Work and Rise!* He worked. Did this man sin? Nay, but someone told how someone said another did – one whom had never seen nor known. Yet for that man's crime this man lieth maimed and murdered, his wife naked to shame, his children to poverty and evil. *Hear us, O heavenly Father!*" For his part, Washington merely responded that the riot's aftermath provided renewed hope for the future: "I believe good in the end will result from the present trials."[55]

The Niagara conferences, offering "faith . . . among the thinking classes," continued for the next several years. The second Niagara meeting – where Du Bois insisted that women be allowed to participate – was held in August 1906 on the campus of Storer College in Harper's Ferry, to commemorate the hundredth anniversary of the radical abolitionist John Brown's birth. Du Bois's stirring "Address to the Country" was read at the final session:

> We claim for ourselves every single right that belongs to a freeborn American, political, civil and social; and until we get these rights we will never cease to protest and to assail the ears of America. The battle we wage is not for ourselves alone but for all true Americans. It is a fight for ideals, lest this, our common fatherland, false to its founding, become in truth the land of the thief and the home of the Slave – a by-word and a hissing among the nations for its sounding pretensions and pitiful accomplishments.[56]

Early in 1907, Du Bois launched another newspaper, *The Horizon: A Journal of the Color Line.* The *Horizon* was characteristically blunt on matters both global and domestic. Socialism, for example, is "the one great hope of the Negro American," he wrote, as it relates not to "the rich but the poor, not the great but the masses, not the employers, but the employees." "THIS IS A RADICAL PAPER," it blared, in terms Elizabeth Cady Stanton surely would have applauded. "It stands for progress and advance. It advocates Negro equality and human equality, it stands for Universal Suffrage including votes for women." The *Horizon* was ultimately fairly short lived, ceasing publishing in 1910, but it proved valuable training ground for Du Bois's next, wildly successful magazine venture begun later the same year. "On us rests to no little degree the burden of the cause of individual Freedom, Human Brotherhood, and universal Peace in a day when America is forgetting her promise and destiny," Du Bois announced in The *Horizon*'s pages. "Let us work on and never despair because pigmy voices are loudly praising ill-gotten wealth, big guns and human degradation. They but represent back eddies in the tide of Time. The causes of God cannot be lost."[57]

In the 1908 presidential campaign, he urged blacks to vote Democratic, commenting that even if "an Abraham Lincoln should [now] arise in the United States and if he should be a Jew in race or a Japanese in color, or a Negro in descent . . . his soul would be pressed and shut out of the republic of the civilized." The "Door of Opportunity" was rapidly closing. "Once we were told: Be worthy and fit and the ways are open," he ruminated at the 1908 Niagara Conference in Oberlin, Ohio. "Today the avenues of advancement in the army, navy and civil service, and even in business and professional life, are continually closed to black applicants of proven fitness, simply on the bald excuse of race and color."[58]

Life in Atlanta during these years was indeed trying for African Americans. Banned from the very public libraries for which their tax dollars were spent, segregation was imposed "more rigorously . . . [and] with more gusto, than in less commercial southern cities," explained Mary Ovington, who noted also the irony that Atlanta had "to endure the knowledge that its most distinguished citizen was black." When Europeans visited the famous Dr. Du Bois, they would stay at hotels "into whose lobby [Du Bois] might not step. They saw a caste system as if a Brahmin had laid out the city. And to acquire wisdom, they went up the hill to see this colored 'untouchable.'"[59]

Meanwhile, the Atlanta conferences continued to thrive. As Du Bois observed, this "small and poor southern college" was the only college or university conducting "systematic and conscientious study of the American Negro," and it established Atlanta University as a serious liberal arts player. Hampton Institute, by contrast, Du Bois explained with characteristic bluntness to a stunned Hampton audience in June 1906, was committing "educational heresy," not just in providing only vocational classes but also in doing so in a "manner and tone that would make Socrates an idiot and Jesus Christ a crank." At Hampton, "the President of the United States can with applause tell young men not to hitch their wagons to a star but to hitch them to mules. . . . [The] great duty before you and me and our people today is to earn a living," but Hampton's approach is "so fundamentally false as to call for a word of warning." It is unsurprising that Du Bois was not invited back to Hampton for another forty-odd years.[60]

In addition to everything else, in late 1908, Du Bois concluded five years of work on a book about John Brown, the abolitionist martyr of Harper's Ferry. Du Bois justified Brown's bloody actions in Kansas, suggesting that Brown was not a revolutionary, because revolution "is always a loss and a lowering of ideals." (By the time the second edition of *John Brown* was published in 1962, though, Du Bois's Marxist views had evolved to the point that he qualified his earlier dismissal of revolution: "But if it is a true revolution, it repays all the losses and results in the uplift of the human race.") Although Du Bois believed *John Brown* was in some ways "one of the best books I ever wrote," sales were decidedly lackluster.[61]

Du Bois's paper and presentation on Reconstruction, "Reconstruction and Its Benefits," at the American Historical Association meeting in December 1909 was (puzzlingly) admired by none other than fellow panelist William Archibald Dunning, the Columbia University history professor whose Southern-biased accounts of the "tragic era" of Reconstruction had influenced generations of historians and falsely skewed millions of Americans' understanding of the post–Civil War years. This paper, previewing his monumental *Black Reconstruction* some twenty-five years later, was Du Bois's first effort to correct the egregious reporting of the Dunning school. He asserted, for example, that Reconstruction's failure to improve the plight of blacks could be explained by the federal government's failure to support the Freedman's Bureau "for ten, twenty or forty years with careful distribution of land and capital and a system of education for the children." Contrary to the conventional wisdom told by the Dunning historians, "[t]he Negro governments in the South accomplished much of positive good.... We may recognize three things which Negro rule gave to the South: 1. Democratic government. 2. Free public schools. 3. New social legislation." Du Bois's paper was essentially ignored by mainstream historians, even though many of his perspectives in this and his later *Black Reconstruction* would be validated generations later as the more accurate by acclaimed professional historians.[62]

Du Bois's days in Atlanta, where he had become an authority of international renown, came to an end (for now) in July 1910, when he accepted the position of director of publicity and research at the brand new National Association for the Advancement of Colored People (NAACP) in New York City. "Stepping, therefore, in 1910 out of my ivory tower of statistics and investigation," he explained, "I sought with bare hands to lift the earth and put it in the path in which I ought to go." The NAACP's origins were in the National Negro Conference, which first convened in a fractious meeting in May 1909, bringing together blacks and whites determined to find a new way forward. "So the conference adjourned," Du Bois reported. "Its net result was the vision of future cooperation, not simply as in the past, between giver and beggar – the older ideal of charity – but," he added hopefully, "a new alliance between experienced social workers and reformers in touch on the one hand with scientific philanthropy and on the other with the great struggling mass of laborers of all kinds, whose condition and needs know no color line."[63]

Du Bois knew that to make real change, he would need to take on and deflate Booker T. Washington (who himself worked actively behind the scenes to discredit the nascent NAACP). In the March 1910 *Horizon,* for example, Du Bois commented, "[F]or the last eight years . . . the sole referee for all political action concerning 10,000,000 Americans" has been Booker Washington. The only ones who have advanced are those who have "giv[en] up . . . agitation and acquiesce[d] in semi-serfdom." "The vested interests who so largely support Mr. Washington's program," he accused, "are to a large extent, men who wish to raise in the South a body of black laboring men who can be used as clubs to keep white laborers from demanding too much." Oswald Garrison Villard (grandson of abolitionist William Lloyd Garrison) provided critical support in an *Evening Post* editorial on April 1, 1910, explaining the rift between Du Bois and Washington: "Eternal vigilance is the price of liberty for the negro . . . and Du Bois is merely living up to the highest traditions of American life when he fights for the rights of his own people to a voice in their government."

When he received word of Washington's propaganda campaign in England asserting that the race problem in America was nearly solved, Du Bois's written response, "An Appeal to England and Europe," was published (even before Washington left England) in the New York *Sun* on December 1, 1910, with signatures of support from twenty-three prominent African Americans. "Mr. Washington's large financial responsibilities have made him dependent on the rich charitable public," Du Bois explained. "He has for years been compelled to tell, not the whole truth, but that part of it which certain powerful interests in America wish to appear as the whole truth." The real truth, Du Bois corrected, is that "[o]ur people were emancipated in a whirl of passion, and then left naked to the mercies of their enraged and impoverished ex-masters."

Washington's statements "[are] like a blow to the face," he concluded. "It is one thing to be optimistic, self-forgetful, and forgiving, but it is quite a different thing, consciously or unconsciously, to misrepresent the truth."[64]

III. The Crisis

> *Boldly and without flinching, I will face the hard fact that in this, my fatherland, I must expect insult and discrimination from persons who call themselves philanthropists and Christian gentlemen.... [M]ay God forget me and mine if... I ever weakly admit to myself or to the world that wrong is not wrong, that insult is not insult, or that color discrimination is anything but an inhuman and damnable shame.*
>
> – W. E. B. Du Bois, 1913

Already late for a public dinner engagement, the man rushed to catch the elevator. Just as he reached the door, appearing beside him, like an apparition, was another late arriver – probably the one person on earth the man would least wish to encounter at that moment.

The man stepped on nonetheless, finding a spot among the other passengers and fixing his gaze on the counter above the door as the attendant closed the gate.

"I cannot believe... he is on this elevator," the man, W. E. B. Du Bois, thought as the elevator began its ascent. "Of all people, the traitorous lunatic – Marcus Garvey."

Marcus Garvey had a similar reaction as he recognized the familiar goateed visage of Du Bois. "Oh God," he muttered to himself. "It's Du Bois, the self-hating 'half-breed' himself."

Some of the other passengers were keenly aware of the irony of the bitterly acrimonious leaders of the two major competing black movements being on the same elevator. The two men had been lobbing bombshells at each other for several years now.

"[Du Bois] is but an unfortunate mulatto who bewails every day the drop of Negro blood in his veins," Garvey, the dynamic Jamaican whose United Negro Improvement Association advocated the Black Zionist goal of repatriating African Americans to Africa, had charged. "That is why he likes to dance with white people and dine with them and sometimes sleep with them."

"Beware The Demagog," Du Bois, the charismatic editor of the NAACP's *The Crisis* monthly, warned of Garvey. "He will come to lead, inflame, lie and steal. He will gather large followings and then burst and disappear...." He sabotages meaningful reform "by exploiting the cleft between our incipient social classes."

But here they were together, standing silently face forward on a Harlem elevator in early 1923 – Garvey trembling violently, Du Bois with nose flaring noticeably. Neither could have known it at the time, but their battle would soon climax – and only one would remain standing.[65]

The primary vehicle Du Bois would use for the next twenty-four years to fight for the rights of his people came in the form of a monthly magazine put out by the NAACP called *The Crisis: A Record of the Darker Races,* edited by Du Bois, "with the cooperation of Oswald Garrison Villard." *The Crisis* (named after James Russell Lowell's poem "The Present Crisis"), was created in 1910 in the best tradition of earlier militant papers like Frederick Douglass's *North Star* and William Lloyd Garrison's *Liberator* and reflected the editor's belief "that this is a critical time in the history of the advancement of men." The magazine came "at the [ideal] psychological moment," Du Bois explained, and the first issue of one thousand sold out immediately, demonstrating that the third time was indeed a charm for Du Bois's efforts at magazine editing. Du Bois imbued the *Crisis* with a quasi-religious passion for justice and progress – along the way engendering a fanatical following, with prominent readers speaking years later of the magazine as having been "just like the Bible to me" or of how the *Crisis* in the childhood home "was strictly inviolate until my father himself had unwrapped and read it – often... aloud."[66]

Du Bois spewed venom from his *Crisis* bully pulpit. Reacting to a 1911 Pennsylvania lynching, he sneered, "Again the burden of upholding the best tradition of Anglo-Saxon civilization has fallen on the sturdy shoulders of the American republic." In this case, the victim had committed a murder, as Du Bois readily acknowledged, but

> the point is he was black. Blackness must be punished. Blackness is the crime of crimes.... It is therefore necessary, as every white scoundrel in the nation knows, to let slip no opportunity of punishing this crime of crimes. Of course, if possible, the pretext should be great and overwhelming – some awful stunning crime, made even more horrible by the reporters' imagination. Failing this, mere murder, arson, barn burning or impudence may do.... We have crawled and pleaded for justice and we have been cheerfully spit upon and murdered and burned. We will not endure it forever. If we must die, in God's name let us perish like men and not like bales of hay.[67]

Another cause Du Bois vigorously championed in the *Crisis* was women's rights (including the rights of black women in the women's organizations) and, in particular, women's suffrage. "Every argument for Negro suffrage is an argument for women's suffrage; every argument for woman suffrage is an argument for Negro suffrage; both are great moments in democracy," he expounded in the September 1912 edition, sounding much like the pre–Civil War abolitionists William Lloyd Garrison and Frederick Douglass at their finest. After five thousand woman suffragists, mostly white, were jeered, jostled, and generally harassed as they marched down Pennsylvania Avenue in Washington, D.C., he wrote with dripping sarcasm in "Hail Columbia" in April 1913, "Again the glorious traditions of Anglo-Saxon manhood have been upheld!" and described how the women "trudg[ed] stoutly" as men tried to "pull girls from their floats" and grab "flags from the elderly women." What impressive "Leaders of Civilization" these "magnificently vindicated white men" were – these men whose approach to women was to "[b]eat them back, keep them down; flatter them, call them 'visions of loveliness' and tell them that the place for woman is in the home, even if she hasn't got a home! Hail Columbia, Happy Land!"[68]

The story of Washington's public embarrassment in March 1911, when he was injured during a tussle with a jealous German American male friend of a woman Washington had been looking for at a reputed brothel on Manhattan's West Sixty-third Street, was met mostly with discreet silence from the *Crisis* and veiled private amusement among Du Bois and the Talented Tenth – but the incident did contribute to Washington's continuing slide. The NAACP's Villard offered condolences and a peace offering and, thereafter, the delegates at the third NAACP Conference in Boston issued a succinct resolution: "Resolved, that we put on record our profound regret at the recent assault on Dr. Booker T. Washington in New York City, in which the Association finds renewed evidence of race discrimination and increased necessity for the awaking in of the public conscience." The rapprochement would prove fleeting, however, after Du Bois published "Starvation and Prejudice" in the June *Crisis*. With Washington firmly in mind, he wrote, "Awful as race prejudice, lawlessness and ignorance are, we can fight them if we frankly face them and dare name them and tell the truth; but if we continually dodge and cloud the issue, and say the half truth because the whole stings and shames ... we invite catastrophe. Let us then in all charity but unflinching firmness set our faces against all statesmanship that looks in such directions."[69]

Forty-five years old in 1913, W. E. B. Du Bois had seen much, and he was mostly discouraged – and disgusted – with what he saw. In personal terms, his influence was increasing, whereas Booker Washington's was declining. "Mr. Washington is now a waning influence in the country amongst the colored people, [while Du Bois is] in the ascendancy," William Ferris wrote in 1913, adding that *Souls of Black Folk* "[is now the] political bible of the Negro race." Of his own widening reach and influence, Du Bois later wrote in *Dusk of Dawn*, "[My] stinging hammer blows made Negroes aware of themselves . . . so much so that today common slogans among the Negro people are taken bodily from the words of my mouth."[70]

As the lack of progress in America toward truly equal racial treatment – now nearly five decades after the heady early promise of Reconstruction – forced the stark realization that the repression of blacks was becoming, if anything, only more solidly entrenched, his words were becoming increasingly strident. With the *Crisis* as his platform, Du Bois delivered a steady stream of insurgent challenges to the establishment. "The jeremiads," he explained, "were needed to redeem a people." Few were immune from his acid pen, and he vigorously defended his writings against antagonists and sympathizers alike. After being questioned by a distinguished white supporter for denouncing as "falsehoods" Theodore Roosevelt's 1914 comments in Brazil that Americans "treat[ed] each man of whatever color absolutely on his worth as a man, allowing him full opportunity to achieve the success warranted by his ability and integrity," Du Bois replied:

> [The African American] has nothing but "friends" and may the good God deliver him from most of them, for they are like to lynch his soul. . . . [D]on't antagonize, don't be bitter; say the conciliatory thing; make friends and do not repel them; insist on and emphasize the cheerful and good and dwell as little as possible on wrong and evil. . . . But [the friend's] feet never walked the ways we tread. He does not know – he cannot conceive this darker world of insult, repression, hunger, and murder. . . . He and . . . millions of others have given no encouragement to lynching except by silence. Except by silence! EXCEPT BY SILENCE![71]

Just as for Elizabeth Cady Stanton and Vine Deloria Jr. with their own respective out-groups, it was always Du Bois's supreme mission to demand equal treatment and justice for African Americans; and his spirited defense of these principles was sometimes abrasive, even to friends. "He does do dangerous things. He strikes out at people with a harshness and directness that appalls me," Ovington admitted to Villard, "but the blow is often deserved and it is never below the belt." Recognizing that for Du Bois, there was no time for patience or lollygagging, Ovington tried to gently tell him that "there was something the matter with *The Crisis* from the viewpoint of its white readers." Must he insult readers "by saying that they are reactionary heathen... when they have no insult in their heart?" she implored. His old friend, the retired Horace Bumstead (president of Atlanta University during Du Bois's tenure there), found "it hard to defend him with friends who come to me with complaints," in light of his attacks in the *Crisis* on the Episcopal Church and others. "Is there something demoralizing in an editor's chair?" Bumstead pointedly asked.[72]

Another complaint among some prominent friends, including Jane Addams, Albert Pillsbury, and Florence Kelley, was that Du Bois was not evenhanded in his approach – he perhaps overcompensated for black grievances by not "absolutely even[ly]... scoring colored wrongdoers precisely as he scores white offenders." During one of his frequent disputes with Du Bois, Villard complained that he "never stops to ask what the facts are on the other side."[73]

The fact is, though, that Du Bois had reason to be vigilant, for many white supporters – even some on the NAACP board – did not truly support full "social" equality. Florence Kelley, for one, in 1920 threatened to resign unless the board renounced Du Bois's *Crisis* comment that social equality was "just as much a human right as political or economic equality." Social equality involved, at its root, the eight-hundred-pound gorilla in the room: interracial sex. The subject of black men with white women, whether or not married, was simply taboo. As Du Bois limned, race relations in America were "at bottom simply a matter of the ownership of women; white men want the right to own and use all women, colored and white, and they resent any intrusion of colored men into this domain." Du Bois was certain, for example, that the usually supportive *Survey*, edited by Paul Kellogg, had rejected one of his essays because he had urged every black to "demand his social rights: His right to be treated as a gentleman, when he acts like one, to marry any sane, grown person who wants to marry him."[74]

The problem Du Bois saw in the efforts of many well-meaning whites – a desire to help but discomfort when blacks were nondeferential or assumed greater responsibility – was a recurring theme. He detected this dynamic at work in the NAACP as well: "Ordinarily the white members [dominated] the committee formed of Negroes and whites. [But] if the

Negroes attempt to dominate and conduct the committee, the whites become dissatisfied and gradually withdraw." During one spring 1913 dispute, for example, Du Bois felt the need to inform NAACP chair Oswald Villard, "I count myself not as your subordinate, but as a fellow officer."[75]

Relations between Du Bois and the rest of the board eased considerably for a time when Du Bois's friend Joel Spingarn assumed the NAACP's chairmanship in 1914. (The two men were soul mates of sorts: "I do not think that any other white man ever touched me emotionally so closely," Du Bois said of Spingarn.) Admitting that he was "tired, too, of the philanthropy of rich white men toward your race," Spingarn told African Americans that he sought to help them "fight your own battles with your own leaders and your own money." Sometimes calling their mission together the new abolitionism, Du Bois and Spingarn orchestrated an aggressive national campaign from the NAACP offices at 70 Fifth Avenue. Even Spingarn's patience wore thin with Du Bois at times, though, as he expressed in a long letter in late 1914: "I do think, however, that like Roosevelt and other men I know and admire, you have an extraordinary unwillingness to acknowledge that you have made a mistake, even in trifles, and if accused of one, your mind will find or even invent reasons and quibbles of any kind to prove that you were never mistaken." Admitting this was a mere "trifle," Spingarn continued:

> Surrounding you always, I may say frankly, I have found an atmosphere of antagonism.... [E]ven some of your most intimate friends feel toward you a mingled affection and resentment.... I realized too (it was your boast) that you could never accept even the appearance of "inferiority" or "subserviency" without treason to the race ideals for which you fight, although on this matter it may be weakness rather than manliness to protest too much.... [Sympathizers] have come to feel that you prefer to have your own way rather than accept another way even when no sacrifice of principle is involved.... Now I shall not hide from you the fact that many people whose devotion to this cause is as deep as yours or mine feel that the time has come to put an end to this tragic trifling.[76]

Coming as it did from Spingarn, a man for whom he had the deepest respect, Du Bois took the letter as well as might have been expected, but true to form, he did not roll over. Some of the criticism was justified, he conceded; and the letter's spirit was "right and that, after all, is the chief thing." He admitted that his personality was "a difficult one to endure" but rationalized that given his "peculiar education and experiences,... it would be miraculous if I came through normal and unwarped." "But for heaven's sake let me do the work. Do not hamper and bind and criticize in little matters."[77]

The very fact that Du Bois maintained an uncompromising approach is an important part of his legacy, and his fierce resolve for equal justice was a major part of the message that has come through to millions of African Americans, then and now. Most blacks in 1915 shared the opinion of the principal of Washington, D.C.'s M Street Public High School, E. C. Williams, for example, that Du Bois's pugnacity "alone justifies the existence of the NAACP." As Lewis explains, "For the emergent class of urban-bred professionals, Du Bois *was* the NAACP" – and the NAACP leadership knew it. Recognizing that it must "attach an extreme value to [Du Bois's] services to the Association and the cause," the board (often grudgingly) "ma[de] the most sweeping concessions in order to give him free play to exercise all his abilities and energy and enthusiasm."[78]

Booker T. Washington's death on November 2, 1915, of kidney failure and high blood pressure brought on by syphilis marked "an epoch in the history of America," according to Du Bois in his respectful but direct obituary in the December *Crisis*. The "greatest Negro leader since Frederick Douglass, and the most distinguished [Southern] man, white or black" since the Civil War, Washington nonetheless also bore the "heavy responsibility for the consummation of Negro disfranchisement, the decline of the Negro college and public school and the firmer establishment of color caste in this land." But "[t]his is no fit time for recrimination or complaint," Du Bois continued, "Gravely and with bowed head let us receive what this great figure gave of good, silently rejecting all else."[79]

Du Bois took the opportunity of globally shifting sands in 1915 to publish "The African Roots of the War," his views on class, race, and capitalism, in the May *Atlantic Monthly*. The nub of his argument was that capital appeased white labor with state welfare and the threat of allowing "competition by colored labor." "By threatening to send English capital to China and Mexico, and by threatening to hire Negro laborers in America, as well as by old-age pensions and accident insurance," he explained, "[English capitalists] gain industrial peace at home at the mightier cost of war abroad." He darkly predicted, though, that unless the "democratic ideal [is extended] to the yellow, brown, and black peoples," colored majorities would someday have the means to rise up, at which point "[t]he War of the Color Line will outdo in savage inhumanity any war this world has yet seen."[80]

Ironically, and perhaps curiously, then, Du Bois welcomed the U.S. entry into World War I on April 2, 1917 – and in so doing, he got himself into a difficult spot with his supporters. Spingarn, who had himself entered the officer corps as a major, began pushing the idea of a special training camp for African American officers in Des Moines, Iowa, and he undertook an ambitious lecture tour to convince educated young African American men of the unique opportunity that service in the military could provide. Du Bois eventually supported Spingarn's idea. Many in the black press and other leaders believed Du Bois's approach was a major miscalculation. Trotter called Du Bois "a rank quitter of the fight for our rights.... [He has a]t last finally weakened, compromised, deserted the fight, betrayed the cause of his race." When Congress ultimately approved Camp Des Moines, Du Bois wrote triumphantly in a June 1917 editorial, "We have won! The camp is granted; we shall have 1,000 Negro officers in the U.S. Army! Write us for information." Responding to his critics, he reasoned (in terms eerily reminiscent of Elizabeth Cady Stanton when she postponed the women's movement during the Civil War): "When the storm is past," he said, "we can take up the idealism of the cause."[81]

An even bigger misstep, however, was his hasty summer 1918 decision to accept Spingarn's offer for a commission in military intelligence. Claiming "no inconsistency with or change of attitude" from his principles, he envisioned "[a] remarkable opportunity for far-reaching work" in the military. (Indeed, looking back, he said that "due to [Spingarn's] influence,... [I was] nearer to feeling myself a real and full American than ever before or since.") An especially unseemly aspect of the affair involved the fact that Spingarn assured officials in the Justice Department that Du Bois had promised to "change the [*Crisis*]" into "an organ of patriotic propaganda hereafter." Sure enough, Du Bois published "Close Ranks" in the July *Crisis*:

> This is the crisis of the world. For all the long years to come men will point to the year 1918 as the great Day of Decision.... We of the colored race have no ordinary interest in the outcome. That which the German power represents today spells death to the aspirations of Negroes and all the darker races for equality, freedom and democracy. Let us not hesitate. Let us, while this war lasts, forget our special grievances and close our ranks shoulder to shoulder with our white fellow citizens and the allied nations that are fighting for democracy.[82]

Although the press and others could not have known at the time of the promised quid pro quo, reaction to "Close Ranks" was severe. The *New*

York News characterized it as "crass moral cowardice"; the Pittsburgh *Courier* opined that "[t]he learned Dr. Du Bois has seldom packed more error into a single sentence." "[I am] unable to conceive that said advice comes from you," Byron Gunner wrote Du Bois. "[Wartime] is the most opportune time for us to push and keep our 'special grievances' to the fore." Du Bois himself recalled that "the words were hardly out of my mouth when strong criticism was rained upon it" by many. In fairly short order, despite initially defending his decision, Du Bois recognized his mistake and was able to concoct a face-saving escape, leaving him free "to work in *The Crisis* which was probably by far the best result." His *Autobiography,* interestingly, fails to mention the "Close Ranks" affair.[83]

Following the Armistice of November 11, 1918, Du Bois was one of fifty-two members of a press delegation who sailed aboard the *Orizaba* on December 8 to cover President Wilson's journey to Versailles. He was moved to tears by a ceremony in the Trocadero where soldiers of all colors were honored by the French Colonial League for their wartime valor, in distinct contrast to the treatment of American black troops. Checking up on the all-black Ninety-second Division in France, he found deplorable conditions for a group that "went through hell," leading Du Bois to comment acidly that "American white officers fought more valiantly against Negroes than they did against the Germans." Du Bois himself was so rudely treated by American army personnel that the local mayor of Domfront felt compelled to apologize and invited Du Bois into his home, where they sang "La Marseillaise" together. While in France, Du Bois also worked to help organize the Pan-African Congress to be held in Paris from February 19–21, 1919. "The African movement means to us what the Zionist movement means to the Jews," he explained. Specifically, it involves "the centralization of the race effort.... To help bear the burden of Africa does not mean any lessening in effort in our own problem at home.... Amelioration of the lot of Africa tends to ameliorate the condition of colored peoples throughout the world."[84]

On his April return, Du Bois penned "Returning Soldiers" for the *Crisis*, largely reconciling much of the acrimony caused by "Close Ranks" the summer before: "We are returning from war!.... But by the God of heaven, we are cowards and jackasses if now that the war is over, we do not marshal every ounce of our brain and brawn to fight a sterner, longer, more unbending battle against the forces of hell in our own land," he lectured. "We return. We return from fighting. We return fighting. Make way for Democracy! We saved it in France, and by the Great Jehovah, we will save it in the United States of America, or know the reason why."[85]

But instead of harmony, postwar America was a tinderbox of racial discord. "Negroes [came] back feeling like men and not disposed to accept the treatment to which they have been subjected," Moorfield Storey explained, and the social upheaval of the great northward migration of blacks, labor strikes, factory shutdowns, and fear of Bolsheviks combined to make the 1919 Red Summer one of the most tumultuous in American history, with racial riots in Longview, Texas; Washington, D.C.; Chicago, Knoxville, Tennessee; and Omaha, Nebraska. Add to that the lynchings in the South; 4 million workers going out on strike; assassination attempts on high-ranking members of the federal executive, judicial, and legislative branches; and anarchist bombings in six major cities culminating in a blast in September 1920 on Wall Street that killed thirty people, and it may have seemed as if the wheels were flying off. Against this backdrop, Attorney General A. Mitchell Palmer aggressively enforced the newly passed federal Espionage and Sedition Acts of 1917 and 1918 with so-called "Palmer raids" and other tactics to root out subversives, leading one historian to comment, "Not for half a century, perhaps at no time in our history, had there been such wholesale violation of civil liberties."[86]

Despite the silencing of a number of publications – especially those expressing communist or socialist sympathies – Du Bois and the *Crisis* managed to continue speaking out defiantly (which, not surprisingly, attracted the attention of the Justice Department). To the charges of political opportunist congressman (and future secretary of state and Supreme Court justice) James F. Byrnes from South Carolina that Du Bois had caused the race riots in Washington and Chicago and posed a grave threat to law and order, Du Bois responded in an October 1920 editorial that it was instead actually Byrnes and people like him who were responsible – not only for the urban riots "but also [for] encouraging for fifty years the lynching of 4,000 Negroes, the disfranchisement of a million and a half voters, the enforced ignorance of three million human beings and the theft of hundreds of millions of dollars in wages."[87]

One reason the *Crisis* was able to continue publishing was because at this early stage Du Bois did not himself advocate Bolshevism in his editorials. "We do not believe in revolution," he wrote in a June 1921 editorial, "The Class Struggle." "We expect revolutionary changes to come mainly through reason, human sympathy and the education of children, and not by murder," he explained, implicitly repudiating Marx's call for bloodshed. He warned, though, that zeal for preventing bloody

PHOTO 4. W. E. B. Du Bois, ca. 1919. Courtesy of Library of Congress.

revolution must not be used as pretext for curbing blacks' [and others'] civil liberties: "[I believe] in free speech and freedom to think, and it is the duty of every Negro to see that the right of black men to think and write and criticize shall not be abridged and taken away under the guise of curbing revolution."[88]

Du Bois continued to sharpen his criticism of the West. Instead of standing for "the possibility of human brotherhood," he said, "America falls far short of that ideal ... as far as black and brown and yellow people are concerned." Truth be told, he averred, "Europe has never produced and never will in our day bring forth a single human soul who cannot be matched or over-matched in every line of human endeavor by Asia and Africa" – including, to name just a few, Nefertari, Jesus, Muhammad, Askia, Confucius, and Buddha. At the second Pan-African Congress in London, Brussels, and Paris in late summer 1921, Du Bois led in crafting the "To the World" manifesto: to "correct maladjustment in the distribution of wealth, ... the outrageously unjust distribution of world income between the dominant and the suppressed peoples." Du

Bois understood that meaningful institutional change would not come easily or any time soon, but he was supremely confident that the messages emerging from this and other Pan-African congresses – for example, that pursuing a "doctrine of racial equality does not interfere with human liberty; rather, it fulfils it" – would eventually change the global power map.[89]

The *Crisis* reached its peak readership during the immediate postwar era, with a total monthly circulation of more than one hundred thousand in 1919. By two years later, however, in the midst of the depression of 1921, circulation had almost halved to fifty-three thousand, contributing to heightening tensions in an NAACP executive committee already annoyed by their famous editor's imperiousness. For a time, Du Bois summarily refused the cost-saving proposals of his fellow directors, until word of his potentially compromising relationship with Madeline Allison, an attractive assistant literary editor, raised sufficient outrage and questions among the board of his fitness to continue serving as editor that in July 1921 he eventually signed the board's take-it-or-leave-it written agreement declaring that "[a]ll special privileges will cease" and imposing greater accountability and supervision over his actions.[90]

The depression of the early 1920s took its toll on another of Du Bois's signature creations, *The Brownies' Book*, a magazine for "children of the sun," which began publishing in January 1920. Du Bois had created *The Brownies' Book* on the reasoning that "[h]eretofore[,] the education of the Negro child has been too much in terms of white people.... All through school life his textbooks contain much about white people and little or nothing about his own race." Through twenty-four issues, the publication presented plays, stories, beautiful illustrations, photographs, letters, and biographical profiles by and about black Americans, young and adult alike. Despite rave reviews and devoted readership, *The Brownies' Book* "cease[d] to be" in the difficult economic climate of December 1921.[91]

Despite these difficulties, Du Bois's renown continued to build. The NAACP's bestowal of the Spingarn Medal on him on the first day of the 1920 NAACP convention merely confirmed his stature as the preeminent black leader during the early postwar era. A few weeks after arriving back from Europe in September 1921, however, Du Bois found himself engaged in a battle he would spend the next several years fighting. Marcus Garvey, a dynamic Jamaican who staked out a position on black issues firmly to the left of Du Bois, had during the prior couple of years attracted a huge, enthusiastic following (parading through the streets of Manhattan and speaking before twenty-five thousand cheering acolytes at Madison Square Garden in August 1920, for example). "I hadn't heard anybody dramatize Africa in the way that Garvey had done it," the historian Charles Wesley observed, adding, "It would have appealed to Du Bois if he'd heard it." Garvey viewed Du Bois as an elitist and equivocator (much as Du Bois had earlier characterized Booker Washington) and, by the end of 1921, Du Bois and the Talented Tenth were becoming increasingly ridiculed and denounced by Garvey and his supporters as, for example, "reactionary under the [pay] of white men." (Others, too, such as *Negro World* editor William H. Ferris, criticized Du Bois's haughtiness – claiming he appeared to view the masses "from the heights of his own greatness.... [Du Bois may be] too aristocratic and hypercritical, too touchy and too sensitive, too dainty and fastidious, too high and holy to lead the masses of his race.") Although Du Bois later acknowledged the overall soundness of much of Garvey's program, he believed Garvey was an insincere opportunist, and he set out to discredit Garvey and some of the more radical views he espoused through his United Negro Improvement Association.[92]

The battle engaged, an unstable Garvey sought to ingratiate himself with the white establishment by suggesting it was patriotic to demonstrate racial bias – and even appealing to the Ku Klux Klan to help advance his agenda of urging black Americans to emigrate to Africa. Du Bois responded by writing that Garvey is the "most dangerous enemy of the Negro race in America and in the world." He is "either a lunatic or traitor...; not even... the hatefulest enemies of the Negro ever stooped to a more vicious campaign than Marcus Garvey, sane or insane, is carrying on." Du Bois, emphasizing that the best hope for the future was in working within the system to own property, become educated, and participate in the democracy, said, "[Garvey] is groveling before [white prejudice], and applauding it; his only attack is on men of his own race who are striving for freedom; his only contempt is for Negroes; his only threats are for black blood." Garvey's fall from grace was swift. He was sentenced to prison for five years on corruption charges and, thereafter, the Liberians (who did not want to accommodate a mass migration from the United States) and others formally distanced themselves.[93]

Attending the Third Pan-African Congress in London in late 1923 and early 1924, Du Bois felt again the sort of release he always experienced while traveling abroad. "My brown face attracts no attention,"

PHOTO 5. W. E. B. Du Bois in *The Crisis* Office, ca. 1920. Courtesy W. E. B. Du Bois Library, University of Massachusetts, Amherst.

he marveled. "I become, quite to my own surprise, simply a man." Following the Congress, he made his first trip to Africa as "special envoy" to Liberia on behalf of the United States, then to Sierra Leone and Senegal. A bit carried away with the possibilities of an official diplomatic position, he told the surprised Liberians that President Coolidge wished to express "publicly and unmistakably... [America's] interest and solicitude" toward its African "sister Republic."[94]

Du Bois's political and economic sympathies were evolving. He supported the progressive Robert "Fighting Bob" La Follette of Wisconsin for president in 1924, whose fourteen-point platform he thought was "one of the best programs ever laid down by a political party in America." (La Follette's impressive total of 4.8 million votes was a record for a third-party candidate but was still only a fraction to Coolidge's 15.7 million.) Increasingly discouraged throughout the 1920s about African Americans' political prospects, he lamented, "The Populists failed. The Socialists failed. The Progressives failed. The farmer-Labor movement failed" – all traceable, he believed, to the Southern-dominated Democratic Party's stranglehold on electoral politics. "The political power of this rump electorate is astonishing," he wrote in the *Nation* in 1928. "What is going to become of a country which allows itself to fall into such an astonishing intellectual and ethical paradox?" he beseeched. "Nothing but disaster," he answered. "Intellectual and ethical disaster in some form must result unless immediately we compel the thought and conscience of America to face the facts in this so-called racial problem."[95]

In addition, whereas five years earlier he had tweaked Russia in editorializing, "We do not believe in revolution," in 1926, he invited readers to consider "with open mind and listening ears," "the astounding effort of Soviet Russia to organize the industrial world." "Here was a people seeking a new way of life through learning and truth," he declared during his first visit to Russia in 1926. "Russia is at work – God how these officials work!" he raved. Observing on his return organized labor's exclusion of blacks in America, together with the victory of Herbert Hoover in 1928 (the "Victory of Wall Street and the KKK," according to Du Bois), he was more pessimistic than ever. "What has the [United States] to contribute to this world problem [of color]?" he asked. The answer: "[Nothing.] Darkness rather than light – paradox rather than logic." Even with his increasingly progressive (verging on radical) politics, Du Bois still had his critics to the left, including the militant *Messenger:* "The sixth award of the Spingarn Medal [went] to the King of Kings, William E. Burghardt Du Bois," it jabbed in 1926, "noted author, famed editor of *The Crisis,* intellectual Grand Lama of Aframerica and coiner of that militant wartime slogan: 'Close Ranks Let Us Forget our Grievances.'"[96]

Although Du Bois was finding it difficult to locate "a clear role for himself in the ranks of the Left," he was encouraged by the development in late 1929 of the League of Independent Political Action, led by John Dewey of Columbia University, with a platform essentially the same as that of La Follette, whom Du Bois had admired in 1924. Also emerging as a competitor for African American hearts was the Communist Party of the USA (CPUSA), which made strong inroads when it rushed to the defense of the Scottsboro boys (nine young black men who were quickly tried, of whom eight were sentenced to death by the Alabama courts for the alleged rapes of two young white prostitutes on a freight train) in April 1931 while the NAACP dithered. Recognizing the CPUSA's attempt to "build on th[e Scottsboro] case an appeal to the American Negro to join the Communist movement as the only solution to their problem," Du Bois returned fire by criticizing the CPUSA for its failure to understand the pervasiveness of racism in America, which Du Bois was convinced would survive even class revolt.[97]

He would hold these views for years, commenting in "Marxism and the Negro Problem" in the May 1933 *Crisis*, for example, that "[c]olored labor has no common ground with white labor.... The lowest and most fatal degree of [their] suffering comes not from capitalists but from fellow white workers." Marxism fell short by failing to "envisage a situation where, instead of a horizontal division of the classes, there was a vertical fissure, a complete separation of classes by race, cutting square across the economic layers.... [I]mported Russian Communism ignored, [and] would not discuss" this "incontrovertible fact," he explained. For their part, Communist Party leaders like Harry Haywood dismissed such assertions, urging instead for the "systematic but persistent struggle against the ideology and influence of petty bourgeois nationalists [that is, Du Bois] among the Negro toilers."[98]

Meanwhile, things were not going well at the *Crisis*. Money problems exacerbated Du Bois's always-touchy relationship with the NAACP board, to the point that even his old ally, Mary Ovington, warned him he was in danger of losing control to the board and particularly to Executive Secretary Walter White. "We do seem to have a good many bouts these days, [but my ability] for hero worship has left me," Ovington wrote Du Bois in 1931.[99]

Something had to give, so in the fall of 1932, Du Bois accepted John Hope's offer of a guest professorship back at Atlanta University for the spring 1933 term – enabling Du Bois, in a face-saving move (orchestrated by Joel Spingarn) to "have it go out to the world that he [was] leaving New York to accept an important post rather than because the paper [was] forced to suspend." Teaching two courses, Karl Marx and the Negro and Economic History of the Negro, Du Bois was pleased to be "again among intelligent and enthusiastic young folk."[100]

Around this time he began promoting new ideas on separation of the races, but he was disappointed with the early response at, for example, the Second Amenia Conference in August 1933. Du Bois had hoped the conferees would understand "the compelling importance of the economic factor" and agree that segregation appeared to be an unavoidable condition. And if this was so, he reasoned, why not work toward building a separate structure that would economically benefit African Americans? His ideas went nowhere, however – and Du Bois was left to conclude that the Talented Tenth conferees had "so subtly become infused with middle-class American 'success philosophy'" that they had forgotten the great mass of "'poor, ignorant, uncounseled and exploited black people.'"[101]

Du Bois continued to press this new separatist message – surprising as it was given his past demands for equal, integrated treatment. "What are we really aiming at?" he asked in "On Being Ashamed of Oneself" in the September 1933 *Crisis* (to which he was still contributing articles). "The building of a new nation or the integration of a new group into an old nation?" By now, he had concluded that it must be the former – the building of a new nation. This would require, if anything, increased segregation, and Du Bois suggested – sounding much like Marcus Garvey a decade earlier – "perhaps [even] migration." Although he was aware that his new posture would be "pounced upon and aided and encouraged by every 'nigger-hater' in the land," Du Bois was insistent. "The next step, then,... involves the organization of intelligent and earnest people of Negro descent for their preservation and advancement in America, in the west Indies and in Africa; and no sentimental distaste for racial or national unity can be allowed to hold them back from a step which sheer necessity demands." He amplified his views in his "Segregation" editorial in the January 1934 *Crisis:* "The thinking colored people of the United States must stop being stampeded by the word segregation.... [T]here should never be an opposition to segregation pure and simple unless that segregation does involve discrimination."[102]

Not surprisingly, Du Bois's words were explosive. Black newspapers opined that Du Bois was "slipping," and African Americans everywhere were stunned. William Hastie, the Interior Department assistant solicitor, could not believe "until my own eyes had convinced me Du Bois himself... (or not himself) making a puny defense of segregation and hair splitting about the difference between segregation and discrimination! Oh, Mr. Du Bois!" Hastie cried, "How could you?!" And, as Du Bois had predicted, some did use his controversial statements as justification to oppose integration.

The NAACP was shaken. Debating what official position to take, the association ultimately agreed on a statement repudiating Du Bois's position in no uncertain terms. "Enforced segregation by its very existence carries with it the implication of a superior and inferior group and invariably results in the imposition of a lower status on the group deemed inferior," the NAACP statement stressed. "Thus both principle and practice necessitate unyielding opposition to any and every form of *enforced* segregation." On May 14, 1934, the NAACP board voted by a strong majority to substantially curtail Du Bois's voice, after which he threatened yet again to resign; however, this time the board accepted his resignation, showing just how irreconcilable the breach had become. As Ovington commented in a letter to Villard, "Now we are rid of our octopus, for of late he has been draining our strength." For his part, Du Bois was philosophical, comforting an upset ally, "All is not yet vanity, and there is plenty to fight for and to do.... I am simply changing because I had to."[103]

And, of course, Du Bois did find plenty to do. He again found a permanent home at Atlanta University, whose board members had been among those who applauded his segregation essays. Aided by a generous Rosenberg stipend of $6,000 originally awarded in 1931, he continued work on a history of the Reconstruction that would correct the record of the egregious misrepresentations perpetrated by generations of Southern-dominated historians (led by William Dunning of Columbia University), who essentially portrayed a South victimized by the passage of the Constitution's Fourteenth and Fifteenth amendments, which opened the door to opportunistic Northern carpetbaggers and incompetent, depraved freed slaves. As Eric Foner writes in his award-winning 1988 book *Reconstruction,* "[The Dunning school's] rewriting of Reconstruction's history was accorded scholarly legitimacy – to its everlasting shame – by the nation's fraternity of professional historians... [and] shaped historical writing for generations."[104]

Black Reconstruction, published in 1935 by Alfred Harcourt (with characteristic late changes to the manuscript by Du Bois that led Harcourt to quip, "I must say that I wish you had had your afterthoughts first"), began exposing the Dunning school's invidious lies – a process fully completed only in the past couple of decades by new generations of historians like Foner. "The work of most of the students whom [Dunning] taught and encouraged has been one-sided and partisan to the last degree," Du Bois explained. "Southern teachers have been welcomed to many Northern universities, where often Negro students have been systematically discouraged, and thus a nation-wide university attitude has arisen by which propaganda against the Negro has been carried on unquestioned."[105]

The book was mostly well received at the time and survives to this day as one of Du Bois's most important works. "If anything finer has been written in English in recent years, [I am unaware of it]," Lewis Gannett enthused. Du Bois's "impassioned attack upon slave-minded historians" was most appropriate, Gannett continued, as was his rehabilitation of Senator Charles Sumner and Representative Thaddeus Stevens, congressional champions of the Thirteenth and Fourteenth Amendments. The

New York Sun praised Du Bois for exposing the "self-satisfied distortions of the period which have passed without challenge for the last thirty years" (some of which even laid fault at the feet of blacks for not being more enterprising during slavery), and the *New York Times* wrote that Du Bois was "absolutely justified in his rancorous onslaught on American historians of the Civil War period" – although he could have used more primary sources, and included fewer interpretations "shot through with Marxian economics." (Indeed, some of the more sustained criticisms of *Black Reconstruction* involved its "completely fantastic attempt," in the words of Talented Tenth critic Abram Harris, "at applying Marxian dogma to history."[106])

It is a telling commentary on American race relations in the 1930s that Du Bois would feel it necessary to write, in all seriousness, that he had told the book's history "as though Negroes were ordinary human beings." As Du Bois explained, even at the end of the Civil War, African Americans were viewed by many simply as subhuman:

> Of all that most Americans wanted, this freeing of slaves was the last. Everything black was hideous. Everything Negroes did was wrong. If they fought for freedom, they were beasts; if they did not fight, they were born slaves. If they cowered on plantations, they loved slavery; if they ran away, they were lazy loafers. If they sang, they were silly; if they scowled, they were impudent.[107]

As noted, such views still persisted nearly seventy years later (thanks in large part to the Dunning school), when Du Bois published *Black Reconstruction*.[108]

IV. Tilt to Asia and Africa: Legacy

> *We know and the saner nation knows that we are not traitors nor conspirators; and far from plotting force and violence it is precisely force and violence that we bitterly oppose.... Peace is not an end. It is the gateway to full and abundant life.*
>
> –W. E. B. Du Bois, 1949

There was a buzz in the air as the 450 doctors, lawyers, businessmen, and college presidents milled about greeting old friends and renewing acquaintances. The group of prominent African Americans was gathering on the campus of Ohio's Wilberforce University to honor the man who had inspired so many of them and countless others to strive for prominent stations in life while the prevailing competing orthodoxy had urged them to settle for a second-class existence of servility.

Conversations trailed off as the distinguished visitors, the embodiment of the "Talented Tenth" of African Americans who would lead the way to reform, found their seats and expectantly awaited the words of their intellectual forebear, eighty-year-old W. E. B. Du Bois, whose visit to Wilberforce on this August 1948 day marked a triumphant return to the site of his first teaching job as a young man more than fifty years before. Following introductory remarks from the lectern, it was Du Bois's turn to speak.

"Karl Marx stressed the fact that not merely the upper class but the mass of men were the real people of the world," Du Bois noted, shortly into his speech.

"OK, fair enough," the visitors thought, despite Du Bois's invocation of the controversial Marx. "After all, the ultimate goal has always been for us to help pull the rest of our people up as well."

The crowd became restless, however, as Du Bois pressed the point. Initially polite, forward-looking expressions turned into impatient sideways glances and whispered comments as Du Bois announced that the Talented Tenth must now "sacrifice and plan for such economic revolution in industry and just distribution of wealth, as would make the rise of our group possible."

This was simply too much. "For years we have worked to pick ourselves up and achieve in line with the exhortations of this man – now he is standing before us saying we must sacrifice all of that for a revolution?" the visitors asked themselves incredulously.

In the end, the answer from the 450 Talented Tenth disciples was no – they would not follow W. E. B. Du Bois on this next adventure. Instead, after his address, they left him sitting, alone, on a Wilberforce University campus bench.[109]

Nearly seventy years old in 1935, during a decade in which he began losing (to old age) friends and acquaintances of his own generation at an increasing rate, Du Bois was awarded a travel fellowship to Germany and Austria by the Oberlaender Trust. In connection with this trip, Du Bois began writing what would become, for the rest of his years, a drumbeat of defenses of the Asian powers Japan, Russia, and China. Writing first in Robert Vann's Pittsburgh *Courier* (for which Du Bois had agreed to write a column titled "A Forum of Fact and Opinion"), he would often stubbornly attempt to defend the indefensible. These writings began to solidify his alienation from mainstream African American supporters that had begun with his "Segregation" essays.[110]

On this occasion, Du Bois arrived in Germany in June 1936, several months after Hitler's invasion of the Rhineland and shortly before the Jesse Owens Berlin Olympics, which he opted mostly to skip, traveling instead to Paris. Du Bois was mightily impressed with the Third Reich's German efficiency, informing *Courier* readers that "public order is perfect." "The whole nation is dotted with new homes for the common people, new roads, new public buildings and new public works of all kinds"; unemployment was low, trains ran on time, and commerce appeared to be booming. He recognized, though, that all was not well. Three years earlier he had suggested that Hitler would be at home at a number of American Southern white universities, where "[t]hey might not understand his German, but his race nonsense would fit beautifully." Now, after departing Germany, he wrote solemnly, as one who had "seen much," that the anti-Semitic activities there "surpassed in vindictive cruelty and public insult anything" else he had ever seen.[111]

Aboard the train traveling across Russia toward his planned visit to Japanese-occupied Manchuria, he ruminated on the revolutionary event he thought was the most important historical development since the French Revolution. "Russia is a World," he wrote. "In any state, a residue of men will sink to the bottom or never rise. Always an elite of ability, training and spirit will lead." In contrast to capitalist societies where a majority is at the bottom, "Russia declares that the majority of mankind can become efficient members of a culture state." Moreover, he added, "Russia says that the bread for the million masses is more important than diamond rings for the hundreds." "The only hope of human unity today lies in the common cause, the common interests of the working classes, in Europe, Africa and Asia."[112]

Once he reached the border at Manchukuo, his friend Hikida Yasuichi's detailed plans and influential contacts were much in evidence. Treated as an honored guest and shepherded with superior service from engagement to engagement on meticulous trains and roads, Du Bois believed Japanese imperialism would spell the overdue end of white Euro-American world domination. Responding to the West's criticism of Japan's expansion into Manchuria, Korea, and elsewhere, Du Bois fumed, "Gorged with the loot of the world, [Great Britain, France, and the United States] suddenly became highly moral on the subject of annexing other people's land. No! they said, and [so] Japan walked out . . . and took Manchuria."[113]

Traveling next to China, where he visited the Forbidden City, the Lama Temple, and the Great Wall, among other attractions, he was struck by the sheer vast quantity of available cheap labor. "Three things attract white Europe to China," he observed. "Cheap women, cheap child labor, cheap men." Du Bois, who thought the Chinese were overly submissive in "the same spirit that animates the 'white folks' nigger' in the United States," spoke his mind freely to a number of influential people in China about the importance of resisting Europe. "I plunged in recklessly," he recalled. "Why is it that you hate Japan more than Europe," he demanded of the Chinese, "when you have suffered more from England, France and Germany, than from Japan?" Europe could be expelled if China simply joined with Japan. The Chinese were not impressed; in fact, given the horrors of Japanese aggression, they were deeply offended – and *China Weekly Review* later accused Du Bois of being a paid Japanese propagandist.[114]

Concluding his travels with a trip to Japan (arriving in Nagasaki in early December 1936), Du Bois was effusive: "Nowhere else in the modern world was there a people so intelligent, so disciplined, so clean and punctual, so instinctively conscious of human good and ill." "Above all," he added, "[Japan is] a country of colored people run by colored people for colored people.... Without exception, Japanese with whom I talked classed themselves with the Chinese, Indians and Negroes as folk standing over against the white world." Du Bois admitted, though, that Japan does curb "freedom of spirit and expression," and "[t]here is poverty...; there is oppression; there is no democratic freedom."[115]

Writing after his return in "China and Japan" in the November 1937 *Courier,* five months after Japan's Rape of Nanking, in which 260,000 Chinese citizens were killed, Du Bois defended Japan even still: "It was Japan's clear cue to persuade, cajole, and convince China. But China sneered and taught her folk that Japanese were devils... Whereupon Japan fought China to save China from Europe and fought Europe through China and tried to wade in blood toward Asiatic freedom." Do not believe that Japan is the first to "kill[] the unarmed and innocent in order to reach the guilty," he lectured, pointing out that white European countries had committed atrocities of their own in South Africa, the Punjab, and Guernica. When Du Bois took these pro-Japan moral relativist arguments on the road to Negro colleges during 1937, Vann, citing declining circulation, cancelled his *Courier* column.[116]

As war clouds gathered over Europe and the Pacific, Du Bois initially urged the United States to abstain, and mocked the crocodile tears shed by the United States and Europe over the Soviet invasion of Poland and Finland. When all those of Japanese descent (whether U.S. citizens or not) in the United States were interned in the months following the attack on Pearl Harbor, Du Bois was one of only a few African American leaders to condemn the action. Commenting generally on the war, he wrote, "We close ranks again, but only, now as then, to fight for democracy not only for white folk but for yellow, brown and black. We fight not in joy but in sorrow with no feeling of uplift," he mused, "but under the sad weight of duty and in part, as we know to our sorrow, because of the inheritance of a slave psychology which makes it easier for us to submit rather than to rebel. Whatever all our mixed emotions, we are going to play the game."[117]

Pensioned at seventy-five years old in 1944 after his five-year contract was not renewed by Atlanta University, Du Bois felt briefly at a loss; but the NAACP (which had become a powerful force over the previous ten years, particularly with the litigation successes of its Legal Defense Fund led by Thurgood Marshall) stepped into the breach with an offer for Du Bois to become its well-compensated Director of Special Research. In making the offer, Executive Secretary Walter White expected Du Bois to say "a proper word now and then and give the association and its secretary moral support"; but, it is little surprise that Du Bois himself had much more ambitious goals for the position.[118]

Together with White (with whom on this occasion he formed an alliance of mutual respect) and black educator Mary McLeod Bethune, he was named one of the NAACP's delegates to the 1945 San Francisco conference to discuss the creation of a new United Nations. In this role, he persistently lobbied the organizing Commission to give greater voice to colonial peoples vis-à-vis the imperial powers, pointing out that nowhere in the drafts were there provisions "even to consider the aggression of a nation against its own colonial peoples," adding that "at least one-fourth of the inhabitants of the world have no part in [the United Nations], [and have] no democratic rights." He moved to include strong anti-colonial language in the Charter. Perhaps predictably, his efforts were unsuccessful.[119]

To Du Bois's and White's chagrin, the United States was failing to lead even on mainstream issues at the UN meetings – such as its failure to propose or advocate a basic human rights provision as a key part of the UN Charter. "Its timorousness and political mindedness has caused the U.S. delegation to lose, perhaps beyond regaining, the bold moral leadership which it should have taken," White scolded. "Russia and China have taken the play away... on the colonial trusteeship, while the smart boys... appear to have outsmarted our delegation on purely political grounds." Testifying before the Senate Foreign Relations Committee on July 11, 1945 (to the extreme annoyance of White, who believed Du Bois was upstaging him), Du Bois urged the Senate to ratify the Charter, but with reservations that the "pressing cries of 750 million unrepresented... were not expressed or [were] even forgotten" at the San Francisco meetings. The Senate ratified the UN Charter on July 28, 1945, without Du Bois's proposed reservations.[120]

Du Bois continued his strident attacks against colonialism in other venues as well – receiving mainstream praise for his 1945 book, *People of Color,* for example, with the *Saturday Review* opining that it contains "enough dynamite to blow up the whole vicious system whereby we have comforted our white souls and lined the pockets of generations of free-booting capitalists." At the Fifth Pan-African Conference in October 1945 in Manchester, England (where George Padmore introduced him as the "father of Pan-Africanism" whose thinking was "more alive than many a youth's"), Du Bois orchestrated the "Challenge to the Colonial Powers," announcing: "We are not ashamed to have been an age-long patient people.... [But we will no longer perform] the world's drudgery, in order to support by our poverty and ignorance a false aristocracy and a discredited imperialism.... We want the right to earn a decent living; the right to express our thoughts and emotions." "We must impress upon the world that it must be Self Government."[121]

His focus shifted then to working with a five-member group at the NAACP to create *An Appeal to the World: A Statement on the Denial of Human Rights to Minorities in the Case of Citizens of Negro Descent in the USA and an Appeal to the United Nations for Redress,* for presentation to the United Nations Commission on Human Rights. Through a couple rounds of discussions in late 1947 and into 1948, there was substantial support among the Charter's signatory nations (including Poland, India, the Scandinavian countries, the Soviet Union and Eastern bloc) for *An Appeal to the World.*[122]

Du Bois's active lobbying did not sit well with the American authorities, however. Even Eleanor Roosevelt was vexed and asked White to arrange a meeting with Du Bois. Mrs. Roosevelt told Du Bois at their June 30, 1948, Park Avenue meeting that the State Department believed "no good could come from such a discussion," so it would be counterproductive "to put *our* petition" on the agenda. Du Bois answered that everyone "ought to know exactly what the situation was in the U.S."[123]

Nor was the NAACP, which by now was aligning with the Truman administration's hard-line position on communism, pleased. Even though Du Bois still leveled some criticisms against communism, he was becoming more sympathetic with the radical left, writing in *The World and Africa,* published by Viking in 1947, "if a world of ultimate democracy, reaching across the color line and abolishing race discrimination, can only be accomplished by the method laid down by Karl Marx, then that method deserves to be triumphant no matter what we think." In mid-May, 1948, his "Open Letter to Stalin" (proposing that the United States and Russia start fresh in their efforts for peace), while praised on Radio Moscow by Josef Stalin himself, was utterly rejected by the Truman administration and harshly criticized as treasonous by the Americans for Democratic Action. The NAACP leadership was further angered when Du Bois's 1946 speech (combining poetry and radical politics) at the communist-dominated Southern Negro Youth Conference in Columbia, South Carolina, was reprinted as a fifteen-page pamphlet in *New Masses,* and widely circulated among the far left. It was not much of a surprise, then, when Du Bois took his radical views to the group that was for so long the very source of his strength, the Talented Tenth, at Wilberforce University in August 1948, as dramatized previously. It was also not much of a surprise, given the successes and material gains of the hundreds of prominent African Americans in attendance, when they essentially showed even the great W. E. B. Du Bois the door.[124]

Indeed, the NAACP and Du Bois's opinions had diverged to such an extent that at its September 13, 1948 meeting, the board voted to inform Du Bois that "at the expiration of his present term, his contract will not be renewed." The action could not have been unexpected – even a couple of years earlier White had threatened such action, commenting, "During the year 1945 certain actions by yourself seriously interfered with the smooth operation of the NAACP as a whole" (including appearing before the Senate Foreign Relations Committee "without notifying the association.") But still Du Bois would not back off – characterizing Truman's plans to arm Greece against Russia, for example, as the "most stupid and dangerous proposal ever made by the leader of a great modern nation," designed patently "for the profit of the American oil millionaires" and the benefit of British imperial designs.[125]

Even with the setbacks of these years (including the defeat of his preferred 1948 presidential candidate, former vice president Henry Wallace of the Progressive Party), Du Bois was characterized in the huge best seller of 1946, *Inside USA*, by John Gunther, as holding "a position almost like that of Shaw or Einstein, being the most venerable and distinguished of leaders in his field"; *Negro Digest* placed him at the head of the list "The Big Ten Who Run America"; and Henry Steele Commager's 1948 list of "Men Who Make Up Our Minds" compared him favorably with Franklin and Jefferson. Had this book and these lists appeared just a few years later, however, it is doubtful he would have been so honored, given how far Du Bois's stature had fallen.[126]

In 1949 and after, Du Bois continued writing for the left – this time, at the suggestion of Herbert Aptheker, for the new radical weekly, *New Guardian*. He was speaking and appearing at many other events as well. At the culmination of the 1949 Cultural and Scientific Conference in New York City, which generated huge anticommunist protests, Du Bois declared the conference a success in a speech at Madison Square Garden: "In a time of hysteria, suspicion and hate," he observed, the organizers had launched one of the "largest gatherings of creative artists and thinkers the world has seen." There were disagreements, yes, "but in one vital respect our agreement is complete: *No more war!*" Speaking to the hysteria in the streets, in the papers, and over the airwaves, he responded (as quoted previously in full): "We know and the saner nation knows that we are not traitors nor conspirators.... What we all want is a decent world.... Peace... is the gateway to full and abundant life." Shirley Graham, Du Bois's regular companion, observed even some of the policemen in the Garden applauding.[127]

Speaking at the World Congress of the Partisans for Peace in Paris in April 1949, attended by two thousand delegates, Du Bois urged, "Let us not be misled. Leading this new colonial imperialism comes my own native land, built by my father's toil and blood.... Drunk with power, we are leading the world to hell in a new colonialism with the same old human slavery which once ruined us; and to a third world war which will ruin the world." After this comment, Morgan State canceled Du Bois's planned June 8 commencement address. Traveling on to Moscow, he spoke to a crowd of six thousand. (On July 1, 1950, his wife, Nina, passed away, prompting his reflection in "I Bury My Wife" that he had essentially sacrificed her happiness to his work for the race. Nina was buried in Great Barrington next to son Burghardt.)[128]

Du Bois took on a new role as chair of the Peace Information Center beginning in 1950. Shortly before departing for Prague in August 1950 to attend the World Youth Conference (where he also visited granddaughter Du Bois Williams, who had moved to Prague and fallen in love with a Czech filmmaker), Du Bois received word that the Justice Department was requiring the Peace Information Center to register as an "agent of a foreign principal within the United States." After his return, in October 1950, the center voted to disband rather than bother with the Justice Department's registration requirement.[129]

The Justice Department would not be dissuaded, however – a grand jury indicted Du Bois to appear on February 16, 1951, in *United States v. Peace Information Center*. On February 16, he was fingerprinted and briefly handcuffed before his grand jury appearance. "It is a curious thing," Du Bois ruminated with reporters afterward, "that today I am called upon to defend myself against criminal charges for openly advocating the one thing all people want – peace."[130]

By the time the trial finally arrived on November 8, 1951, after multiple effective delay tactics by his attorney Vito Marcantonio, much, but not all, of his domestic support had vanished. The NAACP did not take sides, and the Talented Tenth stayed at arm's length, but a remarkable assemblage of groups and individuals from around the world – including Latin America, China, Vietnam, Bulgaria, the Soviet Union, the black Caribbean, Djibouti, French Somaliland, Martinique, and Madagascar – pledged their support. Once the trial began, it soon became clear that the government had a very weak case – and Marcantonio eviscerated the government's arguments of parallelism (that is, that similar approaches by the Peace Information Center and European communist groups proved a subversive connection). The judge, James McGuire, dismissed the case without even sending it to the members of the jury, for to do so would "permit them to speculate on a speculation" – a quick ending to the case that foreclosed the appearance of character witness Albert Einstein, who had offered to do "anything" to help Du Bois. Reflecting on the case and the ostracism that followed, Du Bois said, "It was a bitter experience, and I bowed before the storm. But I did not break."[131]

Du Bois stood as a "tower of strength" throughout the dark McCarthy years. "He was constantly being called upon," his second wife, Shirley Graham Du Bois recalled, "to speak to some embattled harassed group, to appear as a witness before some committee or even in court, to sign a petition, to visit a family bowed in grief because one of its members had been 'taken away.'" By now he was an unabashed ideologue, adopting a mentality where actions of his friends – the Soviet Union and

China – were excusable; but those of his enemies – the United States and Europe – were not, regardless of their merits. He failed to categorically condemn the Soviets' crushing of dissent in Eastern Europe in 1956, for example, and he was "quite prepared to believe that [although] Stalin was at times a cruel taskmaster" (as more fully revealed by Khrushchev at the Twentieth Party Congress in 1956), "the world progresses; men reel and stagger forward; and never before in the history of man, have they made so gallant and successful a struggle as in the Soviet Union."[132]

With the exception of "see[ing] the impossible happen" in *Brown v. Board of Education,* Du Bois was exceedingly pessimistic about the prospects for liberty and equal justice in the capitalist system practiced in America and the West, commenting, for example, that "the organized effort of American industry to usurp government surpasses anything in modern history." He applauded Martin Luther King's Montgomery boycott, but he wished King would address the class-struggle issue – and he was genuinely skeptical of King's Baptist-preacher roots.[133]

With all but the remnants of McCarthyism dormant by the late 1950s, it became less dangerous for the politically correct to associate with Du Bois. His ninetieth birthday celebration at the Roosevelt Hotel in New York in 1958 drew one thousand people (including his two-month-old great-grandson). And "[feeling] like a released prisoner," he was able to travel abroad again for the first time in eight years, after the Supreme Court in 1958 ordered the government to process the passport applications even for those (including Du Bois) who refused to submit an anticommunist affidavit.

That same year he journeyed to England (staying for a month in Paul and Essie Robeson's flat), Eastern Europe (receiving honorary degrees in Prague and in Berlin from his old school, now Humboldt University), the Soviet Union (standing in a place of honor with Khrushchev in Red Square for a parade and being awarded the Lenin Peace Prize), and China (where his birthday was declared a national holiday). In Russia, he defended the ruling class's authoritarianism even while maintaining his Marxist dogma, commenting that "the overwhelming power of the working class as representing the nation is always decisive ... [but] as the workingman is today neither skilled nor intelligent to any such extent as his responsibilities demand, ... [the party is justified in] directing the proletariat toward their future duties." Visiting in China (despite the U.S. government's ban on travel to the People's Republic), he told a group of Chinese university students, "[O]ne thing alone I own and that is my own soul. Ownership of that I have even while in my own country for near a century I have been nothing but a 'nigger.'" To Mao, Du Bois rued that he wished he had done some things differently throughout his career; to which Mao, shaking his head, responded, "['A man's only mistake is to lie down and let the enemy walk over him.'] This I gather, you have never done. You have continued the struggle for your people, for all the decent people of America."[134]

On July 1, 1960, Du Bois returned to Africa, this time to celebrate the creation of the Republic of Ghana. Prime Minister Kwame Nkrumah issued a standing invitation for Du Bois to move to Ghana to do funded research on his *Encyclopedia Africana* – an offer he prepared to take up the following year. Before leaving, however, he mourned the death of daughter Yolande (lamenting, "death should have taken me first").

At the age of ninety-three, when the Supreme Court upheld the McCarran Act (allowing the government to force, at pain of imprisonment and large fines, registration of communist organizations), he formally joined the Communist Party on October 1, 1961, stating: "Today, I have reached a firm conclusion. Capitalism cannot reform itself; it is doomed to self-destruction." Criticizing American two-party politics, he urged reformers to "[m]ake it possible for the people to express their will. Today the rich and powerful rulers of America divide themselves into Republican and Democrats in order to raise ten million dollars to buy the next election and prevent you from having a third party to vote for, or to stop war, theft and murder by your votes." Du Bois did see a shred of hope, however, with the beginnings of student activism: "Students at last to the rescue, even in the West."[135]

Moving to Ghana for good in 1961, W. E. B. and Shirley Graham Du Bois settled into a home in an expensive Accra neighborhood, where they moved about the city and countryside in a Russian Chaika given to them by Khrushchev. There, Du Bois worked on the *Encyclopedia Africana* and met weekly with students and others on his veranda, listening intently and offering occasional comments. University of Ghana's Vice Chancellor O'Brien recalls that on one such occasion, when a student criticized an African leader as "just another Booker T. Washington": "The old man stirred like a tortoise putting its head out of its shell. 'Don't say that. I used to talk like that,'" he said, and remembered an aunt's advice to him many decades earlier: "'Don't you forget that that man, unlike you, bears the mark of the lash on his back. He has come out of slavery.... You are fighting for the rights here in the North. It's tough, but it's nothing like as tough as what he had to face in his time and in his place.'"[136]

Recognizing the old man's failing health, visitors came to pay respects. After the U.S. embassy refused to renew his passport because he was a communist, on his ninety-fifth birthday, Du Bois broke ties with America and formally became a citizen of Ghana. That same day, the University of Ghana gave him an honorary degree, and Prime Minister Nkrumah and his wife joined him for dinner. Du Bois grasped Nkrumah's hand tightly as he prepared to depart, thanking him for allowing him to spend his last days in Africa. He had just one regret: "I failed you – my strength gave out before I could carry out our plans for the encyclopedia. Forgive an old man." Nkrumah left in tears.

Six months later, at 11:40 P.M. on August 28, 1963, W. E. B. Du Bois died – the very day of the massive March on Washington, where Martin Luther King told an assembled throng of 250,000 marchers at the Lincoln Memorial, "I have a dream . . . that my four little children will one day live in a nation where they will be judged not by the color of their skin, but by the content of their character."[137]

"Someday the people in this country," biographer Truman Nelson predicted in a 1958 *Nation* article, "will demand that their own records be set straight, and alongside the political accidents, the Presidents and Senators, will go the enduring and usable truths of the American Prophets. Among these Prophets will be W. E. B. Du Bois."[138]

Few Americans have done as much to shape the social landscape of their day as Du Bois. "Only Frederick Douglass and Martin Luther King, Jr.," Marable suggests, "equalled Du Bois's role in the social movement for civil rights in the United States. But in other respects:

> Du Bois's diverse activities over nearly a century left a larger legacy. Du Bois was the "father of Pan-Africanism" and a central theoretician of African independence; the major social scientist, educator, critic, and political journalist of black America for two generations; and an important figure in the international movements for peace and socialism.[139]

He spent the bulk of his life demanding that African Americans be accorded nothing less than equal justice – as mandated, incidentally, by the inscription on the portico of the U.S. Supreme Court building, which states simply: "Equal Justice Under Law." In a nation unwilling to move fully beyond its slavery-stained history, Du Bois identified, prodded, and often ridiculed a social orthodoxy and official culture that endorsed egregious injustices on the meaningless basis of skin color. In so doing, he created something that had "never existed before, a Negro intelligentsia; and many who have never read a word of his writings are his spiritual disciples and descendants."[140]

At the risk of imprisonment and possible death, Du Bois refused to compromise his principles. "A stubborn determination at this time on the part of the Negro race, to uphold its ideals . . . means victory," he declared; "[whereas] a course of self-abasement and surrender . . . means indefinite postponement of the true emancipation of the Negro race." History provides unhappy examples of those who have capitulated. Another "dangerous soul," for example, Galileo Galilei, "started to know, to observe, to prove, to dream. In doing so he met the Opposition – the obstacles that ever block the way of the man who proposes in thought or deed, something New." But when the Catholic Church threatened him with torture, he renounced his life's work. "Did it pay? Was the truth worth a lie?" Du Bois asked, and answered himself: "[No.] The verdict of civilization must be that not even the splendor of the service of Truth done by Galileo Galilei can wipe away the blot of his cowardly lie. By that lie, civilization was halted, science was checked, and bigotry was more strongly enthroned on its crimson glory."[141]

So, for a radical like Du Bois, he simply had no choice but to continue the fight – even when his pugnacious, sometimes-irascible approach caused him substantial difficulties and alienated even his own friends. (The octogenarian Du Bois knew well the price he paid in sticking stubbornly to his principles, darkly joking, "I would have been hailed with approval if I had died at fifty. At seventy-five my death was practically requested.") Happy is the man, though, he reasoned, "who fights in despair and in defeat still fights."[142]

Like Roger Williams, Thomas Paine, Elizabeth Cady Stanton, and Vine Deloria Jr., Du Bois fought for a more tolerant society – one whose government tolerates people of color as equal members of the American polity and tolerates free expression and association. Truly, he argued, it is not asking too much to "simply . . . make it possible for a man to be both Negro and an American, without being cursed and spit upon by his fellows, without having the doors of opportunity closed roughly in his face." And it is not asking too much, as one who has "obeyed my country's laws even when I thought some of these laws barbarous," to be allowed to "believe in Socialism as well as Democracy" without being called before the courts of the land and threatened with imprisonment. The practice of punishing dissenting thought, Du Bois believed, threatens the very fabric of American democracy: "Such reasoning in the past would have hanged Washington and Jefferson, sent Garrison, Douglass and Phillips to jail for life, and imprisoned Eugene O'Neill and Harry Hopkins."[143]

And like this book's other four radicals, Du Bois identified organized religion as a major source of society's ills. "I have no particular affection for the Church," he wrote in 1907. "I think its record on the Negro problem has been shameful.... So far as the Negro problem is concerned the southern branch of the Church is a moral dead weight and the northern branch of the Church never has had the moral courage to stand against it." His harsh criticism was not reserved to any one Christian faith. Though praising some Catholics for their philanthropic work in the colored South in his 1924 book *The Gift of Black Folk*, he charged that "the Catholic Church in America stands for color separation and discrimination to a degree equalled by no other church in America, and that is saying a very great deal." "[I]t is [a] shame that 'nigger' haters clothed in [the Catholic Church's] episcopal robes," he jabbed in the July 1925 *Crisis*, "should do to black Americans in... segregation and exclusion from opportunity all that the Ku Klux Klan ever asked"; the Christian churches were failing because they had forgotten the true teachings of "Jesus, the Jew." "The church of John Pierpont Morgan," he counseled, "[is] not the church of Jesus Christ."

Although his harshest words were reserved for white Christian churches, he did not hesitate to speak out against black organized religion as well. When black churches in Washington, D.C., forbade Clarence Darrow, an avowed agnostic, from delivering a lecture in 1928, for example, Du Bois wrote, "Such witch hunting would have barred Lincoln and Garrison and Douglass... [and] the greatest of religious rebels was Christ" himself. Speaking at Fisk University in 1938 on the occasion of his seventieth birthday (where he received an honorary doctorate of letters), Du Bois criticized black organized religion for its culpability in the abysmal state of black elementary education. "Instead of building edifices, paying old debts, holding revivals, and staging entertainments," he scolded, the black church needed to modernize – a task for which "the Hebrew Scriptures and the New Testament canon" are ill equipped.[144]

"W. E. B. Du Bois's singular greatness lay in his quest for truth about his own people," the Rev. Martin Luther King said on the centennial celebration of Du Bois's birth in February 1968. "[His] greatest virtue was his committed empathy with all the oppressed and his divine dissatisfaction with all forms of injustice." And his impact extended beyond America as well – he was continually surprised and pleased to be reminded in his later years how much his tireless work for equal justice, African self-determination, and world peace had influenced heads of state, trade unionists, scholars, and other notables in various nations throughout Africa and the rest of the world.[145]

Du Bois was far from perfect – "few would commend," for example, "the ideological and geographical resting places of his final years," David Lewis suggests. "No doubt he was precipitous in totally writing off the market economy, [but he] was right to insist that to leave the solution of systemic social problems exclusively to the market [causes] obscene economic inequality in the short run and irresoluble political calamity in the long run." Martin Luther King Jr. urged that we accept Du Bois in all of his complexity: "Some people would like to ignore the fact that he was a communist in his later years. It is time to cease muting the fact that Dr. Du Bois was a genius and chose to be a communist." More broadly, King suggested, Americans need to begin to see beyond antiquated ideological prejudices: "Our irrational obsessive anticommunism has led us into too many quagmires to be retained as if it were a mode of scientific thinking."[146]

Du Bois's moral relativist defenses of repressive regimes in Japan, the Soviet Union, and China are troubling – it is difficult to understand how a person as finely attuned to injustice as Du Bois could be so blind to the violations of basic human rights perpetrated by other nonwhite countries. At a certain point, however, he became so frustrated and furious after decades of slights, offenses, and abuses against people of color in America and beyond that he began to see things in terms of a kind of global race war, where the goal of resisting white oppression justified virtually any means by people of color.[147]

Du Bois's white-hot anger with an unjust society is reminiscent of the reactions of Roger Williams, Thomas Paine, Elizabeth Cady Stanton, and Vine Deloria Jr. to injustices during their own respective eras. The unique cast of mind of these individuals may offer an explanation, if not excuse, for some of their excesses. As Lewis explains of Du Bois (but that may apply equally to the other four as well): "He was an intellectual in the purest sense of the word – a thinker whose obligation was to be dissatisfied continually with his own thoughts and those of others." All five were intelligent persons who were convinced, to the very core of their beings, of the existence of self-evident truths in the natural order: All human beings, created equal as they are, are possessed of certain inalienable rights – including life, liberty, and the pursuit of happiness – that no government of human design can take away from them. These intuitive values were memorialized – and immortalized – in the Declaration of Independence. In the end, it takes these kinds of stalwart individuals, who refuse to buckle to intense societal and institutional pressures, to effect real and lasting meaningful change.[148]

5

Vine Deloria Jr. (1933–2005)

Betrayals and Bridges

The primary goal and need of Indians today is not for someone to feel sorry for us and claim descent from Pocahontas to make us feel better. Nor do we need to be classified as semi-white and have programs and policies made to bleach us further.... We need fewer and fewer "experts" on Indians. What we need is a cultural leave-us-alone agreement, in spirit and in fact.

– Vine Deloria Jr., 1969

I. Context and Beginnings

From a certain hill on the Pine Ridge Sioux Reservation in South Dakota, it is possible on typical summer afternoons to look out over the expanse to see towering cumulous clouds marching in orderly regiments toward the distant horizon. Lowering one's gaze then to the ravine and meandering creek below, one might imagine the events that occurred at this very spot in 1890.

Focusing intently, it is seemingly possible still to make out within the valley mist the shapes of several dozen ghost tepees, with wisps of smoke curling lazily from their smoke holes, camped near the banks of the creek. In a clearing among the tepees is an ephemeral group of Sioux warriors seated in a circle, surrounded by several ranks of apparitional blue-coated U.S. Army soldiers with locked-and-loaded artillery guns.

"All of you men bring your guns and arms and stack them in the middle," an army officer demands of the Indians. Groups of soldiers then enter the tepees, bringing out axes, knives, and tent stakes, piling them near the guns. "Remove your blankets," the officer orders, "so we can see you are not hiding anything."

It is hard to see exactly what happens next, but as a medicine man, Yellow Bird, defiantly begins chanting a holy song and dancing the steps of the feared Sioux Ghost Dance, a young Sioux of poor reputation, Black Coyote, holds his prized Winchester over his head while shouting that the rifle belongs to him and had cost much. As several soldiers grab him, the rifle discharges – and then all hell breaks loose. A deafening "lightning-sound" of tearing canvas and powder smoke immediately fills the air as the army troops begin indiscriminately firing their carbines into the Indian encampment. Then comes a brief lull in the din.

In the whispering, whistling wind, one can almost hear the wails of the defenseless women and children.

Then, from that very spot on the hill overlooking the scene, the army's Hotchkiss guns begin firing volley after volley of deadly shells – about one every second – spreading grapeshot and shrapnel into the tepees and at the retreating Indian men, women, and children. In the end, some three hundred Sioux men, women, and children are dead.

"We tried to run," Wounded Knee survivor Louise Weasel Bear said, "but they shot us like we were buffalo."[1]

Vine Deloria Jr. visited the site of the 1890 Wounded Knee Massacre as a young boy in the late 1930s–early 1940s – an event he later called the "most memorable" of his early childhood. The visit must have left a lasting impression on Deloria of America's harsh treatment of Indians – an impression that ultimately led, after an adolescence and young adulthood of trying to escape his Indian past, to four decades of lecturing, writing, and cajoling on behalf of Native American peoples. His was a strong, articulate, unifying voice for all Indians.[2]

Like Roger Williams, Thomas Paine, Elizabeth Cady Stanton, and W. E. B. Du Bois, Vine Deloria Jr. detested oppressive authority, and he spoke out passionately for broad recognition and tolerance by the dominant U.S. government of Indian sovereignty, self-determination, and traditions. "What we [Indians] need," he demanded, "is a cultural leave-us-alone agreement, in spirit and in fact."

Deloria, as we shall see, sought to educate people that under the terms of their historically unique political arrangement with the United States, Indian tribes are entirely separate (albeit dependent) sovereigns. As such, they are entitled, under well-established principles of international law, to the respect given any other such sovereign state. Early on, the U.S. Supreme Court (if not the president and Congress) recognized these principles. "The settled doctrine of the law of nations is, that a weaker power does not surrender its independence – its right to self government, by associating with a stronger, and taking its protection," Chief Justice John Marshall wrote in reference to Indian tribes in the 1832 *Worcester v. Georgia* case. "A weak state, in order to provide for its safety, may place itself under the protection of one more powerful, without stripping itself of the right of government, and ceasing to be a state.... 'Tributary and feudatory states,'" Marshall continued, quoting the Swiss scholar Emmerich de Vattel, perhaps the leading international law scholar of the day, "'do not thereby cease to be sovereign and independent states.'" In short, Deloria explained, the dominant society is duty bound to leave the tribes alone to exercise their sovereign rights of government.[3]

Moreover, Deloria added, Indians stand apart (not more or less favored – just apart) from other minority groups in America. When a federal or state court (as opposed to a tribal court) asserts jurisdiction over people, whether Indian or non-Indian, on reservation land, for example, Deloria and other Indian law experts view the issue as involving tribal political rights as opposed to civil rights or racial justice. "The larger issue at stake in nearly all Indian law cases," Professor David Getches has written, "is the relationship of tribes to the United States – a matter rooted in centuries-old policy created as part of the nation's constitutional framework."[4]

Also like Williams, Paine, Stanton, and Du Bois, Deloria – himself deeply spiritual – was harshly critical of Christian religious dogma. "The track record of individual Christians and Christian nations is not so spectacular as to warrant anyone seriously considering becoming a Christian," he declared. "From pope to pauper, Protestant to Catholic, Constantinople to the U.S., the record is filled with atrocities, misunderstandings, persecutions, genocides, and oppressions so numerous as to bring fear into the hearts and minds of non-Christian peoples." More than the others, however, Deloria was critical of dogma of any sort – including that of Western science, which he believed had itself become like a religion to many. He saw danger in the zealousness of rationalist thought wherein scientists "act like priests and defer to doctrine and dogma when determining what truths would be admitted, how they would be phrased, and how scientists themselves would be protected from the questions of the mass of people whose lives were becoming increasingly dependent on them."[5]

PHOTO 1. Vine Deloria Jr., ca. 1975. Courtesy of Philip J. Deloria.

Dubbed early in his career "the Rousseau of the new Indians" and "the red man's Ralph Nader," Deloria's influence has been profound; however, given the relative recency of his writings, his legacy is still a work in progress. As Indian law scholar Charles Wilkinson opined on Deloria's 2005 death, "If you mark down the great figures of the American West in recent times, he belongs there because of his role in reshaping Indian country.... I think in the last 100 years, he's been the most important person in Indian affairs, period." Clifford Lytle, his coauthor on two books, added, "It is a rare issue that does not have his footprints somewhere in the background."[6]

In addition to his quick, intuitive intelligence, Deloria's effectiveness is also attributable to the wealth of experience he acquired during his lifetime in many aspects of the dominant government and culture – first in receiving a degree in theology from a Lutheran missionary school; then directing the National Conference of American Indians, which put him in close touch with policy making in the federal executive and legislative branches; then earning a law degree, giving him a deep understanding of the federal judiciary and its decision making; and finally, working for years as an academic in the American higher education system. By the time he began publishing in his mid-thirties, Deloria had more than the normal insider's view. All these experiences provided him with especially keen insights into the workings of the dominant culture – insights that he leveraged into an advocacy that was at once strident and humble. Even though he "has been connected with most of the major movements in Indian politics" since the 1960s, Lytle explained, Deloria, true to his tribal heritage, "adopted a style of action that seeks to minimize public presence" – on the reasoning that fame can distract from important substantive issues.

Vine Deloria Jr. is known primarily for his advocacy of tribal sovereignty and self-determination. Yet there was another aspect of his work that may eventually transcend even his political efforts: his exploration of Native religions and, toward the end of his life, his brilliant work synthesizing Western rational thought and science with Native spirituality through the person of Swiss psychologist Carl Gustav Jung. "It is almost as if, looking down from a distance, we can watch as Sioux, Jungian, and scientific cosmologies draw close," Deloria observed in this final work, *C.G. Jung and the Sioux Tradition,* published posthumously in 2009: "Where Jung would say, 'Theoretically it should be possible to 'peel' away the collective unconscious, layer by layer, until we came to the psychology of the worm, and even of the amoeba,' the Sioux would simply say that such a demonstration proves we are related to all life and that possibility is self-evident. As the psyche is the world, so too is the Great Mystery."

These ideas resonate deeply with modern-day people of all nationalities. It is here, perhaps, that Deloria shares characteristics with his fellow radicals Roger Williams, Thomas Paine, Elizabeth Cady Stanton, and W. E. B. Du Bois on a deeper level. Might all five have been intuitively more closely attuned than most others to the great universal mystery – a state in which the common interconnectedness of all of creation (living and inanimate alike) allows as the only acceptable moral approach one in which the natural principles of liberty, equal justice, and tolerance are fully internalized and freely practiced?

A profound culture gap has always existed between the two major groups that have inhabited North America throughout human history – Native Americans first and the European settlers who followed. Indians have practiced a form of pagan spirituality premised on the unity between sacred landscapes and one's own existence, whereas Europeans were primarily agrarian Christians. Indians believed in the harmonic interconnectedness of all beings and things, whereas the newcomers viewed humans as placed on Earth by a stern God to rule and tame a wild planet.

It is perhaps inevitable that two neighbors with such divergent worldviews have conflicts – especially when they live in such close proximity. So long as each respects the other's boundaries, however, their differences – say, one neighbor prefers to keep her yard in its natural wildflower state and the other favors a more manicured lawn – should be of little concern. No worries. But when one of the neighbors – indeed, the noisy newcomer – begins to bully and eventually forcibly subjugates the other because of its desire for the old-time neighbor's land, it becomes an unconscionable ethical breach.

This is essentially what has happened over the centuries in North America with the original Indian occupants and newcomer Europeans. Early on, when "the Indian nations were the equal of any power on earth [,t]he European nations scraped and bowed before the Indian chiefs, hoping for allies to insure the existence of their colonies," Deloria explained. "Without the Hurons," for example, "the French would have been unable to exist in North America, and the Iroquois enabled the English colonies to withstand the might of the French and their Indian allies."[7]

Needless to say, the newcomers generally respected the Indians' boundaries during this era, although they advanced various dubious theories for superior title to the land based on their "higher" agricultural use as opposed to the "lesser" use of the itinerant Indians. (Deloria acknowledged, however, that not all Europeans held such views, including, specifically, fellow radical Roger Williams.) The 1786 Northwest Ordinance unequivocally laid out the new nation's deferential policy on Indian affairs:

> The utmost good faith shall always be observed towards the Indians; their land and property shall never be taken from them without their consent; and in the property, rights, and liberty, they never shall be invaded or disturbed, unless in just and lawful wars authorized by Congress; but laws founded in justice and humanity shall from time to time be made for preventing wrongs being done to them, and for preserving peace and friendship with them.[8]

Recognition by the nascent United States of full tribal sovereignty was reflected also in the 1787 Constitution, which expressly identified Indians as independent sovereigns in the all-important commerce clause, which gave Congress the power "to regulate Commerce with foreign Nations, and among the several States, and with the Indian Tribes"; and the taxation-and-representation clause, which excluded from the equation "Indians not taxed." The implication could not be clearer: in the eyes of the nation's founders, Indian tribes were themselves sovereign domestic "nations." Hence, in those days, the United States dealt with the tribes as they would any other nation, by negotiating and entering into treaties.[9]

Consistent with these legislative and constitutional directives, during the nation's early years, the United States adopted a pragmatic expansion-with-honor approach in its land acquisition efforts. As George Washington explained, "I repeat it, again, and I am clear in my opinion, that policy and economy point very strongly to the expediency of being upon good terms with the Indians, and the propriety of purchasing their Lands in preference to attempting to drive them by force of arms out of their Country." More generally, President Washington insisted that the proper mechanism for dealing with Indian tribes was through the treaty process. For its part, early Congresses agreed – providing, for example, in the Indian Trade and Intercourse Act of 1802, that tribal land cessions should occur only pursuant to treaty.[10]

After a few short decades, though, as the newcomers' power and security solidified, their voracious hunger for land increased and they began breaking promises – eventually taking over the Indians' land outright.[11] Reflecting on this history, a centenarian Creek Indian named Speckled Snake said around 1830:

> Brothers! I have listened to many talks from our great white father. When he first came over the wide waters, he was but a little man . . . very little. His legs were cramped from sitting long in his big boat, and he begged for a little land to light his fire on. . . . But when the white man had warmed himself before the Indians' fire and filled himself with their hominy, he became very large. With a step he bestrode the mountains, and his feet covered the plains and valleys. His hand grasped the eastern and the western sea, and his head rested on the moon. Then he became our Great Father. He loved his red children, and he said, "Get a little further, lest I tread on thee."
>
> Brothers! I have listened to a great many talks from our great father. But they always began and ended in this – "Get a little further; you are too near me."[12]

There would be little doubt in whose favor the U.S. Supreme Court would rule in early land disputes. In the 1823 *Johnson v. M'Intosh* case, Chief Justice John Marshall explained that the "discovering" nation had priority to acquire the land, whether through purchase or conquest, from the Native inhabitants. "Discovery gave title to the government by whose subjects, or by whose authority, it was made," Marshall wrote, "against all other European governments, which title might be consummated by possession." The discovery doctrine gave Indians the right of occupancy, to be honored and protected in law, of their own ancestral homelands – but such right could be revoked unilaterally by the discovering nation. Deloria emphasized that the discovery doctrine "did not invalidate Indian rights, since it only went to the power to extinguish [land title,] and that power rested solely with the hand of the federal government." Chief Justice Marshall specified that only "Christian people" could invoke the discovery doctrine, however. "An indigenous seafaring tribe, by contrast, could not plant a flag in the British Isles or on the beaches of Normandy and make comparable claims to England or France," Professor N. Bruce Duthu observed. "The potentates of the old world found no difficulty in convincing themselves that they made ample compensation to the inhabitants of the new, by bestowing on them civilization and Christianity."[13]

Writing a year after the eighteen-month 1969–70 Indian occupation of Alcatraz Island in San Francisco Bay, Deloria asked: "Is the U.S. any more justified in its claim to the land than the Indian militants of Alcatraz who claim also by Discovery? Do they not have the same claim to lands? Can one people simply 'discover' someone else's land and take it by force or trickery?" He answered: "To be consistent the U.S. government should re-examine its position as successor to the European invaders. If it intends to purchase the whole continent, however belatedly, it should do so. If not it should cede Alcatraz and other disputed lands."[14]

Despite *M'Intosh*'s self-serving discovery-doctrine rationale regarding property rights, the early Supreme Court nonetheless still believed that broad-based tribal sovereignty was mandated in the nation's constitutional structure. In 1832, for example, after Georgia courts sentenced a white missionary, Samuel Worcester, to four years of hard labor for violating a law making it a crime for a white person to reside in the limits of the Cherokee nation without having taken an oath to support and defend Georgia, Chief Justice Marshall emphatically announced in *Worcester v. Georgia* that "Indian communities are distinct political communities, having territorial boundaries, within which their authority is exclusive." Because the Constitution exclusively reserves the power to interact with sovereign Indian tribes to the federal government, it follows that it is entirely inappropriate for states to engage in Indian affairs.

Marshall explained that international law principles apply to United States–tribal relations because Indian tribes are sovereign nations that existed before the founding of the United States; and because they did not participate in the framing of the Constitution, they are outside the Constitution's scope. As with any other nation, the primary means to engage in nation-to-nation relations is through the treaty-making process. Following from the *Cherokee Nation v. Georgia* case the year before recognizing Indian tribes as "domestic dependent nations," *Worcester* described the relationship between the federal government and tribes as a form of trust arrangement, analogous in some ways to "that of a guardian to its ward." "Implicit in the relationship," Deloria explained, "is recognition of a degree of independence by the stronger to the weaker."[15]

Even during the first third of the nineteenth century when Chief Justice Marshall was elucidating the Supreme Court's deferential tribal sovereignty posture in *Worcester,* the other branches of the federal government took a radically different approach. In the executive branch, President Andrew Jackson was an unmitigated disaster for the tribes, with his views that Indians' choices were either to assimilate and be subjected to state authority or to move west beyond the Mississippi River. Indeed, after Marshall decided *Worcester,* Jackson reportedly said, "John Marshall has made his decision, now let him enforce it." Jackson disagreed with President George Washington's earlier assertion that the proper manner of dealing with tribes was through the treaty process, stating instead that the "proper guardian is the legislature of the Union." In this declaration were the seeds of the doctrine that survives to this day – that Congress has plenary power over Indian tribes. In other words, the European newcomers – who had been so anxious just fifty years earlier to enter into treaties with Indian tribes so as better to secure their own survival – considered themselves the Indians' masters and forced them to abide by their set of rules.[16]

The Cherokee tribe in Georgia did not wish to go along with Jackson's plans, however, and reminded the United States of its obligations in a memorial to the nation dated around 1830: "The treaties with us, and laws of the United States made in pursuance of treaties, guarantee our residence and our privileges, and secure us against intruders. Our only request is, that these treaties may be fulfilled, and these laws executed." Continuing, the Cherokee memorial appealed to Americans' sense of honor:

> We intreat [Americans] to remember the great law of love. "Do to others as ye would that others should do to you." . . . We pray them to remember that, for the sake of principle, their forefathers were compelled to leave, therefore driven from the old world, and that the winds of persecution

> wafted them over the great waters and landed them on the shores of the new world, when the Indian was the sole lord and proprietor of these extensive domains – Let them remember in what way they were received by the savage of America, when power was in his hand, and his ferocity could not be restrained by any human arm.... Let them bring to remembrance all these facts, and they cannot... fail to remember, and sympathize with us in these our trials and sufferings.[17]

All of this, alas, fell on deaf official ears. Congress acceded to Jackson's wishes and in 1830 passed the Removal Bill, "the first general law passed," Deloria explained, "giving authority to the executive branch to negotiate with the tribes to remove westward to avoid conflict with the advancing tide of white settlement." As the historian Howard Zinn detailed in his groundbreaking *A People's History of the United States* (1980), the Removal Bill offered tribes in Georgia, Alabama, and Mississippi a "choice": "The Indians would not be 'forced' to go West. But if they chose to stay they would have to abide by State laws, which destroyed their tribal and personal rights and made them subject to endless harassment and invasion by white settlers coveting their land. If they left, however," Zinn added, "the federal government would give them financial support and promise them lands beyond the Mississippi." The state of Georgia, supported by the federal government in the person of President Jackson who renegotiated the treaties with a small minority of wealthy Cherokees who were willing to leave, simply ignored Chief Justice Marshall's firm admonitions in *Worcester* and proceeded to put Cherokee land on sale, employing militia to crush any Cherokee objections.[18]

The "support and assistance" provided by the federal government in moving the tribes west during the ensuing years was criminal in its cruelty and incompetence, resulting in the deaths of as many as four to five thousand Choctaws and (later) Cherokees on the Trail of Tears, to cholera, pneumonia, heat, and exposure. "Marshaled by guards, hustled by agents, harried by contractors," Dale Van Every commented in his book *The Disinherited,* the Indians "were being herded on the way to an unknown and unwelcome destination like a flock of sick sheep."[19]

All of this was too much for some Americans. Chief Justice John Marshall himself privately commented that it was to his "greatest astonishment that, after hearing the arguments in both houses, Congress could pass [the Removal Bill]" and believed that it "affects deeply the honor, the faith and the character of our country." Author Ralph Waldo Emerson wrote an open letter in April 1838 to President Martin Van Buren, objecting to the injustice of the removal treaty with the Cherokees, which had been duplicitously signed without the approval of an overwhelming majority of the tribe. "The soul of man, the justice, the mercy that is the heart's heart in all men, from Maine to Georgia, does abhor this business," Emerson lamented. "[This is] a crime that really deprives us as well as the Cherokees of a country, for how could we call the conspiracy that should crush these poor Indians our government?" Emerson then challenged Van Buren directly: "You, sir, will bring down that renowned chair in which you sit into infamy if your seal is set to this instrument of perfidy; and the name of this nation, hitherto the sweet omen of religion and liberty, will stink to the world."[20]

Unmoved, Van Buren smugly reported in a December 1838 address to Congress: "It affords sincere pleasure to apprise the Congress of the entire removal of the Cherokee Nation of Indians to their new homes west of the Mississippi. The measures authorized by Congress at its last session have had the happiest effects."[21]

In the judicial branch, soon John Marshall had passed from the scene, replaced during the middle decades of the nineteenth century on the Supreme Court by justices unwilling to honor the nation's original obligations regarding Indian sovereignty. Now the Supreme Court completed the picture of all three branches of the federal government essentially aligned against tribal interests. Courts in states and territories were even worse. Little more than a generation after Marshall's thoughtful *Worcester* opinion, what passed for judicial wisdom in 1869 was of altogether different timber:

> The idea that a handful of wild, half-naked, thieving, plundering, murdering savages should be dignified with the sovereign attributes of nations, enter into solemn treaties, and claim a country five hundred miles wide by one thousand miles long as theirs in fee simple, because they hunted buffalo and antelope on it, might do for beautiful reading in Cooper's novels or Longfellow's *Hiawatha*, but is unsuited to the intelligence and justice of this age, or the natural rights of mankind.[22]

These dishonorable words, shocking from the supreme court of a territory (New Mexico) in a great nation, in fact epitomized the beginning of a concerted century-long U.S. effort to solve the Indian "problem" by essentially trying to eliminate the tribes – first through the systematic repudiation of treaties; then through various means including allotment and assignment of Indian children to boarding schools; then after a more hopeful (but equally vexed) period in the 1930s corresponding with the Indian Reorganization Act (IRA), through the morally bankrupt termination policies of the 1950s. Only with President Richard Nixon's 1970 directive to Congress "[to reject] the extremes of termination and paternalism because it resulted in the erosion of Indian initiatives and morale" did this sorry chapter end.[23]

Andrew Jackson's antitribal approaches became standard operating procedure for the federal government through the middle decades of the nineteenth century. "After 1834 it was merely a matter of time before the Congress usurped the self-governing powers of Indian tribes and substituted a large and cumbersome administrative agency to direct the lives of Indians," Deloria explained. "Gratuitous expenditures to encourage civilization soon became coercive measures to force assimilation. Indians were given no relief from this pressure, and by the 1880s almost everything that happened on Indian reservations was under the control of the federal government."[24]

Chief Justice John Marshall's offhand remark in *Worcester* that Indians were as wards to the United States' guardian, Deloria stated, "was transformed by the federal courts and Congress into a full-blown theory of wardship under which Congress had unlimited and plenary power to dispose of the lives and property of the Indians without any more justification than that it had the power and... wisdom to do so." When it suited the United States to consider Indian tribes wards, they were wards; when it suited the United States to consider them independent separate entities, they were separate entities.[25]

After the Supreme Court ruled in *Cherokee Tobacco* (1870) that "a treaty may supersede a prior act of Congress, and an act of Congress may supersede a prior treaty," Congress wasted no time ending the practice of treaty making in 1871: "That hereafter no Indian nation or tribe within the territory of the United States shall be acknowledged or recognized as an independent nation, tribe, or power with whom the U.S. may contract by treaty." Fulfilling Andrew Jackson's prophecy, Congress increasingly began claiming power to regulate affairs "*of* the Indian Tribes" – instead of "*with* the Indian Tribes," as expressly mandated in the Constitution.[26]

Beginning in the 1880s, Congress created the allotment system, a key aspect of the government's policy of forced assimilation of Indians into Western culture. Under the General Allotment Act of 1887 (Dawes Act), the president was directed to negotiate agreements with the tribes for the allotment of their lands among tribe members, with rights to the U.S. government to purchase any "surplus" and open it up to homesteaders.

Instead of proceeding in a measured, prudent manner, the Bureau of Indian Affairs (BIA) instead "pushed the policy on Indians as rapidly as possible," Deloria reported. "By the 1920s, Indians had lost a substantial portion of their land, and the BIA was leasing a major portion of their remaining lands either through the device of exercising a 'trust' over the property of the individual 'incompetent' Indians" or declaring a person competent and then quickly selling the land – sometimes without the person's knowledge. Indians who objected were labeled "irreconcilables," subject to arrest, incarceration, and forced apportionment. All told, between 1887 and 1934 (the year Congress repudiated the allotment system), total Indian landholdings diminished by almost two-thirds, from about 138 million acres to around 48 million acres.[27]

To little avail, tribal leaders tried to hold the federal government at bay by referring to treaties that specified the terms under which land cessions would occur. By 1895, "it was apparent that the U.S. was going ahead with tribal dissolution regardless of the treaty rights," Deloria explained. Typical of the "negotiations" undertaken during this period was the Great Sioux Agreement of 1889, which superseded parts of the 1868 Fort Laramie Treaty: "With General Crook sitting at the table the Sioux were reminded that if they didn't agree to cede their lands the Army would come in and exterminate them. In spite of the pressure, less than 10 [percent] of the adult males signed the paper agreeing to the cession," Deloria wrote. "Claiming total accord, the negotiators rushed to D.C. and pushed the agreement through Congress as a statute." As a result, the huge territory – almost all of western South Dakota – "was broken into a number of smaller reservations with separate agencies, each declared as executive-order reservations, thus depriving them of treaty-reservation status which holds a superior right to self-government."[28]

As noted previously, by the later decades of the nineteenth century and the turn of the twentieth century, the federal judiciary as well had become a full participant with the other federal branches in stripping tribes of their land and rights. In *United States v. Kagama* (1886), the Court endorsed the idea that under Congress's commerce-clause power, it possesses virtually unlimited "plenary" guardianship authority over Indian people and tribes. Ignoring Chief Justice Marshall's earlier international law analysis regarding the sovereignty of domestic dependent states, the Court reasoned, "The Indian tribes are the wards of the nation. They are communities dependent on the United States. Dependent largely for their daily food. Dependent for their political rights." It follows, the Court reasoned, that "from their very weakness and helplessness, so largely due to the course of dealing with the Federal Government with them and the treaties in which it has been promised, there arises the duty of protection, and with it the power" of Congress.[29]

Then, in *Lone Wolf v. Hitchcock* (1903), the Court held that Congress had always had the unilateral power to abrogate treaty obligations – "an assertion fraudulent on its face," Deloria charged. Phrasing the holding as necessary for Indians' own "care and protection," the Court reasoned that to require Congress always to obtain Indian consent (to obtain land for use in the allotment system, for example) would deprive it "in a possible emergency, when the necessity might be urgent for a partition and disposal of the tribal lands, of all power to act, if the assent of the Indians could not be obtained." Congress's guiding principles were "considerations of justice as would control a Christian people in their treatment of an ignorant and dependent race."[30]

"It was not only a shock, but a breach of common decency when Congress decided that it had absolute power over the once-powerful tribes," Deloria fumed. "When the Supreme Court also decided that such should be the policy in *Lone Wolf,* the silent conquest of unsuspecting tribes was complete.... That decision slammed the door on the question of morality and justice. It was like appointing a fox to guard the chicken coop." *Lone Wolf*'s outrageous effect was that "Indians had no chance whatsoever to acquire title or rights to lands which had been theirs for centuries."[31]

Deloria argued that Indian tribes never would have so willingly sacrificed their sovereignty, at least not without a struggle:

> Few tribes would have signed treaties with the United States had they felt that the U.S. would violate them. The promises of self-government found in a multitude of treaties, the promises of protection by the U.S. from wrongs committed by its citizens, the promises that the tribes would be respected as nations on whose behalf the U.S. acted as a trustee before the eyes of the world, were all vital parts of the treaty rights which Indians believe they have received from the U.S.[32]

In fact, the nation's earliest federal policy "was to contain the western frontier by getting the tribes to view the U.S. as a benevolent union which they might someday join," Deloria explained. "Indian nations were to be dealt with as sovereign entities on an equal footing with the United States." "In neither the Delaware [1778] nor the Cherokee treaty [1785]," for example, "is any claim made regarding the primacy of the U.S. over the self-governing functions of the tribe." He emphasized, moreover, that the various theories offered by the justices in *Cherokee Nation* do not "in any way support the extravagant claims now made by the U.S. and the Department of the Interior about their absolute power over the lives and lands of American Indians."[33]

Under long-standing international law principles, Deloria explained, the fact that Indian tribes elected to become dependent on the United States for some purposes in no way diminishes their sovereignty and rights of self-determination. "Indian tribes still have the right to be recognized among the nations of the earth," he emphasized, "even with the domestic legal doctrines of the U.S. guaranteeing the validity of their titles as held in a protected status by the U.S. against the European nations."[34]

In any event, Congress promptly cashed the blank check given it in *Lone Wolf* with multiple instances of opening up the Indian lands of the Plains and Mountain West for allotment. The allotment land grab continued well into the twentieth century, until the political climate changed sufficiently – largely because of the 1928 Meriam Report, attacking the Dawes Act, and the efforts of John Collier, "probably the greatest of all Indian commissioners," to force a change of policy by the federal government in the early 1930s. In 1934, Congress passed the IRA ("perhaps," Deloria remarked, "the only bright spot in all of the Indian-Congressional relations"), which expressly repudiated allotment and initiated programs enabling Indian recovery of lost lands, resulting in an increase of Indian holdings from 48 million to 52 million acres within a period of years. In addition, the IRA provided for Indian self-government of the reservations, whereby each tribe was given a right to have a constitution and charter under the law. "It was then up to the tribe to plan its own development to fit its own needs," Deloria commented. The constitutions had to be modeled after the American constitutional design, however, which substantially limited the tribes' governance options. Moreover, all plans had to be approved by the commissioner – and John Collier could be "quite dictatorial in enforcing his visions on tribes," suggests Professor Philip Deloria (Deloria's son).[35]

As much of an improvement as the IRA was, it was not all that it might have been. As originally proposed, "not even the most farsighted of Indian advocates was able to anticipate Collier's vision," Deloria said. Overall, "[a]s a reform measure, Collier's [actually, Felix Cohen's] original draft of the IRA was so thoughtful, philosophical, and ahead of its time that it had a hard time gaining credibility." After convening a number of Indian congresses around the country, "[o]n his return to Congress, Collier saw the program virtually gutted. The final version of the act, after all of the compromises forced by the Indians and the several Senators and Congressmen, did not remotely approach Collier's [and Cohen's] original version." "Perhaps the most important omission from the new law," Deloria later concluded, "was the absence of a provision creating a Court of Indian Affairs." Had the original plan for a national Court of Indian Affairs been followed, it "would have gone a long way in correcting the neglect and inattention that federal courts extended to Indian issues. The Anglo-American courts seemed both incapable and unwilling to address themselves to these Indian needs."[36]

Beginnings

This was the tumultuous cultural heritage into which Vine Deloria Jr. was born on March 26, 1933 (shortly before enactment of the monumental IRA). Born in Martin, South Dakota, on the border of the Pine Ridge Reservation, Deloria was the first child of Vine Deloria Sr., a prominent Dakota Sioux Episcopal missionary priest (and the first Indian to hold a national position in the church) and his Anglo wife Barbara Eastburn. Vine Jr. was descended from great-great-great-grandfather Philippe des Lauriers (anglicized later to Deloria), a French fur trader who married the daughter of a Yankton Sioux headman.

Philippe's grandson (and Deloria's great-grandfather) Françoise, pronounced "Saswe" in the Sioux, became a medicine man at the age of eighteen on the basis of a powerful visionary experience he had at the time. Saswe settled on the Yankton Reservation in 1858, serving thereafter as a trusted healer and leader of the White Swan community. He embraced the arrival of Presbyterian and Episcopal missionaries and welcomed their traditions, baptizing his children and grandchildren and sending some of them to parochial day schools.[37]

According to tradition, Saswe's status as a medicine man committed his descendants to serve as intermediaries with white society, a legacy begun when Saswe's first son (Deloria's grandfather) Philip Joseph Deloria (born Tipi Sapa – "Black Lodge") decided in 1870 at the age of sixteen to become an Episcopal priest, with the goal of helping his people adjust to life on the reservation. He did so for many decades, along the way becoming ordained as deacon in 1883 and priest in 1892, then overseeing all Episcopal mission work on the Standing Rock Reservation until his 1925 retirement. For his lifetime of service (some of which is described in a 1918 book, *The People of Tipi Sapa*), Philip is commemorated in the carvings behind the altar at the National Cathedral in Washington,

D.C., one of only three Americans among ninety-eight "Saints of the Ages."

Philip's only son, Vine (Deloria's father), also went into the ministry. Born at Standing Rock in 1901, Vine Sr. attended military school in Nebraska at the age of fifteen after his mother died and then went on to college in New York, where he considered attempting a professional sports career. After graduating from Episcopal seminary in New York City in 1931, he returned to serve at various parishes on and near Pine Ridge for seventeen years, then at Sisseton Mission in eastern South Dakota and an Iowa Anglo parish for three years each. He was named in 1954 assistant secretary for Indian missions in the National Council of the Episcopal Church (the first Indian national denominational executive) – a bureaucratic job he found extremely frustrating, so he left after four years to return to Iowa to another Anglo parish. Shortly thereafter, he was appointed archdeacon of all South Dakota Indian parishes, a post he held until his 1968 retirement.

"People came to my father for all sorts of things," Deloria recalled many years later. "He knew all kinds of medicine songs, [and] held on to the two cultures without much conflict until the late sixties." By that point, Vine Sr. was fed up with church orthodoxy. "The church put tremendous pressure on the Indians to integrate," Deloria explained, to which his father replied, "'We don't have to. We can be what we are without getting into the melting pot.'" This sentiment was common in Indian country, according to Deloria: "There are thousands of Indian Christians who looked upon Christianity in the old Indian way. The message of Jesus wasn't all that big. But a lot of the Indians were turned off and ended up with no religion. My father just gave up on Christianity."[38]

As a youth growing up on and near the Pine Ridge Reservation during the 1930s and 1940s, given his father's work, Deloria naturally participated in the ceremonies of the Sioux Episcopal Church; he also enjoyed traveling occasionally to the more traditional tribal dances. One of the most memorable events of Deloria's childhood, as dramatized earlier, was visiting the nearby site of the 1890 Wounded Knee Massacre, some of the survivors of which he would still see on the reservation during his boyhood. He went to an off-reservation school in Martin attended by an even mixture of whites and mixed-blood Indians.

"They taught us Rudyard Kipling's world view," Deloria recalled. "It was a simplistic theory that societies marched toward industry and that science was doing good for us. The U.S. has never been on the wrong side of anything. The government has never lied to the people. The FBI is there to help you, and if you see anything suspicious, call them." Unsurprisingly, there was "nothing about the slaves. Minority history just didn't exist. The world somehow is the garden of the white people, and everybody else kind of fits in someplace. And it's not demeaning to fit in, 'cause that's the way God wants it. You're not being put down. Western civilization's finding a place for you." About those teachings, Deloria reflected many years later, "It takes you a long time to realize these things aren't real." Before he came to this realization, though, Deloria went through a period during adolescence and young adulthood where he wanted nothing to do with his Indian heritage.[39]

II. Coming of Age: Tribal Sovereignty and Self-Determination

> *Who is to say that Indians cannot regain their independence some time in the future? Can one view the re-creation of the state of Israel after two thousand years of exile and seriously maintain that the Oglala Sioux will never again ride their beloved plains as rulers of everything they see? Or that the might of the Iroquois will not once again dominate the eastern forests? Consider. Consider.*
>
> – Vine Deloria Jr., 1974

"Son, what *am* I going to do with you?"

"I don't know, Dad," the teenage boy sheepishly replied, looking downward, accustomed to these little father-son talks.

The exasperated father was at his wit's end. His son – a bright, spirited boy – was finding too much trouble for himself.

First it was setting off a thunderous fireworks display over the gym during the high school graduation. Then it was jacking up cars outside church, placing wood under their axles and laughing at the whir of the spinning wheels as the parishioners attempted to depart.

The boy peeked up at his strict, old-school father standing with arms crossed and a stern look on his face.

The father had to suppress a chuckle in spite of himself. Even with his benign delinquency, the boy had a good heart.

But now with this latest transgression – leaping out of the classroom window during a lecture in favor of rabbit hunting – the father knew a change was needed.

"I'm going to send you away to school," Vine Deloria Sr. announced to his namesake son, Vine Jr. "It was good for me at your age, and it would be good for you as well."

And so it was decided – sixteen-year-old Vine Deloria Jr. would leave his home in South Dakota to enter Kent School, a private college-prep school in Connecticut, beginning in the fall term of 1949.[40]

The 1950s and 1960s

After graduating from Kent School in 1951, Vine Deloria Jr. attended college at the Colorado School of Mines in Golden before flunking out and then served a few years in the Marine Corps as a telephone repairman – an experience he remembered with fondness for the rest of his life.

He met his future wife, Barbara, after enrolling at Iowa State University in 1956, where he earned his bachelor's degree in general science in 1958 and was married that same summer. Yet to find his calling, Deloria pursued his best-available opportunity and moved with his bride of one year to Rock Island, Illinois, where he matriculated in 1959 at the Augustana Lutheran School of Theology to study theology and philosophy (working as a welder on the side to make ends meet).

The move into the ministry was not completely unforeseen – he had considered it earlier, but remembering his father's later dissatisfaction with church hierarchy, he had delayed. Although Deloria relished the life of the mind possible in such a setting, he criticized its lack of practical value. "[The] seminary," he said, "in spite of its avowed goals and tangible struggle with good intentions, provided an incredible variety of food for thought but a glaring lack of solutions or patterns of conceivable action which might be useful in facing a world in which the factors affecting human life change daily."

After graduating with a master's degree in theology in 1963, he worked on the staff of the United Scholarship Service (a church-supported philanthropy focusing on expanding educational opportunity) in Denver, directing a new program that helped find scholarships for Indian students to attend elite East Coast schools. Believing in the importance of setting rigorous criteria focusing on high academic performance, Deloria placed thirty students with scholarships in his first year. Despite these impressive results, the church hierarchy, accusing him of elitism, was unhappy with his nonpaternalistic approach.

Not surprisingly, Deloria was ready to move on, and the next year, an opportunity presented itself when he attended the National Congress of American Indians (NCAI) meeting in Sheridan, Wyoming. The organization he found there was struggling – in debt, with a conflicted philosophy, and a precipitously dwindling membership. Deloria was surprised, for example, that no one at the NCAI office in 1964 had even heard of the

PHOTO 2. Vine Deloria Jr., ca. 1955. Courtesy of Philip J. Deloria.

important 1959 U.S. Supreme Court *Williams v. Lee* opinion endorsing tribal sovereignty.

He was appalled, moreover, at the overall state of Indian advocacy, so he decided to run for executive director of the NCAI in 1964 and won. Recognizing the opportunities presented during the early years of the civil rights era, Deloria was determined to reform the NCAI into a viable organization. "What you could see," Deloria remembered, "was that the tribes just had to be more aggressive. The government was so terrified by civil rights that if we just threatened to act, we could prevail."

His three years at the NCAI – where he revived the organization from a moribund shell of 19 tribes to an assertive advocacy group of 156 tribes arguing in Washington against termination and in favor of increased tribal sovereignty – substantially heightened his own national profile.

The New Indians, for example, an important 1968 book by Stan Steiner reporting on the growing red-power movement, cited Deloria more than any other single individual. Deloria received a rapid education about tribal politics and white liberal paternalism while at the NCAI: "I learned more about life in the NCAI in three years," he remembered, "than I had in the previous thirty." The NCAI provided foundational intellectual experience as well. "This is when I started writing," he recalled. "I wanted to give good briefings before Congress. I got to love old documents and learning how to root around in them."

By now, Deloria and Barbara had three children: Philip born in 1959; Daniel, in 1960; and Jeanne, in 1963. Philip recalls that his father's move to advocacy starting in the mid-1960s did not come without a price. "Having Vine Deloria, Jr. in the family meant many things. In the NCAI, ... it meant he was absent for months at a stretch. It meant the sound of the typewriter clicking behind the walls all night long, and no phone calls until noon," Philip remembered. "It surely did not mean help with homework, or attendance at school events and baseball games, or relaxing family trips and vacations. It did mean having our phone tapped." Moreover, "it meant sharing him, first with hundreds, then thousands, and then millions of people, and it meant that there was no choice, really, about whether one wanted to share or not."

A frequent vacation destination for Deloria and his young family (as it had been for his own parents on an almost-annual basis during Deloria's own childhood) was, somewhat ironically, Mount Rushmore. Rushmore was located in the sacred Black Hills, after all, and thus was subject to the indigenous critique that "its imagery represents lethal practices of colonial & imperial domination; its location makes a mockery of the sacred Black Hills; its tourism asks visitors to forget the history and the presence of Indian people on the land." Nonetheless, a couple of generations of Delorias (so far) have developed a kind of "odd respect" for Rushmore with their frequent visits. (Deloria's son Philip related the family lore that during his father's childhood visits, Rushmore's sculptor Gutzon Borglum "held my father up (as he apparently did in every [visit]), proclaim[ing] that my father's skull was the most perfect skull in the world for sculpting, and he longed for the day when he could sculpt something of my father. I heard the story many many times on our nearly annual visits.")[41]

While at the NCAI, Deloria became increasingly convinced that the scarcity of trained Indian lawyers who could defend tribal sovereignty and treaty rights in the American legal system was a serious problem; so, practicing what he preached, in 1967, he resigned as NCAI executive director and enrolled at the University of Colorado Law School. He remained active while in law school, serving on the boards of several national organizations and as a consultant with the NCAI. There – like Stanton before him with the *Revolution* and Du Bois with the *Crisis* – he found a print outlet for his ideas in the *Sentinel*, a quarterly newsletter of the NCAI. His short *Sentinel* columns provided a preview of the caustic sense of humor and biting commentary on matters both inside and outside Indian country that would be a hallmark of Deloria's later writing.

Vine Deloria Jr. came of age just at the beginning of the hated termination era in the 1950s, during the "barren years" from 1945 to 1965 when "self-government virtually disappeared as a policy and as a topic of interest." As Deloria later described the era, "Indian affairs became a minor element in the American domestic scene; Indians became subject to new forms of social engineering, which conceived of them as a domestic racial minority, not as distinct political entities with a long history of specific legal claims against the U.S." In 1953, Congress passed two laws seriously threatening tribal existence, let alone autonomy: one ending tribal wardship status and terminating federal obligations to tribes (H.R. Conc. Res. 108) and the other giving broad permission to the states to assert authority over Indian tribes (P.L. 280). The Urban Relocation Program transferred Indian residents from reservations to cities; then the various termination acts, which ended the United States' political relationships with certain tribes, were the capstone.[42]

The overall effect, Deloria explained, was that tribes "in the 1950s and early 1960s ... had to spend all of their time defending their lands and treaty rights from terminationists. Little was done to develop the reservations because all energies went into saving them from obliteration." With the federal retreat, the affairs of many tribes were largely left up to the whims of the states.[43]

The federal judiciary got into the act again as well, when the Supreme Court held – just nine months after its landmark decision in *Brown v. Board of Education* (which had so cheered Deloria's fellow radical W. E. B. Du Bois) that, notwithstanding the Fifth Amendment's takings clause, which requires Congress to pay just compensation when it takes private property for public use, Congress could extinguish Indian land title without paying just compensation to the tribes. The Court reached this surprising result in *Tee-Hit-Ton v. United States* (1955) by rationalizing that Indian title is not property under the Constitution. In so holding, the

Court reverted back to some of the antiquated judicial language of Indian savagery employed in the original Indian land case nearly a century and a half before, *Johnson v. M'Intosh*.

In the important 1959 *Williams v. Lee* case, however, the Court held that a state court could not reach a reservation-based contract dispute between a non-Indian creditor and Indian debtor, on the reasoning that to allow state courts to hear the case would "undermine the authority of the tribal courts over Reservation affairs and hence would infringe on the rights of Indians to govern themselves." Even with its positive result, however, the *Williams* infringement test – "whether the state action infringed on the right of reservation Indians to make their own laws and [to] be ruled by them" – still left the door open for a state to "protect its interest up to the point where tribal self-government would be affected," whereas *Worcester* in 1832, in acknowledging Indians' exclusive authority in their own territory, had categorically closed the door to state interference. This infringement test has been used in the modern Court's stark turn against Indian tribal interests beginning in the mid-1980s – which, as we shall see, has kicked the door wide open in allowing state intrusions into Indian country.[44]

In the early 1960s, the National Indian Youth Council (NIYC) was formed with the express goal of renewing pride in Native traditions among Indians. This led then to a number of so-called fish-ins beginning in 1964 in Washington State, and the NIYC began to take a more active, militant role in Indian affairs. "Once the ideology of traditionalism was accepted by Indian youth," Deloria commented, "it slowly made its way across the age spectrum of Indian society, creating an exceedingly more aggressive edge to Indian relations with non-Indians."[45]

During the late 1960s, Congress began to become more active again in regulating Indian affairs, passing the controversial 1968 Indian Civil Rights Act (ICRA), which applied some of the rights contained in the Bill of Rights and the Fourteenth Amendment to tribes. (The ICRA was designed to protect Indian individuals from "arbitrary and unjust actions of tribal governments" while also taking into account the tribes' "unique political, cultural, and economic needs.")

In practice, Deloria explained, "ICRA radically changed the substance of tribal courts," forcing them to decide disputes in ways that newly "restrict[ed] the powers of Indian tribes with respect to their own membership." On the positive side, it "more clearly defined appeal procedures from tribal court to federal court," and it lessened the problem of Public Law 280 (which had ceded tremendous authority to the states to regulate

Indian affairs when passed in 1953). *Cohen's Handbook*, the foremost authority on federal Indian law, observes that ICRA has been an equal-opportunity target of criticism, however, from both those "who believe it went too far and those who believe it did not go far enough in constraining tribal actions." Although "ICRA was understood by most people as a major step toward the fulfillment of Indian self-government," Deloria wondered whether it "was... what Indians really wanted." Especially after such events as Alcatraz and Wounded Knee, "when we compare sacred pipe [traditional] and tribal court [modern] as two competing means of reconciliation and problem-solving, the two sides in the conflict become readily apparent."[46]

First principles beg the question of whether Congress even has the authority to enact such legislation as ICRA over sovereign (albeit dependent) Indian nations. Deloria notes the irony of a statute that would, in Senator Sam Ervin's words, "confer upon the American Indians the fundamental constitutional rights which belong by right to all Americans," when, by its express terms, "the Constitution does not apply to American Indians in their tribal relations, [and] does not protect Indian tribes." Indeed, the Supreme Court made precisely this point in 1896 in *Talton v. Mayes,* a case Deloria called "a great decision, which still has relevance to every Indian tribe that operates its own tribal courts." *Talton,* Deloria enthused, held that "the Bill of Rights did not apply to the relationship between the Cherokee Nation and its citizens because the Cherokee Nation had enjoyed self-government before the Constitution had been adopted! As did every other tribe!" The *Talton* opinion squares well with Chief Justice John Marshall's view of Indian tribes as existing in a state of tutelage, assuming at some date in the future "full status as nations in the world community. There was never an indication," Deloria explained, "that the tribes were to be destroyed and their individual members merged into the great American mass as citizens."[47]

Indeed, the civil rights issue ultimately goes back to the question of Indian citizenship – itself a matter of considerable dispute. Whereas almost every treaty signed between 1871 and the early 1900s (and then the 1887 General Allotment Act) provided that individual Indians could forswear their rights to treaty annuities and tribal assets in return for farming land allotments and citizenship, in practice, Indians who accepted citizenship on these terms did not get the full range of rights and privileges enjoyed by other citizens. In *Elk v. Wilkins* (1884), for example, John Elk, who had left his tribe's jurisdiction to move to Omaha and become a taxpaying homeowner and member of the Nebraska militia, was nonetheless held by the Supreme Court not to be a citizen entitled to vote. Then, in *United States v. Nice* (1916), the Court held that Indians remained subject to Congress's plenary authority even after they became U.S. citizens. It is little surprise, then, that "Indians soon got the message that equality was merely a guise under which their lands could be put up for sale while they were systematically denied any privileges of citizenship," Deloria criticized. "Thus, when Senators and Congressman speak today about giving 'full citizenship' and 'freeing the Indians,' it is an immediate tip-off that they've hatched some new scheme to deprive the tribes of further lands."[48]

Finally, Congress passed a one-paragraph law giving blanket citizenship to Indians in 1924. Indians have viewed the 1924 Citizenship Act with mixed feelings. Some tribes and Indians have disputed Congress's unilateral action – as late as the early 1970s, for example, the Pueblo of New Mexico "challeng[ed] the right of Congress to impose its foreign law," and the Iroquois "maintain that citizenship can't be forced upon them by the U.S. without their consent," Deloria remarked. "They refuse to vote and pay taxes and deny any citizenship but their own, even to the point of issuing their own passports to be used in traveling across the U.S.-Canada border."[49]

About the same time Deloria was beginning law school in 1967, following from the heightened militancy of the earlier NIYC efforts, "[t]he power movements... now began to affect Indians," Deloria recalled, and "'Red Power' naturally became a rallying cry." From Mohawk activists blocking the Cornwall Bridge across the St. Lawrence River in December 1968, claiming Canada had violated the Jay Treaty of 1794 (an event broadly covered in the fifty-thousand-circulation Indian newspaper *Akwesasne Notes*), to the organized Indian watch groups of police in Minneapolis–St. Paul resulting in dramatically reduced police arrests of Indians, to a short-lived landing by nineteen Indian students on Alcatraz Island in 1969, Native groups were increasingly finding their voices.[50]

New groups like the American Indian Movement (AIM), formed in St. Paul, were emboldened to speak out more forcefully about the poor treatment of Indians across the nation by outsiders and insiders alike (tribal leaders who were more interested in maintaining cozy relationships with federal bureaucrats than looking out for their people). When two hundred "Indians of All Tribes" captured Alcatraz on November 19, 1969, demanding title to the island from the federal government, the story of Indians' grievances went global. "Alcatraz became the focal point of

Indian protest and the inspiration of Indians everywhere," Deloria wrote. "Many Indians regarded the capture of Alcatraz as the beginning of a new movement to recapture the continent and assert tribal independence from the U.S.," he added. "Tribal elders publically expressed abhorrence at the illegal invasion . . . , while privately they were delighted that some young Indians were tweaking the federal government's nose."[51]

A more productive approach was taken the next year by the Indian occupiers of Fort Lawton in northwestern Seattle, who "used an old federal statute that allowed the use of abandoned federal military posts as Indian schools," Deloria explained. "Negotiating aggressively[,] the Seattle Indians were able to secure a long term lease on some of the land and then built the Daybreak Star Center which is still a major part of the social services available to the Puget Sound Indian Community."[52]

In that same seminal year of 1969, toward the end of Deloria's second year in law school, his first book, *Custer Died for Your Sins: An Indian Manifesto*, burst onto the American cultural scene. There had never been anything like it, Professor Charles Wilkinson explained. "Laced with historical references and vignettes of contemporary conditions and personalities, . . . *Custer* spared hardly anyone." Embodying Deloria's "sarcastic, witty, iconoclastic, and lightning quick, always poking, sparring, and jabbing" personality, Wilkinson continued, it "skewered the usual suspects – the bureau, missionaries, and dominant social values – but he also went after Democrats, liberals, and Indian tribes, including his own – all, in sum, who fell short or dissembled."[53]

Raw and passionate, *Custer* poured forth decades – and centuries – of tribal frustrations and grievances. Deloria chafed, for example, at America's lack of gratitude for Indians' early assistance to the colonies: "When Indian people remember how weak and helpless the U.S. once was, how much it needed the good graces of the tribes for its very existence, how the tribes shepherded the ignorant colonists through drought and blizzard, kept them alive, helped them grow," it is small wonder "they burn with resentment." "There is not a single tribe," he explained, "that does not burn with resentment over the treatment it has received at the hands of an avowedly *Christian* nation."

Conceding that the "thrust of Christian missions was to save the individual Indian," he explained that their larger impact, in fact, "was to shatter Indian societies and destroy the cohesiveness of the Indian communities." Another persistent problem he identified was the social scientists who "look[] into Indian society from a self-made pedestal of preconceived ideas coupled with an innate superior attitude toward those different from themselves. Many times anthropologists and sociologists have acted as if we couldn't do anything if they didn't first understand it and approve of it. Those days," Deloria announced, "are gone."[54]

Custer is livid, moreover, about America's history of broken treaties: "Indian people laugh themselves sick when they hear these statements" from the U.S. government criticizing other countries' unreliability. "America has yet to keep one Indian treaty or agreement despite the fact that the U.S. government signed over four hundred such treaties and agreements with Indian tribes." "In looking back at the centuries of broken treaties," he added, "it is clear that the U.S. never intended to keep any of its promises.... When the crisis had passed, it promptly proceeded on its way without a backward glance at its treachery." America needs to "begin[] to build a moral record in her dealings with the Indian people," he insisted. "America has been sick for some time. It got sick when the first Indian treaty was broken. It has never recovered. Is it any wonder," he queried, "that other nations are extremely skeptical about [America's] real motives in the world today?"[55]

Custer rued that it did not have to be this way: "There were many avenues open for the government besides wholesale theft. In Canada, for example, there are Indian reservations in every province. Indians have not had their basic governmental forms disturbed. They still operate with chiefs and general councils. Nor were they forced," moreover, "to remove themselves whenever and wherever the white man came. Nor did they have their lands allotted and then stolen piece by piece from under them." In America, "[t]here was no need for the government to abruptly change from treaty negotiations to a program of cultural destruction, as it did in 1891 with its Indian assimilation bill. And when the Five Civilized Tribes" of Georgia, Alabama, and Mississippi "had adapted to a semi-white political structure[,] the government could have supported the great experiment of the Cherokees instead of removing them to Oklahoma. Even in the closing years of the last century, when the tribes had by and large adapted from hunters to ranchers, the government could have kept its promises and left the tribes alone."[56]

The book offered concrete solutions. "Many things can immediately be done to begin to make amends for past transgressions," Deloria remarked. "Passage of federal legislation acknowledging the rights of the Indian people as contained in the treaties can make the hunting and fishing rights of the Indians a reality," for one. "Where land has been wrongfully taken... it can be restored by transferring land now held by the various governmental departments within reservation boundaries to the tribes

PHOTO 3. Vine Deloria Jr., ca. 1973. Courtesy of Philip J. Deloria.

involved." It is time, he demanded, for a change. "Mythical generalities of what built this country and made it great must now give way to consideration of keeping contractual obligations due to the Indian people. Morality must begin where immorality began." To that end, he insisted, treaty relations between the United States and Indian tribes must be fully restored. "Congressional policy should recognize the basic right to tribal sovereignty. Such sovereignty should include all promises contained in treaties and should recognize the eligibility of tribal governments for all federal programs which are opened to counties and cities."[57]

As for *Custer*'s impact, Professor Wilkinson remarked that it "altered the political landscape in two ways.... For whites, it humanized Indians,... lucidly explain[ing] the distinctive cultures and needs of Native peoples." Moreover, "Deloria's Indians are resourceful people, survivors who endured wave upon wave of tragedy yet somehow never lost either their lightheartedness or the grit to preserve their ways of life. For Indians," in contrast, "*Custer* inspired empowerment and pride. It offered hope in a time when hope seemed the province of all in America save Natives. It allowed Indians to dream their own real dreams." Steve Pavlik added, "*Custer* inspired a generation of American Indian activism and brought [Deloria] wide recognition as being the intellectual voice and legal mind behind the Indian civil rights movement.[58]

The 1970s

After graduating from law school in 1970, for the following eight years, Deloria worked consulting and teaching at a variety of colleges, including Western Washington University in Bellingham, Washington; the American Indian Studies Center at the University of California, Los Angeles; the Pacific School of Religion; and Colorado College in Colorado Springs. The dam having been broken in 1969 with *Custer Died for Your Sins*, he wrote prolifically during this time – publishing some ten books, including, notably, *We Talk, You Listen: New Tribes, New Turf*, in 1970 (suggesting that American Indian tribalism, with its values of group identity and community, could be a potential antidote for many of the ills of modern American society); *Of Utmost Good Faith* in 1971 (providing ultimately hopeful commentary paired with texts of a collection of relevant legal documents, cases, and laws relating to Indian sovereignty); *Behind the Trail of Broken Treaties: An Indian Declaration of Independence* in 1974 (detailing the protests of the 1960s and early 1970s at Alcatraz, Wounded Knee, and elsewhere, and suggesting that the best way forward for U.S.–tribal relations was a resurrection of the treaty-making process); *God Is Red* in 1975; and *The Metaphysics of Modern Existence* in 1979 (the two latter books offering Deloria's thoughts on the importance of Native religion to the very future of life on the earth).

In 1970, the Indian fishing rights issue was a continuing conflict among Indians and non-Indians in the Pacific Northwest. Dating back to 1854 and 1855 treaties, Indians had ceded land in return for the guarantee of the right to continue fishing at traditional sites. As with most other treaties, whites later began reneging on their earlier promises. A number of earlier U.S. Supreme Court cases affirmed the Indians' treaty rights, but the State of Washington continued to attempt to find ways to prevent the Indians from fishing. Things came to a head in September 1970, when three hundred Tacoma city police, state game wardens, and state police silently surrounded a Nisqually and Puyallup Indian fishing camp, lobbed in tear gas, and rushed and beat the Indian men and women. "People in the camp were arrested for disorderly conduct although the disorder was police inspired," Deloria recounted. "The camp was leveled, the Indians' cars were impounded and taken to Tacoma where they were virtually destroyed while in police custody." "Public opinion turned in the Indians' favor," Deloria remembered, when "Dick Cavett allowed me to show pictures of the attack on the Indian camp on his national television show resulting in a great public outcry against the actions of the police. As a result of the pressure, the federal government filed suit against the State of Washington and eventually won a ruling that entitled Indians of the State to receive an allocation for half the fish in the state."[59]

As talk of treaty reform grew, several additional factors (together with such mobilizing events as Alcatraz, Fort Lawton, and the police attack on the Puyallup, together with Deloria's *Custer* call to action) further galvanized Indian activists in the early 1970s. First, the activists (mostly urban Indians and some younger reservation Indians) found allies in traditional Indians on the reservations. The traditionals were largely full bloods who lived in the backcountry of the reservations and "who had preserved the tribal customs and generally boycotted the tribal governments set up under the Indian Reorganization Act of 1934," believing the IRA was the ultimate bureaucratic betrayal and violation of the 1868 treaty. "These people represented the Indian traditions in the best sense, were generally leaders in the tribal religious ceremonies, and were eager to see something done about the treaties," Deloria explained. "They took the activists seriously when they talked about treaties, and they began to give fairly substantial support" for a more militant form of cultural renewal.[60]

As these groups coalesced, they "made ready to push the Indians who had accommodated the white man off the reservations.... By mid-1972," Deloria continued, "the middle ground of progressive ideology in Indian affairs was fast eroding, and desperate confrontation was in the air over the issue of the nature of the modern Indian community."[61]

After a scrap involving fishing rights in Minnesota and a rally in Gordon, Nebraska, over the mob killing of an Indian (one of a number that year) that drew one thousand protesting Indians, AIM and other activist groups organized the Trail of Broken Treaties caravan to travel across the country, stopping at reservations along the way, to present the Twenty Points Indian reform program to the Nixon administration in

Washington, D.C., a week before the 1972 presidential election. Arriving in Washington on November 3, the Friday before the election, the Indians waited in the BIA auditorium until arrangements for their housing could be made. As the large group made its way out of the building toward the designated Department of Interior auditorium, "some of the guards began to push the younger Indians out the door. Instantly the situation changed," Deloria recounted. "Fearful that they were being pushed out to face the D.C. riot squad, the Indians seized the building.... The caravan leaders could barely keep their followers under control. Sporadic efforts by the police to harass the occupants created a constant state of fear." Finally, six days later, the Indians left the building under a promise from the administration that it would consider the twenty points and would file no criminal charges. The participants also received $66,000 in travel money to get back to their reservations.[62]

The AIM and the other activists "seethed" when they received the administration's dismissive response to the twenty points two months later, and they "vowed never again to surrender without receiving a definite commitment from the administration." "Indians had come to realize," Deloria remarked, that "political activism was their only hope. Even assuming the best of intentions by Congress, they could not achieve a modicum of justice."[63]

Tensions continued into 1973, when another mob killing of an Indian in Buffalo Gap, South Dakota, drew a large group of protesting Indians, and then a large protest occurred in Rapid City. Thereafter, the AIM leaders Russell Means, Dennis Banks, and a few others decided to visit the Oglala Sioux reservation in Pine Ridge, South Dakota. "All things considered, it was the last place on Earth they should have gone," Deloria suggested, if what they wanted was a rest. This was the home, after all, of the tribe that had "waged a successful war against the U.S. from 1864–68 under the famous Red Cloud," resulting in the triumphant Fort Laramie Treaty of 1868 and, in June 1876, had routed Custer at Little Big Horn. Just a few dozen miles away on the reservation was the site of one of the most egregious massacres of defenseless Indians in the nation's history, Wounded Knee – a name that had entered the popular lexicon as shorthand for U.S. governmental duplicity and dishonor, thanks in part to the massive 1971 best seller *Bury My Heart at Wounded Knee*, by Dee Brown.[64]

When Oglala Sioux tribal chair Richard "Dickie" Wilson – who objected to AIM's tactics and opposed the reform-minded traditionals and militant younger Indians – heard the AIM leaders planned on visiting Pine Ridge, he barred them from entering. They came anyway – and "soon the tribal police were brutalizing and harassing tribal members who were suspected of being members of AIM. Believing they had exhausted all legal remedies, [Means, Banks, and] the people got into their cars and headed for Wounded Knee to make their stand" and to issue their "defiant cry of political independence to the world."[65]

The BIA promptly dispatched federal marshals and funds to support their man Wilson. But "Means had his allies also, and Indians from all over the nation, not simply AIM members, began to rush to the reservation in support of the protest." On the second day, the leaders issued a bold demand that the Senate Foreign Relations Committee, chaired by Senator F. William Fulbright, conduct hearings on the issue of U.S. obligations under the Sioux treaties. "Indians across the nation paused and looked at the Wounded Knee occupation in a different vein when the demand for hearing went out," Deloria explained. "It was one thing to issue rhetorical demands but quite another to gather the support of the Indian people themselves for such a demand, and people were very interested to see what would happen." Indeed, the "nature of the occupying force astounded all in its breadth – young Indians, traditionals, medicine men, holy men, representatives of the Iroquois League," with the result that "the more Indian people saw of the Wounded Knee protest, the more seriously they began to take it."[66]

On Sunday, March 11, AIM leader Russell Means made an audacious announcement on national television: the Oglala Sioux Nation declared its independence from the United States and would shoot anyone who violated its borders as defined by the treaty of 1868. Thereafter, "they sent emissaries to New York, and Indians began to show up at the United Nations seeking the assistance of friendly nations which might raise the question of the Sioux treaty before that body. After five more weeks," Deloria recounted, the occupation ended at the end of seventy-two days, when the White House agreed to send negotiators to discuss the treaty of 1868 with traditional Oglala Sioux chiefs and medicine men. Both sides considered the outcome a moral victory.[67]

"While few tribal governments openly supported the Wounded Knee people," Deloria recalled, "Indian country secretly glowed with the knowledge that the mouse had finally roared. And not a few tribal officials began to examine their own treaties with the U.S. to determine how they could respond to the general cry for reform of the treaty relationship." Russell Means "told a story of watching three little Indian boys playing. The two more aggressive boys chose to be Means and Banks. They pointed at the third boy and said, 'You have to be Dickie Wilson.'

The third boy went home crying. He was ashamed," Deloria related, "to even pretend to be a traitor to his own people. Somehow, through all of the protests and symbolic gestures, a different sense of the Indian identity was born."[68]

The Late 1970s and 1980s

In 1978, Deloria and family moved to Tucson, where he took a position as tenured professor of law and political science at the University of Arizona. There, as chair of the American Indian Studies program, he developed the first master's degree in that discipline. He also continued actively writing, publishing a number of articles and books focusing mostly on tribal political and legal history, including *American Indians, American Justice* (1983) (with Clifford Lytle); *Aggressions of Civilization: Federal Indian Policy since the 1880s* (1984); *The Nations Within: The Past and Future of American Indian Sovereignty* (1984) (with Clifford Lytle); and *American Indian Policy in the Twentieth Century* (1985). In addition, *Custer Died for Your Sins* was reprinted in 1988 with a new preface in which Deloria marveled at the changes that had occurred in two decades and reasserted the importance of pointing out to people the injustices being perpetrated against Indian tribes and peoples.

The same year that Deloria joined the Arizona faculty, the federal executive, legislative, and judicial branches all acted to produce legal rules affecting tribal sovereignty. The activism of the early 1970s had prompted activity in the legislative and executive branches that generally improved the lot of Indian tribes. Congress, operating on the recommendations of the May 1977 Final Report of the American Indian Policy Review Commission (created by Congress in 1975), passed two important pieces of legislation in 1978: the Indian Child Welfare Act (ICWA) (restoring much of tribal authority for removal of children from homes) and the American Indian Religious Freedom Act (AIRFA) (protecting "the "inherent right of freedom to believe, express, and exercise the traditional religions of the American Indian including but not limited to access to sites, use and possession of sacred objects, and the freedom to worship through ceremonials and traditional rites").[69]

The judicial branch, by contrast, generally diminished tribal sovereignty and autonomy in three 1978 decisions, a foreshadowing of the more aggressive actions taken by the modern Supreme Court beginning in the mid-1980s and continuing to this day. Specifically, whereas the Supreme Court had previously allowed state law to apply to non-Indians (but not to Indians) in Indian country only under narrow circumstances, in *Oliphant v. Suquamish Indian Tribe* (1978), the Court much more broadly held that tribes simply lack the inherent sovereign authority to exercise criminal jurisdiction in Indian country over non-Indian defendants. Justice Rehnquist reasoned: "Upon incorporation into the territory of the U.S., the Indian tribes thereby come under the territorial sovereignty of the U.S. and their exercise of separate power is constrained so as not to conflict with the interests of this overriding sovereignty."[70]

It was little surprise, then, when the Court held in *Montana v. United States* (1981) a few years later that the Crow tribe could not regulate the hunting and fishing of nonmembers on the fee-simple lands within the reservation, explaining that the tribe had authority only over those lands belonging to the tribe or held for the tribe in trust by the United States (trust lands) (recall that large portions of the reservations had been converted to fee title during the allotment era). In advancing the broad proposition that tribal authority does not extend to nonmembers of the tribe except in limited narrow circumstances, the Court reasoned that the "exercise of tribal power beyond what is necessary to protect tribal self-government or to control internal relations is inconsistent with the dependent status of the tribes, and so cannot survive without express congressional delegation."[71]

In a highly unusual criticism, a lower federal court castigated the Supreme Court for failing to require the United States to meet its sacred treaty obligations to Indian tribes:

> It may well be that non-Indians who acquired land inside the reservation never expected to be subjected to regulation by the Indians. But likewise the Indians themselves never expected . . . that reservation land opened without their consent to non-Indians would be removed from their jurisdiction. The Indians' expectations rest on the explicit guarantees of a treaty signed by the President and Secretary of State and ratified by the Senate. The non-Indians' expectations rest not on explicit statutory language, but on what is presumed to have been the intent underlying the allotment acts – a policy of destroying tribal government to assimilate the Indians into American society. It is difficult to see why there should be an overriding federal interest in vindicating only the latter expectations – especially when the anti-tribal policy on which they rest was repudiated over fifty years ago.[72]

The 1990s and 2000s

In 1990, Deloria moved to the University of Colorado faculty as professor of history and American Indian studies, with adjunct appointments in law, political science, and religious studies – a broad portfolio representing the stature he had achieved. During the 1990s, he continued providing leadership for various organizations and began accumulating awards and honors, some for lifetime achievement, and the move to the state of Colorado (where he had first attended college as an unmotivated undergraduate some thirty-five years earlier) was a homecoming of sorts.

The primary focus of his writing shifted in the 1990s from issues involving Indian sovereignty and politics to those involving Native religion and spirituality, which we will discuss in more detail shortly. Starting with a collection of essays titled *Indian Education in America* (1991), he also published a second edition of *God Is Red: A Native View of Religion* (1994) (the only one of his many books he revised for republication), and he published the new books *Red Earth, White Lies: Native Americans and the Myth of Scientific Fact* (1995) (questioning the integrity of Western science); *For This Land: Writings on Religion in America* (1999); *Singing for a Spirit: A Portrait of the Dakota Sioux* (1999); and *Tribes, Treaties, and Constitutional Tribulations* (with David Wilkins) (1999).[73]

During the 1990s and 2000s, tribal relations with the federal legislative and executive branches continued to improve. "Since the termination era ended, congressional activity has been less headstrong, with anti-Indian politicians indulging in only occasional forays that would curtail tribal authority or rights," Professor Getches explains. During those years, Congress implemented a self-determination policy toward the goal of enhancing tribal sovereignty. Having "appear[ed] to have internalized the lesson of history.... The last two generations of Indians, under the prevailing self-determination policies, have had to cope only with the pockets of poisonous gases that linger from old federal policies."[74]

Starting in the 1980s, Congress began passing measures that have significantly enhanced tribal control in a number of areas, such as the environment and natural resources, cultural resources, and economic development. In 1990, for example, it reenacted the federal Indian Arts and Crafts Act (originally passed in 1935), and it enacted the Native American Graves Protection and Repatriation Act (NAGPRA), enabling tribes to recover ancestral remains from museums and others. For its part, the executive branch in the 1980s and 1990s began negotiating agreements setting up bilateral federal-tribe frameworks for enforcing federal environmental statutes, which also served the purpose of enhancing tribal sovereignty.[75]

Partly as a result of the greater autonomy allowed in these legislative and executive improvements, one of the most profound changes in Indian country in the past few decades has been the dramatic improvement in socioeconomic conditions according to almost all census-measured indexes – largely through the advent and expansion of gaming operations on tribal land, with roots in bingo and garage-style casinos as early as the late 1960s and into the 1970s. Deloria explained that "the success stories of Indian gaming generally revolve around the programs initiated by those tribes that have invested their gaming income in community projects." "The tribal gambling industry did not arise because the federal government accorded 'special rights' to a tiny segment of the American population," Duthu added, "but because tribal governments embraced the opportunities to fund their government operations and to offer services and benefits to tribal citizens."[76]

The federal judiciary, in marked contrast with the legislature and the executive's improved treatment of Indian tribes in recent decades, has gone in the exact opposite direction. "The current Court is in the process, and has been for nearly two decades," federal Judge Monroe McKay said in 1995, "of eroding those protections of the power of tribes to govern their own affairs within their territorial boundaries." Since William Rehnquist became chief justice in 1986, Deloria commented in 1999, "Supreme Court decisions involving Indians [had] taken a radical turn for the worse." And that's saying quite a lot, Deloria remarked, considering that, "on the whole, the Supreme Court has been inattentive, flippant, and disrespectful of Indian rights" through most of its history. Rather than seeking to be a neutral arbiter of disputants, the Court has instead "seen its task as one of finding arguments that will make actions by the other two branches appear legal."[77]

It is most ironic that, when Congress and the executive during the past nearly fifty years have come around to a more charitable attitude toward Indians, the Supreme Court has decided to give less deference to Congress and instead take a more active role itself. This has been a disastrous development for Indian tribes. Prior to 1986, Professor David Getches suggests, the Court generally "construe[d] laws in light of the nation's tradition of recognizing independent tribal powers to govern their territory and the people within it. In interpreting ambiguous treaties and laws," he adds, "the Court regularly employed canons of construction to give the benefit of doubt to Indians, and it deferred to the political branches whenever congressional policy was not clear. Now these legal traditions are being almost totally disregarded."[78]

Getches suggests that a majority of the justices on the modern Supreme Court are motivated not so much by racial bias (with the possible exception of late Chief Justice Rehnquist) as by a desire to advance ideologically driven objectives involving federalism, minority rights, and mainstream values. And the Court "ignores precedent, construing statutes, treaties, and the Constitution liberally to reach results that comport with" these objectives, virtually without exception. To the extent that these attitudes are implicated in Indian cases, they are likely to determine the outcome, change Indian law, and reshape Indian policy, even if the Court is indifferent about Indian law as a distinct field.[79]

Perhaps the most prominent area in which the Supreme Court has elevated state (and sometimes federal) interests to the substantial detriment of Indian tribes is in the area of religious freedom. Although Indians had hoped in 1978 that the AIRFA would finally protect against intrusive governmental actions, what actually happened was that the act produced a deluge of conflict, leading to two decisions about a decade later that effectively neutered any protections Indians may have thought AIRFA provided. "Because of these two opinions," Deloria reported, "American Indians were basically stripped of whatever protection they might have expected from the federal courts and the American Constitution regarding the practice of traditional tribal religions."[80]

First, in *Lyng v. Northwest Indian Cemetery Protective Association* (1988), tribal members from the Yurok, Tolowa, and Karok tribes failed to prevent the U.S. Forest Service from completing a logging road through certain sacred tribal lands, when the Court held that "unless there was specific governmental intent to infringe upon a religion or the government's actions coerced individuals to act contrary to their spiritual beliefs, the first amendment provided no protection for Indian peoples to practice traditional religions even against federal action that potentially could destroy Indian sacred sites."[81]

Two years later, in *Employment Division Department of Human Resources of Oregon v. Smith* (1990), the Supreme Court held that the state's denial of state benefits to Indian Alfred Smith because he had been convicted of using peyote (a federally criminalized drug) during a Native American Church ceremony did not violate Smith's first amendment rights to free exercise of religion, explaining that "the disfavoring of minority religions was nothing more than a logical consequence of democratic government." Justice Antonin Scalia then "encouraged disadvantaged religious individuals and groups to use the political process – that is, to approach Congress and seek legislative religious exemptions."

With this opinion, "Scalia sent a stunning message to all religious groups," "one that was especially unnerving to Indians and practitioners of other minority religions because these individuals and groups typically lack the political clout necessary to effectively lobby Congress or State legislatures for exemptions," Deloria blasted. "And for members of the Native American Church who had already secured just such an exemption in many States and from the federal government, the blow was even harder to fathom. This decision vividly showed," he continued, "that as the last decade of the twentieth century began, American Indians . . . were still without fundamental religious liberties."[82]

More generally, the Supreme Court has long held that Congress has plenary power under the commerce clause to unilaterally usurp tribal authority, and there is little sign the modern Court is willing to revisit the issue. Deloria and other Indian law experts suggest this expansive interpretation of the commerce clause is fundamentally flawed. They argue that, by its terms – "Congress shall have Power . . . To regulate Commerce with foreign nations, and among the several States, and with Indian Tribes" – and history, the commerce clause recognizes Indian tribes as separate sovereigns, akin to foreign nations, and the clause merely specifies that the federal legislature (not state legislatures) are authorized to deal with these quasi-foreign nations. Nonetheless, the Court, in its biased-enabler role, long ago ratified Congress's power grab in cases such as *Kagama* (1886) and *Lone Wolf* (1903). Thereafter, Deloria explained, because the Court's assertion of "the doctrine of plenary power was not challenged or disclaimed by either the Congress or the president," it "has come to be regarded as constitutional law." "The modern Court has done no better [than *Kagama* and *Lone Wolf*] in articulating the legal basis for Congress's assertion of vast power over Indian tribes," Duthu added. "In short, the plenary power doctrine stands as the most potent reminder of America's rejection of respectful, bilateral relations with Indian tribes, and its abandonment of the fundamental principle that our national government is one of limited powers."[83]

The Court's most recent affirmation of Congress's plenary power over Indian tribes occurred in *United States v. Lara* (2004), in which the Court acknowledged Congress's freedom, "with its 'plenary power' in Indian affairs, rooted in the Indian Commerce Clause, . . . to make adjustments in 'judicially made' federal Indian law."[84]

One concurring opinion in *Lara* suggests, however, that one day the Supreme Court may reevaluate its long-held acceptance of the plenary-power theory. Concurring in *Lara*, Justice Thomas wrote: "I cannot agree that the Indian Commerce Clause 'provides Congress with plenary power to legislate in the field of Indian affairs.'" Thomas added:

> The Court should admit that it has failed in its quest to find a source of congressional power to adjust tribal sovereignty.... We might find that the Federal Government cannot regulate tribes through ordinary domestic legislation and simultaneously maintain that the tribes are sovereigns in any meaningful sense. But until we begin to analyze these questions honestly and rigorously, the confusion that I have identified will continue to haunt our cases.[85]

Taken at face value, Justice Thomas's call for the Court to "analyze these [plenary-power] questions honestly and rigorously" is well taken. But because Congress generally has been friendly to Indian tribes in recent decades, some scholars now view Congress as offering Indians their best chance for fair treatment from the federal government – hence, they somewhat paradoxically now support, as the tribes did in *Lara,* the plenary-power doctrine. "Times change," reasons the Indian law scholar Matthew Fletcher – and in the early twenty-first century, the Supreme Court should properly defer to modern congressional policy that, for example, favors tribal justice systems and economic development.[86]

III. Native Spirituality

> *When are we going to free ourselves up and just look at these things? I have been in ceremonies. I have talked to spirits. I'm an educated man, I have three degrees. I'm no damn fool. [T]hose experiences are as real to me as anything in the world.... I don't believe that people having spiritual experiences are necessarily deluded. The experience is a valid experience.*
>
> – Vine Deloria Jr., 1996

The new professor admired his surroundings as he wandered through the gorgeous University of Colorado campus hard beneath the Flatirons rock formations. Breathing in deeply the warm, pine-scented air as he made his way slowly in the late-summer afternoon, he approached one of the many attractive red-tile-roof, Spanish-style classroom buildings on campus.

He had enjoyed his time so far at the university in the late summer of 1990, although he was surprised to hear from his students that some professors were beginning their courses with a recitation of the Bering Strait theory of the peopling of the Western hemisphere.

"They are simply repeating dogmatic folklore which has no solid factual source," he told anyone who would listen.

As he opened the door to enter the cool shade of the building, several other faculty members conversing in the hallway abruptly stopped talking, leaving an awkward silence.

"Odd," the professor thought.

But later he learned that some of those same faculty members, in a series of secretive e-mails, had decided he was a "racist reactionary trying to destroy their fictional Bering-Strait enterprise," and agreed not to invite him to speak to them.

"Had they tendered an invitation," Vine Deloria Jr. told the world seven years later in *Red Earth, White Lies,* "I doubt if I would have appeared, so perhaps a point was scored on each side."[87]

In 1968, while still in law school at the University of Colorado, Deloria was elected to the Executive Council of the Episcopal Church, where he rattled cages with his memorandum titled "More Real Involvement," which proposed sweeping reforms to the church's bureaucracy to better facilitate self-determination among Indian churches (shades of Roger Williams's incendiary internal letter to William Bradford). Labeled by some a "theological superstar" as early as 1974, for the rest of his years Deloria was recognized as a highly original thinker on the intersections of religion, theology, and science.

In 1975, he published *God Is Red* (republished with updates in 1992), his most influential book after *Custer Died for Your Sins,* in which he compared and contrasted Western and Native religions. The book meant to ask, "What are religions? How do they originate? And what can you anticipate [experiencing] in an ongoing religious life?" he later explained, answering that religion "is a force in and of itself" that "calls for the integration of lands and peoples in harmonious unity." Throughout the rest of his life, Deloria amassed a comprehensive body of work on spirituality to accompany *God Is Red,* with such other works as *The Metaphysics of Modern Existence* (1979); *Red Earth, White Lies: Native Americans and the Myth of Scientific Fact* (1997); *Evolution, Creationism, and Other Modern Myths* (2002); and the groundbreaking, posthumously published *C. G. Jung and the Sioux Traditions: Dreams, Visions, Nature, and the Primitive* (2009). In the early works, he primarily described and critiqued Western and Indian religious practices; then he moved into sharply critical accounts of Western science's near-cultlike dogmatism; and finally, addressing the mind-matter relationship with the work of Carl Jung as common link, he began building bridges between Western science and Indian spirituality, a potentially transformative effort with profound long-term implications in reconciling the teachings of Western science and Native traditions.[88]

Religion

Like his fellow radicals Williams, Paine, Stanton, and Du Bois, Deloria believed Christian religious orthodoxy was the source of many of society's ills. "At one time or another," he posited, "slavery, poverty, and treachery were all justified by Christianity as politically moral institutions of the State. Economic Darwinism, the survival of the fittest businessman, was seen as a process approved by God and the means by which He determined His Chosen for salvation." "Where the cross goes," he acerbically added, "there is never life more abundantly – only death, destruction, and ultimately betrayal."[89]

From the time Europeans first began colonizing North America, they sought to convert Indians to Christianity. Responding to the entreaties of a Massachusetts missionary, the renowned Seneca orator Red Jacket replied: "You say there is but one way to worship and serve the Great Spirit. If there is but one religion, why do you white people differ so much about it? Why not all agree, as you can all read the book?" Continuing, he declared: "Brother, we do not understand these things. We are told that your religion was given to your forefathers, and has been handed down from father to son. We also, have a religion which was given to our forefathers, and has been handed down to us, their children." Red Jacket patiently explained: "We worship in that way. It teaches us to be thankful for all favors we receive; to love each other, and be united. We never quarrel about religion, because it is a matter which concerns each man and the Great Spirit," he added, sounding much like Roger Williams.[90]

Indians saw nothing to recommend adhering to white people's demands to adopt their ways and religion. To do so, Red Cloud explained, "you [would have to] begin anew and put away the wisdom of your fathers. You must lay up food and forget the hungry. When your house is built, your storeroom filled, then look around for a neighbor whom you can take advantage of and seize all he has." Sitting Bull, for his part, explained why he did not surrender and come back from Canada to the U.S. reservation: "I am a red man. If the Great Spirit had desired me to be a white man he would have made me so in the first place. He put in your heart certain wishes and plans, in my heart he put other and different desires. Each man is good in his sight. It is not necessary for eagles to be crows."[91]

During the years from 1870 to 1930, when tribal religions were banned and Christianity was established as the official religion of Indian reservations (despite the seeming prohibition on such action by the First Amendment establishment clause), Christian missionaries formed Indian congregations on nearly every reservation west of the Mississippi. "Indian people were continually mystified by the seeming hypocrisy of the Christian churches," Deloria explained. "The churches preached peace for years yet have always endorsed the wars in which the nation has been engaged." "Often rows of sullen former warriors filled rickety wooden chapels to hear sermons on the ways of peace. They were told that the life of war was the path of destruction. Eternal hell, they were assured, awaited the man of war. Then the service would be closed with the old favorite hymn, 'Onward, Christian Soldiers, Marching as to War.'"[92]

The hypocrisy extended to mundane matters as well. "Churches struggled to make the Indians cut their hair because they felt that wearing one's hair short was the civilized Christian thing to do," Deloria reported. "After the tribal elders had been fully sheared, they were ushered into church meetings, given pictures of Jesus and the Disciples, and told to follow these Holy Men. Looking down at the pictures, the ex-warriors were stunned to discover the Holy Dozen in shoulder-length hair!" All of which led Deloria to bluntly conclude: "For me at least, Christianity has been a sham to cover over the white man's shortcomings. Yet I spent four years in a seminary finding out for myself where Christianity had fallen short."[93]

Indians found subversive ways to maintain their own traditions during these decades of oppression. "Choosing an American holiday or Christian religious day when the whites would themselves be celebrating, traditional Indians often performed their [own] ceremonies 'in honor of' George Washington or Memorial Day, thus fulfilling their own religious obligations while white bystanders glowed proudly to see a war dance or rain dance done on their day," Deloria explained. In the end, though, "Indian people obediently followed the way of the white man because it was the path of least resistance. The Great Spirit was exchanged for Santa Claus with some misgivings," however. "Substituting toys for spiritual powers created a vacuum, ... and the tribes secretly preferred their old religion over the religion of the Easter bunny." More recently, he wrote in 1969, "the impotence and irrelevancy of the Christian message has meant a return to traditional religion by Indian people. Tribal religions are making a strong comeback on most reservations. Only in the past few years," for example, "have the Oglala Sioux and Rosebud Sioux revived their ancient Sioux Sun Dance," as have other tribes with their own traditions.[94]

Virtually all Native religious traditions have certain elements in common. First and foremost is an emphasis on place – that is, on the tribe's oneness with the land and nature. "The structure of their religious traditions," Deloria explained, "is taken directly from the world around them, from their relationships with other forms of life":

> The places where revelations were experienced were remembered and set aside as locations where, through rituals and ceremonials, the people could once again communicate with the spirits. Thousands of years of occupancy on their lands taught tribal peoples the sacred landscapes for which they were responsible and gradually the structure of ceremonial reality became clear.... The vast majority of Indian tribal religions, therefore, have a sacred center at a particular place, be it a river, a mountain, a plateau, valley, or other natural feature. This center enables the people to look out along the four dimensions and locate their lands, to relate all historical events within the confines of this particular land, and to accept responsibility for it.[95]

The Great Spirit – or Great Mystery – required that people tolerate all life forms. "Behind the apparent kinship between animals, reptiles, birds, and human beings in the Indian way stands a great conception," Deloria instructed. "Other living things are not regarded as insensitive species. Rather they are 'people' in the same manner as the various tribes of human beings are people." For example, "[i]n the same manner the Plains Indians considered the buffalo as a distinct people, the Northwest Coast Indians regarded the salmon as a people. Equality is thus not simply a human attribute but a recognition of the creatureness of all creation." Given that animals are creatures that demonstrate complex mental process and possess considerable knowledge of the world, we must change, Deloria suggested, how we conceive of their thought processes and means of communications.[96]

"Sioux people understood that *Wakan Tanka* – a word that defies easy definition but reflects the 'great mysterious' – is in everything, so there was no doubt that humans shared certain elements with all other creatures," Deloria explained. "As we probe more deeply into the mystery of life, we come to learn how closely related we are to other creatures." Further, "[r]ecognition of the parity of other creatures in terms of psychological and spiritual capability was the hallmark of the Sioux understanding of other living things," he continued. "This was not a 'worshipping,' ... but rather the adoption of a posture of humility before an aspect of nature that they did not fully understand." "Instead of formulas derived from an instrumental encounter with nature," he added, "the Sioux opened themselves to communications from nature, allowing nature to speak to them in dreams or visions. Birds, animals, and even rocks... educated the people."[97]

Deloria quoted Walking Buffalo, a Stoney Indian from Canada, for the idea of the unity of all creation: "'Did you know that trees talk? Well they do. They talk to each other, and they'll talk to you if you listen. Trouble is, white people don't listen.... But I have learned a lot from trees; sometimes about the weather, sometimes about animals, sometimes about the Great Spirit.'"[98]

Or as Billy Frank Jr., a leading activist for tribal fishing rights of the Nisqually Nation in Washington, explained his spirituality in the 1970s: "I don't believe in magic. I believe in the sun and the stars, the water, the tides, the floods, the owls, the hawks flying, the river running, the wind talking. They're measurements. They tell us how healthy things are. How healthy we are. Because we and they are the same. That's what I believe in."[99]

Regarding the Native belief in the unity of all creation, Vine Deloria's son Philip Deloria shares a couple intriguing stories of his experience working with his mother and collaborator Jerome Bernstein in completing the *C. G. Jung and the Sioux Traditions* manuscript after his father's 2005 death. While driving back home with his mother from northern Michigan, just as Philip broached the sensitive subject of consolidating two of his father's chapters into one, "a rock appeared out of nowhere" and smashed the windshield, whereupon Phil turned to his mother and said, "On second thought, Mom, I think we'll just leave the chapters as they are." Then, when Jerome left momentarily during the final stages of copyediting in Santa Fe, a bird flew into the room, landed on the mantle, and stared directly at Phil as he made edits to the book's "animal chapter." The bird then flew away just as Jerome returned – prompting Phil's observation, "I think my father has just paid me a visit."[100]

The sacred connection of Indian people to the land was poignantly expressed by Curley, a Crow Indian chief, in declining the federal government's requests in 1912 to sell more land:

> The soil you see is not ordinary soil – it is the dust of the blood, the flesh, and the bones of our ancestors. We fought and bled and died to keep other

> Indians from taking it, and we fought and bled and died helping the Whites. You will have to dig down through the surface before you can find nature's earth, as the upper portion is Crow. The land as it is, is my blood and my dead; it is consecrated; and I do not want to give up any portion of it.[101]

"This sentiment," Deloria suggested, "speaks of an identity so strong as to be virtually indistinguishable from the earth itself, the human being, as it were, completely in harmony with the Mother Earth and inseparable in every way. Nowhere else on this planet do we find this attitude." Indeed, Indian songs and chants "frequently do not even mention a deity or the Great Mystery at all"; rather, "[t]hey are directed to plants, birds, animals, and the earth asking for assistance in performing rather mundane tasks. When they do specifically address the Great Mysterious power, their pleas... do not flatter; they are more in the nature of an objective admission of the fact of human finitude." In their religious ceremonies, "Indians virtually eliminate the human element... and concentrate on representing the physical universe." They "pray to the 'four directions,' lay out elaborate sandpaintings to represent the cosmos, and see in pipe bowls and sweat lodges a model of the larger cosmic whole."[102]

Young Chief, a Cayuse Indian, when refusing to sign the Treaty of Walla Walla on the belief the rest of the creation was inadequately consulted in the transaction, expresses well this concept of natural unity:

> I wonder if the ground has anything to say? I wonder if the ground is listening to what is said?... The water says the same thing.... The grass says the same thing.... The ground says, It was from me man was made. The Great Spirit, in placing men on earth, desired them to take good care of the ground and to do each other no harm.[103]

As might be expected, tribal and Christian attitudes substantially diverge on the topic of death as well. Whereas many Christians fundamentally "fear death more than any other part of human existence," in Indian traditions "we find a notable absence of the fear of death.... Because people saw the tribal community and the family as a continuing unity regardless of circumstance, death became simply another transitional event in a much longer scheme of life," Deloria explained. These attitudes were "a result of the much larger context in which Indians understood life. Human beings were an integral part of the natural world and in death they contributed their bodies to become the dust that nourished the plants and animals that had fed people during their lifetime." Christians seek "salvation," whereas "Indians see themselves returning to nature, their bodies becoming the dust of Mother Earth, and their souls journeying to another place across the Milky Way or sometimes being reborn in a new generation of the tribe."[104]

In short, in most tribal traditions, the unity and continuity of all creation transcends death. The Potawatomi chief Metea referred to this continuity in reluctantly signing a land cession treaty in Illinois country in 1821:

> A long time has passed since first we came upon our lands, and our people have all sunk into their graves. They had sense. We are all young and foolish, and do not wish to do anything that they would not approve, were they living. We are fearful we shall offend their spirits if we sell our lands; and we are fearful we shall offend you if we do not sell them. This has caused us great perplexity of thought, because we have counseled among ourselves, and do not know how we can part with our lands. My father, our country was given us by the Great Spirit, who gave it to us to hunt upon, to make our cornfields upon, to live upon, and to make our beds upon when we die.[105]

Similarly, near the end of his life, the Nez Percé chief Joseph instructed his son Young Chief Joseph:

> Always remember that your father never sold his country. You must stop your ears whenever you are asked to sign a treaty selling your home. A few more years and the white men will be all around you. They have their eyes on this land. My son, never forget my dying words. This country holds your father's body. Never sell the bones of your father and your mother.[106]

"This conception of land as holding the bodies of the tribe in a basic sense pervaded tribal religions across the country," Deloria reported. "It testified in a stronger sense to the underlying unity of the Indian conception of the universe as a life system in which everything had its part."[107]

Community

The reliance on the larger tribe in helping cope with death in tribal traditions is just part of the all-encompassing emphasis on community. "Religion is not conceived as a personal relationship between the deity and each individual," Deloria explained. "It is rather a covenant between a particular god and a particular community." The Indian "does not so much live in a tribe; the tribe lives in him," Harvey Cox suggested in *Secular City*. "He is the tribe's subjective expressions." It follows that "[i]t is virtually impossible to 'join' a tribal religion by agreeing to its doctrines. People couldn't care less whether an outsider believes anything. No separate religious standard of behavior is imposed on followers of the religion's tradition," Deloria explained, "outside of the requirements for the ceremonies – who shall do what, who may participate, who is excluded from which parts of the ceremony, who is needed for other parts of the ceremony. The customs of the tribe and the religious responsibilities to the group are practically identical."[108]

The fact that the tribal focus was on community is not to say, however, that the individual was completely subsumed. "The fears that [some] express as to the lack of personal self among tribal peoples is unwarranted.... [For example, o]ne of the most notable features of Indian tribal cultures is the custom of naming individuals," Deloria shared. "Indian names stand for certain qualities, for exploits, for unusual abilities, for unique physical characteristics, and for the individual's unusual religious experiences. Every person has a name given in religious ceremonies in which his uniqueness is recognized" – in contrast to the largely generic names given in white culture. "Individual worth was also recognized in other ways in the tribal religions. The keepers of the sacred medicine bundles, for example, were people who had been carefully watched for their personal characteristics and were chosen to share some of the tribal mysteries and responsibilities in a religious sense," he continued. "The priesthoods of some of the tribes were filled with people who had been carefully trained after they had demonstrated their personal integrity.... In almost every way, tribal religions supported the individual in his or her community context."[109]

Tribal traditions and spirituality, Deloria added, informed customary tribal approaches to governance as well: "Laws as such did not exist within tribal societies. Law was rejected as being force imposed from without, whereas peoplehood required fulfillment from within the individual. Insofar as there were external controls, Indians accepted only the traditions and customs which were rooted in the tribe's distant past." Most tribes had never defined power in authoritarian terms:

> A man consistently successful at war or hunting was likely to attract a following in direct proportion to his continuing successes. Eventually the men with the greatest followings composed an informal council which made important decisions for the group. Anyone was free to follow or not, depending upon his own best judgment. The people only followed a course of action if they were convinced it was best for them. This was as close as most tribes ever got to a formal government.[110]

PHOTO 4. Vine Deloria Jr., with Second Favorite Dog, Bob, ca. 2002. Courtesy of Philip J. Deloria.

Another way in which the tribal value of respecting all members of society played out was in the lesson that "sharing one's goods with another human being was the highest form of behavior," a tradition Indian people have tenaciously held onto "in spite of all attempts by churches, government agencies and schools to break them of the custom." "Christianity came along and tried to substitute 'giving' for sharing," Deloria declared. "There was only one catch: giving meant giving to the church, not to other people.... Stewardship," in short, "meant saving money and giving a percentage of the savings to the church." Indeed, suspicions of avarice and ulterior motives have long permeated Indian attitudes of Christian missions. As the old Indian joke goes: "[When the missionaries] arrived they had only the Book and we had the land; now we have the Book and they have the land."[111]

This tribal focus on the common good was real, which led one white guide, who had spent some time traveling with a band of Indians in 1912 and 1914, to report:

> I tell you I never saw more kindness or real Christianity anywhere. The poor, the sick, the aged, the widows and the orphans were always looked after first. Whenever we moved camp, someone took care that the widows' lodges were moved first and set up first. After every hunt, a good-sized chunk of meat was dropped at each door where it was most needed. I was

treated like a brother; and I tell you I have never seen any community of church people that was as truly Christian as that band of Indians.[112]

Scientific Dogma

More than anything else, it seems, Vine Deloria Jr. detested dogma of any sort. Seeking to "plant seeds of ideas and raise doubts about what we believe," he rejected "mindless orthodoxy in favor of approaching all issues with an open mind." As a result, Steve Pavlik reported, he "was often viewed by 'the establishment' as being well outside the mainstream of accepted dogma."[113]

Squarely in the crosshairs of Deloria's criticism were scientists who insist that science has a monopoly on truth and who correspondingly refuse to acknowledge any role for the spiritual in their formulations. "Like almost everyone else in America, I grew up believing the myth of the objective scientist," he reported, but he later became disillusioned after noting that honest, good-faith questions were met with scorn and ridicule from supposedly open-minded scientists who themselves came to behave like priests with the only set of keys to the vault of knowledge.[114]

Moreover, "[a] deeper problem exists," he suggested. "Science is our religion today. Because it officially produces not concepts of divinity, it is regarded as neutral on the question of origins." But, in fact, it is anything but neutral, he argued, firmly grounded as it is "in a crude materialism that precludes the possibility of divinity, indeed even rejects any hint of teleology – the sense of purpose and meaning – in its explanation of the world we live in." Such views naturally wreak havoc with the possibility that the hard sciences thoughtfully consider spiritually based American Indian traditions.[115]

Deloria insisted that Native creation stories, for example, contain potentially valuable information, if people are willing to listen: "What we have previously been pleased to call creation stories might not be such at all. [Rather, t]hey might be simply the collective memories of a great and catastrophic event through which people came to understand themselves and the universe they inhabited." "Creation stories," he posited, "may simply be the survivors' memories of reasonably large and destructive events." In the interest of all in acquiring a more comprehensive understanding of Earth history, it stands to reason that everyone would want to listen if "we find in the tribal traditions a memory that is not only more correct in many aspects than that of the Western religions, but . . . [rather a] longer and more extensive history of humankind." "That prospect," however, Deloria commented, "has not been considered by Westerners.

Yet it is precisely the consideration that must be released from their religiously ethnocentric universe."[116]

The fact is, "[r]egardless of what Indians have said concerning their origins, their migrations, their experiences with birds, animals, lands, waters, mountains, and other peoples, the scientists have maintained a stranglehold on the definitions of what respectable and reliable human experiences are. The Indian explanation," Deloria complained, "is always cast aside as superstition, precluding Indians from having an acceptable status as human beings, and reducing them in the eyes of educated people to a prehuman level of ignorance. Indians must simply take whatever status they have been granted by scientists."[117]

Deloria especially scorned the absolutist attitudes of many evolutionists, as epitomized by John Huxley, who declared, "The first point to make about Darwin's theory is that it is no longer a theory, but a fact"; or of George Gaylord Simpson, who added, "[t]hose who do not believe in [evolution] are, almost to a man, obviously ignorant of scientific evidence"; and Richard Lewontin, who announced, "[Western science is] . . . the only begetter of truth." Michael Ruse posited that "[e]volution is a fact, *fact*, FACT!" and Richard Dawkins displays the ardent evolutionists' hubris in concluding that "[i]t is absolutely safe to say that if you meet somebody who claims not to believe in evolution, that person is ignorant, stupid, or insane (or wicked, but I'd rather not consider that)."[118]

Such statements, Pavlik suggested, "betray an arrogance that far transcends what is appropriate for the defense of a mere theory. This is the language of *zealots*." Aside from any substantive objections Deloria might have had to such conventionally accepted examples of scientific wisdom as the Bering Strait theory, the overkill (of mammoths) thesis, or evolution (the most sacred cow of all), he demanded that scientists should exhibit more procedural openness and less dogmatism as they go about their work. "'Science' should drop the pretense of having absolute authority with regard to human origins and begin looking for some other kind of explanation that would include the traditions and memories of non-Western peoples," he asserted. Moreover, "We have been so well trained to accept uncritically anything that anyone alleging to be a 'scientist' tells us that we do not really know what kind of evidence exists supporting evolutionary doctrines."[119]

To make things worse, Pavlik added, "These people are the *gatekeepers*. Such people possess the ability to make or break careers, and their students know that" – which naturally bodes ill for open, critical inquiry in our universities. "Does anyone believe for a moment that [Richard Dawkins] would hesitate to *destroy* a student with the audacity to challenge his cherished beliefs about evolution?" Pavlik asked. "It is no small wonder then, that Native American students, along with their non-Native counterparts, go meekly along, like so many lambs to the slaughter, with what their professors and the scientific establishment claim to be the truth."[120]

"We are living in a strange kind of dark ages where we have immense capability to bring together information, but when we gather this data, we pigeonhole it in the old familiar framework of interpretation, sometimes even torturing the data to make it fit," Deloria rued. "Discordant facts and experiments are simply thrown away when they do not fit the prevailing paradigm. Once a theory such as the progression of human evolution, the Bering Strait land bridge, or the big-game hunters is published," he added, "it is treated as if it was *proven* and it is then popularized by people who rarely read the original documents, and vigorously defended by scholarly disciplines more fiercely than they would defend our country if called upon to do so."[121]

Deloria suggested that once we understand that some scientists are interested mostly in "protect[ing] the social and economic status of scientists," we should more critically question their conclusions. "Scientific theories are often built on the most tenuous of evidential foundations and survive only because of the gentleman's agreement within scientific peer groups not to embarrass colleagues," he charged. "Untangling the confusion is almost impossible because many subjects under discussion are so immense that most scholars must take the word of other scholars. There are no umpires to determine what is valid and what is not." In short, he bitingly concluded, "As many lies are told to protect scientific doctrine as were ever told to protect 'the church.'"[122]

Deloria notes the irony in the fact that the most profound achievements in modern physics – the Planck and quantum theories, Einstein and relativity theory, De Broglie and matter-wave equivalence, Schrodinger and wave mechanics, Heisenberg and the uncertainty principle, Pauli and the exclusion principle, for example – themselves would never have been possible had these sorts of dogmatic views prevailed at the times of their respective development. The English philosopher H. David Foster said in *The Philosophical Scientists*: "Not one of these was reasonable or common-sense, but all were true and *they worked*. They were the result of 'inspiration.'" "While the discoveries of modern physics, the most successful of our physical sciences, may be described using complex geometries and mathematics, the *source* of many important and fundamental theories in physics," Deloria added, "is mysticism." "Needless to say, Einstein had an intuitive mystical insight and then expressed it in a mathematical form that his colleagues could understand. It did not happen the other way around." "The great breakthroughs in science," Foster concluded, "were almost all of a mystical nature in which an emotion of 'problem solved' preceded the solution in Queen's English or mathematical symbols."[123]

Indeed, Charles Darwin himself was aware of the danger of such unthinking dogma among scientists. "[Darwin] thought that scientists were too committed to the old conception of species to admit new ideas on the subject," Darwin biographer Gertrude Himmelfarb wrote, and so he "predicted that his book would find more favor with intelligent laymen than with professional scientists."[124]

Having said all of that, Deloria emphasized that "[t]here is no need to abandon science, because we have acknowledged that it is simply our best guess, though a mighty sophisticated one, as to what exactly we are facing when we try to make sense of the physical world. Indeed," he allowed, "American society is so constituted that it would be impossible to abandon the scientific enterprise. In the eyes of most Americans, it is considered outrageous even to criticize science. We can, however, modify science's claims . . . that it alone possesses absolute and truthful knowledge." How can this be done? "Any group that wishes to be regarded as the authority in a human society must not simply banish or discredit the views of their rivals," Deloria answered. Rather, "they must . . . defend their status and the power to interpret against all comers by providing the best explanation of the data."[125]

A New Synthesis

Taking to heart his own advice to explain the data and work for greater cross-cultural tolerance, in the last two decades of his life Deloria sought to identify common ground between modern science and Native spirituality. This effort regrettably remained uncompleted with his death in 2005. Recognizing the potential importance of the project, Deloria's wife, Barbara; son, Philip; and collaborator Jerome Bernstein completed the work and published it posthumously as *C. G. Jung and the Sioux Traditions: Dreams, Visions, Nature, and the Primitive* (2009).

The Swiss psychologist Carl Gustav Jung's thinking deeply influenced Deloria. "[A]s far as my father was concerned," Philip Deloria recalled,

PHOTO 5. Vine Deloria Jr., ca. 2004. Courtesy of Philip J. Deloria.

"Jung had been willing to open his mind to new ways of thinking about the world, about history, and about our human relation to it," and Deloria saw in Jung's approach a possible conceptual bridge between Western scientific thought and time-honored Indian traditions. "In the exchange between Carl Jung and the Sioux traditions," Deloria said, "we can find new sources of insight, vigorous comparisons, and synthetic opportunities, all of which should be considered vital to a continuing exploration of our world." Deloria's project, then, was to educate the Western mind of "the wisdom of the indigenous mind and culture as well as what he perceived to be its superior attitudes, values and practices," in the belief that these cultural lessons could help restore balance to "a great culture that had become too one-sided in its overly rationalistic orientation to life and itself."[126]

To Deloria's mind, Jung's psychology "was the only system of Western thought whose theories could hold and make sense of much of American Indian religion and medicine from the Western perspective," Deloria's Jungian collaborator Jerome Bernstein explained. "Jung's theories of the collective unconscious,... along with the prominence given to the role of mythology in explaining the archetypal foundations of culture and individual psychology, provided a unique lens through which to view the rich world of the American Indian.... Most important," Bernstein concluded, "Jung's psychology remains the only school of thought that considers the religious/spiritual domain as indispensable and integral to the understanding of the human psyche. [And t]here is no understanding of Indian culture or the individual Indian without an appreciation of their religion."[127]

The interest was mutual – Jung himself had been profoundly and permanently influenced by the Native spirituality he witnessed during a 1925 visit to Taos Pueblo. Jung, too, was troubled that rationalist Western culture had lost something very important in its rush to modernity, namely its essential connection to nature. "No wonder the Western world feels uneasy, for it does not know how much it has lost through the destruction of its [sacred concepts].... Its moral and spiritual tradition has collapsed and has left a worldwide disorientation and dissociation," Jung wrote. "Through scientific understanding our world has become dehumanized.... [Our] immediate communication with nature is gone for ever, and the emotional energy it generated has sunk into the unconscious.... We have been that mind, but we have never known it," he lamented. "We got rid of it before understanding it."[128]

Native thinking, in contrast, is characterized more than anything else by a belief that all of creation is linked in an egalitarian sort of cosmic unity, as discussed earlier. Unlike Western thinkers, Deloria explained, "the Sioux did not separate their thoughts into categories and disciplines.... Their view of life was holistic." "Everything was practical, economic, political and religious all at once. Indeed, they had a word for this totality, Wounicage, which simply meant 'our way of doing things.' They accorded other people the right to have their own ways also" – a posture of tolerance that Deloria's fellow radicals Williams, Paine, Stanton, and Du Bois surely would have applauded as well.[129]

Specifically, Deloria explained, "the Sioux developed sets of relationships with other entities that they believed shared the same status":

> Sioux people expected that through living intermediaries, such as stones, animals, plants and birds, they would be led to an understanding of their world and lives. There is no symbolism or hierarchy here in the Jungian sense. Instead, spirits, sometimes human, sometimes not, sometimes birds and animals, appeared physically before them in visions and befriended them. With the assistance of these entities and through their strength, individuals were able to exercise useful powers and to live constructively.[130]

The point is that it was the experience – whether waking or dreaming – that mattered: "All experiences were carefully analyzed and remembered, and beliefs always had an empirical referent."[131]

Dreams, Deloria suggested, are where "we find the largest and most intriguing distinctions between Jung and the Sioux" because "[b]oth groups rely heavily on dreams for information about the future." To the Sioux, dreams are the carriers of symbols, "a wholly different experience than everyday life, comparable in some ways to the near-death experiences described by a number of doctors." "Everyone was expected to open themselves to the greater mystery sometime during adolescence, and few people failed to receive a response of some kind," he shared. "Dreams required public performance, and public performance meant the shared experience of manifested power.... [A]n important dream is immensely practical, warning of danger or informing the dreamer about future events. These kinds of dreams are common enough that people do not regard them as extraordinary."[132]

Jung also saw dreams as conveyors of divine inspiration. The dream was his "most important analytical tool" – "to the psyche as an x-ray is to the body, it truthfully pictures the actual state of a portion of the whole organism/psyche":

> [Dreams] are not subject to our control but obey their own laws.... We do not know the source of their motives, and we therefore say that dreams come from the unconscious.... [I]n dreams we put on the likeness of that more universal, truer, more eternal man dwelling in the darkness of primordial night. There he is still the whole, and the whole is in him, indistinguishable from nature and bare of all egohood. Out of these all-united depths arises the dream.... [Dreams] are therefore fitted, as nothing else is, to give us back an attitude that accords with our basic human nature when our consciousness has strayed too far from its foundations or runs into an impasse.[133]

Dreams, in other words, provided access to the unconscious in Jungian thought, which in turn provided access to information about a much more profound unity among all present and past living organisms. To Jung and other early-twentieth-century psychologists, "the conscious consisted of those bits of information, feelings, experiences and memories which could be easily and quickly retrieved by the willful act of individuals, the unconscious, on the other hand, was an entirely different creature." To Jung, "the unconscious was the ultimate repository of *all* of the experiences of organisms on this planet, of the imprints of ancient learned patterns of survival, of the collective memories of our species," Deloria elaborated, "and of the historical remembrances of the many societies as well as the ancestral family traits inherited by the individual and, of course, his or her set of repressed memories."

Then, "as time passed," he continued, "the unconscious expanded to incorporate new experiences of the biosphere.... Jung came to believe that the psyche and the atom could be understood as essentially the same thing." Jung posited: "Sooner or later, nuclear physics and the psychology of the unconscious will draw closer together as both of them, independently of one another and from opposite directions, push forward into transcendental territory, the one with the concept of the atom, the other with that of the archetype."[134]

Jung acknowledged that "a merger of the results of observation and controlled experimentation was not possible then – and may not be possible now." He added, however, that "[s]ome Quantum physicists today maintain that the indeterminate methodology in subatomic physics is itself evidence of such a unity, a unity that might easily include the psyche." Indeed, "Jung conceived of the psyche in terms of mind and matter, then, which led him to an exploration of physics," Deloria explained. Specifically, "the deeper 'layers' of the psyche lose their individual uniqueness as they retreat farther and farther into darkness." Jung said:

> "Lower Down," that is to say as they approach the autonomous functional systems, they become increasingly collective until they are universalized and extinguished in the body's materiality, i.e., in chemical substances. The body's carbon is simply carbon. Hence "at bottom" the psyche is simply "world." The microphysical world of the atom exhibits certain features whose affinities with the psychic have impressed themselves even on the physicists. Here, it would seem, is at least a suggestion of how the psychic process could be "reconstructed" in another medium, in that, namely, of the microphysics of matter.

Stated another way, Jung continued, "It is not only possible but fairly probable, that psyche and matter are two different aspects of one and the same thing," leading Deloria to comment: "If the psyche could act in a manner similar to 'matter' as we know it, then it seems likely that space and time are not the boundaries we have been taught to believe."[135]

Jung speculated on "the hypothetical possibility that the psyche touches on a form of existence outside space and time" and therefore "presents a scientific question-mark that merits serious consideration for a long time to come.... Modern science," Deloria suggested, "has often been an expression of a deeply materialistic practice that aggressively asserts a position largely devoid of the metaphysical." "Ironically, Western science's insistence on material proof for such entities as 'the soul' stands in stark contrast to the fantastically abstract technological world and culture that has created science and in which it functions" – indeed, recall that the greatest breakthroughs in modern physics have come largely from metaphysical inspiration.

Deloria offered that "Jung's proposed extension of the psyche to a fundamental place in the material world – at least to the world that we have been taught to believe as material – gives us a possibility for the unification of knowledge and a metaphysics that is neither ethereal nor material, but which consists of 'mind-stuff' or 'thinking matter.'" Jung's archetypes, he imagined, may become considered something akin to the equivalent of the formulas describing the physical universe in physics, and may well be seen as comparable to the prophecies of [Sioux] visions, as they give us access to other spaces and superior, non-chronological time."[136]

In summary, we "begin with the recognition that the fundamental reality in our physical world is a strange kind of energy that is found within everything – from stars to humans to stones to quantum energy fields," Deloria posited. "Here we have the opportunity to unite psychology and religion with the energy fields of quantum physics. As the English physicist and mathematician Sir James Jeans, the theoretical physicist F. David Peat, and others have proposed, the world might simply be something like a giant thought." Interestingly, "many Indian tribes start from similar propositions."[137]

IV. The Way Forward: Legacy

> *Within the traditions, beliefs, and customs of the American Indian people are the guidelines for society's future.... Who will listen to the trees, the animals and birds, the voices of the places of the land?... The future of humankind lies waiting for those who will come to understand their lives and take up their responsibilities to all living things.*
>
> – Vine Deloria Jr., 1975

The white visitors from the east were aghast at the conditions in which they found the esteemed Sioux elder, Red Cloud.

The venerable old chief, who in the years immediately following the Civil War had led the Lakota in successfully resisting white occupation of traditional hunting grounds (culminating in the Fort Laramie Treaty of 1868), lived now at the turn of the century in squalor in a one-room dirt-floor cabin at the Pine Ridge Reservation, with just a single potbellied stove to cut the brutal cold of the South Dakota winter.

His female relatives brought him a single bowl of soup daily, and people still came to him for advice, but to the Western eye this was no way for a man of Red Cloud's stature to be living.

"We will send you some things that will allow you to live more comfortably," they announced. And so they did, organizing a charity drive in Boston and sending him fine blankets, money, clothing, and rugs for the dirt floor.

When the white visitors returned the following year, the goods were nowhere to be seen in Red Cloud's cabin. One man, very angry, wanted to know where they were.

"What happened to those things we sent?" he demanded.

"I gave them to the people," Red Cloud replied.

"What? That's crazy – you have nothing! You're a chief! You shouldn't be living like this!"

Red Cloud patiently explained, "I gave those things away *because* I am a chief."[138]

Vine Deloria Jr. retired from full-time teaching in 2000. Thereafter, he was still much in demand as a speaker, continuing until his death in 2005 to agitate for an indigenous way of life embracing (among other things) the great Red Cloud's values: that the sharing of one's possessions with others is the highest possible form of behavior. "Maturity, in the American Indian context," Deloria once commented, "is the ultimate goal of all human existence."[139]

Now a (somewhat reluctant) elder himself, Deloria remained as outspoken as ever on many topics. Among the objects of his critical eye during these years was American higher education: "The institutionalization of knowledge in the academic setting," he charged in 1995, "has made status more important than accomplishments or ideas when determining the canon of truth that will give the best explanation of our planet." "[After retiring,] I realized that academia had been a very stifling, cowardly environment," he recalled in a 2002 speech. "Everyone lived in fear of the institution, of the administrators, of their colleagues in the department, and especially of the profession to which they had pledged undying loyalty. Most annoying to me was the fear of what colleagues might say if I had an original thought."[140]

"We fight desperately to maintain what we call "intellectual freedom" for academics," he continued. "But what is academic freedom in the U.S.? My conclusion is that academic freedom in the U.S. is the right to support whatever doctrine the senior scholar or scholars in a particular field favors" – a conclusion with which W. E. B. Du Bois would have sympathized, we may recall, given the egregiously skewed account of Reconstruction told by several generations of Southern-sympathetic Dunning school historians. "Niels Bohr once noted that new theories arise when the proponents of the old theories die out. Surely we can do better," Deloria admonished, relating a Chinese scholar's quip: "Why is it in China we can criticize Darwin, but not the government, and in the United States you can criticize the government, but not Darwin?"

"The realization that this quip adequately and eloquently describes our situation today continues to haunt me," Deloria admitted. "I came to academia believing the traditional picture of the scholar after nearly two decades of political activism. Joining the University of Arizona," he recalled, "I was very interested in learning more about political theory. For over a year, I patiently went to lunch with my colleagues hoping to engage in heated analyses of the central tenets of our profession. [Instead,] I learned mostly about the politics of getting an edge with the administration for more benefits."[141]

Ever challenging convention, Deloria concluded, "Let's free up graduate education, treat grad students as colleagues, open avenues for minorities, and become aware of the struggles over meaning occurring in the streets around us. Let's tear into existing dogmas asking, 'But what if?'"[142]

The Way Forward

After detailing the many betrayals and broken promises endured by Indian tribes over the centuries at the hands of the United States, Vine Deloria Jr. never hesitated to offer prescriptive advice. "[A] massive correctional effort is needed," he wrote in 1999, "to bring forward the misapplications and omissions of American history so that we can create a coherent and consistent interpretation of the relationship of tribal nations to the U.S. government (and the constituent states) and to the Constitution."[143]

"As the country nears the third millennium," he declared, "it is long overdue that the federal government once again restrict itself to the exercise of the only clear traditional manner of dealing with Indian tribes – the treaty relationship." This was a point he and other Indian activists had been making for more than a quarter-century since even before the Alcatraz and Wounded Knee uprisings. "The best way to restore dignity to the tribes," he had written in 1974, "is to fulfill the original promises made to the tribes in the treaties and agreements of former years" and to return to treaty making for any future negotiations as well.[144]

Moreover, Deloria insisted, the Supreme Court and Congress's mistaken, long-overinflated interpretation of the commerce clause must finally be corrected. Rather than giving Congress plenary power over Indian tribes, "[t]he commerce clause should [instead] be [recognized as] authority primarily for Congress to adjust the domestic law of the U.S. to conform to [its] obligations and responsibilities... as a result of the treaties it makes with the Indian tribes." Tribes are, after all, "preexisting [separate] sovereigns who live surrounded by states and the federal government, the latter-day sovereigns." This last echoes Deloria's earlier statements as well: "Affirmative action by the Congress of the U.S. to define Indian tribes as smaller nations under the protection of the U.S. would be the first step in defining the nature of the new relationship." "In effect, this action would mean a surrender by the U.S. of its right to extinguish Indian aboriginal title, and would freeze the present Indian lands within the context of national boundaries rather than reservation boundaries."[145]

By recognizing Indian tribes under international law principles, he averred, "states would have no more power to interfere with tribal governments or reservation affairs than they would to interfere with the operation of the Canadian or Mexican government. The lines of civil and criminal jurisdiction would be clearly set." Moreover, "Congress could provide a special federal court to handle all questions arising under the treaties, agreements, and laws pertaining to Indians." "We already have various federal courts that deal with specific subject matter," he observed, "and the justification of each of them is that they require a special knowledge and deal with a special body of law and hence relieve the regular federal courts from having to deal with technical subjects with which they might not have expertise."[146]

The specialized court is especially necessary now, Deloria would suggest, in light of the regressive modern Supreme Court. The idea of a special court of Indian affairs was actually one key part of John Collier's comprehensive dream for the IRA in 1934, only to be vastly watered down in the legislative process. Collier's broader vision for the IRA is still relevant today – indeed, Deloria has said, "One of the interim steps which the federal government could take in its effort to create a new Indian policy would be to recognize the genius of John Collier's original suggestions and reconsider the titles contained in his original proposal as separate pieces of legislation today."[147]

Legacy

Vine Deloria Jr. was a central figure in providing a unifying intellectual, political voice to Native Americans past, present, and future in their battles for self-determination and for reclaiming tribal heritage. "For a long time," he told a largely ignorant American public in 1969, which still carried a largely romanticized Cowboys-and-Indians view of the American West, "an Indian was not presumed capable of initiating an action in a court of law, of owning property, or of giving testimony against whites in court. Nor could an Indian vote or leave his reservation. Indians were America's captive people without any defined rights whatsoever."[148]

Although things had improved from those bleakest days from 1880 to 1934, Indian tribes in 1969 were still profoundly disfavored and disadvantaged relative to their rightful status as sovereign nations. Deloria spent a good part of his life working to change this, repeatedly emphasizing, "Indians are alive, have certain dreams of their own, and are being overrun by the ignorance and the mistaken, misdirected efforts of those who would help them."[149] Indeed, he bitterly charged, not all of those efforts were well meaning:

> America has always been a militantly imperialistic world power eagerly grasping for economic control over weaker nations. The Indian wars of the past should be rightly regarded as the first foreign wars of American history. As the U.S. marched across this continent, it was creating an empire by wars of foreign conquest just as England and France were doing in India and Africa. Certainly the war with Mexico was imperialistic, no more or less than the wars against the Sioux, Apache, Utes, and Yakimas. In every case the goal was identical: land.... There has not been a time since the founding of the republic when the motives of this country were innocent.[150]

Continuing, Deloria insisted that, "[i]f morality is to be achieved in this country's relations with other nations, a return to basic principles is in order." And "the first step toward introducing morality into American foreign policy" would be for the federal government to honor its existing treaty obligations to Indian tribes. "Until America begins to build a moral record in her dealings with the Indian people," he concluded, "she should not try to fool the rest of the world about her intentions on other continents." As for the "long-forgotten" Indians themselves, Deloria predicted that as they "rise and begin to reclaim their ancient heritage, they will discover the meaning of the lands of their ancestors. That is when," he added provocatively, "the invaders of the North American continent will finally discover that for this land, God is red."[151]

Deloria reported in 1974 that, "[f]or the first time in history[,] American Indians are exploring the old legal doctrines, the cultural attitudes of themselves and white society, and the history of the peoples of the world to find an answer to the present confusion." With their inquiries came "a realization that the tribe must stand before history and reclaim its political and cultural identity and independence." Deloria's own tribe, the Sioux, "submerged their feelings and suffered in silence but never forgot the defeats they had inflicted upon the white man in numerous battles," he revealed. "Beneath the façade of defeat was the urgency to have one more battle, losing perhaps to overwhelming odds, but in losing finding that eternal affirmation that it is a 'good day to die' and thus confirming that it did mean something to be a Lakota." Nor were these feelings restricted to the Sioux. "[F]or nearly a century," Deloria elaborated, other tribes also "kept their feelings well hidden from the white man but simmering just beneath the surface so if the time should arise when a chance existed to reclaim freedom, there would never be a question whether the price was too high."[152]

Indians implicitly understood all of this, Deloria said – and sure enough, in the mid-1960s "the movement began to get its bearings, first in political ideology, then in religious doctrine, then back again to practical politics, and finally in the explosions of Alcatraz, Fort Lawton, and other invasions of federal lands." Then, "[f]rom the initial protests, one can draw a straight line in ideology and type of confrontation from the first invasion of Alcatraz in 1964 to the snowy hills of Wounded Knee, South Dakota, in 1973" – all revolving substantively around "the treaty of 1868 as symbolic of the hundreds of treaties and agreements that had proven less valuable than the paper they were printed on."[153]

In addition to his invaluable work on the political status of tribes in America, Deloria also brought a greater understanding of tribal traditions and Native religion to the broader non-Indian audience. Beyond the inherent value in such efforts of promoting greater cultural awareness, he undertook – in what may indeed turn out to be his greatest long-term legacy – the ambitious attempt, through the device of Jungian psychology, to bridge the gap between materialist Western science and Native spirituality.

Deloria acknowledged that "[t]he difficulty in opening this dialogue comes from a point of significant difference: the Sioux saw everything as a matter of personal relationships... between and among sacred powers that stood as equals to each other; Jung, following a scientific format, used words that conveyed the sense of objectivity required of scientists." Deloria proposed, though, that "[n]ew perspectives from contemporary science and psychology allow us to see a number of ways in which his psychology greatly resembles the Sioux traditions. It is worth pursuing this overlap and resemblance," he added, "for with almost every topic we have discussed, the Sioux had a broader vision that opens up new questions of both science and psychology. A recounting of Sioux traditions also offers us additional practical physical data to support further inquiry into the philosophical framework offered by Jung."[154]

Deloria's collaborator Jerome Bernstein commented that Deloria's point was not to convince non-Indians to begin practicing tribal rituals. Rather, it was to develop a new measure of cross-cultural respect for other approaches to science and spirituality. "Jung attempted to build a conceptual and psychic bridge to that realm from which Western culture became severed," Bernstein explained. "Vine Deloria Jr. saw Jung's effort, and... has built a conceptual and psychic bridge from his side of the river to meet Jung's. I have an image of the two of them meeting somewhere on that span, sitting and smoking together, arguing and having one hell of a palaver, all the while appreciating and respecting what the other brings."

It is fitting that Deloria and our first radical, Roger Williams – though separated in time by some 350 years – were together in spirit as outspoken advocates for Native rights. From his earliest days in Massachusetts Bay Colony in 1632, Williams intuitively understood that simple principles of decency and fairness prohibited the newcomer Europeans from defrauding the continent's Native inhabitants by taking their land without compensation – and he spoke out about how English kings were seriously morally mistaken for suggesting otherwise. Those same core principles of decency and fairness motivated Vine Deloria Jr. in his outspoken efforts to reclaim for Indian tribes their rightful status as sovereign nations entitled to practice their own traditions free of American government interference.

In the four hundred years between Williams's birth and Deloria's death, those same core principles of decency and fairness – as translated into the larger concepts of liberty and equal justice – informed the belief systems and activities of Thomas Paine regarding the basic rights of man, Elizabeth Cady Stanton on women's rights, and W. E. B. Du Bois on the status of blacks in America. That all of these radicals, each of whom did so much to advance America along the arc of justice in his or her respective ways, shared such core beliefs and experiences during their lifetimes provides, in the end, a fine testament to the Native concept of the timeless "roundness of things."[155]

Notes

Introduction

1. The California measure, Proposition 8, followed an earlier decision by the California Supreme Court holding that the state constitution requires equal treatment of gay marriage.
2. Loving v. Virginia, 388 U.S. 1, 3, 6 (1967).
3. Martin Luther King Jr., "Remaining Awake through a Great Revolution," Mar. 31, 1968. "We shall overcome because the arc of a moral universe is long, but it bends towards justice," King explained. "We shall overcome because Carlyle is right – no lie can live forever. We shall overcome because William Cullen Bryant is right – truth crushed to earth will rise again. We shall overcome because James Russell Lowell is right – 'truth forever on the scaffold, wrong forever on the throne, yet that scaffold sways the future, and behind the demon known, stands a God within the shadow, keeping watch above his own.'" Indeed, truth is already beginning to sway Proposition 8's wrongful discrimination. Shortly before this book went to press, a federal district court struck down the law, explaining that "California's obligation is to treat its own citizens equally, not to 'mandate [its] own moral code.'" "Excerpts From the Judge's Ruling on Proposition 8," *New York Times*, August 8, 2010. The case, *Perry v. Schwarzenegger*, will likely reach the Supreme Court within the next couple years.
4. Amy Chua, *Day of Empire* (New York: Doubleday, 2007), xxxii.
5. Under Howard Zinn's quasi-Marxist view, in which virtually any political conflict may be reduced to a conflict among the classes of society, even the Revolution itself was driven primarily by class interests. "Around 1776," Zinn speculates, "certain important people in America made a discovery that would prove enormously useful for the next two hundred years." "It is pretended that, as in the Preamble to the Constitution, it is 'we the people'

who wrote that document, rather than fifty-five privileged white males whose class interest required a strong central government. That use of government for class purposes, to serve the needs of the wealthy and powerful, has continued throughout American history, down to the present day." Howard Zinn, *A People's History of the United States, 1492–Present* (1980; New York: Harper Perennial: 2005), 59, 684. "The movement for the Constitution," Charles Beard explains, "was originated and carried through principally by four groups of personal property interests which had been adversely affected under the Articles of Confederation: money, public securities, manufactures, trade and shipping." Charles Beard, *An Economic Interpretation of the Constitution of the United States* (New York: Macmillan, 1913), 324–5.

6. Williams, Paine, Cady Stanton, Du Bois, and Deloria are not the only potential worthies – we might also examine the lives of any number of others (some iconic, some not), including William Penn, Benjamin Franklin, Thomas Jefferson, George Washington, William Lloyd Garrison, Thaddeus Stevens, Ralph Waldo Emerson, Henry David Thoreau, Abraham Lincoln, Susan B. Anthony, Frederick Douglass, Malcolm X, Martin Luther King, Julian Samora, Gloria Steinem, Harry Hay, Cesar Chavez, and Howard Zinn, to name just a few.
7. Roger Williams, *The Hireling Ministry None of Christs* (1652).
8. Elbert Hubbard, "Thomas Paine," *Little Visits to the Homes of the Great* (William Wise, 1916), 170; Jack Fruchtman Jr., "Foreword," *Common Sense, Rights of Man and Other Essential Writings of Thomas Paine* (New York: Signet Classics, 2003), x.
9. Herbert Aptheker, "Du Bois, The Historian," in *W. E. B. Du Bois, A Profile*, ed. Rayford W. Logan, 256 (New York: Hill and Wang, 1971), from *Negro History Bulletin* 32, no. 4 (April 1969), 6–16.
10. Vine Deloria Jr., *Custer Died for Your Sins: An Indian Manifesto* (New York: Macmillan, 1969), 103; Kirk Johnson, "Vine Deloria Jr., Champion of Indian Rights, Dies at 72," *New York Times*, Nov. 15, 2005.
11. Thomas Paine, *The Rights of Man* (1792; London: Watts & Co., 1906), 27–8; Thomas Paine, *Common Sense: Addressed to the Residents of America* (1776; New York: Peter Eckler Publishing, 1918), 1–2; Michael Anthony Lawrence, "Government as Liberty's Servant: The 'Reasonable Time, Place and Manner' Standard of Review for All Government Restrictions on Liberty Interests," *Louisiana Law Review* 71 (2007), 1.
12. Bernard Bailyn, *The Ideological Origins of the American Revolution* (1967; Cambridge, MA: Harvard Belknap, 1992), v–vi; Eric Foner, *The Story of American Freedom* (New York: Norton, 1998), xiii.
13. J. S. Mill, *On Liberty* (1859; Cambridge, UK: Cambridge University Press, 2000), 13; John Locke, *Two Treatises of Government and a Letter Concerning Toleration* (New Haven, CT: Yale University Press, 2003).
14. Olmstead v. United States, 277 U.S. 438, 478 (1928) (Brandeis, J., dissenting); West Virginia State Board of Education v. Barnette, 319 U.S. 624, 642 (1943); Lawrence v. Texas, 539 U.S. 558, 562 (2003).

15. Thomas Paine, "Dissertations on Government," *The Political and Miscellaneous Works of Thomas Paine*, vol. 1 (London: R. Carlile, 1819). For example, in a 2007 case, *Ledbetter v. Goodyear Tire & Rubber Co.*, the Supreme Court applied an inappropriately narrow interpretation of the Civil Rights Act of 1964 in denying Lilly Ledbetter's equal-pay claim. Congress, in response, passed the "Lilly Ledbetter Fair Pay Act of 2009" to make clear that, under the statute, claims such as Ledbetter's should be considered by the Court. *Countermajoritarian-difficulty* refers to the doctrinal problem posed in a democracy when an unelected judiciary negates the act of democratically elected majority. Alexander M. Bickel, *The Least Dangerous Branch* (1962; New Haven, CT: Yale University Press, 1986), 16.
16. Michael Walzer, *On Toleration* (New Haven, CT: Yale University Press, 1997), 98.
17. Thomas Paine, *Age of Reason* (1794; New York: Truth Seeker Press, 1898), 10–12.
18. Roger Williams, *The Bloudy Tenent of Persecution for Cause of Conscience* (London: Haddon, 1848), 1, 11, 66.
19. Paine, *Age of Reason*, 6, 9–12; Theodore Roosevelt, *Gouverneur Morris* (1888; Boston: Houghton Mifflin, 1898), 251. Roosevelt added, "There are infidels and infidels, but Paine belonged to the variety... that apparently esteems a bladder of dirty water as the proper weapon with which to assail Christianity."
20. Ann D. Gordon, ed., *The Selected Papers of Elizabeth Cady Stanton and Susan B. Anthony* (Piscataway, NJ: Rutgers University Press, 2006), 4:442; Kathi Kern, *Mrs. Stanton's Bible* (Ithaca, NY: Cornell University Press, 2001), 67; Vivian Gornick, *The Solitude of Self: Thinking about Elizabeth Cady Stanton* (New York: Farrar, Straus, and Giroux, 2005), 119; Elizabeth Cady Stanton, *The Woman's Bible* (1895; Boston: Northeastern University Press, 1993). See generally Elisabeth Griffith, *In Her Own Right: The Life of Elizabeth Cady Stanton* (New York: Oxford, 1984).
21. Herbert Aptheker, ed., *The Correspondence of W. E. B. Du Bois: Selections, 1877–1934* (Amherst: University of Massachusetts Press, 1973), 131, 311; Manning Marable, *Black Radical Democrat* (Boston: Twayne Publishers, 1986), 125; Malaika Home, "Jesus Christ," in *W. E. B. Du Bois: An Encyclopedia*, ed. Gerald Horne and Mary Young (Westport, CT: Greenwood Press, 2001), 181. See generally David L. Lewis, *W. E. B. Du Bois: Biography of a Race, 1868–1919* (New York: Henry Holt, 1993); David L. Lewis, *W. E. B. Du Bois: The Fight for Equality and the American Century, 1919–1963* (New York: Henry Holt, 2000).
22. Vine Deloria Jr., *God Is Red: A Native View of Religion* (1972; Golden, CO: Fulcrum Publishing, 1994), 189; Deloria, *Custer*, 104.
23. Gloria Steinem, *Outrageous Acts and Everyday Rebellions* (1984; New York: Henry Holt, 1995), 383; W. E. B. Du Bois, "Galileo Galilei," in *The Education of Black People: Ten Critiques, 1906–60* (1908; New York: Monthly Review Press, 1973).

24. Bailyn, *Ideological Origins*, 57–8; Alexis de Tocqueville, *Democracy in America*, trans. Arthur Goldhammer (1835; New York: Library of America, 2004), 819.
25. Harpo Films, *The Great Debaters* (2007).
26. Metro-Goldwyn-Mayer, *The Wizard of Oz* (1939).
27. Theodore Seuss Geisel, *Yertl the Turtle and Other Stories* (New York: Random House, 1958).
28. Declaration of Independence of the United States of America.
29. Jefferson to Roger C. Weightman, June 24, 1826, in *The Writings of Thomas Jefferson, 1816–1826*, ed. Paul Leicester Ford (New York: G. P. Putnam's Sons, 1899), 391.
30. Gaspar G. Bacon, *The Constitution of the United States in Some of Its Fundamental Aspects* (Cambridge, MA: Harvard University Press, 1928), 96.

1. Roger Williams (1603–1683): *Freeborn*

1. The vignettes throughout this book's five chapters are closely based on factual information available in the cited sources. They are written in accordance with common practice among historians of "remembering as a personal experience an event at which [they] had not been present in the flesh." Margaret Atwood, "In Search of *Alias Grace*: On Writing Canadian Historical Fiction," *American Historical Review* 103, no. 5 (1998), 1505. "[B]eing scrupulous," the Yale University history professor Jonathan Spence added, "we [historians] may draw conclusions that are equivalent to filling gaps.... We may juxtapose pieces of information in such a way as to imbue them with new meanings, or at least hint at their interconnections. We do not need the circumlocutions of schoolday essays – 'surely he must have been thinking,' or 'no doubt she was aware of' – to perform the same sleight of hand." Jonathan D. Spence, "Margaret Atwood and the Edges of History," *American Historical Review* 103, no. 5 (1998), 1523–4. In the interest of clarity, original archaic spellings are not retained.
2. Cyclone Covey, *The Gentle Radical: A Biography of Roger Williams* (New York: Macmillan, 1966), 116–17; Ola Elizabeth Winslow, *Master Roger Williams: A Biography* (New York: Macmillan, 1957), 119–20.
3. Martin Luther King Jr., *Letter from Birmingham Jail* (April 16, 1963), in *Literary Classics of the United States, Reporting Civil Rights, Part One: American Journalism 1941-1963* (New York: Library of America, 2003), 791–2.
4. Ibid.; Samuel H. Brockunier, *The Irrepressible Democrat Roger Williams* (New York: Ronald Press, 1940), 9; Covey, *The Gentle Radical*, 3.
5. Covey, *The Gentle Radical*, 5, 14; Brockunier, *The Irrepressible Democrat*, 13–14. Lord Edward Coke became an outspoken advocate for the common law against interference by the church hierarchy and the king. Imprisoned in the Tower of London by King James for seven months in 1621 for his work on a protestation for Parliament's ancient rights, he did some of his greatest

work in 1628 at the age of seventy-seven when, as a member of Parliament, he led the House of Commons' effort to pass and impose on King Charles the Petition of Right, which reasserted Englishmen's rights against the king.

6. Winslow, *Master Roger Williams*, 56–7; Brockunier, *The Irrepressible Democrat*, 13.
7. Brockunier, *The Irrepressible Democrat*, 19–20; Winslow, *Master Roger Williams*, 61, 69–70.
8. Covey, *The Gentle Radical*, 7–8; Rev. William Wilson, *The Thirty-Nine Articles of the Church of England* (London: Oxford, for T. Hamilton, 1821), 4.
9. Edwin S. Gaustad, *Roger Williams* (New York: Oxford, 2005), 1–2; Covey, *The Gentle Radical*, 8. The king's action led to an immediate repudiation from Parliament, after which Charles dissolved Parliament until 1640.
10. Gaustad, *Roger Williams*, 3.
11. John Garrett, *Roger Williams: Witness beyond Christendom, 1603–1683* (New York: Macmillan, 1970), 14–15; Covey, *The Gentle Radical*, 56; Williston Walker, *The Creeds and Platforms of Congregationalism* (Philadelphia: Pilgrim Press, 1969), 89–91.
12. Covey, *The Gentle Radical*, 8. The Puritan underground involved organizations of clergy, lawyers, and merchants who hired Puritan preachers as ministers for their groups. Ibid., 9.
13. Ibid., 8; Garrett, *Roger Williams*, 13, 74; Samuel Eliot Morison, *Builders of the Bay Colony* (Boston: Houghton Mifflin, 1930), 64–5; Arthur Percival Newton, *The Colonising Activities of the English Puritans* (Port Washington, NY: Kennikat Press, 1966); Frances Rose-Troup, *John White: The Patriarch of Dorchester and the Founder of Massachusetts, 1575–1648* (New York: G. P. Putnam's Sons, 1930); Larzer Ziff, *The Career of John Cotton: Puritanism and the American Experience* (Princeton, NJ: Princeton University Press). Williams also met the young Oliver Cromwell, four years his senior, at the Masham household. Garrett, *Roger Williams*, 13, 74; Edmund S. Morgan, *The Puritan Dilemma: The Story of John Winthrop* (Boston: Little, Brown, 1958), 34–53; Morison, *Builders of the Bay Colony*, 64.
14. L. Raymond Camp, *Roger Williams, God's Apostle of Advocacy: Biography and Rhetoric* (Lewiston, NY: Edwin Mellen Press, 1989), vi.
15. Covey, *The Gentle Radical*, 14.
16. Winslow, *Master Roger Williams*, 97; John Winthrop, *The History of New England from 1630 to 1649* (Boston: Little, Brown, 1853), 1:340; Caldwell, *Complete Writings*, 4:461.
17. Winslow, *Master Roger Williams*, 97.
18. Ibid.
19. Ibid., 100; Camp, *Roger Williams, God's Apostle*, 121; James D. Knowles, *Memoir of Roger Williams, the Founder of the State of Rhode-Island* (Boston: Lincoln, Edmands, 1834), 43–4; Charles M. Andrews, *The Colonial Period of American History* (New Haven, CT: Yale University Press, 1934), 1:435 nn1–3.

20. Henry Chupack, *Roger Williams* (New York: Twayne Publishers, 1969), 44; Covey, *The Gentle Radical*, 42; Winslow, *Master Roger Williams*, 101.
21. Garrett, *Roger Williams*, 14; William Bradford, *Of Plymouth Plantation, 1620–1647*, ed. Samuel Eliot Morison (New York: Alfred A. Knopf, 2002), 257; Covey, *The Gentle Radical*, 49. During Williams's stay in Plymouth, the colony was undergoing rapid economic development, leading to scrambles for land and diminished interest in religion, leading Williams to write Winthrop that religion was "a duty not so frequent with Plymouth as formerly." Covey, *The Gentle Radical*, 44–5.
22. Roger Williams, *The Bloody Tenet Yet More Bloody*, in Caldwell, *Complete Writings*, 4:461; Covey, *The Gentle Radical*, 94; Garrett, *Roger Williams*, 196; Gaustad, *Roger Williams*, 9. The colonies' self-rationalizations are epitomized by Winthrop's comments in 1633, in countering Williams: "[A]nd if God were not pleased with our inheriting these parts, why did he drive out the natives before us? And why does he still make room for us, by diminishing them [through smallpox] as we increase?" Covey, *The Gentle Radical*, 94.
23. Winslow, *Master Roger Williams*, 104–5; Covey, *The Gentle Radical*, 51; William Bradford, *History of Plimoth Plantation* (Boston: Wright & Potter Print Co., 1898), 2:369–70.
24. Winslow, *Master Roger Williams*, 102; Covey, *The Gentle Radical*, 42; Garrett, *Roger Williams*, 15; Williams, *The Bloody Tenet Yet More Bloody*, in Caldwell, *Complete Writings*, vol. 4.
25. Covey, *The Gentle Radical*, 77; Roger Williams, *Mr. Cotton's Letter Examined and Answered*, in *The Complete Writings of Roger Williams*, ed. Reuben Aldridge Guild (New York: Russell & Russell, 1963), 1:31–112.
26. Covey, *The Gentle Radical*, 77, 80.
27. Ibid., 74; Camp, *Roger Williams, God's Apostle*, 122; Chupack, *Roger Williams*, 44–5; James Kendall Hosmer, ed., *Winthrop's Journal "History of New England, 1630–1649* (New York: Charles Scribner's Sons, 1908), 1:113, 139. In 1637, Williams and Skelton's fears came true as a synod approved allowing civil enforcement of the First Table, with mere "advice" from the ministers. Chupack, *Roger Williams*, 45.
28. Edmund S. Morgan, *Roger Williams: The Church & State* (1967; New York: Norton, 2006), 19–20; Chupack, *Roger Williams*, 60; *Collections of the Rhode Island Historical Society* (Providence: Knowles, Vose & Co., 1839), 4:111. All of this explains why Williams was never a member of another organized religion after 1635.
29. Morgan, *Church and the State*, 83–4; "King Philip," a Wampanoag sachem from near Plymouth, engaged in a destructive war with the colonies in 1675. "As a result, once the war was over, the Narragansetts were crushed forever as a future threat to the settlers, but not before the members of the [New England] Confederation suffered heavy losses of life [and property]. Providence alone had more than one hundred of its original one hundred

and twenty-three houses destroyed." Chupack, *Roger Williams*, 60; Brockunier, *The Irrepressible Democrat*, 273–5; Garrett, *Roger Williams*, 33. Prior to the war's outbreak, Williams's services were called on for the last time to negotiate with the Narragansett; this time, he failed to avert major hostilities.

30. Morgan, *Church and the State*, 110, 113; Caldwell, *Complete Writings*, 4:243; Miller, *Complete Writings*, 7:224.
31. Covey, *The Gentle Radical*, 94–5; John Winthrop, *Winthrop's Journal, 1630–1649*, ed. J. Franklin Jameson (New York: Charles Scribner's Sons, 1908), 1:116.
32. Covey, *The Gentle Radical*, 82, 94–5; Chupack, *Roger Williams*, 46; Richard S. Dunn, James Savage, and Laetitia Yeandle, eds., *The Journal of John Winthrop, 1630–1649* (Cambridge, MA: Belknap Press, 1996), 1:108.
33. We see an example of questionable historical reporting with Massachusetts Bay historian William Hubbard, who, in his *General History of New England*, places responsibility for the incident solely at Williams's feet, whereas the record clearly demonstrates otherwise. See Chupack, *Roger Williams*, 46; Brockunier, *The Irrepressible Democrat*, 51–2; Camp, *Roger Williams, God's Apostle*, 122–3; Covey, *The Gentle Radical*, 102–3. See also Winslow, *Master Roger Williams*, 114 (reporting that King James placed the cross on the flag in 1606).
34. Covey, *The Gentle Radical*, 102–4.
35. Ibid.
36. Ibid., 111–12; Chupack, *Roger Williams*, 46–7; Brockunier, *The Irrepressible Democrat*, 58–60; Gaustad, *Roger Williams*, 10; Winslow, *Master Roger Williams*, 116; Glenn W. LaFantasie, ed., *The Correspondence of Roger Williams, 1629–1653* (Hanover, MA: Brown University Press and University Press of New England, 1988), 1:19.
37. Winslow, *Master Roger Williams*, 117; Covey, *The Gentle Radical*, 114; Sarah Vowell, *The Wordy Shipmates* (New York: Penguin Group, 2008), 101–3.
38. Covey, *The Gentle Radical*, 114–15.
39. Brockunier, *The Irrepressible Democrat*, 62–3.
40. Ibid.; Chupack, *Roger Williams*, 48; Covey, *The Gentle Radical*, 116; Winthrop, *The History of New England*, 1:340.
41. Winslow, *Master Roger Williams*, 118; Covey, *The Gentle Radical*, 116–17; Brockunier, *The Irrepressible Democrat*, 64–5; *Master John Cotton's Answer to Master Roger Williams*, ed. Rev. J. Lewis Diman, in *Publications of the Narragansett Club*, 1st ser. (Providence, RI: George Taylor Paine, for the Narragansett Club, 1867), 2:178n60.
42. Covey, *The Gentle Radical*, 116–17; Winslow, *Master Roger Williams*, 118–19; Chupack, *Roger Williams*, 48–9; Winthrop, *The History of New England*, 1:204. The contrary position of a good number of Williams's ministerial colleagues was made clear in a tract they wrote titled *A Model of Church and*

Civil Power, in which they authorized the right of civil magistrates to intervene in church affairs threatening to cause divisions or separation. Chupack, *Roger Williams*, 48.

43. Brockunier, *The Irrepressible Democrat*, 68, 77, 83–4.
44. Ibid., 84–5; Covey, *The Gentle Radical*, 119–20.
45. Covey, *The Gentle Radical*, 120; Brockunier, *The Irrepressible Democrat*, 86.
46. Winslow, *Master Roger Williams*, 125–6.
47. Ibid., 113; *Gov. Winthrop's Letter to Mr. Endicott about Roger Williams*, in *Proceedings of the Massachusetts Historical Society, 1871–1873*, by Massachusetts Historical Society (Boston: Historical Society, 1873), 344. The Bay colonists never knew when the king's men might show up at their doors. On July 29, 1634, the Bay authorities agreed to fortify Castle Island, a defensive position. A couple of months later, on September 18, word came via the *Griffin* that a Captain Woodhouse, together with troops, might be on his way to impose a governor-general on the Bay. Also arriving on the *Griffin* was a copy of a commission naming Archbishop Laud as head of a committee intended to govern foreign plantations. These ominous news items gave conservative authorities an excuse to pass strict new laws regulating tobacco, dress, and the like, and they hastened funding for the improvements at Castle Island. Covey, *The Gentle Radical*, 102, 111, 94.
48. Covey, *The Gentle Radical*, 120–1.
49. This is part of a poem included in an 1861 book by Daniel C. Eddy describing the courageous resilience of the many Baptists persecuted over the centuries, including Roger Williams. Daniel C. Eddy, *Roger Williams and the Baptists: An Historical Discourse* (Boston: Andrew F. Graves, 1861), 95.
50. Williams to Major Mason, Providence, June 22, 1670, in *Proceedings of the Rhode Island Historical Society, 1874–5* (Providence, RI: Providence Press Co., 1875), 77; Covey, *The Gentle Radical*, 122–5, 128. Williams wrote: "When I was unkindly & unchristianly as I believe driven from my house & land, & wife & children in the midst of New England winter . . . , That ever honored Governor Mr. Winthrop privately wrote me to steer my Course to the Nahigonset Bay & Indians, for many high & heavenly & public Ends, encouraging me from the freeness of the place from any English claims or patents. I took his prudent motion as a hint & voice from God, & waiving all other thoughts & motions I steered my course from Salem (though in Winter snow which I feel yet) unto these parts, wherein . . . I have seen the Face of God." Winthrop's *Journal* reports that the winter of 1635–6 was a "very bad season." Winslow, *Master Roger Williams*, 127.
51. Williams to Major Mason, Providence, June 22, 1670, in *Proceedings of the Rhode Island Historical Society, 1874–5* (Providence, RI: Providence Press Co., 1875), 77; Covey, *The Gentle Radical*, 125–8; Winslow, *Master Roger Williams*, 126. Ousamequin (Massasoit) is better known as the high sachem who first visited and offered friendship to William Bradford and the Pilgrims

on March 22, 1621, in Plymouth – the site of a former Wampanoag village where thousands died of the plague around 1617.

52. Covey, *The Gentle Radical*, 127–9; Winslow, *Master Roger Williams*, 128; C. H. Simmons, ed., *Plymouth Colony Records* (Camden, ME: Picton Press, 1996), 2:87 (recording ten fathom of beads as the price "for his land at Seacunk").

53. Covey, *The Gentle Radical*, 128; Winslow, *Master Roger Williams*, 128 (quoting Williams's 1661 Testimony, taken at Providence, Dec. 13, 1661, John Russell Bartlett, ed., *Complete Writings of Roger Williams,* 7 vols. [New York: Russell & Russell, 1963], 6:316).

54. Covey, *The Gentle Radical*, 129–31; Winslow, *Master Roger Williams*, 129 (describing some of the differing permutations of the legend, including the suggestion that the "What cheer, Netop?" greeting actually occurred during a preliminary scouting trip made alone by Williams and Angell or that Williams was perhaps the first to call out "What cheer, Netop?" to the Narragansett on the shoreline).

55. Morgan, *Church and the State*, 122–3; Sydney V. James, *Colonial Rhode Island: A History* (New York: Scribner's, 1975), 5–6. It was partly for similar reasons that Williams's friend Ousamequin (Massasoit) himself first welcomed the Pilgrims in 1621 – as a hedge against his traditional enemies, the Narragansett, to the west, to whom the Wampanoag had been losing ground. Winslow, *Master Roger Williams*, 122–3.

56. Covey, *The Gentle Radical*, 131–2. As Williams commented on August 25, 1658, about Aquidneck (the island of Rhode Island): "It was not price nor money that could have purchased Rhode Island. Rhode Island was purchased by love."

57. Ibid., 131. The boundaries of the original purchase were memorialized on March 24, 1638, with a written deed, executed in an elaborate ceremony at Pettaquamscutt Rock. Winslow, *Master Roger Williams*, 132–3; Howard M. Chapin, *The Documentary History of Rhode Island* (Providence: Preston and Rounds Co., 1916), 1:61–9.

58. Covey, *The Gentle Radical*, 133–5.

59. Ibid., 135; Chupack, *Roger Williams*, 52; Winslow, *Master Roger Williams*, 138; Bartlett, ed., *Complete Writings,* 6:316; Williams to John Winthrop, 1636 or 1637, in *Publications of the Narragansett Club*, 1st ser. (Providence, RI: George Taylor Paine for the Narragansett Club, 1874), 6:3–7.

60. Chupack, *Roger Williams*, 53; Winslow, *Master Roger Williams*, 138–9; Bartlett, *Complete Writings*, 6:3–7.

61. Winslow, *Master Roger Williams*, 139.

62. Ibid., 137–8 (quoting John Russell Bartlett, ed., Rhode Island Colonial Records, 10 vols. (Providence: State of Rhode Island, 1:14); Chupack, *Roger Williams*, 52 (citing same) [emphasis added].

63. Chupack, *Roger Williams*, 52 (quoting Williams's 1677 Testimony, Rider's *Historical Tracts*, no. 14, 55); Bruce C. Daniels, *Dissent and Conformity*

on Narragansett Bay the Colonial Rhode Island Town (Middletown, CT: Wesleyan University Press, 1983), 11 (citing General Assembly to General Assembly of Massachusetts Bay, Mar. 1658); Gaustad, *Roger Williams*, 60; Rufus Jones, *The Quakers in the American Colonies* (London: Macmillan, 1923), 54–6.

64. Daniels, *Dissent and Conformity*, 1, 11; Covey, *The Gentle Radical*, 145–6; see also Gertrude S. Kimball, *Providence in Colonial Times* (New York: De Capo Press, 1972).
65. What bothered Williams most about government's involvement was the damage it did to Christ's church and religion. Morgan, *Church and the State*, 95–6, 121, 128, 137; Covey, *The Gentle Radical*, 136, 140, 143.
66. Covey, *The Gentle Radical*, 136–7 (quoting Winthrop on the *Arbella*).
67. Ibid., 140–1.
68. Daniels, *Dissent and Conformity*, 9, 11–13 (citing Bartlett, ed., *RICR* 1:156, 204–205, 210–211, 334–5).
69. Chupack, *Roger Williams*, 57–8; Knowles, *Memoir of Roger Williams*, 279, 351; Bartlett, *Complete Writings*, 6:279.
70. Morgan, *Church and the State*, 136, 142; Gaustad, *Roger Williams*, 109; Bartlett, *Complete Writings*, 6:329. See also Daniels, *Dissent and Conformity*, 4–5.
71. Morgan, *Church and the State*, 128, 135–7. The U.S. Supreme Court, at least into the middle of the twentieth century, stated that it was within state governments' "police power" to regulate for the benefit of citizens' health, safety, welfare, and morals.
72. Winslow, *Master Roger Williams*, 136–7; Covey, *The Gentle Radical*, 143.
73. Anthony M. Kennedy, "Law and Belief," *Trial* 34, no. 7 (1998), 23–6; LaFantasie, *Correspondence of Roger Williams*, 2:535–6.
74. Winslow, *Master Roger Williams*, 130–1; Covey, *The Gentle Radical*, 123.
75. Winslow, *Master Roger Williams*, 136–7.
76. Daniels, *Dissent and Conformity*, 6; James, *Colonial Rhode Island*, xiii, 8–9. Some of the settlers founded the other early settlements around Narragansett Bay, such as Anne Hutchinson's group, with William Coddington leading (Portsmouth and Newport) and Samuel Gorton (Warwick).
77. Chupack, *Roger Williams*, 54–5; Garrett, *Roger Williams*, 24.
78. Garrett, *Roger Williams*, 21; Champlin Burrage, *The Early English Dissenters in the Light of Recent Research (1550–1641)* (London: Cambridge University Press, 1912), 1:171–5, 317–18. Harry Vane himself had been banished from Massachusetts for supporting Anne Hutchinson. Garrett explains that the Bay leaders "wondered whether they had been chosen by the Lord to prepare in New England a foretaste of the rule of the saints, the prelude to the millennium. John Cotton, in particular, believed the time might have arrived for this Western dawning to grow to full day in God's chosen England." Garrett, *Roger Williams*, 22; William Bradford,

Of Plimouth Plantation (Boston: Wright & Potter Printing Co., 1901), 49–51.

79. Winslow, *Master Roger Williams*, 159–60. Williams's stated goals in publishing the *Key* were two: First, as "'a private help to my own memory, that I might not by my present absence lightly lose what I had so dearly bought in some few years hardship and charges among the Barbarians.' Second, some of his 'worthy friends, of all sorts' needed to know the Indian language as he had need to know it. *Ibid.* at 161–62 (citing Bartlett, ed., *Complete Writings*, 1:19); Garrett, *Roger Williams*, 22, 82; Gaustad, *Roger Williams*, 57–8; LaFantasie, ed., *Correspondence of Roger Williams*, 2:410.
80. Gaustad, *Roger Williams*, 57–9.
81. Ibid., 59–60 (citing Edmund S. Morgan, *Roger Williams: The Church and the State* [New York: Harcourt, Brace & World, 1967], 130–42); Chupack, *Roger Williams* 55 (citing Bartlett, ed., *RICR*, 1:143–6).
82. Brockunier, *The Irrepressible Democrat*, 145–6 (quoting Thomas Lechford in 1642); Robert Baillie, *Dissuasive from the Errours of the Time* (London: Samuel Gellibrand, 1645), 60.
83. Brockunier, *The Irrepressible Democrat*, 149–51.
84. Ibid., 153; Gaustad, *Roger Williams*, 60–1; Garrett, *Roger Williams*, 24; Winslow, *Master Roger Williams*, 208–10. The request from Parliament for Williams's safe passage was signed by twelve "diverse lords and others of the parliament," testifying to their impressions of Williams's "good affections and conscience" and requesting that he be shown "all friendly offices." Winslow, *Master Roger Williams*, 208.
85. Daniels, *Dissent and Conformity*, 10; Chupack, *Roger Williams*, 54–5; Winslow, *Master Roger Williams*, 210–11, 218–19.
86. Daniels, *Dissent and Conformity*, 13.
87. Chupack, *Roger Williams*, 55–6; Gaustad, *Roger Williams*, 64–6.
88. Gaustad, *Roger Williams*, 66–7; Chupack, *Roger Williams*, 56; Brockunier, *The Irrepressible Democrat*, 201, 212; LaFantasie, *Correspondence of Roger Williams*, 1:353–4, 366–7.
89. Brockunier, *The Irrepressible Democrat*, 212; Gaustad, *Roger Williams*, 67.
90. Gaustad, *Roger Williams*, 67–8, 70; Chupack, *Roger Williams*, 55; Brockunier, *The Irrepressible Democrat*, 201, 212, 214–16; LaFantasie, *Correspondence of Roger Williams*, 1:367. In 1653, Cromwell dismissed the council and dissolved Parliament by threat of force, becoming protector in name and dictator in fact.
91. Brockunier, *The Irrepressible Democrat*, 202–7.
92. Ibid., 208–11.
93. Chupack, *Roger Williams*, 56.
94. Ibid., 56–7; Gaustad, *Roger Williams*, 68–9; LaFantasie, *Correspondence of Roger Williams*, 1:399–402.
95. Chupack, *Roger Williams*, 57–8 (citing Bartlett, ed., *RICR* 1:327).

96. Gaustad, *Roger Williams*, 70; Brockunier, *The Irrepressible Democrat*, 255–6; *The Charter Granted by King Charles II*, 8 July 1663, in *Collections of the Rhode Island Historical Society*, 4:243; John Russell Bartlett, ed., *Records of the Colony of Rhode Island* (Providence: A Crawford Greene, 1857), 2:3–21. Chupack, *Roger Williams*, 58–9; Brockunier, *The Irrepressible Democrat*, 255–6. Perhaps the most contentious issues for Providence and the other towns (indeed, perhaps the most contentious for any government) were matters involving land. Chupack, *Roger Williams*, 53 (quoting Howard M. Chapin, *Documentary History of Rhode Island* [Norwood, MA: Plimpton Press, 1916, 1919], 1:76–8).
97. Daniels, *Dissent and Conformity*, 15–16; Bartlett, ed., *RICR* 1:513–15.
98. Chupack, *Roger Williams*, 59; Gaustad, *Roger Williams*, 128; Bartlett, *Complete Writings*, 6:319.
99. Eddy, *Roger Williams and the Baptists*, 93–4.
100. Ibid., 90–4. The *Commentaries on the Constitution* (3 vols., 1833), by Justice Joseph Story (who sat on the U.S. Supreme Court from 1812 to 1845), were required reading for generations of Americans throughout the nineteenth and twentieth centuries.
101. Eddy, *Roger Williams and the Baptists*, 90–1; Gaustad, *Roger Williams*, 122–4.
102. Morgan, *Church and the State*, 103, 118.
103. Covey, *The Gentle Radical*, 147.
104. Ibid., 115 (quoting John Cotton, as told by William Coddington to the Quaker founder George Fox in 1677); Gaustad, *Roger Williams*, 114. William Penn knew firsthand about religious persecution, having been victimized along with other Quakers in England and Ireland. Ibid.
105. Ibid., 115–17; John Locke, *John Locke: Political Writings* (New York: Penguin Books, 1993), 395–6.
106. Gaustad, *Roger Williams*, 117–19; James Madison, *The Papers of James Madison*, ed. William T. Hutchinson et al. (Chicago: University of Chicago Press, 1962–77), 8:298–304; Thomas Jefferson, *Bill for Establishing Religious Freedom*, in *The Papers of Thomas Jefferson*, ed. Julian P. Boyd (Princeton, NJ: Princeton University Press, 1950), 2:545–6.
107. See James Madison, *The Journal of the Debates in the Convention Which Framed the Constitution of the United States, May–September, 1787*, ed. Gaillard Hunt (New York: G. P. Putnam's Sons, 1908), 2:359.
108. Winslow, *Master Roger Williams*, 124.
109. Ibid., 120, 124. Such what-ifs are intriguing, if chilling. What would have happened, for example, if the South had won the Civil War (see MacKinlay Kantor, *If the South Had Won the Civil War* [New York: Forge Books, 2001]), or if Charles Lindbergh had been elected president (see Philip Roth, *The Plot against America* [New York: Houghton Mifflin, 2004]).
110. Morgan, *Church and the State*, 142. Descartes' (1596–1650) appeals to reason ("I think, therefore I am") are said to have initiated modern philosophy.

2. Thomas Paine (1737–1809): *Revolution*

1. Thomas Paine, *The Rights of Man* (1792; London: Watts & Co., 1906), 144–5.
2. Craig Nelson, *Thomas Paine: Enlightenment, Revolution, and the Birth of Modern Nations* (New York: Viking), 17.
3. Eric Foner, *Tom Paine and Revolutionary America* (New York: Oxford 1976), 79.
4. Jack Fruchtman Jr., *Thomas Paine: Apostle of Freedom* (New York: Four Walls Eight Windows, 1994), 91–2; Harvey J. Kaye, *Thomas Paine and the Promise of America* (New York: Hill and Wang 2005), 5.
5. Fruchtman, *Apostle of Freedom*, 256.
6. Ibid.
7. Foner, *Revolutionary America*, 2; Fruchtman, *Apostle of Freedom*, 17, 19, 20. As the daughter of a Thetford attorney, Frances married below her station in pairing with artisan Joseph, eleven years her junior. Joseph earned about thirty pounds per year – as compared to ten to twenty pounds for a schoolmaster, eight pounds for a plowman, one pound for a common laborer, and ten thousand pounds for the Duke of Grafton. Ibid., 19.
8. Nelson, *Enlightenment, Revolution*, 15. Thetford in 1737 was a small market town of about two thousand residents with a relatively stable economy. Foner, *Revolutionary America*, 4.
9. Fruchtman, *Apostle of Freedom*, 21; Nelson, *Enlightenment, Revolution*, 16; Foner, *Revolutionary America*, 4.
10. Nelson, *Enlightenment, Revolution*, 16; Fruchtman, *Apostle of Freedom*, 22.
11. Fruchtman, *Apostle of Freedom*, 21–2.
12. Foner, *Revolutionary America*, 1; Nelson, *Enlightenment, Revolution*, 22; Fruchtman, *Apostle of Freedom*, 22; Kaye, *Promise of America*, 22.
13. Nelson, *Enlightenment, Revolution*, 20; Fruchtman, *Apostle of Freedom*, 22–3. Privateers were privately owned ships, operated under authority of the Crown, to attack and take cargo from enemy merchant ships. Fruchtman, *Apostle of Freedom*, 24.
14. Nelson, *Enlightenment, Revolution*, 20; Kaye, *Promise of America*, 23; Fruchtman, *Apostle of Freedom*, 25. Sources disagree on how long Paine spent at sea with the *King of Prussia*, ranging from six months to one and a half years.
15. Fruchtman, *Apostle of Freedom*, 26.
16. Kaye, *Promise of America*, 23–4.
17. Fruchtman, *Apostle of Freedom*, 26; Nelson, *Enlightenment, Revolution*, 38; Foner, *Revolutionary America*, 3; Kaye, *Promise of America*, 24–5.
18. Nelson, *Enlightenment, Revolution*, 38; Kaye, *Promise of America*, 25. "There has been a great deal of speculation, by Paine's enemies and partisans alike, that he had little sexual interest in women, although he often flirted with them and enjoyed their company." Fruchtman, *Apostle of Freedom*, 27.

19. Foner, *Revolutionary America,* 2; Fruchtman, *Apostle of Freedom,* 27.
20. Kaye, *Promise of America,* 25–6; Nelson, *Enlightenment, Revolution,* 39; Fruchtman, *Apostle of Freedom,* 28; Foner, *Revolutionary America,* 2. According to a couple sources, at least, Paine might have been framed or scapegoated by his supervisor, William Swallow.
21. Fruchtman, *Apostle of Freedom,* 28–9; Foner *Revolutionary America,* 2–3, 6; Nelson, *Enlightenment, Revolution,* 36.
22. Nelson, *Enlightenment, Revolution,* 36. Paine's interest in science remained with him for the rest of his days. Foner, *Revolutionary America,* 6–7.
23. Seventeen Protestants were executed in Lewes during Bloody Mary's sixteenth-century reign, and as a traditional republican stronghold during Cromwell's mid-seventeenth-century Commonwealth, the radical antipopery tradition still prevailed when Paine arrived in 1768. Foner, *Revolutionary America,* 12; Nelson, *Enlightenment, Revolution,* 37.
24. Fruchtman, *Apostle of Freedom,* 30–1; Kaye, *Promise of America,* 26–7; Foner, *Revolutionary America,* 14.
25. Kaye, *Promise of America,* 27; Fruchtman, *Apostle of Freedom,* 31.
26. Kaye, *Promise of America,* 27–8; Nelson, *Enlightenment, Revolution,* 44.
27. Kaye, *Promise of America,* 26–7; Fruchtman, *Apostle of Freedom,* 35; Nelson, *Enlightenment, Revolution,* 44; Foner, *Revolutionary America,* 7, 15, 10.
28. Nelson, *Enlightenment, Revolution,* 45–6; Kaye, *Promise of America,* 28; Foner, *Revolutionary America,* 15.
29. Fruchtman, *Apostle of Freedom,* 36; Nelson, *Enlightenment, Revolution,* 46.
30. Fruchtman, *Apostle of Freedom,* 38.
31. Ibid., 38–9.
32. Nelson, *Enlightenment, Revolution,* 49–50. Franklin's own son Francis had died of smallpox as a child; his other son William, a British loyalist, would renounce his father during the American Revolution. Ibid., 49.
33. Fruchtman, *Apostle of Freedom,* 90–2.
34. Ibid., 39; Nelson, *Enlightenment, Revolution,* 13–14.
35. Nelson, *Enlightenment, Revolution,* 53; Fruchtman, *Apostle of Freedom,* 39; Foner, *Revolutionary America,* 72.
36. Fruchtman, *Apostle of Freedom,* 42, 43 (quoting Bernard Vincent, ed., *Thomas Paine ou la Republique san frontiers* [Nancy, France: Presses Universitaires de Nancy, 1993], 42). Foner, *Revolutionary America,* 20.
37. Gary B. Nash, *The Unknown American Revolution* (New York: Penguin, 2005), 189; Nelson, *Enlightenment, Revolution,* 52.
38. Foner, *Revolutionary America,* 71, 73; Fruchtman, *Apostle of Freedom,* 45. Adopting the common practice of the day of writing under pseudonyms drawn from antiquity, Paine wrote as "Comus," "Atlanticus," or "Amicus" (or, after 1776, "Common Sense").
39. Fruchtman, 49; Nelson, *Enlightenment, Revolution,* 64; Fruchtman, *Apostle of Freedom,* 5; Foner, *Revolutionary America,* 80.

40. Nash, *Unknown American Revolution*, 152; Nelson, *Enlightenment, Revolution*, 65. It seems likely there were more slaves, apprentices, and servants in Philadelphia in 1775 than free laborers. Foner, *Revolutionary America*, 43.
41. Fruchtman, *Apostle of Freedom*, 51–2. Fruchtman explains that at least one scholar disagrees that Paine is the author of some of these unattributed or pseudonymous letters and essays. Ibid., 42nn33, 35, 38.
42. Nash, *Unknown American Revolution*,189; Nelson, *Enlightenment, Revolution*, 77 (quoting *Pennsylvania Magazine*, July 1775). American militiamen skirmished with 1,200 British soldiers who had come to relieve the colonists of a cache of arms in Concord, leaving 8 Americans and 273 British troops dead. Fruchtman, *Apostle of Freedom*, 59.
43. Foner, *Revolutionary America*, 136; Fruchtman, *Apostle of Freedom*, 60–2. Part of Paine's motivation in completing the work quickly, he explained, was to please his mentor, Franklin. Nelson, *Enlightenment, Revolution*, 80.
44. Nelson, *Enlightenment, Revolution*, 89; Foner, *Revolutionary America*, 136; Fruchtman, *Apostle of Freedom*, 60–1. Paine had immediate disputes with Bell over royalties, so he arranged and paid for another publisher, the brothers William and Thomas Bradford, to print and sell the pamphlets for one shilling (about seven dollars and fifty cents today) instead of the two shillings charged by Bell. Nelson, *Enlightenment, Revolution*, 90.
45. Nash, *Unknown American Revolution*, 189; Nelson, *Enlightenment, Revolution*, 89–92; Kaye, *Promise of America*, 43; Foner, *Revolutionary America*, 79. A comparable per capita number today would be 35 million copies sold in the first year alone. Nash, *Unknown American Revolution*, 189.
46. Nelson, *Enlightenment, Revolution*, 90, 92–3; Foner, *Revolutionary America*, 79, 86.
47. Nelson, *Enlightenment, Revolution*, 93.
48. Thomas Paine, *Common Sense: Addressed to the Residents of America* (1776; New York: Peter Eckler Publishing, 1918), 29–30. Foner, *Revolutionary America*, 82, 83; Nash, *Unknown American Revolution*, 190. Although his words ring clearly from his publications, writing was not an easy task for Paine – he wrote slowly and agonized frequently over proper phrasing and word choice. Fruchtman, *Apostle of Freedom*, 62.
49. Paine, *Common Sense*, 19–20, 22; Kaye, *Promise of America*, 5; Foner, *Revolutionary America*, 77; Nelson, *Enlightenment, Revolution*, 87. Paine also ingeniously embraced the devout in suggesting that monarchy was incompatible with the will of God: "The will of the Almighty," he wrote, "expressly disapproves of government by kings." Foner, *Revolutionary America*, 80–1.
50. Paine, *Common Sense*, 13–15.
51. Foner, *Revolutionary America*, 75.
52. Thomas Paine, *Common Sense*, 1–3.
53. Alexander Hamilton, John Jay, and James Madison, *The Federalist* (Indianapolis: Liberty Fund, 2001), No. 51 (Madison), 267.

54. Bernard Bailyn, *The Ideological Origins of the American Revolution* (1967; Cambridge, MA: Harvard Belknap, 1992), 344–5, 371; Nelson, *Enlightenment, Revolution,* 62. Virtuous government was the watchword for the Roman Republic, which was the very epitome of good government in the founders' view, and it was the ideal prominently expressed by Montesquieu, the single most influential philosopher to the founding generation.
55. Thomas Paine, "Dissertations on Government," in *The Political and Miscellaneous Works of Thomas Paine* (London: R. Carlile, 1819), 1:9; Foner, *Revolutionary America,* 89; Nelson, *Enlightenment, Revolution,* 90, 103. Thomas Jefferson wrote, for example, in his last years: "All, all dead, and ourselves left alone amidst a new generation whom we know not, and who knows not us.... I regret that I am now to die in the belief that the useless sacrifice of themselves by the generation of 1776... is to be thrown away by the unwise and unworthy passions of their sons, and that my only consolation is to be, that I live not to weep over it.... I have sometimes asked myself whether my country is the better for having lived at all." Nelson, *Enlightenment, Revolution,* 4–5, 337.
56. Foner, *Revolutionary America,* 120; Howard Zinn, *A People's History of the United States* (1980; New York: HarperCollins 2003), 70. Time did not soften John Adams's dislike for *Common Sense* – at the age of eighty-four in 1819, Adams wrote to Jefferson: "What a poor, ignorant, malicious, short-sighted, crapulous mass is Tom Paine's *Common Sense.*" Foner, *Revolutionary America,* 190.
57. Nelson, *Enlightenment, Revolution,* 96; Foner, *Revolutionary America,* 123, 201–2.
58. Nelson, *Enlightenment, Revolution,* 96.
59. Ibid., 94.
60. Foner, *Revolutionary America,* 126; Fruchtman, *Apostle of Freedom,* 84–5.
61. Fruchtman, *Apostle of Freedom,* 84.
62. Nelson, *Enlightenment, Revolution,* 97, 99.
63. Ibid., 98.
64. Foner, *Revolutionary America,* 103.
65. Fruchtman, *Apostle of Freedom,* 88, 89; Nelson, *Enlightenment, Revolution,* 102. Elements of Paine's *Common Sense* adopted by the Pennsylvania Constitution included greatly expanded suffrage, a unicameral legislature, a popularly elected vetoless plural executive, requirement of open legislative meetings and printed records, reapportionment every seven years, and liberal guarantees of freedoms and procedural protections. Nelson, *Enlightenment, Revolution,* 273–4; Foner, *Revolutionary America,* 131–2, 138. Paine greatly admired General Greene, writing many years later that he had been "the best general in the American army." Fruchtman, *Apostle of Freedom,* 89–90.
66. Nelson, *Enlightenment, Revolution,* 103.
67. Ibid., 105, 106; Fruchtman, *Apostle of Freedom,* 89–90.
68. Nelson, *Enlightenment, Revolution,* 106.

69. Ibid., 106, Kaye, *Promise of America*, 57.
70. Nelson, *Enlightenment, Revolution*, 106–7.
71. David McCullough, *1776* (New York: Simon & Schuster Paperbacks, 2005), 268–9, 273.
72. Fruchtman, *Apostle of Freedom*, 90–1; Nelson, *Enlightenment, Revolution*, 107.
73. Nelson, 108.
74. Ibid., 107–9; Fruchtman, *Apostle of Freedom*, 90–1.
75. McCullough, *1776*, 271–2; Nelson, *Enlightenment, Revolution*, 107, 108.
76. Fruchtman, *Apostle of Freedom*, 92–3; Nelson, *Enlightenment, Revolution*, 108–9; McCullough, *1776*, 264.
77. Ibid., 274–8.
78. Sources disagree on the length of the battle – McCullough, for example, says less than forty-five minutes; Nelson says ninety. Ibid., 281; Nelson, *Enlightenment, Revolution*, 111.
79. McCullough, *1776*, 283.
80. Ibid., 290–2; Nelson, *Enlightenment, Revolution*, 111.
81. McCullough, *1776*, 284.
82. Fruchtman, *Apostle of Freedom*, 91–2.
83. Asked about the British occupation of Philadelphia, Benjamin Franklin quipped: "You mistake the matter. Instead of Howe taking Philadelphia, Philadelphia has taken Howe." Nelson, *Enlightenment, Revolution*, 116.
84. Thomas Paine, *The Rights of Man*, 27–8.
85. Fruchtman, *Apostle of Freedom*, 322–3.
86. Nelson, *Enlightenment, Revolution*, 111, 146. Some suggest Paine may have suffered from bipolar disorder, which, if true, could explain some of his difficulties.
87. Foner, *Revolutionary America*, 153–7, 181. Paine held a series of jobs during the war years – as a publicist for Congress (losing this job after disclosing, while attempting to expose government corruption, secret diplomatic correspondence with France); as a clerk to the head of the Pennsylvania Board of War; and again as a secret publicist for the U.S. government. Ibid., 139, 158–61, 189; Nelson, *Enlightenment, Revolution*, 111, 139, 148.
88. Much of Paine's time in the mid-1780s was occupied trying to persuade Congress and the states to provide him a stipend for his revolutionary contributions. Nelson, *Enlightenment, Revolution*, 167. In 1785, Congress provided $3,000 (about $250,000 today); Pennsylvania gave five hundred pounds (about $90,000 today); and New York gave him 277 acres of land and a farmhouse, near New Rochelle, abandoned by a loyalist who had fled to Canada. Nelson, *Enlightenment, Revolution*, 169, 170; Foner, *Revolutionary America*, 192.
89. Regarding the new American Constitution that was being hammered out in Philadelphia that very summer of 1787, Paine, somewhat against form, supported the John Adams–supported charter of separated powers and

a bicameral legislature, believing that a strong national government was needed to enable the United States to prosper in international trade and commerce. Nelson, *Enlightenment, Revolution,* 145.

90. Ibid., 176.
91. Ibid., 176; Foner, *Revolutionary America,* 213.
92. Nelson, *Enlightenment, Revolution,* 179; Fruchtman, *Apostle of Freedom,* 221.
93. Foner, *Revolutionary America,* 213. On October 5 and 6, 1789, the king and queen were forced by a large mob to return to Paris from Versailles. Fruchtman, *Apostle of Freedom,* 208.
94. Foner, *Revolutionary America,* 213; Nelson, *Enlightenment, Revolution,* 190; Fruchtman, *Apostle of Freedom,* 211. Around this time, Lafayette gave Paine a key to the Bastille to present to George Washington in honor of his leadership during the American Revolution. Fruchtman, *Apostle of Freedom,* 197, 201. The key hangs, to this day, in the hallway at George Washington's home at Mount Vernon.
95. Nelson, *Enlightenment, Revolution,* 193.
96. Burke, after all, had commented in an early August 1789 letter, "As to us here our thoughts of everything at home are suspended by our astonishment at the wonderful spectacle which is exhibited in a neighboring and rival country. What spectators and what actors!" he exclaimed. "England gazing with astonishment at a French struggle for liberty, and not knowing whether to blame or to applaud!" Fruchtman, *Apostle of Freedom,* 207.
97. Ibid., 213–18. *Reflections* reasoned that humans are weak, with dangerous, strong passions – and that tradition and firm religious grounding are important barriers that prevent human depravity from overtaking the good. Without those barriers, Burke continued, life is meaningless, and the French (and others similarly situated) would suffer through awful spells of chaos and darkness. Ibid., 209.
98. Nelson, *Enlightenment, Revolution,* 202. A novel normally sold a total of 1,250 copies and nonfiction sold about 750.
99. Thomas Paine, *The Rights of Man*, 57–8.
100. Thomas Paine, *The Rights of Man,* 10–11, 75; Nelson, *Enlightenment, Revolution,* 199; Foner, *Revolutionary America,* 216.
101. Thomas Paine, *The Rights of Man,* 17.
102. Ibid., 63.
103. Ibid., 27–8.
104. Ibid., 27. Paine elaborates: "Natural rights are those which appertain to man in right of his existence. Of this kind are all the intellectual rights, or rights of the mind, and also all those rights of acting as an individual for his own comfort and happiness, which are not injurious to the natural rights of others. Civil rights are those which appertain to man in right of his being a member of society. Every civil right has for its foundation some natural right pre-existing in the individual, but to the enjoyment of which his individual

power is not, in all cases, sufficiently competent. Of this kind are all those which relate to security and protection." Ibid.

John Stuart Mill further developed this concept, calling it the "harm principle" in his 1859 book *On Liberty*: "[T]he only purpose for which power can be rightfully exercised over any member of a civilized community, against his will, is to prevent harm to others." J. S. Mill, *On Liberty* (1859; New York: Cambridge University Press, 2000), 13. A proposal to shift the current judicial standard for reviewing government actions to a presumption-of-liberty approach that better reflects these principles may be found in Michael Anthony Lawrence, "Government as Liberty's Servant: The 'Reasonable Time, Place and Manner' Standard of Review for All Government Restrictions on Liberty Interests," *Louisiana Law Review* 71 (2007), 1.

105. Nelson, *Enlightenment, Revolution*, 214.
106. Ibid., 202.
107. Ibid., 208. Adams reportedly said of *The Rights of Man,* with hand on chest, "I detest that book and its tendency, from the bottom of my heart." Answering such sentiments, Paine remarked, "I had John Adams in mind when I wrote the pamphlet, and it has hit as I expected." Ibid., 205, 207.
108. Ibid., 209–10; Fruchtman, *Apostle of Freedom*, 218.
109. Nelson, *Enlightenment, Revolution*, 211; Fruchtman, *Apostle of Freedom*, 234. The people were furious with the king's attempted abandonment, and six thousand armed citizens marched alongside members of the National Assembly escorting the royal family back into Paris, past silent crowds along roads posted with the sign: "Anyone who applauds the King will be beaten; Anyone who insults him will be hanged." Nelson, *Enlightenment, Revolution*, 211.
110. Nelson, *Enlightenment, Revolution*, 212. Maximilian Robespierre, leader of the Jacobins, and Jean-Paul Marat of the Cordeliers both believed a "republic with a monarch" was far preferable. Ibid.; Fruchtman, *Apostle of Freedom*, 235.
111. Nelson, *Enlightenment, Revolution*, 212–13; Fruchtman, *Apostle of Freedom*, 237. "[Duchalet] and Paine had acted alone," Etienne Dumont recalled. "An American and an impulsive nobleman had put themselves forward to change the whole governmental system of France."
112. Nelson *Enlightenment, Revolution*, 213–14. Shortly before he returned to London, Paine dined with Gouverneur Morris, who recalled him "inflated to the eyes and big with a litter of revolutions." Ibid., 214. "He seems to become every hour more drunk with self-conceit." Fruchtman, *Apostle of Freedom*, 240.
113. Fruchtman, *Apostle of Freedom*, 242, 247–8; Nelson, *Enlightenment, Revolution*, 221.
114. Nelson, *Enlightenment, Revolution*, 216.
115. Fruchtman, *Apostle of Freedom*, 253–4, 256–7.
116. Ibid., 258–9.

117. Ibid., 259; Foner, *Revolutionary America,* 219.
118. Foner, *Revolutionary America,* 219; Nelson, 220.
119. Nelson, 219; Foner, *Revolutionary America,* 220–1.
120. Foner, *Revolutionary America,* 220–2.
121. Ibid., 223–4.
122. Ibid., 226; Nelson, *Enlightenment, Revolution,* 226. "We have [always] disclaimed the foolish idea of *leveling property,*" a speaker in Sheffield said, "because our own property, the fruit of our labour, or of our talents, might, by the example, be exposed to the invasion of the first intruder." Foner, *Revolutionary America,* 226.
123. Foner, *Revolutionary America,* 228. Weeks before the book was published, Gouverneur Morris predicted the reaction of the Pitt government, writing in his diary after reading Paine's manuscript, "I am really afraid he will be punished. He seems to laugh at this, and relies on the force he has in the nation." Nelson, *Enlightenment, Revolution,* 225.
124. Nelson, *Enlightenment, Revolution,* 225–6. Pitt's resolve was reinforced after receiving a deputy's information-gathering reports from around the country suggesting that "the seditious doctrines of Paine and the factious people who are endeavoring to disturb the peace of the country had extended to a degree very much beyond my completion" – and that civil war was possible. *The Rights of Man* was now "as much a standard book in this country, as *Robinson Crusoe* and *The Pilgrims Progress,*" one bookseller opined, adding "if it has not its effect today, it will tomorrow." The Home Secretary advised Parliament that Paine's work was being "sedulously inculcated throughout the kingdom." Ibid., 226–7.
125. Ibid., 227.
126. Ibid., 227–8; Fruchtman, *Apostle of Freedom,* 263, 264.
127. Nelson, *Enlightenment, Revolution,* 228–9.
128. Many booksellers selling Paine's work and other sympathizers were fined, arrested, or imprisoned. Nor did the government soon cease its efforts – some twenty years later, publisher Richard Carlile spent three years in jail starting in 1819 for selling Paine's forbidden writings. Ibid., 227–8; Fruchtman, *Apostle of Freedom,* 263, 291.
129. Nelson, *Enlightenment, Revolution,* 229.
130. Ibid., 333; Foner, *Revolutionary America*, 233.
131. Nelson, *Enlightenment, Revolution,* 229–30. Thomas Paine appeared in court for his trial on June 8 to find his case had been postponed until December. Fruchtman, *Apostle of Freedom,* 265. Several months after his September 1792 departure, Paine was tried in absentia, where a handpicked jury quickly found him guilty as charged of sedition. If he ever returned to Britain or was captured on the high seas, he would be promptly hanged. Soon after, medallions proclaiming "End of Pain" and other curios were being sold in the street. Nelson, *Enlightenment, Revolution,* 246–7.
132. Fruchtman, *Apostle of Freedom,* 266.

133. Ibid., 267–8; Nelson, 234.
134. Nelson, *Enlightenment, Revolution*, 235; Fruchtman, *Apostle of Freedom*, 269, 277.
135. Nelson, *Enlightenment, Revolution*, 230; Jay Winik, *The Great Upheaval* (New York: Harper Perennial, 2007), 286–8. The other European kingdoms – Austria, Prussia, and England – viewed France with great trepidation, fearing the same sorts of uprisings among their own peasantry. War between France and the other countries broke out in the spring of 1792. Fruchtman, *Apostle of Freedom*, 219. Lafayette, with previous ties to the monarchy, had his military commission withdrawn; then he surrendered to the Austrians and went to prison for five years rather than returning to Paris for probable execution. The National Assembly dissolved itself and ordered a new election for a constitutional Convention of 749 delegates. Nelson, *Enlightenment, Revolution*, 230–1; Fruchtman, *Apostle of Freedom*, 271; Winik, *The Great Upheaval*, 290.
136. Fruchtman, *Apostle of Freedom*, 279–80; Foner, *Revolutionary America*, 219; Nelson, *Enlightenment, Revolution*, 276; Winik, *The Great Upheaval*, 295–7. In October, Paine was elected to a Girondin-dominated committee to prepare a constitution; he, along with Condorcet, was appointed to prepare the preliminary draft, which was ultimately soundly rejected by the Convention. Fruchtman, *Apostle of Freedom*, 280–1; Nelson *Enlightenment, Revolution*, 238, 250.
137. Fruchtman, *Apostle of Freedom*, 274; Foner, *Revolutionary America*, 237, 240. Paine, with his preferences for free-market economics and distrust of popular mobs, identified most closely with the Girondins. Foner, *Revolutionary America*, 240.
138. Fruchtman, *Apostle of Freedom*, 274.
139. Ibid., 293–4; Winik, *The Great Upheaval*, 307.
140. Fruchtman, *Apostle of Freedom*, 294, 295; Winik, *The Great Upheaval*, 308–9, 312; Nelson *Enlightenment, Revolution*, 241–2. Speaking to the convention on November 20, 1792, Paine argued that Louis's trial "can serve to prove to the world the flagitiousness of governments in general, and the necessity of revolutions, [and France] ought not to let slip so precious an opportunity." Fruchtman, *Apostle of Freedom*, 294; Nelson, *Enlightenment, Revolution*, 240.
141. Nelson, *Enlightenment, Revolution*, 244. "It happens, unfortunately," Paine told the convention, "that the person now under discussion is regarded in America as a deliverer of their country. I can assure you that his execution will there spread universal sorrow, and it is in your power not thus to wound the feelings of your ally." Fruchtman, *Apostle of Freedom*, 243.
142. Winik, *The Great Upheaval*, 364–5, 372, 394; Nelson, *Enlightenment, Revolution*, 250; Fruchtman, *Apostle of Freedom*, 273–4, 277, 314. In March 1793, the convention formed the Committee for General Security (with authority to arrest anyone suspected of disloyalty) and the Revolutionary

Tribunal to try the suspects. Executions became so frequent that neighboring residents complained of the sewers being clogged with blood. Nelson, *Enlightenment, Revolution*, 237–8.

143. Winik, *The Great Upheaval*, 387–9; Fruchtman, *Apostle of Freedom*, 277, 312; Nelson, *Enlightenment, Revolution*, 257.
144. Fruchtman, *Apostle of Freedom*, 313; Nelson, 255, 258, 260; Foner, *Revolutionary America*, 243–4.
145. Nelson, *Enlightenment, Revolution*, 251, 257–8, 260.
146. Ibid., 259, 274.
147. Fruchtman, *Apostle of Freedom*, 323–4; Nelson, *Enlightenment, Revolution*, 277. Paine replied to Morris: "You must not leave me in [this] situation.... You know I do not deserve it, and you see the unpleasant situation in which I am thrown.... They have nothing against me – except that they do not choose I should be in a state of freedom to write my mind freely upon things I have seen. Though you and I are not on terms of the best harmony, I apply to you as the Minister of America.... At any rate I expect you to make Congress acquainted with my situation." Nelson, *Enlightenment, Revolution*, 277.
148. Fruchtman, *Apostle of Freedom*, 322; Nelson, *Enlightenment, Revolution*, 282.
149. Fruchtman, *Apostle of Freedom*, 322.
150. Winik, *The Great Upheaval*, 405.
151. Ibid., 409; Fruchtman, *Apostle of Freedom*, 274; Nelson, *Enlightenment, Revolution*, 250. The Terror would not completely end with Robespierre's execution. Both in Paris and elsewhere, mobs continued to operate with abandon. Fruchtman, *Apostle of Freedom*, 335–6.
152. Fruchtman, *Apostle of Freedom*, 330–1.
153. Nelson, *Enlightenment, Revolution*, 285. "In many respects," Nelson suggests, "the great Thomas Paine of *Common Sense* and *Rights of Man* had been done away with as effectively as if he had been guillotined." Ibid., 286.
154. Thomas Paine, *The Age of Reason* (1794; New York: Truth Seeker, 1898), 6.
155. Ibid., 260, 263; Foner, *Revolutionary America*, 81, 245–6.
156. The major immediate purpose of *The Age of Reason*, then, was to give French citizens hope in the midst of widespread murders of priests, looted churches, vandalized cemeteries, and church bells melted into artillery. Nelson, *Enlightenment, Revolution*, 262–3.
157. Paine, *The Age of Reason*, 10; Nelson, *Enlightenment, Revolution*, 262, 266; Fruchtman, *Apostle of Freedom*, 326.
158. Paine, *The Age of Reason*, 6, 7.
159. Ibid., 7.
160. Ibid., 28, 29; Foner, 246; Fruchtman, *Apostle of Freedom*, 325.
161. Nelson, *Enlightenment, Revolution*, 261. Deism had roots in Aristotle, Epicurus, Cicero, and Newton. Albert Einstein described modern deism in terms

that were essentially a point-by-point elucidation of *The Age of Reason.* Ibid., 272.

162. Paine, *The Age of Reason,* 175.
163. Ibid., 133, 143; Foner, *Revolutionary America,* 246–7.
164. Paine, *The Age of Reason,* 12, 18, 27; Fruchtman, *Apostle of Freedom,* 327; Paine, 359.
165. Nelson, *Enlightenment, Revolution,* 267; Fruchtman, *Apostle of Freedom,* 267, 269. The book sold especially well on college campuses – to the point that a worried Harvard College felt compelled to offer a rebuttal, distributing free copies of *Apology for the Bible* to all students. Fruchtman, *Apostle of Freedom,* 269.
166. Nelson, *Enlightenment, Revolution,* 268–9. The aftereffects of the harsh government actions were long lingering – the library in Paine's hometown of Thetford, for example, did not carry his books until 1908. Ibid.
167. Ibid., 269.
168. Foner, *Revolutionary America,* 256.
169. Ibid., 255–7.
170. Nelson, *Enlightenment, Revolution,* 270–1.
171. Foner, *Revolutionary America,* 257.
172. Fruchtman, *Apostle of Freedom,* 331, 334.
173. Nelson, *Enlightenment, Revolution,* 290; Foner, 94, *Revolutionary America,* 249. In *Agrarian Justice,* which was originally a proposal for the French government, Paine reasoned that "all accumulation . . . of personal property, beyond what a man's own hands produce, is derived from living in society." Therefore, "he owes . . . a part of that accumulation back to society from which the whole came." Too often, individual wealth is 'the effect of paying too little for the labor that produced it; the consequence of which is that the working hand perishes in old age, and the employer abounds in affluence." Importantly, however, Paine also expressly denied any intention to interfere with existing systems of private property. Thomas Paine, *Collected Writings* (New York: Literary Classics, 1955), 408. Foner, *Revolutionary America,* 249, 251, 94; Nelson, *Enlightenment, Revolution,* 290.
174. Nelson, *Enlightenment, Revolution,* 294; Fruchtman, *Apostle of Freedom,* 344–5, 349–50; 352, 353.
175. Nelson, *Enlightenment, Revolution,* 294; Fruchtman, *Apostle of Freedom,* 353.
176. Fruchtman, *Apostle of Freedom,* 369, 371; Nelson, *Enlightenment, Revolution,* 296. Still suffering the effects from his imprisonment and deeply disaffected with the direction the French Revolution had taken, Paine resumed drinking and started thinking more seriously about spiritual matters. Fruchtman, *Apostle of Freedom,* 372–3.
177. Paine and Napoléon were not on such complimentary terms a few short years later. Foner, *Revolutionary America,* 253; Nelson, *Enlightenment, Revolution,* 299.

178. Nelson, *Enlightenment, Revolution,* 303; Foner, *Revolutionary America,* 253.
179. Nelson, *Enlightenment, Revolution,* 307; Foner, *Revolutionary America,* 258.
180. Nelson, *Enlightenment, Revolution,* 306; Fruchtman, *Apostle of Freedom,* 386.
181. Foner, *Revolutionary America,* 258; Nelson, *Enlightenment, Revolution,* 309. In 1806, Paine wrote Jefferson asking if he could receive some further reward for his Revolution work. Jefferson did not respond to his first two inquiries. "After Paine wrote a third time, now suggesting he be named special envoy to Napoleon's France, Jefferson replied thanking Paine for the suggestion but telling him America had no need for additional envoys." Nelson, *Enlightenment, Revolution,* 317.
182. Nelson, *Enlightenment, Revolution,* 308. Again drinking heavily, he retired from New York City to his New Rochelle farm before living out the rest of his days with a succession of friends in the New York City area. Nelson, *Enlightenment, Revolution,* 314–15, 318–19; Foner, *Revolutionary America,* 260.
183. Nelson, *Enlightenment, Revolution,* 322–4. With the exception of one critical poem in a Federalist newspaper, Paine's death went unnoted in the press. Foner, *Revolutionary America,* 260–1. In September 1819, a Paine acolyte (and former antagonist), Peter Cobbett, seeking to restore Paine's reputation, removed his bones from the grave and returned them to England. There, Cobbett met with disdain and ridicule, instead of the hoped-for acclaim. Nelson, *Enlightenment, Revolution,* 1–8.
184. Foner, *Revolutionary America,* 254.
185. Nelson, *Enlightenment, Revolution,* 11.
186. Foner, *Revolutionary America,* 264.
187. Kaye, *Promise of America,* 165. The famous preacher Lyman Beecher published "The Sketch of the Life of Thomas Paine" in his magazine *The Spirit of the Pilgrims,* for example, essentially repeating scurrilous points from Cheetham's flawed biography. Ibid., 131.
188. Ibid., 120.
189. Ibid., 120–1.
190. Ibid., 183. Similar allusions followed, especially as the country became enmeshed in war. In addition, Wilson's proposed Fourteen Points for the League of Nations echoed concepts first raised by Paine in *The Rights of Man.* Ibid., 197–8.
191. Ibid., 226; Ronald Reagan, *Nomination Acceptance Speech, 1980 Republican National Convention,* July 17, 1980, http://www.nationalcenter.org/ReaganConvention1980.html.
192. Barack Obama, *Presidential Inaugural Address*, Jan. 20, 2009, available at http://www.nytimes.com/2009/01/20/us/politics/20text-obama.html.
193. Nelson, *Enlightenment, Revolution,* 123.

194. Kaye, *Promise of America,* 127–8.
195. Ibid., 168.
196. Kaye, *Promise of America,* 265; Foner, *Revolutionary America,* 266; Nelson, *Enlightenment, Revolution,* 335. The "Jubilee Association of the Daughters and Sons of Toil," a truly unique labor union of Philadelphia textile workers both Christian and radical, counted Moses, Jesus, and Paine among its heroes. Outside of the early labor movement, however, one still needed to be a deist or "worse" to participate in most Paineite groups, which well into the 1840s still focused primarily on radical religious issues. Foner, *Revolutionary America,* 266.
197. Kaye, *Promise of America,* 147, 150. The most militant abolitionist of them all – John Brown – read *The Age of Reason* with his men while preparing for their action against the federal arsenal at Harper's Ferry in 1859. Ibid., 155.
198. Ibid., 150, 128.
199. Ibid., 152. As discussed in Chapter 3, Stanton played a leading role in organizing the first Women's Right Convention in Seneca Falls, New York, in 1848, and in drafting the Declaration of Rights and Sentiments demanding political and social equality for women.
200. Ibid., 153.
201. Ibid., 157.
202. Ibid., 171. Emerson eventually came around in 1844 to crediting Paine's influence as the true voice of the founding. The almost-unbelievably-prolific Lippard relentlessly redeemed the reputation of the "heroic" Thomas Paine, the patriot whose "unfailing quill" wrote the words "that shall burn into the brains of kings like arrows winged with fire and pointed with vitriol." Ibid., 147. The name of the merchant ship in Herman Melville's *Billy Budd* was *Rights-of-Man,* the owner of which was "an admirer of Thomas Paine." Ibid., 143–4, 178. Poet Walt Whitman spoke proudly of Paine and of how "determined" he was to "help set the memory of Paine right." Ibid., 144. And Mark Twain was about twenty when he first read Paine, quoting *The American Crisis* in letters home while traveling east in the mid-1850s. Ibid., 171.
203. Foner, *Revolutionary America,* 268; Nelson, *Enlightenment, Revolution,* 256, 269.
204. Kaye, *Promise of America,* 181.
205. Ibid., 186–8, 215. Defending Debs in his infamous sedition trial was the noted trial lawyer Clarence Darrow, who had raised Paine's name in court at least once: "How [the overzealous prosecutor's] mouth would have watered if he had been given a chance to convict Thomas Paine for daring to proclaim the rights of man!" Ibid., 187, 189–90. The communist author Howard Fast wrote *Citizen Tom Paine* in 1943, which was withdrawn in 1947 from all New York City public school libraries because of excessive "vulgarity"; in 1949, the FBI chief J. Edgar Hoover ordered agents to remove and destroy all

of Fast's titles from major libraries. Even Clark Clifford, President Truman's special counsel, had to explain why he had given gifts of fifty copies of *Citizen Tom Paine*. Ibid., 231.

206. Ibid., 182, 206, 210–11.
207. Ibid., 192, 194, 195.
208. Ibid., 195. Americans have especially embraced Paine in wartime. In a 1924 Memorial Day dedication of a monument to America's World War I soldiers, General John J. Pershing remembered that Paine's "inspiring words... became an encouragement to Washington's troops as they met and defeated the enemy," and those same "sentiments filled the breasts of those who passed this spot to battle against tyranny beyond the seas." General George Patton and World War II pilot Captain Marvin Hilton inspired both themselves and their men with Paine's "Tyranny, like hell, is not easily conquered" – Patton as he exhorted his troops across Europe, and Hilton as he flew bombing runs with the immortal words painted on the fuselage of the "Tom Paine," his B-17 Flying Fortress. Ibid., 206, 221; Nelson, *Enlightenment, Revolution*, 336.
209. Kaye, *Promise of America*, 243–4.
210. Ibid., 246, 253, 255.
211. Ibid., 254.
212. Ibid., 171.
213. Ibid., 11.
214. Nelson, *Enlightenment, Revolution*, 9.

3. Elizabeth Cady Stanton (1815–1902): *Gender Wars*

1. Ann D. Gordon, ed., *The Selected Papers of Elizabeth Cady Stanton and Susan B. Anthony: Against an Aristocracy of Sex, 1866–1873* (Piscataway, NJ: Rutgers University Press, 2000), 2:156–7.
2. Stanton, "The Solitude of Self," Jan. 18, 1892, in *Elizabeth Cady Stanton, Susan B. Anthony: Correspondence, Writings, Speeches*, ed. Ellen Carol DuBois (New York: Schocken Books, 1981), 246; Ellen Carol DuBois, *Woman Suffrage and Women's Rights* (New York: New York University Press, 1998), 62–3; Elisabeth Griffith, *In Her Own Right: The Life of Elizabeth Cady Stanton* (New York: Oxford University Press, 1984), xvii (citing Elizabeth Cady Stanton, Susan B. Anthony, and Matilda Joslyn Gage, eds., *History of Woman Suffrage, 1848–1861* [New York: Fowler and Wells, 1881; Salem, NH: Ayer Company, 1985], 4:189–91).
3. Geoffrey C. Ward, *Not for Ourselves Alone: The Story of Elizabeth Cady Stanton and Susan B. Anthony* (New York: Knopf, 1999); Elizabeth Frost and Kathryn Cullen-DuPont, *Women's Suffrage in America: An Eyewitness History* (New York: Facts on File, 1992), 2.

4. Frost and Cullen-DuPont, *Eyewitness*, 12; William Lyman, *A Virtuous Woman the Bond of Domestic Union, and Familiarly Illustrated* (New London, CT: S. Green, 1802), quoted in Nancy F. Cott, *The Bonds of Womanhood: "Woman's Sphere" in New England, 1780–1835* (New Haven, CT: Yale University Press, 1977), 85; Suzanne M. Marilley, *Woman Suffrage and the Origins of Liberal Feminism in the United States, 1820–1920* (Cambridge, MA: Harvard University Press, 1996), 5, 18.
5. Marilley, *Woman Suffrage*, 6; John Cosens Ogden, *The Female Guide; or, Thoughts on the Education of That Sex* (Concord: George Hough, 1793), 26; John Stuart Mill, *Texts, Commentaries*, ed. Alan Ryan (New York: W. W. Norton, 1997), 133–215; George Klosko and Margaret G. Klosko, *The Struggle for Women's Rights Theoretical and Historical Sources* (Upper Saddle River, NJ: Prentice Hall, 1999), 58; Frost and Cullen-DuPont, *Eyewitness*, 3.
6. Wright's legacy as the first public figure in America to actively advocate for women's rights continued to be felt for decades afterward, with her name "virtually an epithet for monstrous female independence." Frost and Cullen-DuPont, *Eyewitness*, 1; DuBois, *Woman Suffrage*, 83, 285. Her own philosophy evolved from English polemicist Mary Wollstonecraft, who was an enthusiast (together with Thomas Paine, Thomas Jefferson, and other early Republicans) of the French Revolution and its principles of natural human rights. Matilda Joslyn Gage, "Preceding Causes," in *The Concise History of Woman Suffrage: Selections from the Classic Work of Stanton, Anthony, Gage, and Harper*, eds. Mari Jo and Paul Buhle (Urbana: University of Illinois Press, 1978), 61–2; Celia Morris Eckhardt, *Fanny Wright: Rebel in America* (Cambridge, MA: Harvard University Press, 1984), 1–3, 282–3; Barbara Taylor, *Eve and the New Jerusalem: Socialism and Feminism in the Nineteenth Century* (Cambridge, MA: Harvard University Press, 1993), 1–18, 65–70.
7. Frost and Cullen-DuPont, *Eyewitness*, 5, 9–19, 31; DuBois, *Woman Suffrage*, 55. The literacy rate for women was much lower than for men in the nation's early decades (the women's rate was just half that of men in 1776, for example). Through the efforts of many women (who themselves were of widely varying opinions on the role of women in the home and society), educational opportunities for women improved dramatically throughout the first half of the nineteenth century, to the point that the literacy rate disparity was eliminated, with the 1850 federal census reporting "equal and universal literacy skills among white native-born New England men and women." Frost and Cullen-DuPont, *Eyewitness*, 5, 9–19, 31; DuBois, *Woman Suffrage*, 55. It must be noted that opportunities for African American women during this same period remained virtually nonexistent, even in the North. These factory jobs themselves became exploitive with worsening working conditions brought on by great increases in numbers of poor immigrants during the 1840s, leading to rising militancy in the female workforce. Frost and

Cullen-DuPont, *Eyewitness*, 5; DuBois, *Woman Suffrage* 55; Eyewitness 9 et seq., 31, 10, 5.

8. *Watson v. Mercer*, 6 Serjeant and Rawle 49 (1820), in *Women of America: A History*, Carol Ruth Berkin and Mary Beth Norton (Boston: Houghton Mifflin, 1979), 111; Frost and Cullen-DuPont, *Eyewitness*, 1–2, 14.
9. Frost and Cullen-DuPont, *Eyewitness*, 20–1; Eleanor Flexner, *Century of Struggle: The Woman's Rights Movement in the United States*, rev. ed. (Cambridge, MA: Harvard University Press, 1975), 62; Lydia Maria Child to Ellis Gray Loring, Wayland, Feb. 24, 1856, in *Letters of Lydia Maria Child with a Biographical Introduction by John G. Whittier and Appendix by Wendell Phillips* (Boston: Houghton Mifflin, 1883), 74.
10. Frost and Cullen-DuPont, *Eyewitness*, 2, 13–14; Ellen Carol DuBois, *Feminism and Suffrage: The Emergence of an Independent Women's Movement in America, 1848–1869* (Ithaca, NY: Cornell University Press, 1978), 45; Berkin and Norton, *Women of America*, 97.
11. Frost and Cullen-DuPont, *Eyewitness*, 19–22; Alexis de Tocqueville, *Democracy in America*, trans. Henry Reeve (London: Colonial Press, 1900), 2:211; Joseph Richardson, "A Sermon on the Duty and Dignity of Woman," Apr. 22, 1832, in Cott, *The Bonds of Womanhood*, 159.
12. Garrison began publishing his own antislavery paper, *The Liberator,* in 1831 and in the following two years helped found the New England Anti-Slavery Society and then the American Anti-Slavery Society, with which he sought to make the immediate emancipation of all slaves a national issue (the national government, for its part, had avoided the slavery question, defining it as a "sectional" issue). Garrisonians consciously avoided aligning with any political party. DuBois, *Woman Suffrage*, 62; Marilley, *Woman Suffrage*, 19–21.
13. Marilley, *Woman Suffrage*, 19, 23; Frost and Cullen-DuPont, *Eyewitness*, 28; William Lloyd Garrison to Sarah M. Douglass, Boston, March 5, 1832, in *The Letters of William Lloyd Garrison*, eds. Walter M. Merrill and Louis Ruchames (Cambridge, MA: Belknap, 1971), 143–5; Afro-American Studies, ed., *Selections from the Writings and Speeches of William Lloyd Garrison* (New York: New American Library, 1969), 127 (emphasis in original).
14. Lucretia Mott was one of the first to answer the call, forming the Philadelphia Female Antislavery Society in 1833, just a few days after Garrison formed the American Anti-Slavery Society, together with other mostly Quaker women, white and black. It was to the Philadelphia Society that sisters Sarah and Angelina Grimké, who were born in Charleston, South Carolina, but moved to the North in opposition to their family's slaveholding, gravitated on their arrival in the North. Buhle and Buhle, *Concise History*, 69; Marilley, *Woman Suffrage*, 22.
15. Sarah Moore Grimké, *Letters on the Equality of the Sexes, and Other Essays* (New Haven, CT: Yale University Press, 1988), 16; Marilley, *Woman Suffrage*, 31–4; DuBois, *Woman Suffrage*, 60; Marilyn Richardson, ed., *Maria*

W. Stewart: America's First Black Woman Political Writer (Bloomington: Indiana University Press, 1987), 68; Larry Ceplair, ed., *The Public Years of Sarah and Angelina Grimke: Selected Writings, 1835–1839* (New York: Columbia University Press, 1989), 62.

16. Margaret Hope Bacon, *Valiant Friend: The Life of Lucretia Mott* (New York: Walker and Company, 1980), 77; Marilley, *Woman Suffrage*, 33; Buhle and Buhle, *Concise History*, 70, 73; Frost and Cullen-DuPont, *Eyewitness*, 28. "*The women of the South can overthrow* this horrible system of oppression and cruelty, licentiousness and wrong," Angelina Grimké wrote. "Such appeals to your legislatures would be irresistible, for there is something in the heart of man which *will bend under moral suasion*. There is a swift witness for truth in his bosom, which *will respond to truth* when it is uttered with calmness and dignity." Marilley, *Woman Suffrage*, 26–7 (citing Larry Ceplair, ed., *The Public Years of Sarah and Angelina Grimke: Selected Writings, 1835–1839* [New York: Columbia University Press, 1989] 37, 66 [emphasis in original]).
17. Marilley, *Woman Suffrage*, 34; Frost and Cullen-DuPont, *Eyewitness*, 28–9; "Pastoral Letter of the Massachusetts Congregationalist Clergy," Boston, Aug. 11, 1837, in *Up from the Pedestal: Selected Writings in the History of American Feminism*, ed. Aileen S. Kraditor (Chicago: Quadrangle Books, 1968), 51.
18. Ann D. Gordon, ed., *The Selected Papers of Elizabeth Cady Stanton and Susan B. Anthony: In the School of Anti-Slavery, 1840–1866* (New Brunswick, NJ: Rutgers University Press, 1997), 1:559–60; DuBois, *Woman's Suffrage*, 64.
19. DuBois, *Woman Suffrage*, 59.
20. Griffith, *In Her Own Right*, 4–9; Stanton to Susan B. Anthony, Peterboro, Sept. 10, 1855, in *Elizabeth Cady Stanton: As Revealed in Her Letters, Diary, and Reminiscences*, ed. Theodore Stanton and Harriot Stanton Blatch (New York: Harper and Brothers, 1922), 2:59. Daniel Cady had wanted nothing more than to pass his legacy on to a son – a desire that was dashed when all six of his sons died in childhood or young adulthood, whereas his five daughters (Tryphena, Harriot, Elizabeth, Margaret, and Catharine) lived full lives. "It was easily seen," Elizabeth later reflected, "that while my father was kind to us all, the one son filled a larger place in his affections and future plans than the five daughters together."
21. Oberlin College, which opened in 1833, was the first college to admit women, beginning in 1837. Frost and Cullen-DuPont, *Eyewitness*, 3–4, 31; Stanton and Blatch, *Elizabeth Cady Stanton*, 1:35; Elizabeth Cady Stanton, *Eighty Years and More, 1815–1897: Reminiscences of Elizabeth Cady Stanton* (London: T. Fisher Unwin, 1898), 33, 44–5; Jean H. Baker, *Sisters: The Lives of America's Suffragists* (New York: Hill and Wang, 2005), 97.
22. Griffith, *In Her Own Right*, 25–6, 33; Stanton, *Eighty Years and More*, 60, 72; Stanton to Rebecca R. Eyster, Seneca Falls, May 1, 1847, in Stanton

and Blatch, *Elizabeth Cady Stanton*, 2:16. Henry was the sort of impractical radical that Judge Cady despised and was a man of little means, as well (her other sisters had married, or would later marry, more respectably – a lawyer, a journalist, or law clerks in her father's firm). Ibid.

23. Geoffrey C. Ward, *Not for Ourselves Alone* (New York: Knopf, 1999), 20; Frost and Cullen-DuPont, *Eyewitness*, 56.
24. Frost and Cullen-DuPont, *Eyewitness*, 57; Stanton, Anthony, and Gage, *History of Woman Suffrage*, 1:419–20.
25. Stanton, *Eighty Years and More*, 81–2; DuBois, *Woman Suffrage*, 58; Stanton to Susan B. Anthony, Peterboro, Sept. 10, 1855, in Stanton and Blatch, *Elizabeth Cady Stanton*, 1:79, 2:59–60; Stanton, Anthony, and Gage, *History of Woman Suffrage*, 1:420; Griffith, *In Her Own Right*, 188; Susan B. Anthony to Lucy Stone, Albany, Feb. 9, 1854, in Gordon, *School of Anti-Slavery*, 1: 239.
26. Stanton, Anthony, and Gage, *History of Woman Suffrage*, 1:419–22; Frost and Cullen-DuPont, *Eyewitness*, 57; Griffith, *In Her Own Right*, 35–40; Stanton, *Eighty Years and More*, 148.
27. Later, during the early 1850s, some women reformers began wearing bloomers, Turkish-style long pants under a shorter, knee-length skirt. Stanton loved the dress, for its convenience and message of rebellion. Stanton at first refused to bend to the withering, sustained criticism of bloomers in the press, arguing "I'll never take it off for now it involves a principle of freedom." Nonetheless, fearing that such a trivial matter as choice in clothing was deflecting attention from more important issues, Stanton and most of the other women reluctantly gave up bloomers by 1853. Stanton to Daniel C. Stanton, Seneca Falls, Oct. 14, 1851, in Stanton and Blatch, *Elizabeth Cady Stanton*, 2:35–6; Frost and Cullen-DuPont, *Eyewitness*, 100, 108; Baker, *Sisters*, 56.
28. Stanton, *Eighty Years and More*, 145–7; Griffith, *In Her Own Right*, 48–50.
29. Stanton and Blatch, *Elizabeth Cady Stanton*, 1:131; Stanton, *Eighty Years and More*, 133, 136; Griffith, *In Her Own Right*, 44.
30. Griffith, *In Her Own Right*, 51; Stanton, *Eighty Years and More*, 148–9; Stanton, Anthony, and Gage, *History of Woman Suffrage*, 1:68–9.
31. Griffith, *In Her Own Right*, 52–3; Stanton, Anthony, and Gage, *History of Woman Suffrage*, 1:68–71.
32. Specifically, in the first few years after returning from London, Elizabeth and Henry had been busy with the birth and care of three sons and getting on their feet financially. They lived, successively, in Johnstown, Boston, Albany, Boston again, then Seneca Falls in 1847, at which point her frustration with her life reached a boiling point. Elizabeth only dabbled in politics during these years (lobbying the New York legislature in 1843 and 1845 for the Married Woman's Property Act, for example) but declined any leading roles either in politics or in the abolitionist movement. Stanton, *Eighty Years and More*, 133; Griffith, *In Her Own Right*, 60–1.

33. Frost and Cullen-DuPont, *Eyewitness*, 81 (citing HWS 1:68–73). The crowd of one hundred seemed surprisingly large to the women, including Lucretia Mott, who had feared "[t]he convention will not be so large as it otherwise might be, owing to the busy time with the farmer's harvest." Griffith, *In Her Own Right*, 55.
34. Buhle and Buhle, *Concise History*, 95, 97.
35. Gordon, *School of Anti-Slavery*, 1:83n3; Frost and Cullen-DuPont, *Eyewitness*, 86–87; Frederick Douglas, *The North Star*, July 28, 1848, in *Frederick Douglass on Women's Rights*, ed. Philip S. Foner (Westport, CT: Greenwood Press, 1976), 49–51; Buhle and Buhle, *Concise History*, 96; Stanton, Anthony, and Gage, *History of Woman Suffrage*, 1:72–3; Elizabeth Cady Stanton, "Address Delivered at Seneca Falls," July 19, 1848, in DuBois, *Correspondence, Writing, Speeches*, 31–2; Sally G. McMillen, *Seneca Falls and the Origins of the Women's Rights Movement* (New York: Oxford University Press, 2008), 98.
36. Frost and Cullen-DuPont, *Eyewitness*, 85–8; Judith Nies, *Nine Women: Portraits from the American Radical Tradition*, rev. ed. (Berkeley: University of California Press, 2002), 82; Griffith, *In Her Own Right*, 57. Other newspaper accounts included the *Worcester Telegraph*, which complained under an editorial titled "Insurrection among the Women" that "the Amazons [intend] in spite of all the misrepresentations and ridicule, to employ agents, circulate tracts, petition the State and National legislatures, and endeavor to enlist the pulpit and the press in their behalf. This is bolting with a vengeance."
37. Buhle and Buhle, *Concise History*, 99–100; Nies, *Nine Women*, 81–2; Flexner, *Century of Struggle*, 76–7; Stanton to Amy Kirby Post, Grassmere, Sept. 24, 1848, in Gordon, *School of Anti-Slavery*, 1:124.
38. Stanton to Lucretia Mott, Seneca Falls, Sept. 30, 1848, in Stanton and Blatch, *Elizabeth Cady Stanton*, 2:20–2; Frost and Cullen-DuPont, *Eyewitness*, 90.
39. Frost and Cullen-DuPont, *Eyewitness*, 93. It was at one such local meeting in Akron, Ohio, on May 28 and 29, 1851, that the former slave Sojourner Truth, who could neither read nor write and whose back was covered in scars she had received from whippings by slave owners, delivered her celebrated "Ain't I a Woman?" speech.
40. Stanton, *Eighty Years*, 162–3; Frost and Cullen-DuPont, *Eyewitness*, 103, Griffith, *In Her Own Right*, 73.
41. Ward, *Not for Ourselves Alone*, 154.
42. Griffith, *In Her Own Right*, 54; Buhle and Buhle, *Concise History*, 96; Stanton, *Eighty Years*, 151.
43. Griffith, *In Her Own Right*, 54.
44. Thomas Paine, *Rights of Man: Being an Answer to Mr. Burke's Attack on the French Revolution*, ed. Moncure Daniel Conway (New York: G. P. Putnam's Sons, 1894), 304–5; Kathi Kern, *Mrs. Stanton's Bible* (Ithaca, NY: Cornell University Press, 2001), 66; Stanton to Susan B. Anthony, Seneca Falls, July 4, 1858, in Stanton and Blatch, *Elizabeth Cady Stanton*, 2:72–3.

45. Mill is most famous for his articulation of the harm principle (quoted also in Chapter 2): "[T]he only purpose for which power can be rightfully exercised over any member of a civilized community, against his will is to prevent harm to others." J. S. Mill, *On Liberty* (1859); *The Subjection of Women*, in Mill, *Texts, Commentaries*, 133, 174; Klosko and Klosko, *The Struggle for Women's Rights*, 58; Gordon, *Against an Aristocracy of Sex*, 2:260; Stanton and Blatch, *Elizabeth Cady Stanton*, 2:122. In response to Stanton's request for a letter of support for the women's cause in America, Mill wrote Stanton as well: "[T]he cause in America has advanced beyond the stage at which it could need a recommendation from me, or from any man," he wrote. "It is not to be believed that the nation which is now engaged in admitting the newly liberated negro to the plenitude of all political franchises, will much longer retain women in a state of helotage which... is now more degrading than ever, because, being no longer shared by any of the male sex, it constitutes every woman the inferior of every man." Gordon, *Against an Aristocracy of Sex*, 2:260.
46. Buhle and Buhle, *Concise History*, 49; Stanton, Anthony, and Gage, *History of Woman Suffrage*, 1:25–42.
47. Gordon, *School of Anti-Slavery*, 1: 491–2; 1: 514; Baker, *Sisters*, 69. Stanton and Anthony had disagreed at the time on the strategy to suspend, but Stanton prevailed on this occasion. "We should be ready to pledge our time, our means, our talents, and our lives to freeing the slaves," she argued. "After this cause made for the Negro will come a peace made for both blacks and women." To which Anthony pleaded in response, "But I have not yet seen *one good reason* for the abandonment of all our meetings, and am more and more ashamed and sad that the means must be sacrificed to the end." Baker, *Sisters*, 70.
48. Griffith, *In Her Own Right*, 103. In addition to Daniel (1842), Henry (1844), and Gerrit (1845), born before the convention, she and Henry had four more children in the 1850s: Theodore (1851), Margaret (1852), Harriot (1856), and Robert (1859). Henry was typically absent ten months of the year registering patents and trying cases. Stanton sought a well-rounded life, taking pride in her mothering and domesticity. Her views on sexuality were liberated, true to her progressive feminism demanding equality in all areas of life beyond suffrage alone. She was not an advocate of "free-love," however; commenting, "I've lived with one husband for over thirty years and I suppose I'll be with him until the end." Ibid., 230; Kern, *Mrs. Stanton's Bible*, 220.
49. Frost and Cullen-DuPont, *Eyewitness*, 99; Griffith, *In Her Own Right*, 83.
50. Stanton to Susan B. Anthony, Peterboro, Sept. 10, 1855, in Stanton and Blatch, *Elizabeth Cady Stanton*, 2:59; DuBois, *Correspondence, Writing, Speeches*, 58; Ward, *Not for Ourselves Alone*, 77; Griffith, *In Her Own Right*, 85; Nies, *Nine Women*, 86. Her earlier delight in the births of her children gave way to greater resignation and bitterness at her fate with the births of Harriot in 1856 and Robert in 1859. In letters to Anthony, she

admitted, "I am very happy that the terrible ordeal is past and that the result is another daughter. But I feel disappointed and sad at the same time at this grievous interruption of my plans"; and "Imagine me, day in and day out, watching, bathing nursing and promenading the precious contents of a little crib in the corner of my room. I pace up and down these chambers like a caged lion, longing to bring nursing and housekeeping cares to a close. I have other work at hand." Stanton to Susan B. Anthony, Peterboro, Sept. 10, 1855, in Stanton and Blatch, *Elizabeth Cady Stanton*, 2:59.

51. Stanton's father Daniel Cady died in October 1859. Although losing her father was difficult for Stanton, his death at the same time freed her from the burden of his oppressive disapproval. Early in the new year, she gave three major speeches on married women's property rights, women's suffrage, and defending divorce.
52. This topic was so threatening to others at the meeting (including Stone, Horace Greeley, and Wendell Phillips) that they sought not only to defeat Stanton's resolutions but also to strike the discussion from the record. Although they were successful in defeating the resolutions, Stanton, with the support of Ernestine Rose and Susan B. Anthony, prevailed on leaving the discussions in the record. Stanton, Anthony, and Gage, *History of Woman Suffrage*, 1:860; Stanton to Susan B. Anthony, Seneca Falls, July 20, 1857, and June 14, 1860, in Stanton and Blatch, *Elizabeth Cady Stanton*, 2:69–70, 82; Griffith, *In Her Own Right*, 100–3; Frost and Cullen-DuPont, *Eyewitness*, 128.
53. Equivocation on the slavery issue was simply not acceptable. In fact, Stanton and other abolitionists had little enthusiasm for Lincoln as he failed to take a strong early stand against slavery.
54. Griffith, *In Her Own Right*, 108.
55. Gordon, *School of Anti-Slavery*, 1:550–1.
56. "I think such mixture [of simultaneously advocating both negro's and women's suffrage] would lose for the negro far more than we should gain for the woman," Phillips wrote to Stanton on May 10, 1865. Baker, *Sisters*, 72.
57. Stanton to Susan B. Anthony, New York, Aug. 11, 1865, in Stanton and Blatch, *Elizabeth Cady Stanton*, 2:105–6; Alma Lutz, *Created Equal: A Biography of Elizabeth Cady Stanton, 1815–1902* (New York: John Day Company, 1940), 132–4; Frost and Cullen-DuPont, *Eyewitness*, 179. Stanton now recognized that Anthony had been correct after all in opposing the strategy to suspend the movement in 1861. "I am now equally sure that it was a blunder," she said, "and, ever since, I have taken my beloved Susan's judgment against the world. I have always found that, when we see eye to eye, we are sure to be right, and when we pull together we are strong."
58. One proposal would restrict voters to literate males age twenty-one and older; another – which would eventually become the controversial section 2 – would condition congressional representation on not limiting male suffrage.

59. Griffith, *In Her Own Right*, 123; Jo and Buhle, *Concise History*, 216–17; Stanton to Editor, *National Anti-Slavery Standard*, New York, Dec. 26, 1865, in Gordon, *School of Anti-Slavery*, 1:550–2, 563–5; James M. McPherson, *The Struggle for Equality: Abolitionists and the Negro in the Civil War and Reconstruction* (Princeton, NJ: Princeton University Press, 1964), 326–8.
60. Buhle and Buhle, *Concise History*, 216; Gordon, *School of Anti-Slavery*, 1:566; Stanton to Martha C. Wright, New York, Jan. 6, 1866, in Stanton and Blatch, *Elizabeth Cady Stanton*, 2:111. The petition called Congress's "attention to the fact that we represent fifteen million people – one-half the entire population of the country – intelligent, virtuous, native-born American citizens; and yet stand outside the pale of political recognition.... [W]e ask that you extend the right of suffrage to Woman – the only remaining class of disfranchised citizens – and thus fulfill your constitutional obligation 'to guarantee to every state in the Union a Republican form of Government.'"
61. Foner, *Frederick Douglass*, 27; Stanton, Anthony, and Gage, *History of Woman Suffrage*, 2:93; Stanton and Blatch, *Elizabeth Cady Stanton*, 2:112; Buhle and Buhle, *Concise History*, 218–19.
62. Stanton and Blatch, *Elizabeth Cady Stanton*, 2:112–13.
63. Buhle and Buhle, *Concise History*, 223; Eric Foner and Olivia Mahoney, *America's Reconstruction: People and Politics after the Civil War* (New York: Harper Perennial, 1995), 91.
64. Griffith, *In Her Own Right*, 89–90; DuBois, *Correspondence, Writing, Speeches*, 89–90; DuBois, *Woman Suffrage*, 98–9.
65. DuBois, *Woman Suffrage*, 89–90; 98–9.
66. Stanton, Anthony, and Gage, *History of Woman Suffrage*, 2:269–70, 284; Gordon, *Against an Aristocracy of Sex*, 2:75–6; Lutz, *Created Equal*, 140–1; Griffith, *In Her Own Right*, 127. Stanton was pleased with herself for her reply to Greeley, recalling the exchange in a letter she wrote later that night to Martha Wright before retiring to bed. "Rather a crushing blow!" she enthused. Stanton and Blatch, *Elizabeth Cady Stanton*, 2:116.
67. Stanton, Anthony, and Gage, *History of Woman Suffrage*, 2:285–7; Gordon, *Against an Aristocracy of Sex*, 2:77n3; Lutz, *Created Equal*, 140–1; Griffith, *In Her Own Right*, 127.
68. Stanton to Emily Howland, New York, Sept. 1, 1867, in Stanton and Blatch, *Elizabeth Cady Stanton*, 2:116–18.
69. Lucy Stone commented, for example, "[Train's] presence as an advocate of woman suffrage was enough to condemn it in the minds of all persons not already convinced." Frost and Cullen-DuPont, *Eyewitness*, 174–6.
70. Frost and Cullen-DuPont, *Eyewitness*, 174–6, 195; Griffith, *In Her Own Right*, 130; Buhle and Buhle, *Concise History*, 247.
71. Frost and Cullen-DuPont, *Eyewitness*, 195; Buhle and Buhle, *Concise History*, 247; William Lloyd Garrison to Theodore Tilton, Roxbury, Apr. 5, 1870, in William Lloyd Garrison, *The Letters of William Lloyd Garrison* (Cambridge, MA: Harvard University Press, 1981), 6:173–4; Stanton to

Edwin A. Studwell, Buffalo, Nov. 30, 1867, in Gordon, *Against an Aristocracy of Sex*, 2:116.

72. Stanton to Thomas W. Higginson, New York, Jan. 13, 1868, in Gordon, *Against an Aristocracy of Sex*, 2:126–7; Stanton and Blatch, *Elizabeth Cady Stanton*, 2:120–1.
73. Gordon, *Against an Aristocracy of Sex*, 2:272–3; Griffith, *In Her Own Right*, 130.
74. Stanton, *Eighty Years and More*, 241.
75. The *Revolution* was housed first in the New York City headquarters of AERA (which itself quickly withdrew), with a primary staff consisting of Stanton as senior editor and author of virtually all of the text, Anthony as office manager, and Parker Pillsbury, the only one of the three with any previous editorial experience, as coeditor. Frost and Cullen-DuPont, *Eyewitness*, 178; Stanton, Anthony, and Gage, *History of Woman Suffrage*, 1:46.
76. Stanton did not shrink from the controversy. In fact, she relished the paper's radical approach, starting with its very moniker. "As to changing the name of the *Revolution*," she wrote Anthony on December 28, 1869, "I should consider it a great mistake. If all these people who for twenty years have been afraid to call their souls their own begin to prune us and the *Revolution*," she warned, "we shall become the same galvanized mummies they are.... The establishing of woman on her rightful throne is the greatest revolution the world has ever known or ever will know. To bring it about is no child's play." "A journal called the *Rosebud* might answer for those who come with kid gloves and perfumes..., but for us...there is no name like *Revolution*." Frost and Cullen-DuPont, *Eyewitness*, 195; Griffith, *In Her Own Right*, 131–2; Ward, *Not for Ourselves Alone*, 112; Ida Husted Harper, *The Life and Work of Susan B. Anthony* (Indianapolis: Hollenbeck Press, 1898), 1:295; Stanton and Blatch, *Elizabeth Cady Stanton*, 2:123. In any event, the *Revolution* would survive only a few more months before closing due to financial difficulties. Frost and Cullen-DuPont, *Eyewitness*, 208; Griffith, *In Her Own Right*, 131–2, 145; Ward, *Not for Ourselves Alone*, 123; Stanton and Blatch, *Elizabeth Cady Stanton*, 2:123.
77. As Lucy Stone wrote the Reverend James Freeman Clarke on October 6, 1869, "Can you not be present to help organize? Our cause suffers today from the lack of the organizing talent of MEN, in its management.... If we can only organize wisely and well, with half our officers men, of the right kind, there will be no end to the good, that will come of it." Marilley, *Woman Suffrage*, 79; Frost and Cullen-DuPont, *Eyewitness*, 202; Griffith, *In Her Own Right*, 140; Leslie Wheeler, ed., *Loving Warriors: Selected Letters of Lucy Stone and Henry B. Blackwell, 1853 to 1893* (New York: Dial Press, 1981), 228–9.
78. Ibid.; *Revolution*, Nov. 24, 1870, in Judith Papachristou, *Women Together: A History in Documents of the Women's Movement in the United States* (New York: Alfred A. Knopf, 1976), 72–3.

79. Kern, *Mrs. Stanton's Bible*, 10; Vivian Gornick, *The Solitude of Self: Thinking about Elizabeth Cady Stanton* (New York: Farrar, Straus, and Giroux, 2005), 80–1.
80. Griffith, *In Her Own Right*, 142–3. Griffith adds, however, that in some ways things had never been better for Stanton. "By 1870 she had become emotionally self-sufficient. She lived apart from Henry in her own establishment in Tenafly. She entertained him as a guest and divided care for the children with him but was financially and socially independent of him." Moreover, "[n]ow that her children were older, she was less involved with them. She had a full-time housekeeper and few qualms about leaving those children still at home. She was not entirely kind to those closest to her, however.... She expected her female friends to support, understand, forgive and sustain her, and on the whole they did," Griffith explains. Stanton "still cared about her family and friends. But most of all she cared for herself and her cause." Ibid.; Stanton, Anthony, and Gage, *History of Woman Suffrage*, 2:320–2.
81. Stanton's talks on the circuit covered a broad range of topics, with lectures including "The Bible and Women's Rights," "Famous Women in the Bible," "The Subjection of Women," "Home Life," "The True Republic," "Coeducation," "Marriage and Divorce," "Marriage and Maternity," "Our Girls," "Our Boy," "Prison Life," "Thurlow Weed, William Seward, and Horace Greeley," and "The Antagonism of Sex." During the summer months, she was at home with her children – who, ranging in age from thirteen to thirty in 1872 and home from school or visiting, were, she said, "intelligent companions... [and] a real pleasure." Griffith, *In Her Own Right*, 147–9.
82. Gordon, *Against an Aristocracy of Sex*, 2:274–5; Baker, *Sisters*, 81, 112; Stanton and Blatch, *Elizabeth Cady Stanton*, 2:131, 133; Stanton to Lucretia Mott, Tenafly, New Jersey, July 19, 1876, in Stanton, Anthony, and Gage, *History of Woman Suffrage*, 3:45–7, Lutz, *Created Equal*, 239. One of the "recent judicial decisions" to which Stanton referred was *Minor v. Happersatt*, which denied the constitutional claim of a woman, Virginia Minor, 1 of about 150 women turned away when attempting to vote in the presidential election of 1872 (chanting "We are Coming, Uncle Sam, with 15 million more"). Some who did manage to vote, including Susan B. Anthony, were subsequently arrested. Gordon, *Against an Aristocracy of Sex*, 2:275, 2:274; Baker, *Sisters*, 81. The outraged reaction to *Minor v. Happersatt* was captured well by the comments of the abolitionist lawyer Horace Dresser: "The great usurpation is now affirmed, legalized, by the degree of the Judicial Department of the government! More than 20,000,000 of the people of this Nation have been declared without the pale of political rights secured to them by the Constitution of the fathers."
83. They completed volume 1, covering the years through 1860, in May 1881; volume 2, covering 1861 to 1876, was completed the following May; and volume 3, bringing the movement up to date through 1885, was published in 1886.

84. Ibid., 188. Elizabeth and Henry were married for nearly fifty years. Although they had their differences, the marriage was satisfactory enough. After Henry's sudden death from pneumonia in 1887, Elizabeth reflected with some warmth, "[We] lived together without more than the usual matrimonial friction, for nearly half a century, had seven children... [all] well sheltered, clothed and fed, enjoying sound minds in sound bodies." But her regrets were clear as well: "Ah! If we could only remember in life to be gentle and forbearing with each other, and to strive to serve nobly instead of exacting service, our memory of the past would be more pleasant and profitable." Griffith, *In Her Own Right*, 188; Stanton and Blatch, *Elizabeth Cady Stanton*, 2:236.
85. Frost and Cullen-DuPont, *Eyewitness*, 267; "The Pleasures of Age," speech by Elizabeth Cady Stanton, in Ann D. Gordon, ed., *The Selected Papers of Elizabeth Cady Stanton and Susan B. Anthony: When Clowns Make Laws for Queens* (New Brunswick, NJ: Rutgers University Press, 1997), 4:457.
86. Griffith, *In Her Own Right*, xiii, 209; Ward, *Not For Ourselves Alone*, 3–9; Lutz, *Created Equal*, 293; *New York Times*, "Elizabeth Cady Stanton: Her Fourscore Years and Services Honored by a Vast Audience," Nov. 13, 1895 (ProQuest Historical Newspapers).
87. Griffith, *In Her Own Right*, 21–3; Stanton, *Eighty Years and More*, 24, 42–4, 47–8.
88. Kern, *Mrs. Stanton's Bible*, 46; Stanton, *Eighty Years and More*, 231, 285. Feminist criticism of Christian orthodoxy was not completely new when the *Woman's Bible* was published in 1895. Among others, the early activists Frances Wright in 1828 and the Grimké sisters in the mid-1830s identified faulty interpretations of the Bible as key reasons for women's subjugation. William Lloyd Garrison became more outspoken in his antipathy for clerics toward the end of the 1830s and into the 1840s; at the 1848 Seneca Falls Convention, Stanton commented, "Woman has too long rested satisfied in the circumscribed limits which corrupt customs and a perverted application of the Scriptures have marked out for her. [She must now] move into the enlarged sphere which her great Creator has assigned her." Lucretia Mott raised the topic during an argument with the Rev. Henry Grew at the 1854 National Women's Rights Convention, charging that "[t]he pulpit has been prostituted, the Bible has been ill-used. It has been turned over and over in every reform."
89. Kern, *Mrs. Stanton's Bible*, 12; Gornick, *The Solitude of Self*, 118–19.
90. Elizabeth Cady Stanton, *The Woman's Bible* (Boston: Northeastern University Press, 1993), xxi xxii (foreword by Maureen Fitzgerald).
91. Stanton, *Eighty Years and More*, 380. The main feature of the January 1885 NWSA convention in Washington was the attempt to pass a series of statements drafted by a committee chaired by Stanton "impeaching the Christian theology – as well as all other forms of religion, for their degrading teachings in regard to woman."

92. Baker, *Sisters*, 133; Kern, *Mrs. Stanton's Bible*, 69. Stanton was profoundly moved by Darwin's work. "Admit Darwin's theory of evolution," she wrote her cousin Elizabeth Smith Miller in 1887, "and the whole orthodox system topples to the ground; if there was no Fall, there was no need of a Savior, and the atonement, regeneration and salvation have no significance whatever." Stanton to Elizabeth Smith Miller, March 5, 1887, Theo Stanton Collection, Elizabeth Cady Stanton Papers NjR. Freethinkers, based on John Locke's theories, questioned the veracity of anything (such as biblical miracles) not based on reason or observation. Kern, *Mrs. Stanton's Bible*, 66. Stanton was especially impressed with the freethinker Robert Green Ingersoll (one of Thomas Paine's greatest defenders), with whom she socialized in New York City in the 1890s. "How long, O how long will mankind worship a book?" asked Ingersoll. "How long will they grovel in the dust before the ignorant legends of the barbaric past?" Kern, *Mrs. Stanton's Bible*, 63–4 (citing Robert G. Ingersoll, *The Lectures of Col. R. G. Ingersoll* [Chicago: Rhodes and McClure, 1898], 787).
93. Kern, *Mrs. Stanton's Bible*, 1, 50, 67, 71, 75–6; Gornick, *The Solitude of Self*, 120–1; Gordon, *When Clowns Make Laws for Queens*, 4:442.
94. Stanton, *Eighty Years and More*, 390; Kern, *Mrs. Stanton's Bible*, 99, 101, 103, 135; Stanton, *Eighty Years and More*, 372, 392; Gordon, *When Clowns Make Laws for Queens*, 4:514.
95. Although throughout the years, Anthony would much preferred to have had Stanton attend the meetings herself (she even paid Stanton's annual dues in the 1880s when Stanton allowed them to lapse), she did rely heavily on Stanton's written contributions. To her credit, Anthony gave recognition where due. Lutz, *Created Equal*, 279–82; Stanton and Blatch, *Elizabeth Cady Stanton*, 2:253–4.
96. DuBois, *Woman Suffrage*, 63; Ward, *Not for Ourselves Alone*, 206; Barry, *Susan B. Anthony*, 293.
97. The group included her close friends and allies Clara Colby, Matilda Joslyn Gage, Helen Gardener, and Lillie Devereux Blake, as well as Sara Underwood, Ursula Bright, Josephine K. Henry, Olympia Brown, and Frances E. Burr – few of whom at the time or thereafter held leadership positions in the mainstream NAWSA. As social outcasts of sorts, these women were unusually close, supporting one another through sickness and in health for decades afterward. Kern, *Mrs. Stanton's Bible*, 135–42, 149–50, 169.
98. Kern. *Mrs. Stanton's Bible*, 167, 150; Stanton, *The Woman's Bible*, 14, 20, 21.
99. Stanton, *The Woman's Bible*, 7–8, 14, 20–1; Kern, *Mrs. Stanton's Bible*, 150, 167.
100. Stanton, *The Woman's Bible*, 2:7–9, 200 (appendix).
101. Stanton, *Eighty Years and More*, 465–7.
102. Ibid., 467.

103. After a summer of fierce, even violent, political battles in Nashville, the Tennessee legislature ratified the Nineteenth Amendment in a close vote on August 18, 1920, when the youngest man in the legislature, twenty-four-year-old Harry Burn of McKinn County, switched his vote in response to his mother's written admonition ("Dear son... Vote for suffrage and don't keep them in doubt.... I have been watching to see how you stood, but have not seen anything yet. Don't forget to be a good boy"), explaining later, "I know that a mother's advice is always the safest for a boy to follow." Kern, *Mrs. Stanton's Bible*, 4–5; Ward, *Not for Ourselves Alone*, 224.
104. Griffith, *In Her Own Right*, xv.
105. Ibid.; Ward, *Not for Ourselves Alone*, x.
106. Griffith, *In Her Own Right*, xvi–xvii.
107. Kern, *Mrs. Stanton's Bible*, 1–4; Kevin P. Phillips, *American Theocracy: The Perils of Radical Religion, Oil, and Borrowed Money in the 21st Century* (New York: Viking, 2006), 368.
108. Mark Twain, *Mark Twain in Eruption: Hitherto Unpublished Pages about Men and Events* (New York: Grosset and Dunlap, 1940), 345.
109. Stanton, *The Woman's Bible*, viii (introduction by Fitzgerald); Mary D. Pellauer, *Toward a Tradition of Feminist Theology: The Religious Social Thought of Elizabeth Cady Stanton, Susan B. Anthony, and Anna Howard Shaw* (Brooklyn, NY: Carlson, 1991), 17, 38.
110. Pellauer, *Toward a Tradition of Feminist Theology*, 15; Phillips, *American Theocracy*, 382–3.
111. Stanton and Blatch, *Elizabeth Cady Stanton*, 2:79–80.

4. W. E. B. Du Bois (1868–1963): *American Apartheid*

1. W. E. B. Du Bois, "Foreword," in *The Souls of Black Folk; Essays and Sketches* (1903; rpt., New York: Johnson Reprint, 1968), 2. Du Bois biographer David Lewis cautions that "the ['wee wooden schoolhouse'] incident must have occurred, and his account of it is certainly psychologically plausible; yet sympathetic skepticism is advisable whenever Du Bois advances a concept or proposition by way of autobiography. Often the truth is not in the facts but in the conceptual or moral validity behind them." David Levering Lewis, *W. E. B. Du Bois: Biography, 1868–1919* (New York: Henry Holt, 1993), 33–4.
2. Lewis, *Biography*, 34; Eric Foner, *A Short History of Reconstruction, 1863–1877* (New York: Harper and Row, 1990), 137, 151.
3. Manning Marable, *W. E. B. Du Bois: Black Radical Democrat* (Boston: Twayne Publishers, 1986), ix; Richard C. Goode, "Jesus Christ," in *W. E. B. Du Bois: An Encyclopedia*, ed. Gerald Horne and Mary Young (Westport, CT: Greenwood Press, 2001), 113; Malaika Horne, "Religion," in Horne and Young, *Encyclopedia*, 181.

4. Lewis, *Biography*, 11, 15, 17; W. E. B. Du Bois, *Dusk of Dawn: An Essay toward an Autobiography of a Race Concept* (New York: Schocken Books, 1968).
5. Lewis, *Biography*, 13–14, 20; W. E. B. Du Bois, *The Autobiography of W. E. B. Dubois, A Soliloquy on Viewing My Life from the Last Decade of Its First Century* (New York: International Publishers, 1968).
6. Lewis, *Biography*, 11, 13, 20–1, 47.
7. Ibid., 21–2, 27; Marable, *Black Radical Democrat*, 2–3 (citing "Du Bois Interview" [William T. Ingersoll, May 1960/Columbia Oral History Project], 3).
8. Lewis, *Biography*, 29, 34, 36–8; Marable, *Black Radical Democrat*, 3–4; Emma Gelders Sterne, *His Was the Voice: The Life of W. E. B. Du Bois* (New York: Crowell-Collier Press, 1971), 12–14.
9. Marable, *Black Radical Democrat*, 9; Du Bois, *Autobiography*, 127.
10. Lewis, *Biography*, 41–2, 46, 52; Du Bois, *Autobiography*, 98; Marable, *Black Radical Democrat*, 6–7. Alexander died in 1886 during Du Bois's junior year of college, leaving him $400 and a cache of papers giving clues of his Franco-Caribbean origins. Lewis, *Biography*, 72.
11. Lewis, *Biography*, 50–3, 56–60; Du Bois, *Autobiography*, 106; Marable, *Black Radical Democrat*, 7–8. Booker T. Washington, "University Education," in *The Booker T. Washington Papers, 1909–11*, ed. Louis R. Harlan and Raymond W. Smock (Chicago: University of Illinois Press, 1981), 10:284–5. Du Bois's and Stanton's shared admiration of Phillips is another thread in the intriguingly interwoven lives of this book's five profiled individuals, although there is no record that Du Bois and Stanton ever met during their twenty-five overlapping years. Booker T. Washington, himself a former slave, recalled of the period directly after the war, "Those were wonderful days.... Suddenly, as if at the sound of a trumpet, a whole race that had been slumbering for centuries... awoke and started off one morning for school."
12. Lewis, *Biography*, 62, 64; Du Bois, *Autobiography*, 107; W. E. B. Du Bois, *Darkwater: Voices from within the Veil* (New York: Harcourt, Brace and Howe, 1920), 14.
13. Lewis, *Biography*, 68–69; Du Bois, *Autobiography*, 114; Marable, *Black Radical Democrat*, 9–10.
14. Lewis, *Biography*, 73–4, 77; Marable, *Black Radical Democrat*, 9.
15. Lewis, *Biography*, 79–82, 84–6, 91; Marable, *Black Radical Democrat*, 11–14. At James's invitation, Du Bois was a regular at the Harvard Philosophical Club, where he attended dinners and read philosophy in the quiet upstairs libraries alongside classmates the likes of George Santayana and others. Lewis, *Biography*, 80.
16. Lewis, *Biography*, 65–6; Marable, *Black Radical Democrat*, 9–11, 16; Du Bois, *Autobiography*, 114, 119–20; Du Bois, *Souls of Black Folk*, 189–91, 250–64.
17. Lewis, *Biography*, 90, 101; Marable, *Black Radical Democrat*, 15.

18. Lewis, *Biography*, 103–8; Du Bois, *Autobiography*, 138; Marable, *Black Radical Democrat*, 14.
19. Lewis, *Biography*, 113–14 (quoting Herbert Aptheker, "Introduction," in *The Suppression of the African Slave Trade to the United States, 1638–1870*, by W. E. B. Du Bois [1896; Millwood, NY: Kraus-Thomson, 1973], 10).
20. Lewis, *Biography*, 116, 120–30; Marable, *Black Radical Democrat*, 16–17; Du Bois, *Autobiography*, 160–2; Du Bois to D. C. Gilman, Berlin, Oct. 28, 1892, in *The Correspondence of W. E. B. Du Bois*, ed. Herbert Aptheker (Amherst: University of Massachusetts Press, 1973), 1:20–1. Du Bois designated Aptheker, a trusted friend and confidant, as "literary executor" to look after his letters and materials. Malik Simba, "Aptheker, Herbert," in Horne and Young, *Encyclopedia*, 11.
21. Lewis, *Biography*, 130–2, 137, 147 (quoting W. E. B. Du Bois, "The Present Condition of German Politics," Student Papers, Du Bois Papers, University of Massachusetts); Marable, *Black Radical Democrat*, 17–18.
22. Lewis, *Biography*, 138–41, 144, 146; Du Bois, *Autobiography*, 173, 175.
23. Lewis, *Biography*, 139–49; Marable, *Black Radical Democrat*, 20; Du Bois, *Darkwater*, 16.
24. Lewis, *Biography*, 150–4, 177; Du Bois, *Autobiography*, 185–7; Marable, *Black Radical Democrat*, 22. Wilberforce was formed near Xenia, Ohio, by White Methodists in 1856 as the nation's first college for Negroes and then purchased in 1863 by the African Methodist Episcopal Church as its flagship college.
25. Lewis, *Biography*, 161–6; Du Bois, *Souls of Black Folk*, 216; Marable, *Black Radical Democrat*, 33–4.
26. Lewis, *Biography*, 154–6, 158–9; Marable, *Black Radical Democrat*, 22. Article 1, section 9, of the Constitution provided: "The migration or importation of such persons as any of the States now existing shall think proper to admit, shall not be prohibited by Congress prior to the year one thousand eight hundred and eight."
27. Lewis, *Biography*, 174–8, 238; Marable, *Black Radical Democrat*, 41–2.
28. Lewis, *Biography*, 174–5; Marable, *Black Radical Democrat*, 42–3.
29. Marable, *Black Radical Democrat*, 52–4; Booker T. Washington to Du Bois, Tuskegee, Alabama, Nov. 8, 1903, in Aptheker, *Correspondence*, 1:54; Lewis, *Biography*, 304.
30. C. C. Harrison to Du Bois, Philadelphia, Aug. 15, 1896, in Aptheker, *Correspondence*, 1:40; Lewis, *Biography*, 179–80, 187–8, 190–1; Marable, *Black Radical Democrat*, 24–5.
31. Lewis, *Biography*, 192–3.
32. Ibid., 189–90, 205–8; W. E. B. Du Bois, *The Philadelphia Negro: A Social Study* (Philadelphia: University of Pennsylvania, 1899), 4, 97; Marable, *Black Radical Democrat*, 25–6.
33. Du Bois, *Philadelphia Negro*, 394–5; Lewis, *Biography*, 208–9.

34. Du Bois, *Philadelphia Negro*, 351–2; Lewis, *Biography*, 208, 210.
35. Lewis, *Biography*, 185–6, 193–7, 354. Du Bois parlayed his Philadelphia work into several additional projects for the Department of Interior Bureau of Labor Statistics. Ibid., 197, 354.
36. Ibid., 169–72.
37. Ibid., 172–3; Marable, *Black Radical Democrat*, 34–6.
38. Lewis, *Biography*, 199–201; Marable, *Black Radical Democrat*, 37–8 (quoting W. E. B. Du Bois, "Striving of the Negro People," *Atlantic Monthly* 80 [August 1897], 194–8).
39. Lewis, *Biography*, 198, 213–19; Marable, *Black Radical Democrat*, 27. Like Fisk, Atlanta University was established by Congregationalist missionaries from the North shortly after the Civil War. Du Bois took his teaching seriously. Asking himself how he might respond to the heartfelt student question, "Do you trust white people?" he wanted to be "natural and honest and frank, but it was bitter hard" – knowing inside that "[y]ou do not and you know that you do not, much as you want to" but replying anyway that she "must trust them, that most white folks are honest, and all the while you are lying on every level, silent eye there knows you are lying... to the greater glory of God." Lewis, *Biography*, 214–17.
40. Lewis, *Biography*, 226, 229–45; Marable, *Black Radical Democrat*, 43–4. After passing on the Tuskegee opportunity, Du Bois made a strong bid for the job as assistant superintendent of colored schools in Washington, D.C., but lost out to an inside candidate – with Washington playing a nuanced political role in his defeat.
41. Lewis, *Biography*, 263–4, 274–5, 339 (quoting W. E. B. Du Bois, "The Evolution of Negro Leadership," *Dial*, July 16, 1901, 53–5 [reproduced in Herbert Aptheker, ed., *Book Reviews by W. E. B. Du Bois* (Millwood, NY: KTO Press 1977), 3–5]).
42. Ibid., 247–51; Marable, *Black Radical Democrat*, 39–40. Du Bois used the "problem of the color line" description numerous times in his most celebrated work, *Souls of Black Folk*, published in 1903.
43. Lewis, *Biography*, 226–8; Marable, *Black Radical Democrat*, 30–1. Years later, Du Bois admitted to wondering how things might have turned out "had we been persons of greater experience." Lewis, *Biography*, 228.
44. Lewis, *Biography*, 251–3, 256, 260. Louisiana had 130,344 registered black voters in 1896 and only 5,320 in 1900; Alabama had only 3,000 registered black voters out of an adult black male population of 181,471.
45. Du Bois, *Souls of Black Folk*, viii; Lewis, *Biography*, 232, 277–81, 291–6; Marable, *Black Radical Democrat*, 47–9; Jay Parini, *Promised Land: Thirteen Books That Changed America* (New York: Doubleday, 2008).
46. Du Bois, *Souls of Black Folk*, 1, 9–10; Lewis, *Biography*, 278–81.
47. Du Bois, *Souls of Black Folk*, 13, 17, 30, 32, 35, 38.
48. Du Bois, *Souls of Black Folk*, 41, 50, 53, 59, 105; Lewis, *Biography*, 283–8; Marable, *Black Radical Democrat*, 46–7, 51.

49. Lewis, *Biography*, 218–21. The conferences of 1902 ("The Negro Artisan"), 1903 ("The Negro Church"), and 1908 ("The Negro American Family") were especially noteworthy. Ibid., 378, 463.
50. Lewis, *Biography*, 300–5; Marable, *Black Radical Democrat*, 47, 53; Louis R. Harlan, *Booker T. Washington: The Wizard of Tuskegee, 1901–1915* (New York: Oxford University Press, 1983), 70.
51. Lewis, *Biography*, 307, 309–11; Marable, *Black Radical Democrat*, 53–4.
52. Lewis, *Biography*, 312–13; Du Bois, "Credo," *Independent* 57 (1904), 787; Du Bois, *Darkwater*, 3–4; Marable, *Black Radical Democrat*, 67.
53. Marable, *Black Radical Democrat*, 55–6; Lewis, *Biography*, 316–17, 321–3.
54. Lewis, *Biography*, 324, 331, 333; Harlan, *Booker T. Washington*, 191.
55. Lewis, *Biography*, 327, 333, 335–6; Marable, *Black Radical Democrat*, 57, 60. During the Atlanta riot, Du Bois rushed back from a Census Bureau Study in Lownes County, Alabama, to sit on his porch with a shotgun to protect Nina and Yolande.
56. Lewis, *Biography*, 327–8, 330 (quoting W. E. B. Du Bois, "Address to the Country," Du Bois Papers/University of Massachusetts [reproduced in Herbert Aptheker, ed., *Pamphlets and Leaflets by W. E. B. Du Bois* (White Plains, NY: Kraus-Thomson, 1986), 64–5]); Marable, *Black Radical Democrat*, 56–7. Niagara was beset by a chronic shortage of money, as well as debilitating infighting between key players Trotter and Morgan, which would spell its demise within several years. Lewis, *Biography*, 340.
57. Lewis, *Biography*, 338, 381–3. Du Bois found time for a four-week respite in England in summer 1907, which, as with all of his trips abroad, brought the contrasts with America into sharp relief: "[I dreamt] of past beauty and present culture, as I fondly dreamed to realize a democracy in which I and my people could find a welcome place." Ibid., 371–2.
58. Ibid., 337–42. Criticizing Theodore Roosevelt at the 1907 Boston Niagara meeting for "swaggering roughshod over the helpless black regiment whose bravery made him famous," afterward Du Bois began calling more frequently for blacks to abandon the Republican Party. Ibid., 339–40.
59. Ibid., 344, 346, 350; Marable, *Black Radical Democrat*, 63; Mary White Ovington, *Portraits in Color* (New York: Viking, 1927), 82–3. In 1909, while at Atlanta University, Du Bois affiliated with Alpha Phi Alpha, the nation's first black intercollegiate Greek letter organization (established in 1906 by the first seven black men to attend Cornell University). Troy S. Brown, interview by Michael Anthony Lawrence, July 23, 2010.
60. Lewis, *Biography*, 344, 346, 350, 353–4; David Levering Lewis, *W. E. B. Du Bois: The Fight for Equality and the American Century, 1919–1963* (New York: Henry Holt, 2000), 232; Du Bois to Leonard Carl Cartwright, Oct. 4, 1928, in Aptheker, *Correspondence*, 1:381–2. Du Bois's advice for an idealistic young Harvard professor offers a rare insight into his innermost views of the struggle. "The world will not give a decent living to the persons who are out to reform it," Du Bois revealed. "How long can you get

the necessary bread and butter by speaking out frankly and plainly? When you can no longer do this, what compromises can you make in unessentials that will allow you to save your soul? Beyond that, is oblivion," he concluded. "The oblivion of complete surrender or of complete silence. The object of life is to avoid either of these." Lewis, *Fight*, 231, 241, 247, 248–9.

61. Lewis, *Biography*, 357, 359–60; Marable, *Black Radical Democrat*, 65–6.
62. Lewis, *Biography*, 383–5.
63. Lewis, *Biography*, 386–8, 391, 393, 395, 407; Marable, *Black Radical Democrat*, 72–4. The new resolve among the NAACP's white and black founders was prompted in part by a race riot in Springfield, Illinois (the home town, sadly enough, of the Great Emancipator himself, Abraham Lincoln) on August 14, 1908. Lewis, *Biography*, 405; Marable, *Black Radical Democrat*, 71.
64. Lewis, *Biography*, 398, 400–2, 414–15.
65. Lewis, *Fight*, 50, 77–8, 82.
66. Lewis, *Biography*, 409–11, 413, 417; Marable, *Black Radical Democrat*, 78–9. The magazine sold 3,000 copies in January 1911; by April 1912, circulation was 22,500. Lewis, *Biography*, 416.
67. Lewis, *Biography*, 426–7 (quoting Du Bois, "Triumph," *Crisis* 2 [Sept. 1911], 195).
68. Lewis, *Biography*, 418–19; Herbert Aptheker, ed., *Selections from* The Crisis (Millwood, NY: Kraus-Thomson Organization, 1983), 1:55–6; Marable, *Black Radical Democrat*, 85, 124.
69. Lewis, *Biography*, 433–4; Marable, *Black Radical Democrat*, 81. Even in the midst of all of his activities at the *Crisis* and elsewhere, Du Bois published his first novel, *The Quest of the Silver Fleece*, during this time. Something had to give – and for Du Bois it was his relationship with Nina and Yolande. He provided for his family financially and made efforts to correspond but was mostly physically absent – finding reasons throughout most of his married years for living apart. Ibid., 443–5, 451–2, 458; Marable, *Black Radical Democrat*, 66–7.
70. Lewis, *Biography*, 466–8; Du Bois, *Dusk of Dawn*, 303. His fame was firmly established, with Du Bois Clubs springing up and babies and even a cigar named after him. Lewis, *Biography*, 505.
71. Lewis, *Biography*, 479 (quoting W. E. B. Du Bois, "The Philosophy of Mr. Dole," *Crisis*, 9 [Jan. 1915]: 94–6); Marable, *Black Radical Democrat*, 80–1.
72. Lewis, *Biography*, 480–1, 483.
73. Lewis, *Biography*, 477, 483; Marable, *Black Radical Democrat*, 79. Some in the organization sniped about Du Bois's perceived favoritism ("People were employed because of personal devotion to [Du Bois], and retained for that reason," charged one), and his free-spending ways (The *Crisis* went "gaily on expanding merrily while the NAACP is forced to retrench and retrench," complained another). Lewis, *Biography*, 477, 483.

74. Lewis, *Biography*, 449–50, 478; Elliott M. Rudwick, *W. E. B. Du Bois: Propagandist of the Negro Protest* (New York: Atheneum, 1968); Thomas Lee Philpott, *The Slum and the Ghetto: Neighborhood Deterioration and Middle-Class Reform, Chicago, 1880–1930* (New York: Oxford University Press, 1978); Du Bois to Joel E. Spingarn, New York City, Oct. 28, 1914, in Aptheker, *Correspondence*, 1:206; Marable, *Black Radical Democrat*, 79–80.
75. Lewis, *Biography*, 468–9, 471; Marable, *Black Radical Democrat*, 79.
76. Lewis, *Biography*, 476, 484–6, 492–4; Joel E. Spingarn to Du Bois, Amenia, NY, Oct. 24, 1914, in Aptheker, *Correspondence*, 1:202; Marable, *Black Radical Democrat*, 80.
77. Lewis, *Biography*, 493, 474, 514, 481, 459–62. The bond between Du Bois and Spingarn would be strengthened at the Amenia Conference (a three-day campout on August 24–26, 1916, at Spingarn's estate), intended to bring together the various factions of black and white leadership. Ibid., 517–18. Marable, *Black Radical Democrat*, 82–3. During the decade, Du Bois's *Star of Ethiopia* production – a three-hour pageant involving hundreds of participants depicting black history from ancient Egypt to the present – was put on in several cities to strong reviews. Lewis, *Biography*, 459–60. Despite the internal drama at the NAACP and *Crisis*, the magazine continued to thrive, steadily increasing in circulation from thirty-three thousand in early 1914 to forty-five thousand in April 1916 and sixty-two thousand by the end of the decade. Ibid., 474–81.
78. Lewis, *Biography*, 471–2, 480, 500.
79. Ibid., 501–3; Marable, *Black Radical Democrat*, 82.
80. Lewis, *Biography*, 503–5; Marable, *Black Radical Democrat*, 94. Woodrow Wilson's first term was a major disappointment for Du Bois and other reformers, as the number of African Americans employed by the federal government vastly decreased, and segregation in federal workplaces increased dramatically. Du Bois's book, *The Negro*, released in 1915, offered broad corrections to the Southern-sympathetic histories foisted on the public by the Dunning school of historians and sought to counteract the filmmaker D. W. Griffith's *The Birth of a Nation*'s racist portrayal of a victimized South – "with the Negro represented either as an ignorant fool, a vicious rapist, a venal or unscrupulous politician or a faithful but doddering idiot," Du Bois observed. Lewis, *Biography*, 507, 509–12.
81. Lewis, *Biography*, 524–5, 529–32; Marable, *Black Radical Democrat*, 95. Du Bois suffered a serious illness in December 1916 and January 1917 in which he lost a kidney. Marable, *Black Radical Democrat*, 97.
82. Lewis, *Biography*, 553–6; Du Bois, "Close Ranks," *The Crisis*, July 1918, in Aptheker, *Selections from* The Crisis, 1:159; Marable, *Black Radical Democrat*, 96–7.
83. Lewis, *Biography*, 555–60. A majority of the NAACP board considered Du Bois's position shameful (one board member, Neval Thomas, opined that

Du Bois had "reversed his whole life, and is no more good to us"). Ibid., 557.

84. Ibid., 561, 565, 569–73. Despite the impediments, black units in fact managed to distinguish themselves in battle. The Ninety-third Division even earned the honor from the French of leading their army into German-occupied territory after the armistice – although the Ninety-third and all other African American units were excluded from the Allied victory parade down the Champs-Élysées later that summer. Ibid., 564–5, 574–7; Marable, *Black Radical Democrat*, 101–2.
85. Marable, *Black Radical Democrat*, 103; Lewis, *Biography*, 578; Du Bois, "Returning Soldiers," *Crisis*, May 1919, in Aptheker, *Selections from* The Crisis, 1:196–7.
86. Lewis, *Fight*, 5; Lewis, *Biography*, 579–80.
87. Lewis, *Fight*, 6, 27. Regarding the disfranchisement issue, Du Bois began promoting the constitutional argument before Congress that Southern states were subject to electoral corrections under section 2 of the Fourteenth Amendment, which mandates reduction of states' representation in Congress in equal proportion to the degree they disfranchise eligible male voters. To the skittish who worried that this argument assumes states actually have a choice to disfranchise black voters, Du Bois properly replied that the Fifteenth Amendment prevents states from taking such measures. About Tuskegee's Robert Moton, one of the skittish who wanted to avoid the constitutional argument, Du Bois commented, "I am continually astonished by his lack of courage." Lewis, *Fight*, 27.
88. Ibid., 4; Du Bois, "The Class Struggle," *Crisis*, June 1921, in *Selections From* The Crisis, ed. Aptheker, 1:303–04; Du Bois, "Radicals," *Crisis*, Dec. 1919, in Aptheker, *Selections from* The Crisis, 1:247; Marable, *Black Radical Democrat*, 103.
89. Lewis, *Fight*, 14–16, 41, 43–4, 48; Du Bois, *Darkwater*, 50; Marable, *Black Radical Democrat*, 103–5. While in Europe, Du Bois prepared the "Manifesto to the League of Nations," and the League's Mandates Commission favorably published the proposals, stating "[We] urge that the League of Nations take a firm stand on the absolute equality of races." Marable, *Black Radical Democrat*, 105; Lewis, *Fight*, 47–8.
90. Lewis, *Fight*, 2, 34–6; Marable, *Black Radical Democrat*, 122–3.
91. Lewis, *Fight*, 32–4.
92. Ibid., 11, 21, 23–5, 50, 66, 77–8; Marable, *Black Radical Democrat*, 115, 129.
93. Lewis, *Fight*, 62, 65–6, 72, 82, 149–50, 152–3; Marable, *Black Radical Democrat*, 116–18. President Coolidge commuted Garvey's sentence in 1927, after which he was deported to Jamaica. He died in 1940 at the age of fifty-two. Drew VandeCreek, "Garvey, Marcus (1887–1940)," in Horne and Young, *Encyclopedia*, 85.

94. Lewis, *Fight*, 114–16, 120–1, 123–7; Marable, *Black Radical Democrat*, 105–6.
95. Lewis, *Fight*, 231, 241, 247–9; Marable, *Black Radical Democrat*, 126–7. Throughout the years, Du Bois continued to indulge his wandering eye, visiting devoted women across the country in the course of his frequent travels. Bemoaning the paucity of serious literary work by African American authors, true to ambitious form, Du Bois wrote a "literary" novel of his own, *Dark Princess*, published in 1928. Ibid., 182; Marable, *Black Radical Democrat*, 133. By some accounts his own "favorite book," *Dark Princess* received generally favorable reviews, including one by *Opportunity*'s Alain Locke, who described it as a "skyscraper problem novel of the Negro intellectual and the world radical... [that] offers the framework of a truly great novel." Lewis, *Fight*, 219. Du Bois never completely bought into the so-called Harlem Renaissance during the 1920s, exclaiming, "I do not care a damn for any art that is not used for propaganda." Ibid., 103, 154, 168, 175, 177; Marable, *Black Radical Democrat*, 131–2.
96. Lewis, *Fight*, 195–6, 198, 200, 250–1, 255. Du Bois stirred up controversy on multiple fronts during the 1920s. Invited to deliver the commencement address at Yolande's graduation from Fisk in 1924, he used the opportunity to initiate a relentless campaign against Fisk's autocratic President Fayette McKenzie as part of his move to reverse what he saw as the decline of quality black liberal arts colleges. Fisk is "choking freedom," he told a surprised audience (including some applauding students, who were later punished for their indiscretion). The Fisk campaign was successful; less successful strikes followed at Howard, Lincoln, and especially Hampton, where the college's president imposed a mandatory pledge of loyalty and obedience. "[T]he most disconcerting thing in the Hampton strike," Du Bois lamented, "is the way in which graduates and parents repudiated their own children." What a far cry from the ideal, he mourned in the *Nation*. "Students are not sent to school to learn to obey. They are sent there to learn to do, to think, to execute, to be men and women." Ibid., 130, 131, 132–3, 135, 136, 137–42, 145–6; Marable, *Black Radical Democrat*, 135–6.
97. Lewis, *Fight*, 252–7 (citing W. E. B. Du Bois, "A New Party," *Crisis* [Aug. 1930], 282).
98. Lewis, *Fight*, 256–60, 263, 265, 308–11; Du Bois, *Dusk of Dawn*, 205; Harry Haywood, "The Struggle for the Leninist Position on the Negro Question in the U.S.A.," in *American Communism and Black Americans: A Documentary History, 1930–1934*, ed. Philip S. Foner and Herbert Shapiro (Philadelphia: Temple University Press, 1991), 93 107; Marable, *Black Radical Democrat*, 142–3. The CPUSA was originally formed in 1925 as the Worker Party. Lewis, *Fight*, 255.
99. Lewis, *Fight*, 274–7, 280, 282, 290; Marable, *Black Radical Democrat*, 138–41.

100. Lewis, *Fight*, 301, 304, 143. Du Bois had extra reason to be pleased, with the birth of granddaughter "Baby" Du Bois Williams in late 1932 to Yolande and husband Arnett Franklin Williams, whom she had married in 1931. Ibid., 289, 304.
101. Ibid., 318–23.
102. Ibid., 331, 336, 345; Marable, *Black Radical Democrat*, 140–1. Du Bois's approach suffered some internal inconsistencies – for example, he advocated segregation but refused to consider the CPUSA's ideas for a separate forty-ninth African American state.
103. Lewis, *Fight*, 335–6, 338, 340–2, 346–8; Marable, *Black Radical Democrat*, 141–3.
104. Lewis, *Fight*, 347, 350–7, 360; Foner, *Reconstruction*, 258–9.
105. Lewis, *Fight*, 347, 350–7, 360; Foner, *Reconstruction*, 258–9. Foner continues: "Few interpretations of history have had such far-reaching consequences as this [Dunning school] image of Reconstruction . . . [which] did much to freeze the mind of the white South in unalterable opposition to outside pressures for social change and to any thought of . . . eliminating segregation, or restoring suffrage to disenfranchised blacks. They also justified Northern indifference to the nullification of the Fourteenth and Fifteenth Amendments." Foner, *Reconstruction*, 258–9.
106. Lewis, *Fight*, 356, 361, 364–6, 375–6; Marable, *Black Radical Democrat*, 145–7. In answer to purist critics of the book's unorthodox Marxism, Herbert Aptheker explained, "Du Bois's use of term 'proletariat' [derived] from the Latin *proletarius,* [meaning] a citizen of the lowest class." Du Bois likely began reading Marx seriously sometime shortly after World War I; by 1933, he would claim that *Das Kapital* ranked with the Bible among "great books of truth." Shawn R. Donaldson, "Marx, Karl (1818–1883)," in Horne and Young, *Encyclopedia*, 135–6 (quoting "Marxism and the Negro Problem," in *Crisis* [March 1933]).
107. Du Bois, *Black Reconstruction in America* (1935; New York: The Free Press, 1998), 1, 125; Lewis, *Fight*, 365, 368. Epitomizing the bigotry of the "redeemed" South was Mississippi governor James K. Vardaman, the "White Chief": "[The Negro was a] lazy, lying, lustful animal which no conceivable amount of training can transform into a tolerable citizen." Lewis, *Biography*, 215.
108. Lewis, *Fight*, 374.
109. Ibid., 538; Marable, *Black Radical Democrat*, 173. Then ten-year-old David Lewis, Du Bois's Pulitzer Prize–winning biographer, witnessed his own attorney father speaking with Du Bois on that August 1948 day at Wilberforce. Lewis, *Biography*, xi.
110. Lewis, *Fight*, 384–5, 388–9; Marable, *Black Radical Democrat*, 154–5. Ostensibly, the fellowship was to study how industrial education in Germany and Austria compared with Booker Washington's achievements in the United States. Du Bois's own views on the question had moderated in the

quarter-century since he had sparred with Washington – he had become more tolerant of industrial education, believing a mixture of industrial and liberal arts education was the model for the future. Marable, *Black Radical Democrat*, 154–5.

111. Lewis, *Fight*, 388, 393, 398, 400–2; Marable, *Black Radical Democrat*, 155.
112. Lewis, *Fight*, 405–7; Marable, *Black Radical Democrat*, 155.
113. Lewis, *Fight*, 390, 409–11.
114. Ibid., 412–14; Du Bois, *Autobiography*, 46.
115. Marable, *Black Radical Democrat*, 156; Lewis, *Fight*, 415–17.
116. Lewis, *Fight*, 414–19; Marable, *Black Radical Democrat*, 156; Robert Fikes Jr., "Japan," in Horne and Young, *Encyclopedia*, 112. Du Bois later explained that he did not favor China less than Japan but that he hated "white European and American propaganda, theft and insult more." Lewis, *Fight*, 461–2; Marable, *Black Radical Democrat*, 156–7.
117. Lewis, *Fight*, 454, 456–7, 62–3, 470. During the war, Du Bois's moral relativism continued mostly unabated, with comments like, "If Hitler wins, down with the blacks! If the democracies win, the blacks are already down." Ibid., 467; Marable, *Black Radical Democrat*, 157. *Black Folk: Then and Now, An Essay in the History and Sociology of the Negro Race*, published in summer 1939, sought to repudiate a eugenics movement given new life by fascist ideologies. Du Bois supported Franklin Roosevelt in the 1940 election, believing that the Works Progress Administration had played an important role in providing subsistence for blacks in the 1930s. Lewis, *Fight*, 455, 464, 505; Marable, *Black Radical Democrat*, 154. During this time, he moved the family to Baltimore, where Nina would live with Yolande (who had escaped her abusive husband Arnett) and granddaughter Du Bois Williams, now eight years old in 1940. Lewis, *Black Radical Democrat*, 471.
118. Marable, *Black Radical Democrat*, 163–4; Lewis, *Fight*, 495, 497–8; Du Bois, *Autobiography*, 327. Despite some of his more recent troubling comments, in 1940, Du Bois was still a commanding force. In the fall of 1940, he published *Dusk of Dawn: An Essay toward and Autobiography of a Race Concept*, dedicated to Joel Spingarn, "scholar and knight," where he admitted that "had it not been for the race problem early thrust upon me and enveloping me, I should have probably been an unquestioning worshiper at the shrine of the social order and economic development into which I was born." Lewis, *Fight*, 472–3; Marable, *Black Radical Democrat*, 152–3. *Dusk of Dawn,* "one of the significant works of Marxian theory in the mid-twentieth century," advanced "the plausibility and advantages of a separate African American cooperative economy in the United States." Kenneth Mostern, "Dusk of Dawn," in Horne and Young, *Encyclopedia*, 65–6. He also undertook the editing duties of another publication, *Phylon: The Atlanta University Review of Race and Culture,* which would be epitomized over the coming years by the resistance offered by the penny-pinching

President Rufus Clement and Spelman College President Florence Read. Lewis, *Fight*, 477, 481, 483; Marable, *Black Radical Democrat*, 150–1, 161.

119. Marable, *Black Radical Democrat*, 163–4; Lewis, *Fight*, 502, 504–5.
120. Lewis, *Fight*, 508, 510.
121. Ibid., 509, 513–15; Marable, *Black Radical Democrat*, 164–5.
122. Marable, *Black Radical Democrat*, 169; Lewis, *Fight*, 528, 533. Work on *An Appeal to the World* was completed in August 1947 and sent to the NAACP board for approval. Lewis, *Fight*, 521–2. Walter White sat on the report, however, until it was trumped in part by the release in October 1947 of a report entitled *To Secure These Rights* by the interracial fourteen-member President's Committee on Civil Rights, which itself advocated meaningful reforms (though more modest than those called for in *An Appeal to the World*). Ibid., 529.
123. Marable, *Black Radical Democrat*, 169; Lewis, *Fight*, 534.
124. Marable, *Black Radical Democrat*, 156; Lewis, *Fight*, 523–4, 528, 530, 537–8. Du Bois's withering criticism of President Harry Truman and his administration became increasingly awkward for the NAACP during these months.
125. Marable, *Black Radical Democrat*, 172, 175; Lewis, *Fight*, 519, 531–2, 534.
126. Marable, *Black Radical Democrat*, 173–4, 181; Lewis, *Fight*, 535–6.
127. Marable, *Black Radical Democrat*, 176; Lewis, *Fight*, 442–3. After losing his *Defender* voice in May 1948, Du Bois would contribute 120 articles to *New Guardian* until 1961, at $50 per article. Lewis, *Fight*, 538, 541.
128. Marable, *Black Radical Democrat*, 176–7; Lewis, *Fight*, 544–5; Du Bois, *Autobiography*, 350.
129. Lewis, *Fight*, 547; Marable, *Black Radical Democrat*, 179–82. Du Bois accepted a position offered by his old friend Paul Robeson to serve as honorary vice chair of the Council on African Affairs in 1949. Marable, *Black Radical Democrat*, 175–6. By July 13, 1950, the center had gathered an impressive 1.5 million signatures from forty states in support of the Stockholm Appeal, an international statement of the World Partisans of Peace signed by a half billion people worldwide calling for the "absolute banning" of atomic weapons. Ibid., 179. Secretary of State Dean Acheson minimized the petition as a "propaganda trick in the spurious 'peace offensive' of the Soviet Union." Ibid., 179.
130. Marable, *Black Radical Democrat*, 182; Lewis, *Fight*, 546–9. After being nominated by the American Labor Party of New York for the U.S. Senate, Du Bois received 205,729 votes. Lewis, *Fight*, 547, 552; Marable, *Black Radical Democrat*, 180–1.
131. Ibid., 186–7; Lewis, *Fight*, 550, 552–4. During the trial, Langston Hughes commented, "[I]f W. E. B. Du Bois goes to jail a wave of wonder will sweep around the world." Lewis, *Fight*, 552.

132. Marable, *Black Radical Democrat*, 192, 198; Lewis, *Fight*, 556; Du Bois to the foreign editor of the *Literary Gazette*, Brooklyn, Sept. 26, 1957, in Aptheker, *Correspondence*, 3:415. Du Bois attempted to soften Stalin's atrocities by equating them with the West's history of slavery, World War I, Nazi death camps, and the like. Lewis, *Fight*, 557.
133. Lewis, *Fight*, 555, 557, 570. In the landmark *Brown* case in 1954–5, the Supreme Court struck down the separate-but-equal doctrine promulgated nearly sixty years earlier in *Plessy v. Ferguson*. Of American capitalism, Du Bois wrote in 1953: "Mass capitalistic control of books and periodicals, news gathering and distribution, radio, cinema, and television has made the throttling of democracy possible and the distortion of education and failure of justice widespread." David Levering Lewis, "Foreword: The Dissenting Temperament of W. E. B. Du Bois," in Horne and Young, *Encyclopedia*, xii (quoting "Negroes and the Crisis of Capitalism in the United States").
134. Marable, *Black Radical Democrat*, 199–200, 203–6; Lewis, *Fight*, 558, 560–2, 564; Du Bois, *Autobiography*, 11, 36; Mary Ellen Wilson, "China," in Horne and Young, *Encyclopedia*, 37–9.
135. Marable, *Black Radical Democrat*, 208–13; Lewis, *Fight*, 565–7; Du Bois to Gus Hall, Brooklyn, NY, Oct. 1, 1961, in Aptheker, *Correspondence*, 3:439–40; David Levering Lewis, "Forward: The Dissenting Temperament of W. E. B. Du Bois," in Horne and Young, *Encyclopedia*, ix.
136. Lewis, *Fight*, 567, 569.
137. Ibid., 569–70 Lewis, *Biography*, 1–3. Some of the rest of King's immortal words: "I have a dream that one day this nation will rise up and live out the true meaning of its creed: 'We hold these truths to be self-evident, that all men are created equal.'... I have a dream that one day on the red hills of Georgia the sons of former slaves and the sons of former slave owners will be able to sit down together at a table of brotherhood.... Now is the time to lift our nation from the quicksand of racial injustice to the solid rock of brotherhood. Now is the time to make justice a reality for all of God's children.... Let freedom ring. And when this happens, and when we allow freedom to ring – when we let it ring from every village and every hamlet, from every state and every city, we will be able to speed up that day when all of God's children – black men and white men, Jews and Gentiles, Protestants and Catholics – will be able to join hands and sing in the words of the old Negro spiritual: 'Free at last! Free at last! Thank God Almighty, we are free at last!'"
138. Lewis, *Fight*, 559 (quoting Truman Nelson, "W. E. B. Du Bois: Prophet in Limbo," *Nation*, Jan. 25, 1958, 76–9).
139. Marable, *Black Radical Democrat*, viii.
140. Ibid., 143 (quoting NAACP, 1934); Du Bois, *Dusk of Dawn*, 314; Du Bois, *Autobiography*, 299.
141. Marable, *Black Radical Democrat*, 187–8 (quoting W. E. B. Du Bois, "Galileo Galilei," in *The Education of Black People* [1908], 17–30).

142. Du Bois, *Dusk of Dawn*, 314; Du Bois, *Autobiography*, 299.
143. Lewis, *Biography*, 201; Marable, *Black Radical Democrat*, 193; Du Bois, *Souls of Black Folk*, 4.
144. Marable, *Black Radical Democrat*, 124–5; Du Bois to the Reverend Samuel H. Bishop, Atlanta, May 1, 1907; Du Bois to Joseph B. Glenn, March 4, 1925, in Aptheker, *Correspondence*, 1:131, 311; Lewis, *Fight*, 441–2; Malaika Horne, "Religion," in Horne and Young, *Encyclopedia*, 181–2.
145. Marable, *Black Radical Democrat*, 209, 217.
146. Ibid., 217; Lewis, *Fight*, 570.
147. Lewis, *Fight*, 421.
148. Ibid., 570. The Declaration of Independence states: "We hold these Truths to be self-evident, that all Men are created equal, that they are endowed by their Creator with certain unalienable Rights, that among these are Life, Liberty, and the Pursuit of Happiness." Moreover, "That to secure these Rights, Governments are instituted . . . and that whenever any Form of Government becomes destructive of these Ends, it is the Right of the People to alter or to abolish it, and to institute new Government, laying its Foundation on such Principles."

5. Vine Deloria Jr. (1933–2005): *Betrayals and Bridges*

1. Dee Brown, *Bury My Heart at Wounded Knee* (New York: Henry Holt, 2000), 442–4.
2. James Treat, introduction to *For This Land: Writings on Religion in America*, by Vine Deloria Jr., ed. James Treat (New York: Routledge, 1999), 7.
3. Worcester v. Georgia, 31 U.S. 515, 520 (1832).
4. David Getches, "Beyond Indian Law: The Rehnquist Court's Pursuit of States' Rights, Color-Blind Justice and Mainstream Values," *Minnesota Law Review* 86 (2001), 329. "There is a profound difference between American Indians and all of these other groups in America," Deloria explained in *God Is Red* (1975). "The Indian is indigenous and therefore does not have the psychological burden of establishing his or her right to the land in the deep emotional sense of knowing that he or she belongs there." Vine Deloria Jr., *God Is Red: A Native View of Religion* (Golden, CO: Fulcrum Publishing, 1994), 60.
5. Deloria, *God Is Red*, 189. Vine Deloria Jr., *Red Earth, White Lies: Native Americans and the Myth of Scientific Fact* (Golden, CO: Fulcrum Publishing, 1997), 5.
6. Treat, introduction to *For This Land*, 13, 16. Kirk Johnson, "Vine Deloria, Jr., Champion of Indian Rights, Dies at 72," *New York Times*, Nov. 15, 2005.
7. Vine Deloria Jr., *Behind the Trail of Broken Treaties: An Indian Declaration of Independence* (New York: Delacorte Press, 1974), 83.

8. Vine Deloria Jr., *Custer Died for Your Sins: An Indian Manifesto* (New York: Macmillan, 1969), 44. Felix Cohen, *Cohen's Handbook of Federal Indian Law* (Newark, NJ: LexisNexis, 2005), 24. See also Frank Pommersheim, *Broken Landscape: Indians, Indian Tribes, and the Constitution* (New York: Oxford University Press, 2009), 18 (recognizing Roger Williams's legitimate purchases of Indian land).
9. U.S. Constitution, art. 1, sec. 8; art. 1, sec. 2(3) (amended by U.S. Constitution, am. 14, sec. 2).
10. N. Bruce Duthu, *American Indians and the Law* (New York: Penguin, 2008), 67, 166. Howard Zinn, *A People's History of the United States 1492–Present* (New York: HarperCollins, 2003), 133.
11. The manner of the takeover depended on the geographic location of the tribe. For tribes east of the Mississippi River, the provisions of the 1830 Removal Act enabled the United States to initiate military forced marches of the Indians to reservations west of the Mississippi, thus allowing white settlers to take over the vacated land. For tribes west of the Mississippi, first came war, then a peace treaty, then five to ten years of waiting out the starving Indians, and finally either a renegotiation of the treaty or an act of Congress abrogating the treaty. Matthew Fletcher, interview by Michael Anthony Lawrence, March 15, 2010.
12. Zinn, *A People's History*, 135.
13. Johnson v. M'Intosh, 21 U.S. 543, 573 (1823); Duthu, *American Indians* 68, 70–71.
14. Vine Deloria Jr., *Of Utmost Good Faith* (San Francisco: Straight Arrow, 1971), 36–7.
15. Vine Deloria Jr., *Behind the Trail*, 98, 108; Cohen, *Cohen's Handbook*, 49 (commenting, "'The acts of our government plainly recognize the Cherokee nation as a state, and the Courts are bound by those acts'"); Philip J. Deloria, interview by Michael Anthony Lawrence, Apr. 27, 2010. Lindsay Robertson provides a fascinating history of how the Court created the "discovery doctrine" in *Johnson v. M'Intosh* for limited application, only to try (without success) to put the genie back in the bottle in *Worcester*. Lindsay G. Robertson, *Conquest by Law: How the Discovery of America Dispossessed Indigenous Peoples of Their Lands* (New York: Oxford University Press, 2005).
16. Cohen, *Cohen's Handbook*, 50; Deloria, *Behind the Trail*, 209.
17. Zinn, *A People's History*, 139–40.
18. Deloria, *Of Utmost Good Faith*, 40–1; Zinn, *A People's History*, 133, 138, 141.
19. Zinn, *A People's History*, 135, 138–9.
20. Duthu, *American Indians*, 10; Zinn, *A People's History*, 146–47.
21. Zinn, *A People's History*, 148.
22. United States v. Lucero, 1 N.M. 422 (1869). Tim Alan Garrison describes how Southern state courts "provided legal legitimacy to the state legislative

assault on Indian rights" during the removal period. Tim Alan Garrison, *The Legal Ideology of Removal* (2002; Athens: University of Georgia Press, 2009), 5.

23. Deloria, *Behind the Trail*, 135, 215–16; Cohen, *Cohen's Handbook*, 81–2; Duthu, *American Indians*, 17. Fully one-third of all Indian children (sixteen times the rate of non-Indian children) were removed from their homes by government agencies. "The educational programs consisted primarily of 'kidnapping' Indian children and taking them off to government boarding schools where they were brain-washed of any memory of their Indian heritage," Deloria explained. "Often the parents were denied treaty annuities unless they allowed their children to be taken away."
24. Vine Deloria Jr., *Tribes, Treaties, and Constitutional Tribulations* (Austin: University of Texas Press, 1999), 75.
25. Deloria, *Behind the Trail*, 210–12, 215, 134.
26. The Cherokee Tobacco, 78 U.S. 616, 621 (1870).
27. Cohen, *Cohen's Handbook*, 77–9; Deloria, *Behind the Trail*, 189–90; Vine Deloria Jr. and Clifford M. Lytle, *The Nations Within: The Past and Future of American Indian Sovereignty* (Austin: University of Texas Press, 1984), 25; Pommersheim, *Broken Landscape*, 130.
28. Deloria, *Of Utmost Good Faith*, 52. "Whereas treaty-right reservations have all rights inherent in the original Indian tribe," Deloria comments, "executive order reservations only have rights implied in their establishment by the executive branch."
29. Lone Wolf v. Hitchcock, 187 U.S. 553 (1903) (quoting United States v. Kagama, 118 U.S. 375, 382–83 [1885]).
30. Ibid., 564, 565.
31. Deloria, *Custer*, 37–8.
32. Deloria, *Behind the Trail*, 136; for general information, see Robert A. Williams Jr., *Linking Arms Together: American Indian Treaty Visions of Law and Peace*, 1600–1800 (New York: Routledge, 1999).
33. Deloria and Lytle, *Nations Within*, 101; Deloria, *Behind the Trail*, 120, 118.
34. Deloria, *Behind the Trail*, 110, 111.
35. Deloria, *Custer*, 37–8, 48; Cohen, *Cohen's Handbook*, 86; Duthu, *American Indians*, 75–6. John Collier entered the field of Indian affairs in 1922 during the Pueblo effort to prevent outright forfeiture of their lands; later in the 1920s, he worked with several Arizona and Montana tribes, including the Navajo and the Kootenai and Salish, in protecting control of on-reservation natural resources. Deloria and Lytle, *Nations Within*, 148, 184; Deloria, *Behind the Trail*, 192–4; Deloria, *Custer*, 144, 48; Philip J. Deloria, interview by Michael Anthony Lawrence, Apr. 27, 2010.
36. Deloria, *Behind the Trail*, 194–6, 198–200; Deloria and Lytle, *Nations Within*, 152–3; Cohen, *Cohen's Handbook*, 87.
37. Although he regularly attended church, Saswe himself was forbidden from becoming a member of the church until the matter of his marriage to three

Sioux women was resolved in 1871 (with the death of one wife and another leaving to return to her home reservation). Treat, introduction to *For This Land*, 6.

38. Studs Terkel, "Vine Deloria," in *My American Century* (New York: New Press, 1997), 36.
39. Terkel, *American Century*, 35–6; Philip J. Deloria, interview by Michael Anthony Lawrence, Apr. 27, 2010.
40. Charles Wilkinson, *Blood Struggle: The Rise of Modern Indian Nations* (New York: Norton, 2005), 106–7.
41. Philip J. Deloria, preface to *Destroying Dogma: Vine Deloria Jr. and His Influence on American Society*, eds. Steve Pavlik and Daniel R. Wildcat (Golden: Fulcrum Publishing, 2006), v, vi; Philip J. Deloria, "Reading Mount Rushmore" (lecture, Michigan State University, East Lansing, MI, Apr. 19, 2007).
42. Deloria and Lytle, *Nations Within*, 190, 192; Cohen, *Cohen's Handbook*, 94–7; Duthu, *American Indians*, xvi–xvii.
43. Deloria, *Custer*, 139; Duthu, *American Indians*, 13. "The readers of Indian anthologies have always been led to believe that no significant statements were made by Indians in modern times until the great Chicago Conference of 1961," Deloria notes. "All through the Eisenhower administration, [however,] without fanfare and publicity, the members of the [NCAI] fought a valiant struggle against the forces of Congressional oppression." Deloria, *Of Utmost Good Faith*, 216–17.
44. Williams v. Lee, 358 U.S. 217, 223 (1959). See also Pommersheim, *Broken Landscape*, 213, 62 (commenting, "[i]n the modern era, the Indian Commerce Clause morphed from a textual restraint on federal power in Indian affairs to a textual accelerant of federal authority").
45. Deloria and Lytle, *Nations Within*, 198–9; Cohen, *Cohen's Handbook*, 100.
46. Cohen, *Cohen's Handbook*, 956, 101–2; Duthu, *American Indians*, 31–3; Deloria, *Tribes, Treaties*, 157; Deloria and Lytle, *Nations Within*, 210–11, 213–14.
47. Deloria, *Of Utmost Good Faith*, 110; Deloria, *Behind the Trail*, 136. Progress did not come without cost, Deloria emphasized a couple decades later in 1999. "Beginning in 1961, Indian tribes were the beneficiaries of numerous federal programs that invested millions of dollars in the reservation and its programs." But, Deloria asked, at what cost? "[W]hen the dust finally clears away and people evaluate [this era], they will realize that the progress of the sixties and seventies was purchased at an enormous price. In order to attach themselves to national social welfare legislation, Indians had to pose as another American domestic racial minority." Because "Indians happened to be a group that fell within the identifiable guidelines," they lost a sense of their altogether unique status as sovereign preexisting nations. Deloria, *Tribes, Treaties*, 215–16.

48. Deloria, *Tribes, Treaties*, 146, 147; Deloria, *Of Utmost Good Faith*, 84, 86.
49. Deloria, *Of Utmost Good Faith*, 94.
50. Deloria, *Behind the Trail*, 34–6; Deloria, *God Is Red*, 8.
51. Deloria, *Behind the Trail*, 36–9. The activists' inexperience eventually caught up with them, however, even while still on Alcatraz before departing a year and a half later; and "during the next two years the Indian activist movement degenerated into sporadic landings on federal property." See also Deloria, *God Is Red*, 9–10.
52. Deloria, *God Is Red*, 10.
53. Wilkinson, *Blood Struggle*, 108.
54. Deloria, *Custer*, 35, 50, 101–2, 265.
55. Ibid., 28, 48–9, 51, 76–7.
56. Ibid., 49–50.
57. Ibid., 51–52, 144.
58. Wilkinson, *Blood Struggle*, 108; Steve Pavlik, introduction to Pavlik and Wildcat, *Destroying Dogma*, xi.
59. Deloria, *God Is Red*, 11–12. That decision, together with a Puyallup boundary settlement in the late 1980s, "put sufficient pressure on the state of Washington that it sought to create better relations with the tribes," Deloria later reported. "In 1990 it established a form of tribe-state compact with mutual recognition for each other's political status. Today the state is seen as the most progressive of the western states in its relations with Indians." Ibid., 13.
60. Deloria, *Behind the Trail*, 40, 41, 187. The major Indian protest groups were AIM, the United Native Americans, and the Indians of All Tribes. Ibid., 41.
61. Ibid., 41.
62. Ibid., 52–6. Highlights of the twenty points included points 1 (restoration of Indian constitutional treaty-making authority); 2 (creation of a new treaty commission within the first year); 4 (commission review of past treaty violations and establishment of ongoing review process); 5 (resubmission of previously unratified treaties to the Senate); and 6, the most fundamental of all (compliance with treaty terms as the basis for all U.S.-tribal relations). Ibid., 44–9.
63. Ibid., 61–3, 145. Deloria had little regard for the federal executive branch's efforts on behalf of Indians, primarily through the BIA ("a rather gooey glob of inertia-bound career bureaucrats," Deloria memorably stated, "surrounded by well-intentioned do-gooders who flit in and out of the mess with complete misunderstanding but the best of motives"). Deloria, *Of Utmost Good Faith*, 3–4.
64. *Bury My Heart at Wounded Knee* sold five million copies and was translated into twelve languages. Hampton Sides, foreword to Brown, *Bury My Heart at Wounded Knee*, xvi–xviii. Deloria, who deeply admired the book, said, "Every Indian will wish he had written it."
65. Deloria, *Behind the Trail*, 63–72; Deloria and Lytle, *Nations Within*, 239.

66. Deloria, *Behind the Trail*, 71–5; Deloria & Lytle, *Nations Within*, 239. "The overtones of potential violence, [and] a possible repeat of the original massacre, made the protest appear to be a nightmare replayed on television every evening before the eyes of a horrified world," Deloria wrote.
67. Deloria, *Behind the Trail*, 77–80. Responding to rumors of a federal attack at Wounded Knee, Indians from all over the reservation "became tense, and . . . could not stand idly by and watch the federal marshals kill their sons, uncles, cousins, and fathers." By Friday afternoon, March 9, "the roads to Wounded Knee were jammed by cars filled with Indians trying to get to the little village. They were determined to stop the marshals from killing their relatives. So instead of confronting a mere three hundred Indians armed with rifles," Deloria recalled, "the marshals faced over a thousand Indians, the majority of them converging on Wounded Knee from behind the federal forces." A seven-mile-long line of cars is "a lot of Indians, no matter how you figure," Deloria quipped. Ibid., 75–7. The takeover lasted another two months. In the end, a federal marshal was paralyzed and two Indian men were shot and killed by gunfire.
68. Ibid., 78–9; Deloria, *God Is Red*, 22–4. Following Wounded Knee, the International Treaty Council (the representative group of American Indian tribes) was given observer status in the United Nations as a qualified nongovernmental organization (NGO). In 1977, the group traveled to Geneva to appear at a UN NGO conference on discrimination against indigenous populations. Deloria explained that these conferences, by providing Indian tribes a forum for discussing their cultures, traditions, and grievances with the United States, were tremendous morale boosters for tribal leaders. Deloria, *Tribes, Treaties*, 241.
69. Cohen, *Cohen's Handbook*, 104–5; Duthu, *American Indians*, 16–18. See also Pommersheim, *Broken Landscape*, 242–6.
70. In developing these distinctions, Justice Thurgood Marshall commented in *McClanahan v. State Tax Commission of Arizona*, 411 U.S. 164, 172 (1973): "[Tribal sovereignty] provides a backdrop against which the applicable treaties and federal statutes must be read. . . . It must always be remembered that the various Indian tribes were once independent and sovereign nations, and that their claim to sovereignty long predates that of our own Government." See also Pommersheim, *Broken Landscape*, 222.
71. Montana v. United States, 450 U.S. 544 (1981). According to *Montana*, the two limited circumstances when the tribe's authority does reach nonmembers are the following: (1) the tribe may tax, license, and the like where nonmembers enter consensual relationships with the tribe or its members through contracts, leases, and so on; (2) the tribe may retain civil authority over non-Indians on fee lands within the reservation when their conduct threatens or directly affects political integrity, economic security, or health or welfare of the tribe. Ibid., 565–6. See also Duthu, *American Indians*, 36–7; Pommersheim, *Broken Landscape*, 212.

72. Confederated Salish and Kootenai Tribes of Flathead Reservation, Montana v. Namen, 665 F.2d 951, 964n30 (9th Cir. 1982).
73. Treat, introduction to *For This Land*, 14.
74. Getches, "Beyond Indian Law," 356–7.
75. Cohen, *Cohen's Handbook*, 105–7; Duthu, *American Indians*, 97. In the environmental area, for example, it amended a series of acts "expressly to provide a regulatory role for tribes in environmental matters, including amendments to the Clean Water Act, the Clean Air Act, the Safe Drinking Water Act and the Superfund Act (CERCLA)."
76. Matthew Fletcher, "Bringing Balance to Indian Gaming," *Harvard Journal on Legislation* 44 (2007), 45; Deloria and Lytle, *Nations Within*, 262; Duthu, *American Indians*, 117, 130.
77. Deloria, *Tribes, Treaties*, 52, 55–6.
78. Getches, "Beyond Indian Law," 267–8. Rather than serving as a neutral, deferential arbiter, the Court now is engaged in determining (in Justice Scalia's words) "what the current state of affairs ought to be."
79. Getches, "Beyond Indian Law," 268, 318, 329. Getches explains that "the conclusion that the Rehnquist court prefers the interests of states has overwhelming statistical support. When a state loses in a lower court and the [Supreme Court] accepts the case, it reverses in favor of the state 93 percent of the time. By contrast, when the state wins below the Court reverses only 47 percent of the time." Ibid., 320. Regarding mainstream values, he adds, "although the justices have diverse perspectives on religion, the majority disfavor minority faiths and are satisfied with the appearance of state neutrality to religions even if it means that mainstream religions will thrive and others ultimately will be unable to survive." Ibid., 322. *Nevada v. Hicks* (533 U.S. 353 [2001]), Getches suggests, "is a stunning example of how it pursues the Justices' larger agendas in Indian cases while ignoring and misapplying Indian law principles." Ibid., 330.
80. Deloria, *Tribes, Treaties*, 112.
81. Ibid., 114–16; Deloria, *God Is Red*, 247; Duthu, *American Indians*, 110.
82. Deloria, *Tribes, Treaties*, 118–19; Cohen, *Cohen's Handbook*, 107–8. In reaching this result, the Court scrapped its well-established compelling-interest test for determining whether government actions infringe the free-exercise clause, stating instead that generally applicable, neutral state laws (even those that cause serious disruptions to free exercise) are subject to a much less rigorous form of review.
83. Getches, "Beyond Indian Law," 200–1; Duthu, *American Indians*, 170.
84. United States v. Lara, 541 U.S. 193 (2004). In *Lara*, Congress did exactly what Professor Getches in 2001 suggested it should do, in "legislat[ing] to correct the Court's misadventures" and "reaffirm[ing] explicitly the principles of tribal sovereignty that were always implicit in its silence." Getches, "Beyond Indian Law," 268, 362. Relying on Congress is no guaranteed fix, however. "Congress certainly has made horrendous blunders – like the

allotment and termination policies, which it later had to reject in embarrassment. Nevertheless," Getches suggested, "the legislative process has an advantage over adjudication in that it is able to frame policy that looks beyond a single fact situation. Moreover, today Indians participate fully in the political process." Getches, "Beyond Indian Law," 276.

85. United States v. Lara, 541 U.S. at 226 (Thomas, J., concurring).
86. Matthew Fletcher, "Preconstitutional Federal Power," *Tulane Law Review* 82 (2007), 509; Matthew Fletcher, "The Supreme Court and Federal Indian Policy," *Nebraska Law Review* 85 (2006), 121.
87. Deloria, *Red Earth, White Lies*, xi.
88. Treat, introduction to *For This Land*, 12.
89. Deloria, *Custer*, 104; Deloria, *God Is Red*, 261.
90. Deloria, *God Is Red*, 200.
91. Ibid., 198.
92. Deloria, *Red Earth, White Lies*, 11; Deloria, *Custer*, 109, 113.
93. Deloria, *Custer*, 109, 124. The Christian missions greatly expanded "in 1870, [when] President Grant simply handed out religious monopolies to the respective denominations in different parts of the country," Deloria related. Concerted efforts were made to eliminate tribal life on the reservations. For example, "Indian students were allowed to read in their own language only if the Bible had been printed in it." Deloria, *Red Earth, White Lies*, 11.
94. Deloria, *God Is Red*, 240; Deloria, *Custer*, 112.
95. Deloria, *God Is Red*, 66–7. "American Indians hold their lands – places – as having the highest possible meaning," Deloria added, "and all their statements are made with this reference point in mind." Ibid., 62.
96. Ibid., 89–90. Deloria explained that Indian tribes do not envision the Great Spirit in human form: "To be sure, many tribes used the term *grandfather* when praying to God, but there was no effort to use that concept as the basis for a theological doctrine by which a series of complex relationships and related doctrines could be developed." Ibid., 73, 79.
97. Vine Deloria Jr., *C. G. Jung and the Sioux Traditions: Dreams, Visions, Nature, and the Primitive*, ed. Philip J. Deloria and Jerome S. Bernstein (New Orleans: Spring Journal, 2009), 14, 187–9. "While Western thinkers are trained to [detect similarities] between humans and animals on a [genus/species] basis, they have had difficulty conceiving of such similarities in psychological terms, having rejected the concept [that] animal thought and emotions" could be closely related to those of humans. Deloria suggested that Native tradition and Jung both understand and respect animals' cognitive capabilities.
98. Deloria, *God Is Red*, 90.
99. Duthu, *American Indians*, 92.
100. Philip J. Deloria, interview by Michael Anthony Lawrence, Apr. 27, 2010.
101. Deloria, *God Is Red*, 148.
102. Ibid., 149, 153–4.

103. Ibid., 81–2.
104. Ibid., 167, 170–2, 155. "Some tribes made up medicine bundles containing bits of hair of the deceased, flesh or claws of the animals and birds most closely related to the family, and other intimate things of the deceased," Deloria disclosed. Then, "[t]his bundle was kept in the family dwelling for a year after the death and treated as if the person was still present with the family," thus extending the trauma "over a period of time [so] people could be comforted that, while the deceased was not visibly present, he or she was spiritually and emotionally present."
105. Ibid., 172.
106. Ibid., 173.
107. Ibid.
108. Ibid., 194–6.
109. Ibid., 195–6.
110. Deloria, *Custer*, 205.
111. Ibid., 121–2.
112. Deloria, *God Is Red*, 200–1 (quoting Ernest Thomson Seton's recollection of Tim Newcomb, who had been his guide in his travels in the West in 1912 and 1914).
113. Pavlik, introduction to Pavlik and Wildcat, *Destroying Dogma*, xi.
114. Vine Deloria Jr., *Evolution, Creationism, and Other Modern Myths* (Golden: Fulcrum Publishing, 2002), xiii, 5.
115. Ibid., 46.
116. Deloria, *God Is Red*, 137–8. The ultimate task of tribal religion, "if such a religion can be said to have a task, is to determine the proper relationship that the people of the tribe must have with other living things and to develop the self-discipline within the tribal community so that man acts harmoniously with other creatures," Deloria asserted. "At no point does any tribal religion insist that its particular version of the creation is an absolute historical recording of the creation event or that the story necessarily leads to conclusions about humankind's good or evil nature. At best the tribal stories recount [the people's experience]." Ibid., 88.
117. Deloria, *Myths*, 7.
118. Pavlik, "Darwin, Deloria, and the Origin of Life," in *Destroying Dogma*, 86; Deloria, *Myths*, 48.
119. Deloria, *White Lies*, 53–4.
120. Pavlik, "Darwin, Deloria," 87. "The assumption of the Western educational system," Pavlik further suggests, "is that the information dispensed by colleges is always correct, and that the beliefs and teachings of the tribe are always wrong." Ibid., 84.
121. Deloria, *White Lies*, 211.
122. Ibid., 93; Deloria, *Myths*, 5. As might be expected given his controversial views on the shortcomings of modern science expressed in these and other works, Deloria had his share of critics. A selection of those criticisms may

be found in the following: George Johnson, "Indian Tribes' Creationists Thwart Archeologists," *New York Times*, Oct. 22, 1996; John C. Whittaker, "Red Earth, White Lies: Native Americas and the Myth of Scientific Fact," *Skeptical Inquirer*, Jan.–Feb. 1997; Bernard Ortiz de Montellano, "Post-Modern Multiculturalism and Scientific Illiteracy," *American Physical Society News* 7, no. 1 (1998), 12; H. David Brumble, "Vine Deloria, Jr., Creationism, and Ethnic Pseudoscience," *American Literary History* 10, no. 2 (1998), 335–46; Bruce Thornton, *Plagues of the Mind: The New Epidemic of False Knowledge* (Wilmington, DE: ISI Books, 1999).

123. Deloria, *Myths*, 57.
124. Ibid., 92.
125. Ibid., 6; Deloria, *Red Earth, White Lies*, 26.
126. Jerome Bernstein, foreword to Deloria, *Jung*, xi; Deloria, *Jung*, 21, 200. "At the same time [Deloria] was piqued and shocked by some of Jung's presumptions and seeming arrogance when observing the world of 'the primitive,'" Bernstein explains. "He determined to respond to Jung as a 'primitive psyche' himself, addressing the many errors in Jung's observations." Bernstein, foreword to Deloria, *Jung*, x.
127. Bernstein, foreword to Deloria, *Jung*, xiv.
128. Ibid., xi. A few years earlier during a visit to Algeria and Tunisia, "Jung seems to have seen for the first time the dark shadow of what was commonly seen as 'progress' and 'civilization,'" Deloria reported, and his visit to Taos further opened his eyes. "Writing to Miguel Serrano in 1960 as a feeble old man, a year before his death, Jung wistfully reflected: 'We are sorely in need of a Truth or a self-understanding similar to that of Ancient Egypt, which I have found still living with the Taos Pueblo.'" Deloria, *Jung*, 17–18, 21.
129. Deloria, *Jung*, 7.
130. Ibid., 13.
131. Ibid., 7.
132. Ibid., 172, 194; Deloria, *God Is Red*, 153.
133. Deloria, *Jung*, 168–70.
134. Ibid., 8–9.
135. Ibid., 184–5.
136. Ibid., 186.
137. Ibid., 184.
138. Tom Holm, "Decolonizing Native American Leaders: Vine's Call for Traditional Leadership," in *Destroying Dogma*, 58–9.
139. Daniel R. Wildcat, "Indigenizing the Future," in *Destroying Dogma*, 145.
140. Deloria, *Red Earth, White Lies*, 211; Deloria, "Plenary Address: Reforming the Future: Where Is the Academy Going?" in *Destroying Dogma*, 4; Philip J. Deloria, interview by Michael Anthony Lawrence, April 27, 2010.
141. Deloria, "Plenary Address," 12; Deloria, *White Lies*, 30–1.
142. Deloria, "Plenary Address," 12. By contrast, "[i]t's much better in Europe," Deloria suggested. "They're challenging major theories. New ideas seem to

be emerging everywhere. Books proposing new alignments of ancient history, new scenarios for earth history, radical revisions of existing doctrines – all kinds of ideas are discussed more freely than in the U.S.," he added. "The difference between what we research and the topics they choose is amazing. They seem to be a century ahead of us.... These people are adventuresome. They're not whining." Ibid., 11.

143. Deloria, *Tribes, Treaties*, ix.
144. Deloria, *Behind the Trail*, 262.
145. Deloria, *Tribes, Treaties*, 161; Deloria, *Behind the Trail*, 252.
146. Deloria, *Behind the Trail*, 254, 260; Deloria and Lytle, *Nations Within*, 265.
147. Deloria and Lytle, *Nations Within*, 265. With the door kicked open by the work of Vine Deloria Jr. and other Indian agitators, tribal leaders in the twenty-first century are engaged in serious efforts to memorialize their return to largely independent status with the U.S. government.
148. Deloria, *Custer*, 7.
149. Ibid., xiii.
150. Ibid., 51.
151. Ibid.; Deloria, *God Is Red*, 292.
152. Deloria, *Behind the Trail*, 249–50.
153. Ibid., 251.
154. Deloria, *Jung*, 199.
155. Hal Borland, *When the Legends Die* (Philadelphia: J. B. Lippincott & Co., 1963). *When the Legends Die* is one of three books – along with *Little Big Man* by Thomas Berger and *Stay Away, Joe* by Dan Cushman – identified by Deloria in *Custer Died for Your Sins* as worthy depictions of Native American life. Deloria, *Custer*, 16.

Index